THE CAPITALIST ERA

The Capitalist Era

THE MAKING—AND UNMAKING—OF THE GLOBAL MIND

JEREMY ADELMAN

PRINCETON UNIVERSITY PRESS
PRINCETON & OXFORD

Published by Princeton University Press
41 William Street, Princeton, New Jersey 08540
99 Banbury Road, Oxford OX2 6JX

press.princeton.edu

GPSR Authorized Representative: Easy Access System Europe - Mustamäe tee 50, 10621 Tallinn, Estonia, gpsr.requests@easproject.com

ISBN 9780691177021
ISBN (epub) 9780691292588
ISBN (PDF) 9780691292151
LCCN: 2026937193

British Library Cataloging-in-Publication Data is available

Editorial: Priya Nelson and Emma Wagh
Production editorial: Sherry Gerstein
Jacket design: Haley Jin Mee Chung
Production: Danielle Capurso
Publicity: James Schneider and Kathryn Stevens
Copyeditor: Holly LaFon

Jacket image: Adapted from Doloves / Shutterstock

This book has been composed in Arno

Printed in the United States of America

10 9 8 7 6 5 4 3 2 1

MIX
Paper | Supporting responsible forestry
FSC® C008955

To my sisters, Shonagh and Rachel

The condition of being strangers and slaves in the land of Egypt brings man closer to his neighbor. In their condition of being strangers, men seek one another. No one is at home. The memory of this servitude creates humanity.

—EMMANUEL LEVINAS

CONTENTS

ILLUSTRATIONS

THE CAPITALIST ERA

INTRODUCTION

A Declaration of Interdependence

PANIC SEIZED the world. Deadly plague spread from Hong Kong to San Francisco. Drought struck northeastern Brazil and the breadbaskets of Russia. Unemployment, strikes, massacres, pogroms—there was even a Broadway play about ruinous bank runs. Newspaper headlines worldwide screamed calamity. Painters turned their palettes away from telluric countrysides to grim landscapes of overtilled fields worked by back-broken peasants. These were years of fear—fear of food and fuel shortages, alarm about losing money, financial turmoil, and unease about migrants from far-flung places. Governments slapped tariffs on trading partners and, with the help of new devices like machine guns and barbed wire, commanders sent soldiers to far-away places to kill people who spoke different languages. The extermination of native peoples reached a gruesome acme. Other new devices transformed how people learned about how blood was spilled and money was lost on the other side of the world. Cheap newspapers, long-distance cables, and portable cameras brought the remote up close. They globalized a *grande peur*, particularly fear of being overwhelmed by foreigners—and fear of being killed by them. The planet felt smaller and more dangerous at the same time.

These were the tumultuous years of the 1890s, a transition from the optimism of a Victorian past to doubt about the future. The buoyancy of Jules Verne's thrilling adventures in unfamiliar lands (*Around the World in Eighty Days* rolled off the press in 1872) gave way to H. G. Wells's visions of a dying Earth, dystopian futures, and pathogenic horror (*The War of the Worlds* hit bookstands in ominous 1898). Today, we scroll through a limitless supply of digitally enhanced variations on Wells's fears of invasion and extraterrestrial extraction wars. We live in times of escalating fear of atmospheric rifts, predatory politics, and everyday graphics of extermination.

Part of the very nature of panics is for people living within them to fail to see them in context, to be unable to see that what feels like endtimes is more often a turning point, a difficult and uncertain transition rather than grand finale. The search for context and meaning is what motivates this book, to understand the rhyming emotions of the past two centuries. To remember earlier anxious and angry times puts our present into perspective. It reminds us that fear always dueled with other emotions, like joy and excitement, that serviced alternative visions of the future on our planet.

Heated emotions, not just the cold calculus of self-interest, have governed how strangers have regarded and treated each other in the capitalist era. Sentiment and self-interest coiled together to shape the rhythms of world capitalism while animating the great debates and contradictions that made and unmade the Global Mind.

This book is a history of how we humans grew to share Earth, whether we like it or not. Strangers are tied together in their search for food, fuel, security, respect, and ideas. This is nothing new for a social species. But the scale of mutual dependence wrought by modern capitalism has changed radically since the industrial revolution. As have the stakes. The scale and stakes involved in depending on strangers have provoked warring feelings—fear and excitement, sympathy and suspicion; the intensity of mutual need produces visions of one-world utopias and existential dread, as well as indifference, confusion, and exhaustion. That war has been conducted as much in our heads as on the ground, high seas, and in the skies. Lately, the sentiment has settled on gloom. A former global optimist slumped into despair. We need fewer pundits and more therapists who, he moaned, "can help us accept who we are."[1]

One temptation is to define this emotional spectrum in terms of its extremes. Grim and foreboding nativists warn of an apocalypse: get back to basics of blood-and-soil loyalties to nation and tribe or face extinction from cultural and demographic annihilation by migrant hordes or unfair economic competition. At the other extreme are one-world universalists for whom only selfless solidarity will redeem humanity from another sort of extinction: ecological ruin or engulfing war. Each extreme has its preferred narrative populated with saviors and villains.

Left out of these narratives are the actual outsiders: the people who are either a threat or in dire need of saving. Because *they* are so needy, they are reduced to cartoonish figures disfigured by stereotypes about strangers. In photographic terms, we need to widen the lens so that strangers who have been left out of the story come into view—to see that they too have relevant and deeply mixed feelings about sharing the planet with "us" because we need them.

Widening the frame has consequences for what we see and how we see. For starters, it means admitting frictions that are intrinsic to the modern condition, the contested necessities of modern life. For the past two centuries, the choice has *not* been whether to live in the purity of the tribe-nation or the bliss of one-world. The choice has been about managing tensions between them. Strangers have often disagreed and fought precisely because they needed what the other had; that's what makes necessity contested. Technologies, markets, and flows of ideas created a *unity* of the world without *unifying* it.

Either-Or

Each side has self-serving blind spots. Tribalists have to reckon with a large avoidance. To claim that one could be independent and restore in-group autonomy without giving up what strangers contribute is to perpetuate an illusion that one might live without the constraints of dependence while enjoying its benefits. At best, this is thoughtless, at worst, malicious. It leads dependent people to take and to deny they are taking. Denial is a step toward dehumanizing those upon whom one depends.

One-worlders also have reckoning to do. Accepting the fractured unity of a world of strangers challenges a universalist dream: the creation of a posthistorical polity integrated under one value system in which humans work together as "global citizens." This oneness fantasy erases the differentiated world of strangers who negotiate, quarrel, and bicker over the distribution of their needs. It denies a self-interest in gain from others, which lies behind the urge to manage, control, and to dominate the people we need. Redemption does not lie waiting as if strangers will all get along because they need each other. Out of *this* denial grows an aversion to accept the toll it asks of others and its own form of cruelty, especially on strangers who never asked to be part of someone else's vision.

The debates that splinter us have never been about interdependence or independence. This dichotomy is misleading. It is dangerous. To be independent would mean poverty, indigence, and shortened, less creative lives; few large-scale social experiments in modern history have truly pursued this regression to isolation. Think Pol Pot in Cambodia. What is more, declarations of independence have never been announcements of solitude, a call to return to a metaphoric island. Rather, they are requests from free people for recognition from other free strangers and pleas for entry into interdependence on their own, undictated terms—and requests from unfree people for recognition of their claims to freedom.

The debate about how we need strangers and how they need us has really been, and remains, about what kind of interdependence should prevail. Will or should the world order be more inclusive, with relatively open borders and welcoming arms? Or will it be predatory and hierarchical, with us grabbing what we need from others while and when we can? How to balance inclusion with hierarchy? What mix of self-interest and sympathy will govern how strangers treat each other?

These questions have challenged us many times over. For over two centuries, our search for answers—fueled by a potent cocktail of compassion, jealousy, fear, and anguish—has shaped the policies, norms, and institutions that regulate our world. With those guidance systems teetering, the questions that gave them force confront us again now.

After two centuries of history, the time has come to square up to the fact that strangers carry mixed feelings about each other; the Global

Mind has always been split. Universalists may tout one-world dreams of unity and the virtues of caring for needy strangers, but they have been less than saintly about their interests and methods. For their part, tribalists may claim to care foremost for their own kin, clan, or nation, while blaming strangers for their misfortunes, but they obscure the ways they need strangers, sometimes loathe them because they need them, and yet find ways occasionally to welcome them.

The either-or style that dominates our arguments misses the essence of interdependent life: to need strangers for survival is to lend strangers a measure of control over resources, over information, over recognition. That is a discomforting condition. It is also inescapable. To be interdependent elicits inner tension no matter who you are because you submit to others a capacity to affect your lifeway. At least among neighbors and citizens there are forums and rituals, from parliaments to parishes, for agreeing upon the rules of sharing life and how to contest them. This is untrue of the ties across societies and among strangers. Whatever one thinks of the United Nations, arms control agencies, climate monitors, or global charities and banks, they do not share the convoking power or legitimacy of neighborly or national affiliations; there is little room for democratic exchange and contestation over technical rules managing global supply chains and vaccine inventories, or nuclear proliferation and carbon emissions, rules that really do determine life-and-death matters like access to vaccines or risks of atomic bombs.

For two centuries, integration across borders reduced dependence among neighbors and augmented dependence among strangers. A gap opened between our needs and our control over the ways we meet them.[2]

The gap has filled with an unstable mixture of cooperation and competition, sharing and hoarding. The balance has shifted and changed over the generations. But one thing is true about the making of the modern world: the mixture has never given way to extremes of one-world unification or a return to blessed isolation. Simplified dichotomies have obscured the real tensions over power and control, over who gets to reap the rewards of interdependence and who distributes the costs. It is time we reckon with our mixed selves, our contested necessity. It is time to reckon with the real turmoil at the heart of an interdependent world.

To help with the reckoning, we need tools. Some come from earlier reflections on the dilemma of interdependence. This book relies on insights from earlier transitions, some of them perilous. One sociologist writing in the late 1930s, Norbert Elias, observed the working of what he called the "affect economy."[3] By affect economy, Elias was referring to the feelings that bind or separate members of society to and from each other, the emotions that glue them together in common pursuits or drive them apart—and at times lead to savagery. A German-born Jew writing from exile in Britain, Elias observed how growing interdependence between peoples augmented the division of their social functions; as people specialized in different tasks and roles, they became more proficient and productive. This expanded the radius of the population brought "into dependence on one another." In this way, interdependence created wealth, science, art, and poetry. But it also spurred shame, repugnance, and fear "of other peoples' gestures of superiority." Unleashed, fears about being controlled by others might lead to aggression, thwarting or even ruining the rewards of interdependence. Which of the jostling emotions would prevail? The answer to that question, Elias argued in his 1939 classic, *The Civilizing Process,* depended on learning moderation, nurturing manners, and developing the ability to curb "spontaneous [negative] impulses and emotions." Fears, anxieties, and resentments still lurked within. After all, more interdependence meant more need for others and more vulnerability to their possible disdain; to manage these feelings required restraint and self-control.[4]

Herein lay a drama of modern life: the struggle over how to regulate the combustible mixture of attachment and fear in a world in which people needed what others had. Many of the actors, norms, and institutions created over the past two centuries have been designed precisely to moderate and to manage the global limbic system through a combination of restraint and reward.

Independence as a Euphemism for Hierarchy

That internal regulatory system, what humans created and learned through experience, has had to contend with a big challenge: moderating emotions was no guarantee that the stranger would behave in the same way. Interdependence—the word itself is a problem. Start with the prefix, "inter-." Inter- means that what is needed for survival and recognition flows both ways, unlike "dependence," which evokes the idea that reliance goes only in one direction.

Adding inter- challenges assumptions about the other, often more uplifting prefix, "in-." *In*dependence. Such a clear, such a certain, word. To grow up and develop means, like saying goodbye to childhood, moving from dependence to independence. To be dependent connotes stuntedness, immaturity, underdevelopment, as if being mature meant autonomy and self-determination. Becoming free has meant breaking away from the control of others, to be unconstrained, a master of one's fate. It has been the credo of secessionists for centuries, from the champions of American "independence" in 1776, to Brexiteering in 2015, to President Donald J. Trump's Liberation Day announcement of massive tariffs on trading partners. The language of the nation has become the vernacular of resistance. Remember the slogan of the 2015 Brexit campaign in Britain, "Take Back Control," as if there was once control and, even more, as if it never implied controlling others.

The prefix *in*-dependence creates the comforting illusion that one can live without others. It also conveniently obscures the hierarchy that has been part of the modern capitalist world; in the shadow of becoming "independent," the grown-ups and the sovereigns all too often defined their autonomy by subordinating, if not exploiting, others, hoarding benefits and externalizing the costs of their needs. Independence has been a euphemism for extraction: power imbalance and hierarchy create incentives for the powerful to claim a greater share of the pie at the expense of the powerless, often in the name of pursuing independence or a natural civilizational hierarchy. For centuries, it has also been a bottomless well into which the aggrieved have dipped their buckets to explain their resentment—against outsiders' deceit, competitors' duplicity, and insiders' disloyalty. Resentment reflects the sense of having given more than they got in the exchange with strangers. The reflex is to declare independence, when what the declarers really yearn for is interdependence on their terms.[5]

Interdependence is also slippery. It is often taken to imply reliance among equals and dismissed as a utopian's pipedream. In practice—and in theory—symmetry is as rare as it is fleeting. What is more, societies might *pursue* asymmetry to extract better terms from strangers and are motivated to do so because they are interdependent. This insight came from a Berlin-born economist Albert O. Hirschman in the 1930s. Like Elias, he worried about the fragility of the world. Hirschman observed the ways Adolf Hitler, in the name of national security, wrung what he could out of neighbors to the south and east of the Third Reich to extort his way to rebuilding imperial grandeur, to make Germany great again. He noted that concentrations of power stirred and rewarded bullies—even if, as he hoped, Hitler were defeated. Having enlisted on the Spanish Republican side during the Civil War and the French army to stop a Nazi invasion—all while penning his thoughts on the nexus between international trade and national power—Hirschman dreamed of a postwar peace, one in which powerful sovereigns learned some basic lessons about the economic causes of war. The lessons began with a recognition of the benefits of restraining themselves or, even better, submitting to international rules and guardrails that had the authority to restrain them from abusing their economic muscle. What would be the point of winning a war against dictatorship only to concede the peace to new economic bullies? If the virtue of self-restraint was one lesson, the other lesson was about the vitality of openness so that smaller, more vulnerable, countries had a diversity of partners that enabled them to wiggle out of coercive impositions that the powerful were always tempted to wield.[6]

Fast-forward: it was not accidental that nativist champions of the twenty-first century spoke in terms of restoring national greatness after globalization. They sprinkled the pixie dust of "security" over just about everything from trade and technology to migration and public health to justify hierarchy. "Taking Back Control," the slogan of Brexiteers in Britain, had not-so-vague appeals to memories of empire. On the U.S. side, the rhetoric of "Make America Great Again" never bothered hiding nostalgia for a time in which "America" could tell others what to do; that's what made it great. Russian leaders nursed a history of past greatness and eyed the breakaway republics like Ukraine as disloyal children. Chinese leaders have their variant on grandeur. Even small countries with outsized military strength, like Israel, fall prey to the temptations to hail a vision of sacred unity to justify grabbing the land of strangers. Calls to redeem a glorious past worry less about the freedom of others than they exude melancholy for hierarchy and restored virility that had been drained by the deceit and disloyalty of others and their self-interests hiding behind a globalist veneer.[7] These word games were such effective responses to the risks of globalization because they portrayed strangers as carpetbagging threats, the real menace to the nation; after all, strangers are the ones with needs, not us! With such simple *in*dependence formulae within reach, why bother with the messy, unsatisfying moral burdens of *inter*dependence? Why not invoke the magical word independence as cover for restoring asymmetrical interdependence?

It is misguided to see backlashing—then and now—as expressions of yearning for splendid isolation. What backlashers have wanted is *not* separation from the world, a divorce from strangers. They do not want to forfeit the benefits that come from interdependence; they want interdependence on their own terms, free of the need to cooperate with, sacrifice for, or listen to strangers, free to deal with risk and threat by hoarding from strangers and calling it *in*dependence. After all, "nation-first" implies that other nations come second, third, last. "Nation-first" denotes hierarchy and control by the powerful over the powerless—coercive interdependence, not blissful independence. "The president is unwavering in his commitment to restore American manufacturing and global dominance," proclaimed Donald Trump's press secretary Karoline Leavitt two months after his return to the White House in early 2025. "The America-last globalist era is ending," to be replaced by an "America-first economic agenda."[8]

If there is solidarity, nation-firsters envision a collusive comradeship of superior nations, races, and creeds prevailing over others. In the nineteenth century, as the first half of this book will show, it was a club of white, European, self-anointed civilizing empires who looked upon the rest as subordinate. Nowadays, the club is less racially striped, though there are some who yearn for bygone days of white, Anglo-Saxon hegemony. But it is no less clubby, no less inclined to carve the world into great power spheres. When the prime minister of Canada, in the sobriety of his dark suit and tie, went to the podium at the World Economic

Forum on January 20, 2026, he invoked a "rupture" in the world, a break from a cooperative era wrapped in a "fiction" that great powers would restrain themselves. In a setting habituated to proclaiming the virtues of sharing from the gilded halls of Davos, Mark Carney laid bare not a future, but the present of bare-knuckled geopolitics, one in which the powerful liberated themselves to pursue their ends at the expense of the powerless.[9] Carney may have been correct; the one-world fantasy was over. But there is an alternative narrative. This rupture can equally be seen as a surfacing of an always latent form of interdependence. That form is extractive and hierarchical. It lurks in the Global Mind, waiting to be stimulated by a specter of rising risks and threats posed by strangers. It would be recognizable to imperialists of the 1890s and 1930s; it emerged from the shadows of globalization's hypocrisies after 2008. The illusions of globalization may have been buried in that Alpine winter of 2026 as Carney's speech ricocheted around the world. But the rewiring of interdependence to favor the empowered with a disregard that shaded into dehumanization of the powerless was not new.

The struggle to resolve the vexing questions about interdependence flows through the last two centuries like a great river. It has yielded major wars and exterminations as well as heroic commitments and solidarities. This is not because some people are bad and others good, some realistic and others naïve, some caring and others cruel. It is because *need* produces mixed sentiments from the same origin point; need elicits a basic tension within the imaginings of the Global Mind. If we can hold the image of diverging urges, competition and cooperation, solidarity and suspicion, in our heads at the same time it might be easier to talk in less either-or, stand-my-ground terms, to see that what binds also divides, to accept that needing others can be comforting and agonizing at the same time.

Little Finger

The trouble with interdependence was sown into early arguments about capitalism before its triumph. In earlier times, strangers appeared in markets and temples where they bought and sold goods and shared prophecies from far away. Migrants settled among natives. Foreign merchants hawked spices and exotic cloths. Face-to-face interactions among strangers in the fairs of medieval Champagne and Samarkand yielded codes of behavior and exchange, subtle nods, handshakes, bows. Biblical Jerusalem was a cacophonous entrepôt of traders and money lenders who spoke many tongues yet were conversant in gestures that promoted trust across cultural and religious divides.[10] The world economy began to change in the eighteenth century. Spreading empires, the seeds of free trade, capital mobility across borders, and mass migration laced a world of connected villages into an integrated, and increasingly interdependent, unit. But those complex codes of personalized trust and mutual regard among localized strangers had difficulty keeping up as trade and migration became more impersonal and larger scale.

Some observers saw new perils on the horizon. Capitalism meant that trade was growing, but the ties between strangers became more anonymous. Observers struggled to understand changes in ways that tangled the cold logic of self-interest with the heat of one's emotions and sympathies. Notably, eighteenth-century pioneers of political economy worried about what has been called the "dilemma of distance." It obsessed them. They saw how the rise of commercial society (the word "capitalism" still didn't exist) could generate bonds of sympathy between people; they also foresaw that as commerce reached into remote corners, it stretched these bonds between strangers and thinned them out.[11]

Let's start with the bonding. The founder of modern economics, Adam Smith, argued that morals and markets worked together to create virtues, trust, politeness, and respect—elements that glued societies together so that commerce could take place without grabbing or feuding. In one of his most famous passages of *An Inquiry into the Nature and Causes of the Wealth of Nations* (1776), Smith argued that the division of labor appealed to self-interest *and* brought people into a common purpose. He noted famously that "it is not from the benevolence of the butcher, the brewer, or the baker, that we expect our dinner, but from their regard to their own interest. We address ourselves, not to their humanity but to their self-love, and never talk to them of our own necessities but of their advantages." For Smith, humans didn't have an innate regard and love for each other; their instinct for self-preservation and pursuit of advantage drove them to reciprocal association with others. It was not noblesse-oblige but necessity that brought people together into mutual regard and tethered them through specialization.

This is crucial: Smith was commenting not just on the needs *of* strangers but the need *for* strangers. It was, he believed, in the self-interest of people to depend on each other. In turn, the need for strangers would trigger regard for strangers' needs. From this flowed a harmony of human forces that pushed societies forward and upward, always mixing economic reason and emotion. What he called the "mutual sympathy of sentiments" served as a bedrock of social relations; sympathy was the underlying fabric that softened self-interest's potentially predatory impulses and restrained dangerous passions, like avarice, to make them more "social."

Smith's friend, David Hume, took the argument for interdependence a step further. It was, he argued, commercial nations that were "both the happiest and most virtuous." In an essay he wrote in 1752, and which deeply influenced Smith, Hume explained that "industry, knowledge, and humanity, are linked together by an indissoluble chain, and are found, from experience as well as reason, to be peculiar to the more polished, and, what are commonly denominated, the more luxurious ages." It was from trade among strangers and the spread of consumption that people learned the habit of "conversing together." And of all trade, the most beneficial, he thought, was foreign trade. Here Hume advanced his case for interdependence to its limits. Foreign trade exposes peoples of the world to different goods, tastes, and desires. It "rouses men from their indolence; and presenting the gayer and more opulent part of the nation with objects of luxury, which they never before dreamed of, raises in them a desire of a more splendid way of life than what their ancestors enjoyed."[12] By being exposed to luxuries, goods, and services beyond one's reach, especially when they came from exotic places, people would become more civilized.

In the course of a prolonged exchange and friendship between Hume and Smith, the potential for harmony became more elaborate. With mutual gain and splendor might also come justice. Hume extended this idea famously in a passage in *An Enquiry Concerning the Principles of Morals* in 1751. The spread of commerce might spread a concern for fairness. "Suppose that several distinct societies maintain a kind of intercourse for mutual convenience and advantage," he told his readers. Then, "the boundaries of justice still grow larger, in proportion to the largeness of men's views, and the force of their mutual connexions." By contrast, in a world in which humans could pluck from the trees all they wanted there would be no need to trade. Music, the arts, and many virtues may flourish. But justice—the defense of others because it is the right thing to do because it is in one's self-interest—would be totally "USELESS" (Hume's caps), "an idle ceremonial, and could never possibly have place in the catalogue of virtues."[13]

Since Hume and Smith's time, this argument about the uplifting effects of integration, lacing human needs to human virtues through a helix of relations between strangers, has been a precept of a fundamentally optimistic view of progress, one that escalated from need to recognition, and from recognition to justice.

If they were optimistic, they also had worries. Smith and Hume could have stopped on an upbeat note. But they did not. There was a problem. Harmony was not a logical or necessary outcome of widening the radius of "mutual convenience and advantage." Did the "largeness of men's views" always follow in proportion to "mutual connexions"? Smith and Hume were not oblivious to intrinsic perils, intrinsic in the sense that risks were inherent to the need for strangers, especially as the encompassing radius of interdependent strangers grew. What happened when strangers became less visible to each other, when exchange relations became more and more anonymous, more remote—when "men's views" lost focus? This is where it is important to reckon with the ways commerce also thinned the bonds of human-to-human relations even as it multiplied and extended them. Distance had been bothering Smith before he made the case for the virtues of self-interest in *The Wealth of Nations*. It was a wrinkle in his scheme from early in his thinking. Could a harmony of sentiment survive the effects of expanding distance; could one be separated and sympathetic at the same time?

To illuminate the problem, Smith engaged in a few thought experiments and added the calculus of pain to a mix of emotions otherwise dominated by the pursuit of pleasure. In his *The Theory of Moral Sentiments* (1759), he speculated on the human capacity to sympathize with the suffering of those far away. He conceded that a human naturally "feels his own pleasures and his own pains more sensibly than those of other people." These were what he called "the original sensations," and they radiated outward to include close kin, then neighbors and friends. But greater happiness and beneficence required more than close ties; the challenge was to identify pleasures and pains of others beyond the tribe and regulate behavior accordingly. Smith's solution was to introduce readers to a third character in the relations between strangers: the "impartial spectator," who judged human behavior and deemed it worthy of trust. Our ability to imagine such a character, a kind of secular God, is what kept people from behaving in beastly and extractive ways because they internalized the perspective of others. Part 3 of *The Theory of Moral Sentiments* began by acknowledging human limits: "We can never survey our own sentiments and motives, we can never form any judgment concerning them, unless we remove ourselves, as it were, from our own natural station, and endeavour to view them as at a certain distance from us." He added: "We can do this in no other way than by endeavouring to view them with the eyes of other people, or as other people are likely to view them."[14] The operation required detachment, an ability to imagine being judged by others as a condition for living in a society greater than a clan bound by blood and soil.

How did the impartial spectator monitor behavior and sympathy when the strangers were far apart, mediated by continents, oceans, and many other layers of transactions? Smith performed another thought experiment. He asked readers to join him in wondering how "a man of humanity" might feel, upon reading the news, about the plight of many Chinese swallowed up by an earthquake? One might imagine this gentleman sipping his tea from Canton, sweetened with tea from slave plantations of the Caribbean. While doing so, Smith noted, this "man of humanity" would study the effects of the earthquake "upon the commerce of Europe, and the trade and business of the world in general."

He considered the effects on his self-interests. And then? What about the victimized? Smith answered, "And when all this fine philosophy was over, when all these humane sentiments had been once fairly expressed, he would pursue his business or his pleasure, take his repose or his diversion, with the same ease and tranquillity [*sic*], as if no such accident had happened." In one of his memorable passages, Smith addressed the diminishing power of sympathy for those suffering far away:

> If he [this imagined man of humanity] was to lose his little finger to-morrow, he would not sleep to-night; but, provided he never saw them [the suffering Chinese], he will snore with the most profound security over the ruin of a hundred millions of his brethren, and the destruction of that immense multitude seems plainly an object less interesting to him, than this paltry misfortune of his own.[15]

Key words in this passage are *provided he never saw them*. That's what distance did: made the fortunes of strangers invisible and difficult to see back home. Distance added to the burden of the impartial spectator. Remember this passage because it will be relevant when we consider the effects of technologies of communication, especially the role of media, which burst upon the stage just as free trade swept liberal thinking in the middle of the nineteenth century. For now, we need to unpack Adam Smith's little finger problem. Does one lose sleep over the plight of endangered far away strangers or the prospect of losing a little finger? Therein lay a disturbing thought. Adam Smith and David Hume worried that "beneficence" tended to fade as a stranger receded from the spectatorial center; it faded while dependency did not. The dynamic resembles, Hume noted in his *Treatise of Human Nature* (book 3, section 3, titled "Of Goodness and Benevolence"), "all objects [that] seem to diminish by their distance." This was how a painful little finger might obsess someone more than the death of thousands of strangers far away even as the man of humanity sipped his Cantonese tea.[16]

Herein lay a dilemma for the prophets of capitalism, one which has haunted us ever since.[17] Normally, Smith and others are read as apostles of free markets. What is often forgotten is that they fretted over the moral consequences of market life. While specialization and mutual need created structural bonds of necessity that pressed the horizons of interdependence into the distance, the regard for strangers followed no such pressure. There was no physical law, no gravitational pull, drawing people to be more social with far-strangers, no automatic trigger to summon what Hume called "tender passions" to accompany the mutuality of cold self-interest. Tenderness sparred with other passions like courage, ambition, and greed, which were potentially destructive and could dispose one to be "a tyrant and public robber." There were, in other words, dueling urges within commercial society and thus dueling collective emotions governing dependence between strangers. And there was little to predict whether tenderness or greed might prevail. The very same commercial society that fostered interdependence, motivated the appreciation of arts and luxuries, and bred good manners also pushed strangers apart; the bonds of sympathy did not automatically keep pace with the spread of self-interest.

How to resolve markets with morals, exchange without exploitation? Smith, Hume, and other prophets of capitalism had only unsettled, contingent, and speculative answers. Later, less hesitant thinkers in the flush of the industrial revolution of free trade would call the effort to reach a humane synthesis either credulous or impossible. But so long as the rewards from strangers were bountiful, there was hope that sympathy would keep pace with self-interest.

There were two noteworthy exceptions for the early prophets. The first was the example of the East India Company's increasing powers in Bengal and monopoly rights to trade. This was a model of bullying strangers. It undermined the sovereign's "natural" obligation to look out for the welfare of its subjects in order to govern virtuously. It was bound to spiral into cruelty and debase the otherwise potentially uplifting effects of trade. The East India Company, in Smith's immortal words, exemplified "the wretched spirit of monopoly."[18] This concern is worth bearing in mind as observers monitored the allure of predation. The second was slavery, a thorn in the side of market optimists and discomforting to Scots in particular, as it is now clear that the Scottish commercial economy was highly dependent on the slave trade and circulation of tropical goods from plantations.[19] One might even say that confronting the suffering of slaves made raw a nerve that connected the senses to the mind of the British empire. Here too the urge of institutions to further extraction illuminated the limits of sympathy—and the power of the temptation to dominate. Smith is spare in his commentary. *The Wealth of Nations* alludes to slavery as an expression of "the pride of man" and his urge to "domineer over others."[20] But of the enslaved themselves scarcely a word; the suffering strangers was, in the end, less concerning than the distortion in the allocation of capital to monopoly interests. The hope was that expanding commercial society would make enslavement obsolete because it would erode monopoly. As the traffic in enslaved labor grew, its cruelty made it a cause célèbre.[21]

In their time, Smith, Hume, and others found the oppression of strangers to be cruel. But in their time, they were in fact more concerned with the feeling of *indifference* among the consumers of Bengali textiles or Caribbean sugar, that is, simply not caring about the fate of others, especially those upon whom we rely for the things we desire. Indeed, concern for the commonwealth rather than the privilege of monopolists would eventually render oppressions obsolete. Meanwhile, it was the specter of indifference that threatened to perpetuate injustice. What they feared was the lack of sympathy for outsiders upon whom people depended—an emptiness, passivity, absence of attachment.

At the cusp of a world market revolution, it was harder to envision more active negative sentiments about strangers produced by interdependence itself. It was only a speck on their horizon that market integration might induce people to act in cruel and exploitative ways *because* they had a self-interest in doing so and claimed a right to do so. Smith and Hume could not quite foresee how the need for strangers might yield active resentments, anxieties, and loathing that drove some strangers to degrade and to dehumanize others as conditions for inhumane integration. The passing of time would show that extraction and its emotional conditions would not wither away. Rather, they set off a debate over the moral conditions of interdependence, a debate over how to share the world.

The Picture Gallery

As capitalism marched across the globe, and technologies of interconnection proliferated, the debate over needing strangers became ferocious because interdependence became observable. The unity came into being just as a revolution in media and representation made strangers more visible to each other in print, on screens, and eventually on devices carried around in pockets.

The debates in our day over the ethical, strategic, and material bonds with strangers, fueled by circulating images, are not new even if they ricochet across the world with an instantaneity that no one could foresee when the first oceanic cables were laid and modern cameras were invented in the middle of the nineteenth century. The rise of modern interdependence coincided with a revolution in communications. Newspapers, televisions, cameras, and eventually, pocketable screens and lenses, as well as actors linked to the spread of modern communications, including journalists, business boosters, social activists, and "influencers"—witnesses of what was happening far away—made these ties visible in ways Adam Smith could not have imagined.[22]

Valuable knowledge flowed across borders as commodities, migrants, and capital did. Indeed, the circulation of information enabled and motivated the flow of products and people in pursuit of opportunities. As a result, strangers lived far away but they were not unseen; global interdependence coiled with the emergence of a society of spectacles, one in which remote social relations were mediated by news, stories, and images. "We are speaking of the elements of the new commercial relationships," noted the German philosopher Jürgen Habermas, "the traffic in commodities and news created by early capitalist long-distance trade." The old vertical relationships of dependence, associated with local life and feudal ways, got eclipsed by "a far-reaching network of horizontal economic dependencies."[23]

Few forces gave more immediacy and visibility to emerging dependencies than the movement of photographic images, which were part of a wider transformation in the economy of information flows. Remember Adam Smith's words: *provided he never saw them*. If Smith anticipated some of the effects of long-distance commerce but could not foresee the changing economy of images, one who did was the African American abolitionist Frederick Douglass. A former enslaved man from Maryland who would go on to world renown as a writer and orator, Douglass was also one of the most photographed men of the nineteenth century; and more than a subject, Douglass was an important protagonist as a magazine editor, publisher, and best-selling author in the burgeoning emotional economy of print capitalism. He had a sense of the power of the reproducible and mobile image in shaping public sentiment about strangers. The camera as we know it was barely a decade old when, on December 3, 1861, months into the U.S. Civil War, Douglass gave an impassioned lecture at Boston's Tremont Temple. It was right after a fierce winter storm. The hall was packed, despite the blizzard. Douglass rose to the stage. He praised great inventors, James Watt (steam), Benjamin Franklin (electricity), Samuel Morse (telegraphy). But, he complained, the inventors of "pictures" never got the recognition they deserved. Louis-Jacques-Mandé Daguerre, the French painter and printmaker who had figured out how to capture light etched onto silver-plated sheets of copper, arguably the first photos, had, according to Douglass, revolutionized the world. "By the simple but all-abounding sunlight," he "has converted the planet into a picture gallery," Douglass said. After his invention, "men of all conditions may see themselves as others see them." Figure 0.1 shows him in 1848 in one of his many portraits posing to defy customary images of Black men as bedraggled slaves, dressed as a gentleman, gazing thoughtfully away from the lens and therefore the viewer, inviting them to ponder what a former enslaved man was thinking.

Douglass was not naïve. He did not believe that strangers simply viewing other strangers would cause sympathy to abound. Photos, like all other commodities, could glut the market. "Next to bad manuscripts, pictures can be made the greatest bores," he joked. His audience laughed. "Authors, editors, and printers suffer by the former while almost everybody has suffered by the latter. They are pushed at you in every house you enter, and what is worse, you are required to give an opinion of them." More presciently, Douglass warned his audience to marvel at the breakthroughs but to be wary of their contradictory

FIGURE 0.1. Frederick Douglass.

effects. The circulation of pictures of others could magnify existing feelings, good and bad: "*All* [my emphasis] wishes, all aspirations, all hopes, all fears, all doubts, all determinations grow stronger and stronger precisely in proportion as they get themselves expressed in words, forms, colours, and actions." In the end, however, Douglass captured the technological optimism of his age, the belief that breakthroughs that brought the world together would ultimately improve the world. The camera was a machine, like the cable, the railway, the steamship, and the spread of print technologies, destined to forge ever more togetherness. Consider some of Douglass's closing words to his rapt audience: "The increased facilities of locomotion, the growing inter-communication of distant nations, the rapid transmission of intelligence over the globe—the worldwide ramifications of commerce—bringing together the knowledge, the skill, and the mental power of the world, cannot but dispel prejudice, dissolve the granite barriers of arbitrary power, bring the world into peace and unity, and at last crown the world with just[ice], liberty, and brotherly kindness."[24]

Douglass's response to Adam Smith's little finger problem was a cautiously optimistic one; while there were reasons to pause and worry, the forces of progress were on the side of a more enlightened togetherness. The camera contributed to the mobility of information and changed how people saw the world, partly because envisioning became more accessible, making the planet into a gallery. But the camera also changed vision itself. Photographs contained the sense of immediacy, of being there, witnessing events without being present; by collapsing the distance between the viewer and the sufferer, the pain (or pleasures) of strangers created a spectacle of togetherness and heightened complex and contradictory affective responses.

One of the effects of the camera—and transformations in printing, broadcasting, and eventually digital communications—was to diffuse the production of images and information so that not only were there more sources, they were more distributed. Creating and sharing a documentary vision, spreading spectatorship, went beyond professionals, a process that began long before the advent of the smartphone. The camera turned its possessor into a chronicler; because it was relatively cheap, mobile, and easy to master, the urge to produce and circulate portraits of distant people and places multiplied the quantity of distant encounters. Family portraiture was decreasingly restricted to members of gentry posing in bucolic settings with their dogs resting at their ankles. Albums, wedding poses, graduations, recordings of the solemn and the celebratory in the form of the snapshot meant that photographic displays proliferated as the camera and printing got cheaper. There was also the travel shot, the postcard, the obligatory ornaments of voyaging and encounter, which themselves were becoming democratized and commodified; from their start, the travel business organized tours in order to stage the traveler to be imaged in the iconic spot—the Eiffel Tower, the Pyramids in Egypt, Disneyland.

In 1965, a French sociologist called photography a "middle-brow" art form that mapped on to the swelling of a middle class in search of its own symbolic capital, its own aesthetic, in the quest for social distinction.[25] Though Pierre Bourdieu, an avid photographer, missed the ways in which the photograph crossed the brows from high to low, he nonetheless pointed to the ways in which the production and circulation of images included the handiwork of amateurs who did not live off the sale of their reporting but who brokered it for other ends to make an interdependent world an intervisible one. One only has to think of postcards in the twentieth century or images taken on smartphones from vacations in the twenty-first century to be posted on Instagram—or, for that matter, the way in which documentarists chronicled police brutality with iPhones during the plague-filled summer of 2020 in Minsk or Minnesota, or the explosion of videoclips of atrocities in Israel and Gaza. The advent of digital photography and social media marked one more stage in the explosion in supply of images that made strangers more commonplace yet ever more liquid.[26]

Documentarists were part of a wider assembly of actors, institutions, and technologies that connected strangers and conjugated understandings of self-interest in and sympathy between them. They could bridge political and spiritual economies that tied people—and their faiths—together. Consider the story of Rev. William A. Smith, a mid-century evangelical missionary who left Canada for China in the early 1930s and whose service to his Lord connected rural folk of the Ottawa Valley to rural folk of Shandong. Born in Scotland before the First World War, he, like millions of others, voyaged to Canada to escape a poverty trap in Glasgow just as Italian farmers moved to Argentina, Ceylonese sharecroppers ventured to Guyana, and Gujarati printers sailed to the Cape Colony. While pounding the pavement in Depression-era Toronto, he met a preacher, converted to an evangelical brand of Protestantism, and found the vocation to preach himself. A few years later, he left Canada to become a missionary in China. En route, his vessel docked in Hong Kong. He clamored down the gangplank to find a camera store to buy a recently invented fast and portable image-making machine of his own: a Leica. Rev. Smith was my grandfather—and he never ceased to marvel at this state-of-the-art German device. As a child listening to his stories, I would watch as he would hold his camera, caressing it like a cat. It would be indispensable for his mission; for the rest of his long, preaching life, there was always a camera within reach to document what he saw for others to see. By the time he reached Hong Kong, the Leica had launched its career as the device of choice to record world events and atrocities like the Italian invasion of Abyssinia and the bombing of Guernica, and my grandfather bicycled and snapped his way across northeast China—until invading Japanese troops drove his family (including my mother) to flee in 1937.

We will return to the fateful hinge years of the mid-1930s in due course in this book. What is important about middle-brow amateurs like Rev. Smith is that making interdependence visible was not just a professional enterprise; it took commonplace and personalized forms and served many purposes. The images he produced were bundled into slide shows and recycled in magazines and posters for parishioners in Canada as part of a spiritual campaign to enlist their prayers and to raise money for the proselytizing business. Rev. Smith's images were one way to stir Canadian sympathies and shake their savings to support a distant

FIGURE 0.2. Shandong, 1936.

mission to rescue the souls of strangers far away. The images yielded a picture gallery of China and its peoples for farmers in the Ottawa Valley. Indeed, for millions of believers around the world, the mission photo created a sense of connection long before proselytizers took to airwaves and social media. There were more secular forms, postcards, travel shots, honeymoon memorabilia, ancestral albums, and mantlepiece images of the distant, the everyday personal picture galleries of the world. The photo shown in Figure 0.2, taken around 1936 of an itinerant vendor who used a sail to propel his barrow across the flatlands of Shandong, was one of my grandfather's favorites. It profiled what he regarded as the stoic ingenuity of the people he was seeking to rescue; it figured in slide shows exhibited to cobelievers in Canada to stir their compassion—and modest financial contributions.

Like so many other missionaries and economists, adventurers and investors, poets and journalists, scientists and technocrats making a world of spectacles and concepts, Rev. Smith contributed to the ways in which strangers regarded each other across streets and oceans, so that every living room and field of a conflict zone merged into connected operating theatres of the global mind. Pros and amateurs were among the many involved in recording an integrating world—rendering it intervisible as it was becoming interdependent. A new stage emerged for debating the world as it was coming into being, a forum for rival narratives and contested arguments triggered by the need for strangers.

1

World of Strangers

Rubble and Remaking

Out of rubble possibilities are often born. Ruining old ways can clear the slate for new ones. By the end of the eighteenth century, a concentration of technological, commercial, and military power brought steamers to the Mississippi River, a European investment spree to South America, and the wonder of plate glass and cast iron to the Great Exhibition of 1851 in London. It materialized dreams of more than a connected world, but an integrated world. It also sent land surveyors to Africa and Argentina and aimed cannons at palaces in India and China to reduce to wreckage the forces that stood in the way of uniting the planet. Demolished buildings and deforested landscapes became repeated scenes as soldiers, merchants, settlers, and land-grabbers made the world anew.

Integration and its rubble became observable. The scenes became spectacles. The world was becoming interdependent and intervisible at the same time, which raised the emotional mercury and set off the first round of arguments among thinkers of modernity about what it meant to need strangers far away. Thanks to the transformation in communications and print technology, and the advent of mechanical visual recording devices, an explosion of new actors and networks turned to documenting what humans could do to and for each other. Creating and destroying were not just imagined; they were imaged, printed in black and white and relayed in mass quantities and with the immediacy of telegraphic communications, the penny press, and popular magazines. Readers and viewers witnessed old worlds crumbling and new ones being born and responded with chest-thumping pride and dismay.

One of the first globe-trotting photographers was Felice Beato. He was born in Venice in 1832, though we know little about his early life moving around the eastern Mediterranean before he laid his hands on a camera. In the 1850s, taking photographs was becoming the rage. The boulevards of Paris sprouted with men with black capes, large boxes, and unwieldly billows capturing images of streets and parks and boasting the marvels of near-instant portraiture. Photographers popped up in Rome, Athens, and at the foot of the Pyramids in Egypt to take photos of and for an expanding world of travelers who wanted souvenirs of their visits. It was inevitable that reporters and photographers would become chroniclers of carnage as well. Images familiarized distant strangers with each other's construction and destruction. They activated the possibility that newsmakers might function as Adam Smith's impartial spectator, holding strangers to account for how they treated each other. Few exemplified this process more than Beato.

It was in Paris that he got his first camera. From there, he took the craft to new heights and pushed it into new frontiers. Beato met James Robertson, coin engraver, superintendent of the Imperial Ottoman Mint, and portraitist, in Malta. From this beehive of commercial and military activity in the middle of the Mediterranean, the two sailed to Constantinople in 1851 and set up a photography studio in the gateway to the Black Sea. Robertson married Beato's sister, Leonilda Maria Matilda. Then, Felice's brother, Antonio, joined the business.

This comfortable, interimperial, transcultural partnership changed forever with the outbreak of the Crimean War in October 1853. The British government had urged one of London's premier photographers, Roger Fenton, to venture to the Black Sea to create images that would drum up support for war against imperial Russia. His photographs would from then on shape war reportage. Panoramas of battlefields, portraits of stoic officers, and stills of industrialized combat fused manly heroism and mechanical brawn into an incongruous mix, a mix that would culminate in the muddy desolation and mournful eyes of shell-shocked soldiers of the First World War. Crimea, in this sense, marked the start of a cycle of exploring how to represent the clash of strangers in distant parts at the dawn of mass communications. It was also the first international war in which the telegraph played a role.

After a bout with cholera and some broken ribs, and depressed at the destruction of Sebastopol, Fenton returned to London to share his plates with Queen Victoria and the imperial patriciate. This cleared the way for Robertson and Beato. They hauled their equipment to battlefields and followed Fenton's epic style. Then they changed it. Instead of gallantry and scale, their record of the siege of Sebastopol was one of ruin. Magazines and newspapers adapted their plates into etchings to simulate reality—which drained electoral support for distant war as wars were becoming more distant and less popular.

After Crimea, Beato parted ways with his family. He rushed to India when he heard about the unrest among East India Company troops, carrying with him the technologies and techniques he had honed in the Black Sea. Arriving in Lucknow in time to shoot the rubble in the interior of Secundra Bagh, the magnificent high-walled garden where some of the fiercest fighting took place during the so-called Mutiny or the First War of Indian Independence of 1857, Beato set up his gear with ten-by-twelve-inch plates. Bystanders helped him arrange bones and skulls across the foreground to add a little drama—something he'd learned from Fenton, who infamously rolled cannon balls across the foreground of his well-known shot of the *Valley of the Shadow of Death* to dramatize the barren landscape of a battle scene after it was over. The devastation in India needed less staging. Mughal glory had been reduced to rubble, akin to Greece, Rome, or Egypt—except that this destruction was not the handwork of ancient invaders or father time; it was British artillery *now*. In ruins, Lucknow became a diorama to exhibit the fossils of a civilization made as dead as the buildings beyond, waiting to be rebuilt by the imperial ingenuities of the Victorian age. It became a site of colonial melancholy for a lost world.[1]

As these images got dispatched to London, Beato followed imperial troops farther east. As he got better at his craft, and troops got more involved in opening Asia, Beato got more daring with the dead—though

FIGURE 1.1. Lucknow.

always portraits of dead strangers—to turn viewers into witnesses of others' misfortunes. If Frederick Douglass had imagined cameras as recording devices to create a "picture gallery of the planet," he had not yet envisioned this documentary style for the world as it was being integrated through trade and invasions. It fell to Beato to pioneer the genre as he worked his way across Asia, photographing distant parts as merchants and soldiers laced them together. Beato made the business of making interdependence visible; his pictures of Asia were seen back in London by the imperial patriciate and great mid-century thinkers, as well as a growing reading and viewing public. They contributed to debates about far-away wars, dreams of opening Asia, and encounters through media that provided the forum for divided responses to the dawn of global unity.

We will return to Beato's career later. In the meantime, the features of Beato's moment need to be underscored. The 1850s shattered longstanding anxieties about diminishing resources, confined markets, and plebian unrest that had crested with protest waves and famine of the 1840s. Hitherto, any theory of prosperity was coupled to fears of scarcity; a theory about the wealth of nations was simultaneously a recognition that most of humanity's existence had been governed by subsistence and want. That, after all, was humanity's steady state before the vast opening of global frontiers and the mobilization of people and capital to exploit them. Rev. Thomas R. Malthus had predicted that surpluses were destined to be consumed by growing populations; there was no escape from the inexorable law of diminishing returns in natural resources against the human propensity to procreate. But the middle of the nineteenth century brought a shift. Malthusian pessimism got driven—at least for a while—from the stage. As tariffs fell, trade boomed. Railways and steamships opened new frontiers, food became more abundant, and euphoria took over. The technological and conceptual breakthroughs of the Victorian age flipped the narrative. Now, access to other peoples, their savings, their lands, and their labor created a sense of limitlessness. For some it was a moment for triumph, for others a plunge into the unknown—one that would become foreboding about what it meant to depend on strangers for survival. This chapter is about the opening moment in that debate, a debate about opening. It is about modern freedoms and modern origins of the right—indeed, the moral obligation—to dominate strangers on a world scale to make the world whole.[2]

A New Unity

The Crimean War launched Felice Beato's career during a profound realignment of commercial, technological, and political forces. At the center of this realignment was a dramatic decline in "transaction costs"—the tolls on commerce arising from the difficulty of getting useful information and enforcing contracts between distant partners. Such costs depressed the ability and motivation to trade or strike bargains between strangers. Before 1800, those firms that were involved in long-distance trade relied upon special privileges (like Crown concessions to collect taxes or to raise armies) and monopolies (like exclusive rights to sell goods and enslaved people in determined markets) to make money. New concepts, technologies, and institutions prompted elites, especially around the rim of the Atlantic world, to seek new bearings.

They found them by creating new scales of coexistence—integrating nation states for emerging citizens and expanding markets for commodities and capital to flow between nation states. Borders, physical as well as conceptual, were surveyed, mapped, and etched with greater precision and into ever more remote parts in order to handle the greater flows of goods, capital, and peoples that crossed them. The idea of territorial nation-states grew up alongside the making of a world market in order to join it, manage it, stoke it; nations became more unified, the lands within them more privatized, and the states that ruled them more centralized—even as these nation-states relied more and more upon the world market for bounty and recognition. This is why territorial expansion of nations and world integration went hand in hand, a process that stretched from the United States and Brazil to Russia and Japan.[3]

Technologies, especially in transportation and communication, girded these new scales by marking boundaries and creating the machinery used to traverse them. By 1913, steam, iron hulls, steel rails, screw propellers, and enlarged ships slashed freight rates to a quarter of what they were a century earlier. Tumbling freight rates and the rise of bulk shipping then slashed intercontinental transaction costs and widened the resource base of the world. The nineteenth century replaced a connected world of old empires, chartered monopolies, and galleons with an interdependent world of financiers, mass migration, and an alliance of cable and steel.[4]

Many forces sutured the world into one unit. Technical breakthroughs, and the rise of social classes encouraged by government willingness to place legal, political, and military resources at the service of an expanding marketplace, released productive forces to link parts of the world together. Much of the exuberance of the 1850s related to marveling at what could be done with iron and glass, carbon and combustion: nearly a million people flocked to London's Great

Exhibition of 1851 to gawk at the engineering and new steam-powered machines of the industrial era.

But for engineering to sweep the imagination, imaginations had to be sweepable. A public had to be readied to consume the news of the world's marvels. A byword of the age, "progress," was synonymous with learning and displays of learning, in particular learning to read—literacy. From there, writing could lead to an expansion of communicative circles beyond the hubs of oral conversation and local life: peoples across longer distances could be reading the same news, instructions, and books at the same time. While the eighteenth century gave birth to a dream of widened literacy, it was in the nineteenth that it spread. When he was editor of *El Nacional* and later Governor of the Province of San Juan, as well as after he became Argentina's president in 1868, Domingo Faustino Sarmiento made schooling one of his causes—to dispel what he considered the relics of superstition and to create virtuous citizens for the new republic. Modern life and civics demanded literacy. His 1862 Statutory Law of Public Education required San Juanino children to attend primary school. The new Meiji regime in Japan, where literacy already went beyond cliques of noble families, launched a campaign to spread public schooling; on the eve of the First World War, military conscript lists revealed that 90 percent of recruits in the country could read. France's Ferry Laws of the 1880s made primary education universal, free, and secular. By century's end, Britain, the Netherlands, and Germany could boast a literacy rate of almost 100 percent. Southern Europe and Russia lagged, but after the 1860s, ridding countries of illiteracy was—at least rhetorically—a measure of success. It was also the gauge of failure. In China, which struggled to shake off the old examination system and the grip of its scribes, reformers pointed to the school system as the reason for the regime's decay.[5]

Schooling was part of a reorientation of politics and policies that widened horizons and the social classes that profited from them—and thus realigned coalitions that favored expansion and opening, especially in Europe and the Americas. The mercantilism that had buoyed early modern empires came under assault from various directions at once; it was this broader, combined pressure across the Atlantic world, fueled by consumers, readers, and the spread of civil society, that gave protectionism, barriers to commerce, and curbs on mobility a bad name—except when migration involved too many of the "wrong" sort of people.[6]

Literacy and technology, normative and physical forces, combined to dismantle commercial barriers even as national boundaries were getting mapped out. It has long been thought that one nation, Britain, first hoisted the flag of free trade philosophy by abrogating the Corn Laws and the Navigation Acts, two of the mercantilist mainstays, in the late 1840s. This is a self-serving myth for English liberals. In fact, the advent of free trade and commercial fusion was more interactive and more driven by interests as well as by ideology. The first countries to throw off the old barriers were in fact the recently seceded Latin American societies; yearning to rid themselves of Portuguese and Spanish fetters and desperate to promote exports to pay off war debts and recover from the collapse of silver mining, most welcomed traffickers from Europe and North America. True, Mexican conservatives feared disorder if the old estates and guilds lost their privileges. But on the whole, republicans and monarchists alike sought a new place in the world market to replace what they lost with political independence. Liberals like Argentina's Juan Bautista Alberdi, who drafted a version of the republic's constitution in 1852, argued for open nations—nations committed to free exchange of goods and peoples as a condition of progress for a region emerging from empire. To Alberdi and many of his contemporaries, it was the promise of progress that motivated Creoles to reject Spanish mercantilism so their nations could join and be recognized by a wider world of interconnected nations. "A *patria* is liberty, order, wealth, and civilization in the native land," he argued, "organized by learning and in the name of this land." In effect, citizens could only have a country with order and liberty, the "principles of civilization," by acknowledging that they came from Europe and that they should be open to Europe's civilizing influence. Civilized America is, he wrote, "Europe within America."[7] There was nothing unpatriotic about interdependence between new and old worlds.

France, often touted as a picture of resilient protectionism, was also a more open and pragmatic trading partner for most of the nineteenth century than its frenemy on the other side of the Channel. In part, this was because French business was less reliant on old protectionism than cousins in Britain that had grown up under the shelter of the Navigation Acts and the Corn Laws. Moreover, many liberals knew full well that keeping up with their British rivals meant competing in new markets. Average British tariffs were almost double the rate of France's through most of the century. If there was concern in France, it was to avoid the spectacle of British pauperism, to avoid igniting another revolution, which still weighed on the minds of elites. France became an exporter of demiluxe industrial products, Jacquard silk, marquetry, furniture, and leather garments; to wear a pair of French gloves was a sign of decency in New York and Tokyo. By the time Richard Cobden and Michel Chevalier took the lead in the Anglo-French Treaty of Commerce (1860), a trade boom was already unfolding. In practice, the treaty was one more step to support exporters on both sides. What it set off, however, was a cascade of bilateral trade agreements and most-favored-nation clauses in the ensuing years. Countries in Europe and the Americas rushed to join the club. Only in the 1980s would we see a similar merger wave again.[8]

For the first time in world history, external trade was an engine of economic growth in the most rapidly growing countries. Over the course of the nineteenth century, the volume of merchant shipping quintupled.[9] From 1800 to 1914, world economic output grew by 7 percent per decade, but world commerce soared by an average of 33 percent per decade, most of this in the years after 1860. Measured as a share of gross output, international trade was more significant in 1914 than it was in 1990.[10] It transformed what people ate and wore, the tools they used, and the weapons they fought with. Europeans got used to buying more of their daily bread baked from American and Russian wheat; they added more and more doses of Caribbean and Brazilian sucrose and caffeine to their diets to replace traditional ales; cotton fibers from the United States, Egypt, and India kept the textile mills of Manchester working to replace traditional rough woolens with cheaper cottons; more and more enslaved Africans were shackled to work New World labor camps, though after 1850 the Atlantic slave trade quickly shrank, only to be replaced by other forms of free and unfree migrant labor.

Finally, mobile capital joined the spread of literacy and commerce to sweep world regions together. "Money is economical power," wrote Walter Bagehot, editor of *The Economist*, on the eve of the financial panic of 1873. And the moneymen of England ruled the rulers because English money was "borrowable money."[11] Strangers merged not just what they consumed but what they saved and what they spent. As magnates and middle classes in parts of Europe grew richer, the pool of investable funds grew. In the absence of capital-hungry warring states, who served as regular—if often feckless—clients, financiers turned to new borrowers. They could be private or public, especially for the subvention of heavy infrastructure like ports, railways, canals. More and more, these clients, eager to reach into hinterlands, to bridge continents, or to connect seas, lay overseas. "Foreign" investment soared after 1850. Boosted by the discoveries of gold in California (1848) and Australia (1851), credit became plentiful. Joint stock banks in Britain, Germany, and France grew. Stock markets became hubs for new railroad, shipping, and communications companies in search of investors to sink money into the very infrastructure that made it possible to get wheat from Ohio, guano from Peru, and cotton from Bengal—and to send settlers and migrants to opening frontiers.

London may have been an epicenter, but world trade created a distributed latticework of bills of trade, credit, and finance that—not unlike in the globalization after 1989—increasingly had no single center. European bankers and their American cousins reached out to—or sent out—sons, daughters, and cousins to intermarry with elites in global entrepôts, and if not relying on wedlock, finding other interlocking means of cosmopolitan business and sociability. So did Baghdadi Jews. David Solomon Sassoon, tired of business with the Pashas and lured by the fortunes of newer empires, went East and set up shop in Bombay, which became the heart of silk, cotton, tea, and above all, opium trading networks. On the heels of the First Opium War, his son, Elias, was sent to Hong Kong to expand the family's commercial enterprises, which diversified from commodities to insurance, shipping, and to cap things off: banking across India and China. Jamsetji Nusserwanji Tata, Parsi founder of a Gujarati dynasty, made his first commercial strike by supplying and supporting British expeditionary forces in Africa and China from the 1860s and would follow the Sassoons in the opium trade, financing the development of ports, roads, and urbanization. Tata would set up subsidiaries in Shanghai, Kobe, and Paris. If anything, the British empire, formal and informal, was the membrane of a polyglot webbing of faiths, cities, and family businesses that thrived off the wars waged under the Union Jack.[12]

Merchant bankers then created a patrician culture of clubby, metropolitan ties that spun the world's commercial hubs into a web of financial borrowing and lending. Jockey clubs, business associations, opera houses, and other sites abounded for high-society hobnobbing of a social class that spread liberal ideas and markets. Oftentimes, Europeans set up branches of their family firms right on the heels of newly laid long-distance cables. These operations fanned out all over: German minions to South America, and French houses to colonies first, then to Singapore, Hong Kong, and Bangkok. They were a cosmopolitan bourgeoisie, lampooned by Karl Marx as pretentious Mr. Moneybags, lodging themselves in hot spots like London and Paris, New York and Shanghai, Buenos Aires and Johannesburg, and their satellites. The nucleus was composed of merchant-financiers who saw themselves as the heralds of individualistic and progressive liberal transformations, replacing archaic despotism and war with commerce and well-mannered, reputable business. Remarkably successful, the world of the Rothschilds, Glyn Mills, Barings Brothers, and other wholesome houses at the apex in London, with junior affiliates (and clients) like Samuel Hale in Boston or Juan Zimmermann in Buenos Aires, sustained this web, thickened with spousal alliances and kinship ties, that drew together a multinational social class with a shared credo of enlightened opportunism.[13]

It was a testament to how quickly global integration transformed the landscape that even merchant bankers had to adapt to a world that threatened to make them obsolete. At first, their business was to fund general trade, like Glyn Mills' promotion of the Bank of Egypt to finance Anglo-Egyptian commerce. As integration created new specialties, many of them got branded. Anglo–South American Bank was known as the "nitrate bank" because of its business in Chile. The Ionian Bank (IB) was the "currant bank." The Bank of Mauritius, the "sugar bank." But what really drew them together was the rise of private portfolio investment—channeling swelling pools of savings into larger destinations for enterprise, especially in the major public works and private infrastructure projects of transportation and communication industries. The IB shifted from currants to banknote issuance for the region and was soon the broker for the Greek government's ties to the London money market. They opened branches, like Chartered Mercantile's outlet in Yokohama in 1863 and the Oriental Bank Corporation in Bombay in 1842 tasked with giving financial advice to the Japanese government, which the government used to advantage after the Meiji takeover and the rush to modernize after 1868, to float Meiji bonds for its first London loans in 1870 and 1873. The British outpost in Hong Kong was the home for the Hongkong and Shanghai Banking Company (now known by the acronym HSBC), whose doors opened in March 1865 as one of the first truly transnational financial firms, with Parsi, Sephardic, German, American, and British controlling interest. As a bank for the treaty port, it was also the financial gateway for the interior of China; only a fool would want to miss out. It would issue the first public loan to China, known as the Foochow loan, in 1874, backed by customs revenues. London's stock exchange and its satellites were the hub of interlocking directorships, shareholders, partnerships, joint-stock companies, and trustees that governed portfolio investment radiating across oceans, languages, and nationalities to create a shared world of credibility and credit.[14]

The worldmaking capstone was the creation of a unified measure of value and set rules—and a system to ensure that countries conformed and played by them. The most famous was, of course, the gold standard, in effect a network that yielded positive externalities as more and more countries joined it, which they did after a particular incident. Keen to humiliate silver-based France after trouncing the Second Republic in the Franco-Prussian War, the German Reich chancellor Otto von Bismarck was eager to join the small but prestigious gold club. He used a portion of his forced French indemnity payment to buy a hoard of gold and thereby adopt the standard in the early 1870s. That set off a frenzy that made gold a near-universal exchange rate system. As with the trade deal flurry of the 1860s, the rush to gold in the next decades revealed a fear of missing out. True, there were other metal standards. The Latin Monetary Union (between France, Switzerland, Italy, and Belgium) aimed to coordinate a bimetallic silver-gold standard. In practice, though, it turned into a stepping stone on the path to gold monometallism, and increasing numbers of countries joined the fraternity of "respectable," credit-worthy countries managed by worldly elites in top hats, waistcoats, and stiff collars who convened in their salons in Bombay and Rio de Janeiro to create an aura of earned privilege measured by a common gilded standard.[15]

Crimean Moment

One restraint on the new world unity had been the high price of information. But just as shipping costs fell dramatically, so too did the cost of creating and circulating information that measured the value of what could be shipped. One might say that the flow of information, which intensified in the 1840s, laid the groundwork for a new system of values. As those values took hold, the premium on information rose, motivating networks of agents and firms to produce and circulate more of it. Information was not just a commodity extracted and produced for sale; information and its packaging determined the value of other commodities. Just as wheat was the staple for bread, information was the staple of the affective world economy.[16]

As news became cheaper and more accessible, it also sparked ever quicker reactions; news of openings and information about prospects for trade, investment, and conquest prompted rushes to exploit them. No sooner were Spanish armies driven from South America in the 1820s than British investors devoured news about mineral discoveries in the Andean foothills. Dreaming of an El Dorado of their own, they poured money into bogus mining ventures and inflated public stocks. Indeed, distant wars not only became the news—they sold the news as new. The outbreak of the Mexican-American War in 1846 created a surge in demand for the latest dispatches from the front. The booming

American print industry published columns about the conflict and the triumph of the occupation of Mexico City. Wars, by turn, were opportunity openers par excellence. Immediately after the Mexican government signed the humiliating Treaty of Guadalupe Hidalgo, there followed the sensational revelations about gold discoveries in the Sacramento Valley, which set off an El Dorado fever that reached China and Peru. Within weeks, migrants from Canton and Hamburg began packing their bags. Nuggets of California gold reached the free port of Hong Kong for Christmas 1848. Farmers from as far away as Chile geared up to ship grains and leather to frenzied forty-niners; by the end of 1849, Chile's foreign office had issued six thousand passports to miners who lined up to book tickets on ships bound for California. When ships from San Francisco docked in Valparaiso to pick up their human cargo, they unloaded bales of newspapers blaring headlines about Californian gold. By the time Midwestern Americans scrambled their way to the West Coast, it was already teeming with non-Anglo miners and merchants from around the Pacific, which set the stage for a mix of cooperation and violence at the edge of the world economy.[17]

Information and its emotional purposes also shaped the meaning of conflict in Crimea, where this chapter began. Russian, French, and British elites vied for supremacy over the Black Sea—which triggered events that attracted a booming news industry. Indeed, information was crucial for drumming up public support and for winning wars. Then, when a merchant steamer reeled out a three-hundred-mile submarine cable from Varna to Balaclava, French and British field commanders suddenly had nearly instant contact with Paris and London. And as reporters flocked to the front, good reporting also became invaluable intelligence. Russian commanders grumbled that they learned more about the movements of their own troops from the London *Times* than from their horse-powered information chains. There was only one paper in the Black Sea area, *Odesskii vestnik*, which didn't even have a correspondent in Crimea and published scanty, censored briefs weeks late. Little did Russian commanders know that British and French commanders were also poring over *The Times* to figure out what was going on—and complaining bitterly about being sabotaged by reporters. The

Russians, quipped the Waterloo-veteran British Commander in Chief Lord Raglan, needn't bother with a "Secret Service" with so much field intelligence out in the open (not that Raglan was particularly astute in his use of secret intelligence, a reminder that getting information and using it well are two different things).[18] The 1854 *Times*—even the name of the paper evoked the idea that readers should be up-to-date with events—became the most influential newspaper in the world thanks in part to its wartime reportage, though it was *The Daily Telegraph* (note the title) that pioneered sensational headlines, stop-and-press columns, and all-important filler. In London, "the painful excitement for information beggars all description," noted British Foreign Secretary Lord Clarendon. This even meant news of horrifically embarrassing losses, like the infamous slaughter of the Light Brigade.[19]

News of the world rolled in. No sooner did the Crimean War end than bulletins arrived by steamer (Atlantic cables did not work until 1866) from the troubled United States of a fast-moving financial panic. In late August, the Ohio Life Insurance & Trust Company failed—and sent a riptide to New York and Europe, stoked by reports of gruesome violence in Kansas and fears of mass farm failure. The result: a first news-fueled global financial crisis, the "Panic of 1857."

Put this in historic context. A generation earlier, it had taken days for Wellington's victory over Napoleon's armies at Waterloo, barely two hundred miles away, to reach London. By the time armies clashed on the Crimean front, a message took a few hours to reach Paris. When the Napoleonic Wars came to a close, it took over four months for news from London to reach India and then New South Wales, two to three months to reach Buenos Aires or Cape Town. The advent of "steamship news" cut the time lags somewhat, and the British Admiralty took over the running of ocean mail packets to make them more efficient. American packet boats muscled into the Royal Mail business, cutting round trips between New York and Liverpool to five weeks.

Policies, informed by new notions of freedom and military pressures, played their part in opening the information economy. Most important was the rise of the idea of "press freedom"—to join the other freedoms in trade and labor. *The Times* excoriated the British government for trying to manage the narrative of conflict in Crimea; the military establishment loathed the newspaper's reporter, William Russell, and struggled, to no avail, to silence officers and soldiers' complaints about their commanders' incompetence and the horrible conditions. Libel laws underwent profound changes, which immunized writers and reporters from prosecution from the powerful. Stamp taxes were removed; magazines could be mailed more cheaply. Information became a valuable private good, personal property, items to exchange between reporters and agencies, newspapers and readers who bought them—not state secrets subject to meddling governments. Only later did modern "security" laws get drafted to recover states' rights to surveil and control. For now, the value of information made it more prized and harder to contain as long as the technologies and agents were decentralized and the fourth estate self-identified as an industry of its own.

Hardware laid the physical infrastructure for a new fluidity of all commodities, including information. Long-distance and submarine cables expanded the reach and increased the rapidity of information gathering. Poles lifted lines above ground and provided clearways for rail lines; more and more, rail and cable went up together, creating corridors of track and poles through the hinterlands. New coating techniques made of colonial Malaysian latex and Bengali hemp allowed electric cables to be laid under water. A cable linked Dover to Calais in 1851; after that, lines stretched all over the planet to link commercial entrepôts. From 1865 to 1903, the global reach of cables went from 4,400 kilometers to 406,000 kilometers. By the century's end, any self-respecting city was wired in and boasted numerous telegraph offices; those that were not wired up in the maps shown in Figure 1.2a and b. hankered for a cable connection of their own to join the shrinking world. The time it took for a message dispatched from London to reach other cities went from one month to 2 days for New York, 145 days to 3 for Bombay, and 97 days to 3 for Buenos Aires. Wiring brought new actors to the stage: the news "agencies" that piggybacked on the cables, and a growing network of information brokers.[20]

Along with a revolution in transportation and communication, there was also a change in printing technologies. It involved not one big

(a)

(b)

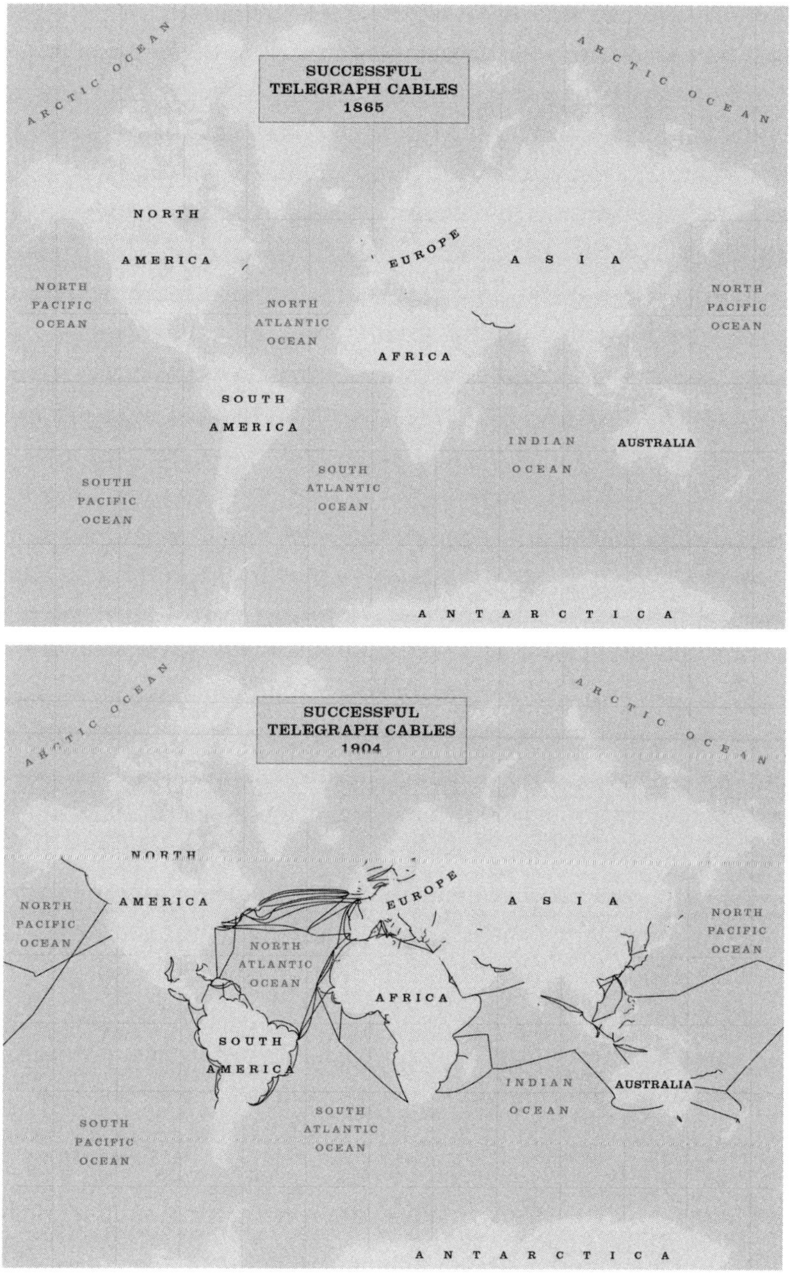

FIGURE 1.2a and 1.2b. The Expansion of Underwater Telegraph Cables, 1865–1904.

breakthrough but a cluster of them; we tend to think of a "print revolution" in the singular, when in fact there were many determinants. Wood blocks gave way to casting metal type. By the late 1860s (as a response to the cotton shortage of the U.S. Civil War), newspapers shifted to wood pulp as a source of paper, ending the use of rags and old clothes as fiber. The effect was to reduce dramatically the cost of paper, creating the prospect for large rolls of printable sheets, and thus unimaginable economies of scale for publishers who sought to render information about the week's—or the day's—events into immediately legible news. Approximately four thousand copies could be produced, without interruption, by printing on rolls of paper up to three and a half miles in length. By 1860, printing on rolls had become a standard practice. Many of the first daily outlets self-identified as newspapers. *The Daily Telegraph* (so named to capture the edge of the new technology) launched in 1855; within three years it could boast print runs of three hundred thousand. Prices dropped sharply, down to one penny (or sou or cent) per issue (with the halfpenny paper, like the *Mercury Leader* and the *Daily Mail*, to follow in the 1890s). Once single stamped sheets gave way to rolls, tinkerers tackled typesetting. By 1890, printers had devised a system known as Linotype, which eventually became an industry standard, though there remained many newspapers that hung on to their own techniques—which gave printers and typesetters important control over production and often made them into vanguards of the labor movement. Still, there was no denying the effect of mechanical casts. By 1900, the Wicks Rotary Typecaster could lay sixty thousand characters an hour.[21]

Buoyed by rising literacy and the declining cost of print production, news became a global commodity to join the flow of rubber, wheat, and cotton, as well as products like coffee, sugar, and opium. News became not just the way in which information got packaged and distant events got represented; news made information an industrial product tied to the new imperialism.

News of the world made strangers familiar, even if they could no longer see each other, unlike in the old market days. The advent of photography and the circulation of reproducible images made strangers ever more intervisible. This too was an industrial byproduct, though it took longer for the photo to join the word of mass circulation. Where photos appeared in mass-circulation periodicals they were rendered as wood engravings. The 1842 launch of *The Illustrated London News* employed artists to copy line drawings (*The Wall Street Journal* keeps up this charming anachronism as part of its brand). Photos on newsprint had to wait until after 1880 with the spread of photomechanical reproduction and halftoning. Until then, photos mainly appeared in pricey books or personal albums.[22]

Iron rails and hulls, mobile steam-powered engines, cables, and chemical reproduction of images about far-away places unleashed forces to open new frontiers and to connect them to metropolitan markets.

Let's return to the 1850s and the Crimean moment. In 1852, the Russian writer Ivan Goncharov set sail aboard the three-masted frigate *Pallada*. His mission: to establish commercial ties with Japan. He was the secretary to Vice Admiral Yevfimy Putyatin. The expedition took two years around Europe, Africa, and Asia, and yielded one of the great travelogues of modern literature at the dawn of the mass genre. The Russian admiral was a devout Orthodox, a man of tradition. He refused the offer of a new steamship in favor of a handsome bowsprit and the majesty of sail—and insisted that the *Pallada* have a chapel. For many seamen, the idea of replacing wind with coal was unmanly and ungodly. The pace allowed Goncharov to take notes of his African and Asian observations, as well as to record his disparaging insights about European greed abroad. When the vessel finally and proudly entered Nagasaki in August 1853, the Russian mariners learned that U.S. Navy warships—fast-moving steamships—had beat them to Japan by a few months. The Russians, who had sailed into harbor properly and obeyed Tokugawa rituals, were late to the party. Still, the epic of the *Pallada,* thanks to Goncharov's observant eye and prolific pen, would become a bestseller in the thriving Russian market for stories about widening horizons and spreading empires.[23]

When American steamships under Commodore Matthew Perry entered Edo Bay with four paddlewheelers belching black smoke on July 8, 1853, the goal was to open diplomatic ties and markets in one show of strength—a show that was meant to be shown. The commodore had insisted that an artist and daguerreotypist, Eliphalet M. Brown, join the expedition and keep a visual record. Perry ordered that seventy-three Paixhans shell guns—which catapulted naval warfare into the steel age because these explosive shells reduced wooden hulls to matchsticks—be trained on the town of Uraga. Gunners set off a volley of blanks at terrified townsfolk. The shōgun's officials, worried about a repeat of the bullying that forced China to accept humiliating terms after the First Opium War, gave in to American demands for extraterritorial rights for its citizens. The same deal curbed Japanese tariff autonomy without committing the United States to reciprocal constraints. An opening so one-sided was bound to provoke a domestic debate in Japan over how to handle unwelcome but irrepressible strangers. The Tokugawa regime cracked, heaved, and eventually made way for the Meiji Restoration, a new regime nursing its own ideas of Japanese expansion.[24]

Meanwhile, news of Japan's opening got back to St. Petersburg and fueled Tsar Nicolas I's growing fear of encirclement. It was no longer the familiar rivals of the French, British, and Ottoman Empires he had to worry about. Now the tsar had to fret about upstarts like Japan, the United States, and soon Germany. In turn, the Russophobia in Britain went on high alert, stoked by the circulation of tales about St. Petersburg's ambition for Eurasian power. Across Europe, liberals pointed accusing fingers at tsarist Russia as the model of Eastern tyranny. They fumed about occupied Poland. There were rumors that Russian spies were sewing discord among soldiers in the East India Company in Bengal. The paranoia went all ways. The Russian commander in Siberia, upon reading the news from Japan of the Taiping Rebellion in China and of British vulnerabilities in Asia, urged the tsar to grab the Amur Valley, which flows into the Sea of Okhotsk, and establish a Far Eastern presence before the British or Americans could get there. But it was to the south that the tsar looked with most unease once the fear of encirclement took hold. His ministers worried about Anglo-French incursions in the neighboring Ottoman Empire and their naval presence on the Black Sea—and thus Russian access to the Mediterranean. The result: a bitter, costly, and undecisive conflagration across Crimea. It led to the first efforts to draft modern laws of war, like rules for treatment of prisoners. It led to the founding of pioneering humanitarian institutions, like the Red Cross. It accelerated the laying of long-distance cable for news dispatching and gave us the war photographer, like Fenton and Beato. It led to more scrambles for territory and influence. It was an early sign of how world integration sowed the seeds of new and more lethal tensions.[25]

A fundamental change took place in the mid-nineteenth century. Iron and steam latched to new means of transportation, new policies, and new systems of communications. The value of news, images, and the work of witnesses, brokers, and intermediaries ensured that strangers were increasingly conscious of their emerging interdependence.

The Civilizing Mission

This alignment of interests and institutions yielded a model, an idea of interdependence—one that could be celebrated at home and exported beyond. The free trade crusader, publicist, manufacturer, and parliamentarian Richard Cobden fiercely defended the notion that expanding commerce was the ticket not just to prosperity but to peace. He argued that as countries became trading partners, they would prefer to cooperate instead of compete, exchange goods instead of bullets. Visionaries made the rivalry that had plagued Europe for centuries a thing of the past—all in the interest of consumers and individuals. What is more, Cobden believed, this international order could export its virtues beyond the "civilized" European orbit and include the "rougher," less virtuous, fringes—and thus promote the universal values of European civilization. One of his followers, James Silk Buckingham, "Oriental Traveler," liberal reformer, founder of the *Calcutta Journal,* and temperance and peace activist, went out on a limb: trade with China and the importation of tea from Canton would help the crusade against drunkenness at home. If commerce was civilizing in Asia, tea was downright liberating for England's vice. For men like Buckingham, free trade, open borders, and peace were all tangled up with the virtues of teetotaling and the spread of tea parties to sober up an unruly working class and eradicate the debasing effects of the pub. On the heels of his triumphal fight against the Corn Laws in 1848, Buckingham rushed to Brussels as a delegate to the World Peace Congress.[26]

"Civilization" was a term that appealed to eighteenth-century French thinkers to depict cultural spheres endowed with forward-leaning powers of learning and accumulation. Picked up by Adam Smith and other Scottish philosophers and adapted (as we will see later) by John Stuart Mill and liberals into a script, "civilization" operated bifocally to address with one creed a basic divide between the advanced and developed, the West and the "barbarian" or "savage" Rest. What was important about attaching the word "mission" to the word "civilization" (as in *mission civilisatrice*) was that, amid interdependence, everyone could be civilized, provided they followed the script written by the "missionaries." Even the stagnant, decaying civilizations of the "East" could be rekindled and aligned with the precepts of Europe's conception of progress and uplift. "Civilization" was a kind of creed for pulling the world's parts together. One-world dreaming of a universal peace, of a humanity united by shared rights, of global citizenship or neoliberal apotheosis, has, ever since, accompanied integration like a shadow.[27]

One of the elixirs of this movement was trade, the expansion of the marketplace, spreading the forces of supply and demand to unleash individualism and civilize by making people interdependent. Material reward and moral respectability proved a powerful combination to motivate rulers in Paris and London to join the free trade bandwagon. Touting freedom to trade, freedom to own property, freedom to practice one's religion, and free labor, European expansionists fanned out. Even the moral politics of abolitionism and the growing chorus calling to rid the world of slavery could be purposed for a brand of European entanglement and expansion abroad. Indeed, abolitionism gained a powerful boost with the faith in the civilizing promise of market integration. Thomas Clarkson, the Cambridge-educated minister's son and pioneering abolitionist, was also cofounder of the Society for the Promotion of Permanent and Universal Peace; he epitomized the convergence of the fight against restrictions on commerce in grains (the Corn Laws) and the fight against the slave trade. As these two movements locked arms, the interest-driven appeals of free trade liberalism provided a mode of action to pursue world peace.[28] When Frederick Douglass, still enslaved in the southern United States, visited England in 1846 to boost the abolitionist cause and to sell copies of his narrative to purchase his freedom, he made sure to visit the aging Clarkson, who took one of Douglass's hands between his palms and in a trembling voice proclaimed, "God bless you, Frederick Douglass!" "It was a meeting of two centuries," Douglass later recalled.[29]

The push to abolish the slave trade and establish open markets became a pretext for intervention in Africa, Asia, and Latin America, tying humanitarian crusading to a capitalist purpose. After many years of arm-twisting, in 1851 the Brazilian government finally gave in to Whitehall pressures: the world's largest importer of enslaved Africans would hereafter prosecute any Atlantic trafficker. That same year, the British consul in Lagos delivered an ultimatum to the ruler of the city, Kosoko, to end shipments of enslaved people, and maneuvered Royal Navy warships to bombard the town. The defenders resisted. But divisions in the ruling family led to Kosoko's fall and the triumph of a puppet regime that promptly signed a treaty to abolish the slave trade—and to guarantee that "the subjects of the Queen of England may always trade freely with the people of Lagos in every article they wish to buy and sell." Within a decade, the port and island of Lagos became a protectorate and eventually got annexed "in order that the Queen of England may be the better enabled to assist, defend, and protect the inhabitants of Lagos," to end the slave trade, to open local markets, and to instill laws that protected property owners—in a word, to make Lagos a model of civilization in Africa, an emblem of the uplifting virtues of Christianity and commerce. The Colony of Lagos would also become an outpost for Saro (from the Yoruba *sàró*) merchants, Creole Nigerians who migrated back to Africa after being emancipated and soon ran the thriving entrepôt business, like Oshodi Tapa. An ex-slave, and ex–slave trader, Tapa became an agent for a European trading house and pioneered the palm oil export trade. Saro merchants like Tapa pushed the market frontiers ever inland and came to champion colonial expansion from the colony. Especially after the arrival of underwater cables in 1886, Saro networks extended not only to the hinterlands but overseas to the Caribbean and Bahia, where many of them had once been enslaved.[30]

A cornerstone of this narrative was the conviction that integrating strangers into the world that Europeans were making could uplift them and spread progress. It became the civilizing mission, and would be picked up and modified by latter-day expansionists looking for a moral pretext for reaching into strangers' domains. Whether strangers welcomed it or not was a nicety little considered amid the euphoria to export the purpose. It was not just an Anglo-American conceit. Or even Protestant. In Argentina, the struggle between what was seen as the barbarism of the countryside and the civilization of city outposts like Buenos Aires was a common literary trope. France dispatched Catholic missionaries to the Levant in the 1840s and 1850s, often on the heels of Lyonese merchants who were looking to expand Jacquard silk cloth sales in Lebanon and beyond. Indeed, Christian monasteries there became important raw silk purveyors in the Levant, exporting back to French manufacturers. Lebanese merchants began to send their sons and daughters to Catholic schools. The Oeuvre d'Orient, created in 1856, was a network that channeled the funds raised in French parishes to support education, conversion, and business activities of the missions across the Middle East and Balkans. It promoted the use of French as the language of business, elbowing out Greek and Italian. By 1860, it was clamoring for French military intervention to rescue Lebanon from Ottoman forces. When the First World War ended in 1918, the Oeuvre d'Orient seized the moment to press for French control of Lebanon. The *mission civilisatrice* transcended religious and national boundaries.[31]

West Europeans and their progeny were not the only sources for the civilizing script; Europeans only claimed to have cornered the market. By the middle of the nineteenth century, Tokugawa elites in Japan were becoming more and more interested in probing beyond the boundaries that divided Japanese subjects from strangers. Often adapting Chinese conceptions of civilization, they set about creating ethnic categories and social hierarchies to explain their relations with distant fringes. The Ainu of Hokkaido, Japan, for instance, fell under the magnifying glass of Japanese explorers and ethnographers who wrestled with whether to treat them as a separate race or culture—asking whether their hairstyles and clothing were signs of their irredeemable backwardness or just displayed more primitive versions of Japanese customs, suggesting they could be uplifted through conversion, commerce, and education. Even before formal colonization of the northern archipelago, there was a crusade to domesticate the Ainu, eradicating "barbarian" customs of public urination and the scandal of mixed bathing.[32] Likewise, in the borderlands of the Amur River that separated China and Russia, from the Yablonovy Range emptying into the Tatar Straits, Slavic settlers moved in the 1840s, accompanying geographers, surveyors, and cultural cataloguers of the people of the region who would soon be regarded as subjects of Russia's Far East. The 1850s saw a flourishing Oriental Renaissance in St. Petersburg as geographical expansion and integration of the empire fueled a desire to know in order to civilize distant parts of the realm—and to make Russia, like America, a nation of peoples that straddled oceans to integrate the world.[33]

"The Character of the Human Race"

From these practices and places emerged moral and material principles that fused into a model, or a creed, to govern how strangers were meant to become interdependent. It grew out of the Scottish insights explored in the introduction but shed the anxieties about whether longer distances would drive a wedge between self-interest and sympathy. Mid-century liberals and civilizers worried less about the ability of ethical commitments to keep pace with economic claims; they either calculated that ethics and economics were necessarily combined in the confidence in the virtues of the marketplace or argued that a gap may open between self-interest and sympathy, but that some sympathy was better than none. The first was a robust case for the civilizing mission, the second an expedient one. Over the course of the latter half of the nineteenth century, especially as the violent and unsavory features of expansion into the lands of strangers was harder and harder to deny, the expansionists tended to dispense with the robust case for the civilizing mission and retreated to the expedient one.

The principal heir to the hopeful strain of the Scottish Enlightenment, that believed that markets could serve morals and self-interest could promote sympathy, was John Stuart Mill. A longstanding employee of the East India Company, Mill was more than casually familiar with the way trade and conquest laced the world together. Like liberals before him, he saw growing interdependence as a process of opening closed societies, spreading freedom, and willing entanglement with strangers, relying *on* them for goods, ideas, and help—and offering the same *for* them.

John Stuart Mill laid out the contours of a liberal vision of the world, one in which the expansion of capitalism could spread liberty abroad and bring prosperity for all. Because of its unique combination of virtues and powers, the model would ineluctably dissolve the obstacles in its way. In a pinch, a bit of pressure might be necessary to break any stubborn obstacle. It is worth pausing over the argument's features, not least because it has enduring appeals, especially to self-described liberal internationalists' views of interdependence. In 1848, at the dawn of the Californian Gold Rush, the abrogation of the Navigation Acts, and the abdication of the French king, Louis-Philippe, Mill published *Principles of Political Economy With Some of Their Applications to Social Philosophy*, a book that laid out a narrative about how commerce could advance and universalize civilization by making societies more interdependent with each other. Following the footsteps of nineteenth-century liberals like Benjamin Constant and his own father, James Mill, another East India Company employee, John Stuart Mill believed that trade could eclipse war—exchange soften the relations between strangers—and submit people to the logic of self-interested commonness. In book 3 of his work, he made a plea for the power of international trade. It had two parts. The first highlighted the sheer efficiency gained by being able to specialize, which the new system afforded. "A more efficient employment of productive forces of the world" made all parts of the integrated market more effective at producing more goods at lower costs.

> If two countries which trade together attempted, as far as was physically possible, to produce for themselves what they now import from one another, the labour and capital of the two countries would not

> be so productive, the two together would not obtain from their industry so great a quantity of commodities, as when each employs itself in producing, both for itself and for the other, the things in which labour is relatively most efficient.[34]

A famous passage, these lines are often read quickly as a paean to the gains from commerce; the ability to produce for a wider market brought more efficiency. Read more closely, they are also about the relations between peoples. Mill insisted that "*the two together*" should be beneficiaries of trade and integration for the formula to work; specializing based on comparative advantage implied that strangers on either side of the deal should reap rewards. The distribution of advantage was necessarily reciprocal. Moreover, it was not just trade that fused societies together. Money played its part. "Capital is becoming more and more cosmopolitan," he observed. Investment moved across borders to stitch societies together. "There is so much greater similarity of manners and institutions than formerly, and so much less alienation of feeling, among the more civilized countries, that both population and capital now move from one of those countries to another on much less temptation than heretofore."[35]

But togetherness did not mean fairness; reciprocity was not the same as equality. Even if isolated societies gained relatively more, they did not necessarily close the gap. Mill did concede that the absolute distribution of rewards from exchange could benefit one side more than the other; he was not naïve about the fairness of the deal. Here there is some murkiness in Mill's theorem. It is unclear whether he believed that this reciprocity enjoyed a corollary—that some people would gain relatively more by making labor and capital more productive if they began from a position of least efficiency because their markets were smaller, more enclosed. Could closed and isolated societies gain relatively more by opening than those that were already open and integrated? Some passages in *Principles of Political Economy* suggest Mill believed that closed societies would gain relatively more from opening than those that were already open; other passages note that the leading openers would gain disproportionately compared to the latecomers. What was important was that reciprocity brought benefits to the laggards. Mill defended the case for the less "civilized" societies, those at "an earlier stage of industrial advancement," to align with the more advanced. "A people may be in a quiescent, indolent, uncultivated state, with all their tastes either fully satisfied or entirely undeveloped, and they may fail to put forth the whole of their productive energies for want of any sufficient object of desire," he wrote. Trade made uncivilized peoples "acquainted with new objects" and tempted them with "the easier acquisition of things which they had not previously thought attainable." For those accustomed to few comforts, he continued, the prospects of getting them would induce them to work harder, to trade, to save, to accumulate "for the gratification of their new tastes."[36]

What was important about commercial fusion was that it unleashed an innate desire for comforts and possessions, the inner consumer lurking in all humans regardless of station or location. Trade spread civilization because it drew out universal propensities to want betterment. Recognizing the prospects for betterment in turn meant recognizing the rewards that flow from the mutual needs of strangers.

There was one more important step in the Mill formula for virtuous interdependence. The transformations it wrought were not just material. They were also "intellectual and moral." If in the past strangers' principal source of contact with each other was conflict and war, trade brought strangers together for a common purpose, not to fight over conflicting ones. In so doing, trade could cause interdependent people to cease eyeing each other with suspicion and envy and instead to approach with curiosity and opportunity. They could even borrow and imitate where they used to resent and repudiate. In a famous passage in book 3 of *Principles of Political Economy,* which he modified in subsequent editions, Mill argued that "commerce is now what war once was, the principal source of this contact" between the civilized and the rest. This contact created an ability for societies to compare "their own notions and customs with the experience and example" of others, because "there is no nation which does not need to borrow from others, not merely particular arts or practices, but essential points of character in which its own type is inferior." Needing, borrowing, and emulating across borders, he continued, were "rapidly rendering war obsolete, by strengthening and multiplying the personal interests which are in natural opposition to it," and international trade, "in being the principal guarantee of the peace of the world, is the great permanent security for the uninterrupted progress of the ideas, the institutions, and the character of the human race."[37]

Here we have a picture of an investor-trader's grand vision for the world, one in which commerce supplanted conflict and spread the frontiers of civilization. Events of his century allowed Mill to see what Smith and Hume could only prophesize, and to develop a more elaborate conception of the virtues of interdependence between strangers. Yet there was a basic condition for this formula. As long as there was open and free communication between strangers, even the "weak, poor, and ill-governed" could see in their dependence upon the "advanced" societies a vision of what they could become. As long as information flowed freely, the more opulent and advanced could send their instruments of civility—capital and commodities—to the have-nots. Mill's formula resolved Smith and Hume's worries about the dilemma of distance. Gone was the anxiety about the gap between sympathy and self-interest, and the prospect that sympathy might wane as the specter of the needy or suffering stranger receded into the horizon. In its place Mill offered confidence in the power of markets, communication, and the multiplication of entangled interests that bound strangers together.

What did Mill have to say when the "weak, poor, and ill-governed" did not share his creed? As news and images reached London about unrest and uprisings, especially in India, his 1848 formula began to look thin. This is where Mill the political theorist and student of his father's own writings on India (which justified British control in the name of civilization's crusade against barbarism) gives us some insights into new dilemmas of distance that he anticipated but could not resolve within his scheme. To make sense of these, he had to step out of it. The imperial mixture of unequal parts required an ordering system with more muscle than the market possessed to hold it together. From the time he was seventeen, Mill was in the employ of the East India Company. He became responsible for correspondence in the Political Department and defended Company rule, arguing that it was the instrument of civilization because it was better suited to understand the national character of India than the British government. Parliament reflected the progressed state of the British character. But where tradition, or "the despotism of custom," held people in thrall to superstition and moral lethargy, governors had to rely on different instruments to hold strangers together than the benevolence of the invisible hand. Giving rights to strangers who did not yet embrace "the progressive principle" of liberty would produce the worst form of tyranny—a people trapped in a past from which they could not, on their own, escape. Mill: "The greater part of the world has, properly speaking, no history, because the despotism of Custom is complete. This is the case over the whole East."[38]

These words are from *On Liberty*, a short book he wrote a decade after *Principles of Political Economy* and only a few years after retiring from the East India Company rolls because he did not agree with the government's takeover of India. In his account, what were once great civilizations were now stuck in their own mud. They gave up their own ancient "progressive" principles and were mired in "stationariness," unable to produce beauty or convenience. The mantle of progress had passed to "us," "we," Europe. "We are progressive as well as changeable: we continually make new inventions in mechanical things, and keep them until they are again superseded by better; we are eager for improvement in politics, in education, even in morals, though in this last our idea of improvement chiefly consists in persuading or forcing other people to be as good as ourselves."

Mill summoned plenty of Orientalist grist for his narrative. He argued that the native states of India were bereft of commerce, manufactures, even of civic history, which required a system of governance to shake the society out of "savagery." The Company, by contrast, had brought railways, education, commerce, and legal rights for individuals, and cleared the way for a moral development that might reverse centuries of stasis and allow eventually for liberty. But his most damning words were reserved for China, which had in ancient times risen so high as to become a "nation of talent" for thousands of years. It was by this time the epitome of enclosed stationariness, however. Nothing exemplified to Mill the trap of backwardness more than the pain of foot-binding women. "To maim by compression," he argued, reflected the Qing commitment to impose a homogeneity on a diverse people. "Its idea of character is to be without any marked character." In an aside, Mill wrote that Europe could "become another China" if it was not vigilant—if it did not foster openness, diversity, and "many-sided development" in which commerce and manufacture produced a "desire of rising" not just among some classes, but all classes.[39] In the meantime, *On Liberty* offered prophecies about China that are often reduced to one, much discussed, line: "If [the Chinese] are ever to be farther improved, it must be by foreigners."[40]

In a short essay published in *Fraser's Magazine* the same year as *On Liberty*, Mill did chart some principles governing the use of force, to distinguish bad from good pretexts for foreign interventions in the capitalist age, so that war would service a dream of peace, as an undesired (if necessary) means for a desired end. It was 1859. The essay was called "A Few Words on Non-Intervention." Ever since, it has been an important essay in the debate over the ethics of intruding into the lives of strangers on the grounds of self-interest. After the end of the Crimean War, in the late days of the Second Opium War, and on the eve of the opening of the Suez Canal, Mill argued that Britain's purpose in the world was not to seek empire but to bring civilization through commerce, manufactures, and civil liberty to strangers. Going to war for aggressive purposes was wrong, criminal even. But some wars, like those to defend the nation against aggression, were just. There were also circumstances in which an "intervention" was justifiable when waged in the interests of strangers. This applied to people who did not (yet) know freedom and thus could not be expected to fight for freedom, even their own. "The virtues of freemen cannot be learnt in the school of slavery," Mill noted; an unfree people had little chance of becoming free without help from outside. But there was a trap: if unfree strangers did not clamor for their own freedom, an outside liberator ran the risk of deluding themselves into thinking they could assist and getting caught in a quagmire. How to free the unfree from the outside in? Mill warned against overeager interventions. But he did not say that they were futile. There were cases in which the intervention was legitimate, like in Suez,

Crimea—and China. In these cases, expanding commerce meant pushing out the frontiers of liberty for Europeans and securing a glimmer of liberty in the East. "Foreigners" had to make the unfree free. But the recipe only worked as long as, behind the gunships, merchants and investors rushed in to pry open competition and enable private property; otherwise, there was little to distinguish intervention from bullying rackets. Force was a virtuous necessity, not to exercise dominion or monopoly, but to open markets so that the East, frozen in time, could rejoin human "history."[41]

Mill offered an uplifting argument for, and a coherent narrative about, knitting the world together; a world of interacting strangers was good for all. In the context of 1850s optimism and bravura, Mill sidestepped what had bothered Enlightenment figures a century earlier about the dilemma of distance. Some might say this was convenient; a stakeholder in the East India Company, he had a personal interest in the story of its purpose. But there was more: a physical and epistemological shift had happened, one that could not have been foreseen a century earlier. Steam, cables, mobile capital, and a new language of freedom seemed to have turned the idea of commercial civilization into a material reality. War and suffering would fade away as reciprocal self-interest created the attachments between strangers, attachments that would have cascading benevolent moral consequences, even if this meant the occasional use of force against stationary regimes that held back their own people—and everyone else. Liberals succeeded in casting off—or at least keeping at bay—doubts that had troubled Smith and Hume. Mill was so influential because he gave voice to the sense of possibility in the miracle of self-interested dependence between strangers. More of it would put an end to strife and misery; it never truly occurred to Mill that more interdependence might yield more strife and misery.

Tearing Down the Walls

It fell to liberalism's critics and, by the 1890s, a growing chorus of self-doubting liberals, to express misgiving about the new unity. One might even say that Mill's own treatise, including his defense of humanitarian intervention in the service of opening, was a response to critics at home who thought that gunship diplomacy overseas was a violation of the creed. The surge of artisan and peasant unrest worldwide through the 1840s, from Mayan resistance to weavers in Berlin barricades to the Taiping Rebellion, suggested that not everyone greeted this new order with enthusiasm. Romantics and socialists denounced the venality of money men and industrial life. Novelists lampooned bourgeois frivolities and exposed the emotional and material toll on the urban poor. Anti-imperialist liberals began to worry about the scattering of British and French troops. These distempers yielded a counternarrative that accented the involuntary nature of interdependence and the broad unease about compelling strangers to rely on each other. Crucially, however, the critics were not yet attuned to the voices from the other side; for the moment, what bothered them more was the effects on the civilizers themselves.

In the counternarrative, violence replaced voluntarism, exploitation took the place of exchange. Then, as now, real-world events gave credence to pessimists. Much of their criticism focused on the "stationariness" of the "East," where European and American behavior fell short of the nations' lofty claims. It was, ironically, an ever-freer press that poked at the hypocrisies of the civilizers. As was often the case, the East India Company was in the middle of the fray. By the 1830s, the firm's monopoly over tea trade in Canton was under assault. Desperate to keep commercial ground and chafing over Qing protection of the Chinese market, the Company had little more than silver to offer China in exchange for tea. The firm turned to opium, which originated from its factories in India, to sell to China.[42]

At first, Qing officials did not bother with smugglers. But when addiction spread, they did. The result was the First Opium War (1839–42). The British did not necessarily want *free* trade. That was low on the priority list of a government still dominated by protectionists. They wanted *their* trade, and they were prepared, when their warships and troops subdued Qing forces, to force the Chinese government into the first of a series of brazenly unfair treaties. Crushed by taxes and famine, and indignant about the concessions to foreign barbarians, Chinese rebels rose up to restore the moral fabric of the Middle Kingdom. The bloodiest civil war in history, the Taiping Rebellion took thirty million lives (some estimates reach one hundred million). By the end of the summer of 1853, the London *Times* reported that the rebellion was "in all respects the greatest revolution the world has yet seen." With its treaty gains at risk, London sent a negotiating party. The Emperor Xianfeng, struggling to preserve his grandeur, ordered the foreigners to kneel as was custom. The delegation negotiator, the multilingual Harry Parkes, accompanied by the *Times* reporter Thomas Bowlby, refused. Any emissary from the queen of England, an equal to the Qing emperor, was not required to kowtow. "Behead them," the emperor told his guards. The furor over protocol degenerated. Parkes, Bowlby, and other foreigners were shackled and dragged to Beijing in carts for execution. The leader of the British forces, Lord Elgin, was enraged and led allied troops on to the Forbidden Palace to release the hostages, but not before fifteen had died in captivity. The hawkish Bowlby was among them. A swarm of maggots, it is said, buried into his mutilated wrists; after three days, his rotting body was strapped to a beam and heaved over the capital's wall to be eaten, legend went, by dogs and pigs. The London press, which could now count its reporters among the victims, crackled with excitement and outrage.[43]

The problem for London was this: it was hard to promote virtues by peddling vices. The opium craze was already alarming at home. Samuel Taylor Coleridge's addiction was well-known. Thomas de Quincey's *Confessions of an English Opium Eater* (first published in *London Magazine* anonymously in 1821) was a sensation. Far away, the reportage was even uglier. Warmonger-merchants in Canton soiled British honor. There were reports of British troops handing over rebel prisoners to Qing authorities and standing by as they got butchered in public. *The Economist* called this hypocritical meddling—using trade as a pretext for conquest. *The Illustrated News of the World* typified the lamenting mood. This was neither chivalrous nor commercial; it seemed senseless to promote a cause that pit "nearly one half of man [in a] deadly feud with the other."[44] The Second Opium War only deepened the misgivings about interdependence. Stirred by fantasies of showing China the virtues of free trade while teaching the Middle Kingdom a lesson in respect, this time British and French forces joined forces against the Qing.

This second round of aggression also produced the first photographs of war in China, which heightened the debate back home. In 1860, Felice Beato, after two years in India, followed British troops into China. He was on hand for the battles, unlike in his previous tour, and had perfected his technique. Taken over an eight-month period, his images for the pages of *Le Monde illustré* and *The Illustrated News of the World*, which assured readers that these were documentary images "taken on the spot," intensified doubts about the purpose of war in Asia. Henry Haring's gallery on bustling Regent Street, blocks from Piccadilly Circus, showcased Beato's photos of conquered India and China to packed visitors. The montage was hardly a portrait of Anglo-French heroism. Some marveled. Others mourned. Some were enraged. The show spurred heated debate. It had been the Chinese troops who had fought, literally, to the last man; European soldiers, absent in much of the battleground imagery, came across as invaders, not liberators. Even as the soldiers lay moaning, Beato insisted that the scene be untouched until he had finished his portraiture of defeat. In the most controversial of all the photos, of the fallen Taku Forts (August 1860), the cadavers of Qing troops lay where they were blown apart, some of their faces looking up to Beato's lens—and thus to the viewer. In compelling spectators to come face-to-face with the dead, Beato made viewers witness to the ruin of strangers' worlds. Beato's images of Taku fueled domestic discord about the legitimacy of using opium and gunships to open the Chinese market. Even swaggering free traders squirmed.[45]

Two months after the slaughter at Taku, Beato took his gear to Beijing; his plates became the first to document the emperor's Summer Palace and the magnificent Pavilion of the Spirit of Literature, and would circulate in albums, books, and magazine pages. Here were images of "real," until now walled-off, China. See for yourself. Look at the splendor. Observe the decay. Even the walls are crumbling. The Middle Kingdom is ripe for "opening."

But one person's opening is another's closure. Beato's images are rare, and rare for a reason. He was the only person to create a photographic

FIGURE 1.3. Taku Forts.

record of the palace interior before its destruction. Lord Elgin flew into a fit when he learned that the negotiators in Peking had been imprisoned. So he ordered the palace demolished. It took four thousand men three days of pillaging and burning to raze it. They slaughtered three hundred hiding eunuchs and palace maids. When the news of the destruction reached Paris, Victor Hugo was appalled. "It betokened to our minds a sad portent of the fate of this antique empire," concluded one of the expedition's translators, Robert Swinhoe, though he consoled himself with the thought that "there is time yet for China to regenerate herself, and by cultivating friendly relations with foreign empires, learn . . . and keep pace with the march of progress."[46] Even as the beams and gables of the building smoldered, sixteen Chinese men dressed in royal crimson liveries carried an irascible Lord Elgin in a sedan chair to

FIGURE 1.4. The Summer Palace.

a ratification ceremony in the capital serenaded by an army band playing "God Save the Queen." The Treaty of Beijing stuck the Qing with an indemnity bill to pay the victors' costs and opened the doors for embassies, missionaries, and merchants to move beyond the old treaty ports. Beato was there to witness the event and made strangers witnesses; a few days later, he recorded a portrait of the man who had signed the treaty for the Chinese side, a shattered brother of the emperor, Prince Gong. At first, Prince Gong thought the camera was a gun; he turned pale, his eyes darted to the British commanders. Lord Elgin assured him it was safe. The prince relaxed. Though much of the image is out of focus, his mournful eyes pierce through.[47]

More conquest meant more integration, and more integration yielded more prospects for a creative opportunist like Felice Beato. He would shadow Europe's and America's armies, creating a visual narrative of the military edge of world unity until he finally settled down in Japan. There he set up a studio in Yokohama. For over two decades, he took portraits of samurai officials, tea house girls, temples, and street scenes, creating an album of Japan's turbulent Bakumatsu period (1853–68). It is tempting to see him as restlessly curious, a cultural emblem of a new

FIGURE 1.5. Prince Gong.

cosmopolitan age, gathering imagery of strangers for curious viewers back home. But his passion was equal parts business; Beato was in it for the money, a motive at least as important to the age of opening as curiosity was. Occasionally, he overreached. Whatever fortunes he accumulated from his craft got wiped out by speculating in the Tokyo Silver Exchange as it was rocked by a bank crisis. He tried to reinvent himself as a merchant and set sail for London, now through the engineering marvel of the Suez Canal, which had opened in 1869. On the way, he got wind of another military expedition, this time to Sudan in 1884. Beato scrambled to Khartoum. By the time he got there, most of the fighting was over. He continued on through the Red Sea to Cairo and to London. No sooner did Beato unpack than imperialists girded for what would be the last Anglo-Burmese campaign before the full annexation of Burma to British India—and the ensuing refugee crisis. Beato hustled back to Asia again too late for the carnage. Events were now ricocheting too fast for him to keep up, thanks to the expanding network of telegraph cables. So he settled down in postwar Mandalay, opened a studio on C Road, and launched a new business model, swapping out officer portraits for Thomas Cook guidebooks and postcards for the burgeoning imperial tourism industry. No longer was it just soldiers and merchants who sought memorabilia of their mobility, but vacationers. In 1898, Beato sold his business, and from there he slips from the records.[48] Maybe he had a hunch that his business model was doomed; the Kodak Brownie camera, introduced in 1900, was portable and inexpensive, had simple controls and film roll, and meant that almost any traveler could take their own photos. A box with a cheap lens, the device cost one dollar. Kodaks put many Beatos of the world out of business. But they also created vast new opportunities for the news industry and in particular the glossy magazine that made the arresting photograph the news.

One avid consumer of the news about European gunboat diplomacy was the exiled German radical Karl Marx, who was settled in London laboring on his magnum opus, *Das Kapital.* He also happened to be fascinated by photography, describing ideology as representing social reality "upside down as in a *camera obscura*" and using visual tropes to lambaste empiricists for believing what they were seeing and idealists for their inability to see.[49] He advocated a new vision for envisioning, to transcend what the mechanics of the lens—like capitalist production—framed and trapped. As a news junkie, Marx likely saw some of Beato's images. The opium trade, he jeered, was a scheme concocted by British merchants to smash a sclerotic Celestial Empire. By banning opium consumption, "the Emperor gave its traffic all the advantages of a religious propaganda" to Anglo-Indian-Canton merchants and the navies behind them. But if Marx spared no kind words for the Qing, he jabbed at the "flagrant self-contradiction of the Christianity-canting and civilization-mongering British Government." Britain's zeal to open the Chinese market in the name of free trade *required* that the drug be illegal for Chinese traders in China so it could be monopolized by self-righteous European merchants. "Whenever we look closely into the nature of British free trade," he mocked in September 1858, "monopoly is pretty generally found to lie at the bottom of its 'freedom.'"[50]

Just as John Stuart Mill gave expression to the uplifting narrative about integration, nobody outlined the dysphoric one more than Karl Marx and Friedrich Engels, the authors of the other great treatise of 1848. If Mill defended the optimistic storyline of interdependence and the virtues of specialization, Marx and Engels saw commercial integration's power to destroy—even to destroy itself. Marx and Engels did not necessarily sympathize with peasants and artisans struggling for a dying cause; what they did do was highlight the ways in which integration was spelling those people's doom. Marx wrote searing essays for the *New-York Daily Tribune* in the 1850s and 1860s about the "Mutiny" in India, slavery in the United States, and the Opium Wars in China. What drove him to distraction was what he considered the hypocrisy of the governments and the monied men puppeteering them, which accounts for his blend of prophetic outrage and calculating realism. Marx was quick to see the implications of opening trade, expanding railways, extending cables—and the rise of a new financial-mercantile class that sought to make a fortune off the integration of the world and the exports of European manufactures.

As Mill finished his treatise on political economy, Marx and Engels labored over a long pamphlet, *The Manifesto of the Communist Party*. Marx dithered. He preferred to read the papers and lecture workers on the inevitable duplicity of free trade; merchants and industrialists proclaimed its moral purpose when really it was all about the money. Pressed by the Communist League, Marx finally buckled down in early 1848 and rushed to finish the pamphlet, adding his friend, editor, and muse, Engels, as coauthor.

Mainly read as a prophecy of socialist revolution, *The Manifesto* can also be understood as a forecast of a different sort of revolution, one that predicted the ways in which markets and their champions would tear down walls. "In the place of the old wants," noted the authors, "satisfied by the productions of the country, we find new wants, requiring for their satisfaction the products of distant lands and climes. In place of the old local and national seclusion and self-sufficiency, we have intercourse in every direction." Indeed, Marx and Engels offered some keys to understanding the economics of the civilizing process: The commercial and technological feats they saw as responsible for this brave new world were creating "universal interdependence of nations." This universal interdependence would sweep away the obstacles that lay in its irreversible course. The system "by the rapid improvement of all instruments of production, by the immensely facilitated means of communication, draws all, even the most barbarian, nations into civilization." In a rhetorical flourish, the authors concluded that "the cheap prices of commodities are the heavy artillery . . . [that] batters down all Chinese walls, with which it forces the barbarians' intensely obstinate hatred of foreigners to capitulate."[51]

Did integration make the British in China liberators or predators? For Marx, the two roles could not be disentangled. The *camera obscura* made the latter seem, in the self-congratulatory rhetoric, like the former. A decade after *The Communist Manifesto,* his prophecies seemed to be coming true. The smoke from crushing the rebellion in India was still in the air while Marx was poring over news from Canton about the British demands to the Emperor Xianfeng (just before he seized the envoys). He noted how the Palmerston government condemned opium while using it to smash the protections of a troubled Middle Kingdom. How convenient, Marx chortled, that battering down China's walls happened to be a bonanza for narcotic exporters from the raj now that India was formally colonized![52]

Prophets of Revolution

In some ways, Marx, Engels, and Mill saw the world in the same way. A new age was upon humans. They agreed that it was irreversible. They agreed that the market was propelled to expand: the age of nations was also one of interdependence between them. They had a sense of the world-changing transformations of their time and struggled to put them into a larger arc. *The Communist Manifesto* "must contain some history," Engels insisted to Marx.[53] The old system of local attachments and feudal hierarchies was dissolving as the power of money and commodities brought the world's parts into one "world market." In the place of guilds and lords, artisans and apprentices, patricians and serfs was a world dominated by a modernizing bourgeoisie.

But what form would interdependence take? Would it lead to more liberty or more exploitation? On these questions, there was vast disagreement. Each side staked out rival views of interdependence as a deliverance or alienation. If Mill underscored the inexorable uplift and took a euphoric view, his socialist counterparts were dysphoric. If Mill dwelled on expanding horizons, Marx and Engels focused on the thinning of social bonds within and across societies. If Mill obscured the widening gaps between winners and losers from integration, Marx and Engels could only see the chasms: this was an order, they insisted, that "has drowned the most heavenly ecstasies of religious fervor, of chivalrous enthusiasm, of philistine sentimentalism, in the icy water of egotistical calculation."[54]

The Scottish Enlightenment thinkers had created a vision of commercialization that blended possibility with apprehension. A century later, there was a clear contest between rival views of this emerging unity, with titans of political economy staking out their competing narratives, ones that would shape the debates over needing strangers for the ensuing generations. As integration became inevitable and interdependence irreversible, would they foster reason and compassion or avarice and hypocrisy?

Soldiers of the Bridge

So long as the Victorian boom boomed, uplifters carried the day. Marxists and other doomsayers lost battle after battle. Marx himself would look upon the defeat of the Paris Commune as a historic defeat, a turning point in revolutionary eschatology, and would retreat from his certainties.

FIGURE 1.6. The Nile.

In the upcycle, language came to reflect the affective conditions of the economics of opening. This included the word "global." Associated with jet-setting in our day, the word popped up in the 1830s in news about trade and finance. It was still an obscure neologism until the travel industry began to take off and steam shipping made tourism cheaper and faster for patrician vacationers from Europe and America. Thomas Cook promoted the use of coupon books with vouchers that could be redeemed at hotels and restaurants—the precursor to the traveler's cheque—to facilitate border crossing without having to exchange money. The empresario launched cruises, like the 1893 dahabeah vessel pictured in Figure 1.6, up the Nile after the British seizure of Egypt in 1884.

With the spread of Thomas Cook's *Tourist's Handbooks*, footwear and binoculars for the well-heeled, and luggage designed to stack on a porter's trolley to be wheeled through train stations and swanky hotel lobbies, the career of the term "global" began. Marie-Eugène Melchior, the viscount of Vogüé, loved to travel. "His ambition," noted *Harper's* magazine, "to use a word of his own, is to be 'global.'"[55] Critic, novelist, amateur historian from a French provincial family, Vogüé would gain recognition above all for his narratives of his pilgrimages to Syria and Palestine published regularly in Europe's posh magazines, like the *Revue des deux mondes*. It was in Russia—a travel destination he especially touted—that he found his calling as a global booster, marrying a general's sister, calling attention to Dostoevsky, and painting a portrait of a connected world of exotic places and peoples. He extolled "Les Voyageurs" (travelers) and wrote essays dedicated to twenty-year-olds around the planet to share his zest for the world now that it was the oyster for the well-heeled—and to manufacture a particular Western gaze.[56]

It would be hard to exaggerate the European, not to say Eurocentric, features of this vision of integration and interdependence. But it was a vision that appealed beyond Europe—and in respects was not a uniquely European invention. The gaze across new horizons went multiple directions.

Peoples of Asia, Latin America, and Africa, the Resterners, also contributed to the dreamscape of integration and togetherness. They were, after all, confronted—often literally—with the same markets and muskets that Europeans and neo-Europeans brought with them. Many of them—Filipino and Peruvian anarchists, Bombay trade unionists—dreamed of a socialist unity as a counterpoint to the capitalist one. For others, the spread of the West created dreams of an alternative for the Rest, a unity that might escape the vices of integration. Jamal al-Din al-Afghani, the Iranian traveler and thinker, reacted to the British seizure of Egypt with pan-Islamic manifestos read widely across the Muslim world, arguing for Muslim ramparts to defend any more penetration.[57]

But most Resterners—at least the rulers and elite literati—who gazed across the horizon yearned for membership in the world order, with plans for internal reform and adaptation to take a seat in international society. A full-throated anti-colonial resistance as an integrated global movement had to wait. There were signs that it was coming. But first came the idea that the Rest could be as "global" as the West. As a young man, Halil Halid, born in Ankara in 1869, believed in the civilizing mission, joined the Orientalist circles in Britain, earned a master's degree at Cambridge, and taught Turkish at the Special Indian Civil Service section at Cambridge. He would eventually grow disillusioned with Christian pieties, becoming shaped by the petty slights of everyday life as a Muslim in Britain and the relentless pressure on Ottoman sovereignty. His *The Crescent Versus the Cross* (1907) would become a classic critique of the double standards of the civilizers. But even this great polemic was less a tirade against civilizational exclusions than an argument that the "East" had its own history of grandeur; it represented a civilization in its own right. Both sides had their work cut out. It was time that the "people of the Crescent" explain to the missionaries what they really thought of their "glorified civilization." Along the way, he urged his Muslim *confrères* to embrace the material breakthroughs that led to their temporary subordination; Easterners had to catch up and demonstrate that they did not need to be civilized from the outside. In so doing, they would recover their moral standing and restore their place at the table of the worldmakers. Europeans in turn had to relinquish their portrait of the East as uncivilized and give up their convenient monopoly over civilization. What Halid called for was not an overthrow of European values as much as an accommodation for others'. Inclusion of the East in a European-made world would yield better understanding and a more peaceful world order.[58]

For many others, however, joining the club meant internalizing its values. The Japanese philosopher and international lawyer Nishi Amane turned to "Western learning" after moving to Edo and eventually to Leiden, where he studied political economy and statistics. He would become one of the most vocal critics of Tokugawa feudalism and isolation. Later, as the personal tutor to the Meiji emperor, Nishi insisted that Japan be part of the Western legal order—by building national sovereignty within an interdependent world.[59] For liberals worldwide, the flow of goods, people, and money could integrate without conquest. Bengal liberals yearned for greater freedoms and progress—in part to construct a sense of a "people" endowed with rights against the private caprice of the East India Company. The quest sent some, like Rammohan Roy, on a journey to meld an "ancient Indian constitution" with liberalism to restrain imperial authorities and their oligarchs. By the latter half of the century, they saw themselves as part of a wider, international current of what the late Christopher Bayly has called "the more evanescent global ideologies of the period."[60] While on a diplomatic mission to Europe in 1858, Juan Bautista Alberdi noted that interdependence was not even an option for countries like Argentina. There was so much *need*. It was the destiny of the periphery to welcome integration because there was no choice. "Nations like England and France can think twice about taking foreign loans . . . ; but poor and sparsely populated countries [like mine] have no cause to hesitate," he wrote.[61]

Among reformers beyond Europe, the liberal creed authorized yearnings to break free from stationariness. For José Martí, the Cuban patriotic poet, the struggle for freedom from stultifying Spain was all about release from enclosure to join the rest of the world. The transformation in communication fascinated him. His articles for Spanish American newspapers were full of news about postal service in Germany and telegraph lines in Japan. From New York, he marveled at the opening of Brooklyn Bridge on May 24, 1883. As literary editor of *La América*, a magazine like so many others around the world published for teeming diasporas, Martí witnessed the inauguration of the miracle of steel cables and industrial masonry. True, he worried about "the excessive love of wealth" and crass commercialism of New York. But feats like the Brooklyn Bridge connected worlds and opened gates for strangers to seek a better life on a more tolerant planet. "No longer are deep trenches dug around embattled fortresses," he noted. "Now cities embrace one another with arms of steel." Martí's wistful essay ended on an upbeat note: "Bridges are the fortresses of the modern world. Better to bring cities together than to cleave human chests. Today, all men are called upon to be soldiers of the bridge."[62]

Even in its time, Martí's vision was dreamy. But if we do not take his and others' hopes for redemptive interdependence seriously, we fail to understand the depth of disappointment and mourning when interdependence became more menacing, as the euphoria of opening gave way to a different emotional register, as the bonds between strangers became tightener and more threatening at the same time, as fear and anxiety of enclosure flowed into the emotional world economy.

2

Earth Hunger and the Moral Crisis of Integration

Moral Witness

The nineteenth century was good for liberals. Moments of widening horizons tend to favor them; it helps to feel less limited to feel liberated. Victorian faith in free trade, the civilizing power of gold-backed money, and redemptive opportunities to spread the New Testament to other continents and colors erased the concerns that once troubled Scottish Enlightenment thinkers. What a surprise, then, that at their zenith, the openers should be confronted with a groundswell of misgiving that they were forced to encircle, contain, and crush—and then bemoan as a burden.

The end of the century was a peak time of integration and exclusion, mobility and extermination, deepening interdependence and growing sense of entrapment, enclosure, and shortage. As the lacing that strapped the world together tightened, people began to view resources, populations, and risk in a new light. The result was a rush to grab what remained of open frontiers. Latecomers to the "opening" acts—Japan, the United States, Germany—were especially keen to claim their share of the planet. To this was added growing risks of interdependence. The explosion of money lending and the consolidation of the gold standard sent financial shocks ripping through the system. Social elites began to eye other countries not just as opportunities but increasingly with suspicion and envy even as interdependence deepened.

As the world was becoming more frenzied, new actors came to the fore to create a spectacle of the moral and material limits and failings of liberal-imperial integration. The philosopher Avishai Margalit has noted that actors like reporters and truth-seekers, charged with the task of representing the success and suffering of others, perform the role of "moral witness." These bear a resemblance to Adam Smith's "impartial spectator," which was capable of holding people to account for how their actions affect strangers. For Margalit, however, the impartial spectator may have been an abstraction, while an active witness is someone who takes some risk to behold anguish firsthand and relays it to audiences and readers elsewhere. At century's end, missionaries, diplomats, reporters, and travelers all filled this role, feeding the circulation of stories and images that showed the darker side of interdependence. As anxiety crept into the discourse about interdependence, they made ties between strangers appear more perilous, menacing even. The word "darkness" became a metonym for the new age. These actors cast light on the dastardly and immoral happenings in the world's shadows. The moral witness simulated encounters with far-away places and peoples without requiring a reader or viewer to leave their living room. It was enough to transport the reader's imagination to consider how the other lived. Or died. In so doing, the moral witness activated emotional responses to interdependence.[1]

We are cycling back to Adam Smith's original dilemma about the balance of self-interest and sympathy. Recall that he had envisioned the stranger as a central figure in commercial society's ethical coordinates. Smith hoped that moral and market attachments might align, that trade would make strangers mindful of each other's needs and tame brute competition and militarism. But he also worried that it might not. What would happen when self-interest and sympathy parted ways—and were seen to part ways as alarm about risks and news of cruelty between strangers coursed into public debate thanks to the work of moral witnesses to market integration?

By 1900, this question haunted liberal worldmakers and spoke to a basic tension. On one hand, there was the ligature of markets that connected distant parts with common barometers of exchange, like convertible currencies, converging prices, and international units of measure, even standardized time. On the other hand, there was the enclosure and partition of lands into an ever more stratified planet. The first heightened the integrative power of common measures, categories, and commensurabilities; the second heightened the capacity to sort into hierarchies. One integrated while the other distinguished and sorted. Between these two forces the world became more unified and divided at the same time.

News of the World

The media played its role in fanning the emotional world economy. Print capitalism and new media practices spread along with market forces. Indeed, sectors of the media had a vested interest in magnifying risks and reasons for tension. Opportunity, conquest, war, and atrocity made headlines. When once asked, "What sells the news?" a *Daily Mail* editor replied, "The first answer is 'war.'" He went on: "War not only creates a supply of news but a demand for it. So deep rooted is the fascination in a war and all things appertaining to it that . . . a paper has only to be able to put up on its placard 'A Great Battle' for its sales to go up."[2] Backed by networked agencies and the syndicated newspapers, reporters fueled and followed conquistadors to bear witness and relay the news to reader-consumers back home. They ensured that the effects of depending on strangers informed public arguments and shaped conflicting narratives about the ethics of integration.

In the early 1890s, American newspapers went into a frenzy about reports of Spanish atrocities in Cuba. William Randolph Hearst was locked in combat with his rival, Joseph Pulitzer; they dueled to outsensationalize each other with stories of distant wrongdoings to sell papers. Hearst's *New York Journal* erupted with indignation on December 12, 1895: "SPANIARDS INHUMAN CRUELTY." During the ensuing conflict, sales of Pulitzer's *New York World* and Hearst's *Journal* soared. Then, when the war turned into a bloody counterinsurgency, headlines changed their tune. Instead of liberators and openers, American troops found themselves accused of inhuman cruelty.[3]

Conflict made news and news sold papers; news became *the news,* a means of buying one's way into an ever more interlinked and instantaneous mode of life. Behind the competition for stories and information was an expanding network of reporters and agencies. Agence Havas in Paris, Julius de Reuter's agency in London, and Wolff in Germany were among the first truly multinational corporations with agents and "bureaus" scattered all over the planet. No sooner did a submarine cable reach a new port than a news agency opened there. The Associated Press (AP) started as a collaborative of five American newspapers to share the costs of conveying news from the Mexican-American War and joined the cable club after the Europeans. These networked firms reflected the imperial molds from which they sprang and partitioned the news market. Reuters made a grab for Asia. AP wanted the Western Hemisphere. Havas mopped up the Middle East and parts of Africa. Australians, Canadians, Japanese, and Russians responded with agencies of their own. The Japanese Foreign Ministry opened bureaus in Shanghai and New York; the Kokusai and Tōhō News Agencies aimed to feed reports to China to create a common "Oriental" sense of camaraderie against the "West." The result was a web of contracts and cables that linked news sources to news readers through daily papers and glossy magazines.[4]

The news regime motivated a growing number of men and some women with pens and pads to venture afield. Eventually, the camera bag would join the reporter's kit. George Eastman's 1888 Kodak was a simple handheld box capable of multiple exposures on negatives; Kodak made capturing everyday life of strangers and strange lands possible—and the goal. At twenty-five dollars (not cheap—but within reach of a middle-class image maker), and advertising "You press the button—we do the rest," the Kodak became a global booster of its own. When the Kodak Brownie came out (one dollar!), the firm saw that the profits lay less in the machine per se but in the repeat sales of film and mail-in processing in the Kodak "lab" (which was really a factory posing as a darkroom). The firm sponsored Hiram Bingham's Yale Peruvian Expedition, equipping it with the tools to showcase the area's marvels, and Bingham was quick to advertise the camera in his visual exposés of Machu Picchu and other finds in *Harper's Weekly* and *National Geographic*—which put on a full spread of over two hundred images in 1913. Kodak in turn used Bingham's Peruvian panoramas in their promotional sales for a new style and class of exotic tourism, one that could be visually recorded by the tourists themselves. Anyone could do this; if you can travel, you can shoot.[5]

Photography reinforced a style shift in reportage. In the late 1880s, it became possible to reproduce photographs reasonably well in mass-printed publications, but the paper quality had to be high. Only after 1897 did photomechanical reproduction and halftoning make it possible to reproduce photographs on cheap newsprint. By 1914, English half-penny papers like *The Evening News* and *The Daily Mail* had conditioned readers to expect a few pictures alongside the text; *The New York World* employed a small battalion of sketch artists to recycle photos into line drawings (as well as comics strips).[6] Images enabled readers to visualize the story—and yielded a greater sense of immediacy and wider sensory reaction. There was also a stylistic shift in journalism. "The truth" became an imperative, compelling journalists to visit the places and events that they reported on—to be witnesses and report from the spot instead of recycling official pronouncements or cabled reports. Rising competition placed greater premium on at least the illusion of accuracy; the camera helped because it seemed so objective. The correspondent was born, hunting for the human-interest story and ready with quotes from "sources" and even interviews. To fill the pages with news stories (with room for revenue-generating advertisements), specialized magazines, supplements, and Sunday editions took off.[7]

This was the context that gave birth to a documentary style of reporting and recording. Exposés of indigence and squalor became a journalistic genre and subjects for early "street" photography with the help of portable cameras and lighting devices to expose the shadows. Using a handheld Kodak and experimenting with flash techniques for night shots, the Danish American police reporter Jacob Riis revealed the squalid conditions in Manhattan's multiethnic working-class neighborhoods, though he was not above the temptation to arrange and pose his subjects—and sometimes paid them. *Scribner's Magazine* published an eighteen-page montage of line drawings of his photos called "How the

FIGURE 2.1. How the Other Half Lives.

Other Half Lives." Later editions reproduced the original images, like the night shot of an alley off Mulberry Street that depicted three boys asleep on a heating vent, two of them barefoot, bearing Riis's sarcastic caption, *STREET ARABS IN SLEEPING QUARTERS*. It is less clear whether this was a spontaneous shot; the image was taken in daylight. One of the boys appears to be smiling. But the image packed its punch, bringing to the eyes of the city's magnates what they preferred to ignore. This "system," Riis jabbed, "is the evil offspring of public neglect and private greed . . . a storm-centre forever of our civilization." In case the reader-viewer missed the point, he asked, "What are you going to do about it?"[8]

Reporting could also shade into fictional genres of moral witnessing. No one made this move more commercially successful than the émigré Pole Joseph Conrad, who joined the British merchant marine and worked his way up to captain. Seafaring and excursions into forbidding parts gave him the stage sets for stories about global encounters. Conrad made the genre his, declaring that "experience [is] pushed a little (and only very little) beyond the actual facts of the case." While working for a Belgian trading company, Conrad found himself navigating steamers up the Congo River, the perfect setting for probing the underbelly of the civilizing mission. His masterwork came out as serialized and illustrated stories in *Blackwood's Magazine* and was later compiled into the world's most famous tropical atrocity novel, *Heart of Darkness.*[9] After describing the horrors of Belgian colonialism in Congo, the raconteur, Charles Marlow, returned home. At the end of the story, Marlow gazed at the horizon from the side of his ship anchored in the Thames and reflected on the merging shadows of Europe and Africa: "The offing was barred by a black bank of clouds, and the tranquil waterway leading to the uttermost ends of the earth flowed somber under an overcast sky—seemed to lead into the heart of an immense darkness." Ever since, some readers have presumed that the heart of this darkness was in Africa. In fact, Conrad conveyed a general sense of overcast skies to reflect what Europeans were doing worldwide; it was not just those he (and others at the time) called "savages" who behaved in inhuman ways. Any human could be savage. This included the civilizer, perhaps especially the civilizer because they had many more means to inflict cruelty in the name of humanity.[10]

As this darkness of the world became the stuff of sensational stories, the press became a forum for debate and disagreement about interdependence. Before becoming a nonviolent activist, Mahatma Gandhi cut his teeth as a barrister-editor in South Africa. His newspaper, *Indian Opinion,* started in Durban in 1903. Aiming to provide an alternative viewpoint to that of the white supremacists and appealing to readers of the raj's diaspora, *Indian Opinion* provided a pastiche of world news from the wire services; pieces from Ruskin, Tolstoy, and Thoreau; and long editorial ruminations on the remembrance of India from afar. Indeed, the drafts of Gandhi's famous anti-colonial pamphlet, *Hind Swaraj* (1909), first appeared as editorials in *Indian Opinion,* albeit surrounded by columns about upheavals of the Boxer Rebellion in China and meltdowns on Wall Street. When Gandhi finally returned to India in 1914, he regarded the printing press and the newspaper as indispensable tools in his nonviolent campaigns to give his readers a sense of location in a wider world.[11]

Enclosing the World

The expansion and integration of print capitalism was one element of an economic makeover. It made visible other elements of the makeover. One of them was the scramble to penetrate, seize, or colonize the lands of strangers in the name of commerce and civilization. Never before had trade been such a motor of economic growth. Exports from Europe from 1870 to 1913 tripled; world trade as a share of world gross domestic product (GDP) doubled. Not until the early twenty-first century would so many people, so many commodities, and so much investment again flow across borders as a share of world output.[12]

Integration brought increasing rivalry. Eurocentrism magnified rivalry: Europe so concentrated world commerce that it spurred contenders who feared being excluded from its markets, because it looked and behaved like a club. Britain and France enjoyed exporter head starts in new markets. But Germany surged after 1880. At the Berlin Conference of 1884–1885, where European leaders partitioned much of Africa, one of the ostensible pretexts was opening the sub-Sahara to trade—and announced "freedom to trade" in the Congo Basin and open traffic on the Congo and Niger Rivers. The pact scarcely disguised the collusive rivalry between delegates. Competition intensified when American and Japanese interests joined the fray. Japan, by 1900, was muscling into British markets in India; Japanese textiles already had a foothold in China. Many other countries yearned to catch up. In fact, Europe's share of a much-enlarged world trade dropped between 1870 and 1913 from 68 percent (a staggering hegemony and an all-time peak) to 57 percent as competitors pressed in.[13] As the German officer and later Admiral Georg Alexander Müller noted in 1896, "World history now stands under the sign of economic struggle. It rages across the whole globe."[14]

And as the industrial revolution shifted into an age of steel, coal, and eventually oil, a scramble for new raw materials—fibers, fuels, and foodstuffs—in turn had powerful effects on the rest of the world. The value of exports from Latin America, Asia, and Africa nearly tripled in the three decades between 1883 and 1913, especially from societies where land was relatively abundant, where incumbent populations, especially peasants, could be displaced and replaced by migrant labor. Tamils went to Ceylon, Italians to Argentina, and Akwapim farmers migrated from the interior hills of West Africa to coastal cocoa plantations. Within a generation, fields, plantations, and mines dominated once pastoral or peasant worlds to make a more integrated world.[15] The result was a massive demographic reshuffle. By 1912, transoceanic migration peaked at 3.3 million, which represented about 1.7 percent of the world population—a share unsurpassed in human history. It was also truly global. Between 1846 and 1940, nearly as many people moved from India and Southern China to the labor camps and mines of Southeast Asia and the Indian Ocean rim as moved from all of Europe to all of the Americas.[16]

Integration and rivalry—competitive interdependence—led to a massive a shift in land use and territorial grab; there is no conception of territory without a boundary and no idea of filling to its limits without a notion of exploiting it. Once employed for local needs, land and labor got repurposed to produce for exports. In all, between 1750 and 1900, especially with the railway boom after 1870, between 1.5 billion and 2 billion acres of the world's most arable land and pasture was submitted to routine processes of cultivation for commodity production, which represented the largest redistribution of property in the history of humanity.[17] Hinterlands became breadbaskets for industrial and urban societies to meet their needs and satisfy their newfound tastes. Hemp, coffee, rice, cotton, rubber, and soon oil would be the staples of the new world order, produced in one place to be consumed somewhere else.

The most significant product was wheat. A small, hardy grain, easily harvested mechanically and put in motion by conveyers, silos, and container railcars and ships, the staple of our daily bread—about 20 percent of the world's daily caloric intake is from wheat—got connected to global supply chains.[18] Grain farmers, once the backbones of peasant societies, found themselves commodity producers par excellence. In the 1840s, European countries were basically self-sufficient in grains. By the eve of the First World War, a third of Europe's wheat was imported; for

Britain, the share was a whopping three-quarters. The flip side were the Dakotas. Seventy percent of their acreage was devoted to one crop, wheat, and 85 percent of the output was exported to Europe. Grain shipments alone accounted for over 40 percent of all freight tonnage from Argentina. One index of this convergence was the unity of wheat prices around the world. Buenos Aires, Chicago, and St. Petersburg gave the same rewards to their farmers. Those who could not produce for less than the world price went out of business, moving to cities or to new frontiers.[19]

John A. Hobson, an English economist, liberal reformer, and public moralist known for his famous tract *Imperialism: A Study* (1902), tried to square free-market internationalism with some protection for the displaced farmers and unemployed workers it produced, and grew increasingly concerned with the effects of foreign competition on "home industries." He noted that "when each village was a virtually self-sufficient economic unit, some sense that he was helping to feed his neighbour must have accompanied the work of the husbandman who tilled the soil." Those days were going or gone; the self-sufficient, unintegrated, or partially integrated peasant was a vanishing figure. "The Dakota farmer," Hobson noted by contrast, "whose wheat will pass into an elevator in Chicago and after long travel will go to feed some unknown family in Glasgow or in Hamburg, can hardly be expected to have the same feeling for the social end which his tilling serves."[20] Astonished by the power of new technologies of transportation and communications, from transcontinental railways and their latticework of grain distribution to the thickening web of underwater cables sending news about stock and future prices halfway around the world in minutes, Hobson's "new liberal" creed mixed awe and concern about the displacing effects of old liberal economic integration at home, as well as a dawning preoccupation about its effects on the imperial fringes.

My Brother the Peasant

Integration upended lifeways especially where arable land was populated by relatively self-sufficient peasantries or pastoralists. For them, integration meant enclosure and enclosure meant pressures on the commons they relied on for survival. The grasslands of the Americas saw perhaps the most dramatic of these transformations as nomads and villagers got swept aside, exterminated, or corralled into reservations to make way for settlers, their commons transformed into global granaries.

Sometimes local populations adapted—but always at a price. Peasant commodity production swept across global countrysides to produce essentials for world trade. When the Crimean War severed the supply chains for Russian flax at the same time that the world commodity bonanza was beginning, Bengal jute farmers mixed jute (a reasonable long fiber substitute for flax) into their rice crop rotation. Though they found themselves locked in a cycle of debt and dependence on the market, peasant producers of the Bengal Delta kept the world supplied with rope and sacks to haul other world products.[21] In Mexico, extracting vanilla relied on Indigenous labor because the plant was a woodland staple best grown naturally in the wet hillsides of the Gulf of Mexico coast and resisted monocrop production. Vanilla was a native spice drawn and cured from a tropical orchid harvested by Totonac people who circled through the forests to drip the juice from wild vines. When the boom in ice cream making hit American markets with the advent of steam-powered refrigeration, the commercial production of ice cream soared. Flavored with vanilla, ice cream became the rage on leisurely boardwalks and in parlors across America. As the historian Emilio Kourí has shown, exploiting the vanilla ice cream frenzy in the United States turned the internal structure of village life inside out. Totonac harvesters began to "plant" and concentrate their crops in limited spaces bounded by private property markers. Some families became prosperous landowners. Others were reduced to wage earners or sharecroppers. Yet the artisanal gathering system from orchids survived, which blunted wholesale dispossession of Indigenous lands.[22]

Portraits from Bengal and Mexico suggest a spectrum of local responses to global integration; enclosure and unification did not dichotomize the world into a mass of dispossessed workers on one side and one-percenter fat cats on the other, despite Marx's prophecies. And yet, the world was becoming unfair. The demise of nomadism and the autonomous peasantry became the stuff of tragic narratives of loss and mourning. Art galleries in Berlin and Paris drew crowds to exhibitions of peasant hardship. Consider the case of the Brazilian witness Euclides da Cunha. Raised a humble mestizo grandchild of a Portuguese slaver, da Cunha was trained at the elite military polytechnical school of Rio de Janeiro. Transatlantic doctrines of scientific uplift made him an engineer, explorer, and an apostle of Brazil's civilizing mission. Brazil, country of sugar, coffee, and rubber harvested from the land to be consumed elsewhere, was an archetype of global economic integration, which brought da Cunha face-to-face with backlanders from the impoverished northeast known as *Sertanejos*—a mixed-race people not unlike him, part Indian, ex-enslaved, and scraping a life out of the scrub or working as indentured laborers. In 1893, thirty thousand of them, led by the messianic preacher Antônio Conselheiro, took refuge in the interior of Bahia in a hamlet called Canudos. Like millions of others who were losing their lands and autonomy, the *Sertanejos* of Brazil defied state authorities; global integration was not for them.

The Brazilian military in response marched to the hinterlands to crush what got labeled as a "rebellion." Their first efforts were a disaster. Legendary commanders, like Colonel "Head-Chopper" Antônio Moreira César, were killed. News of the debacles spread to the capital, Rio de Janeiro. Humiliated, the army countered ferociously. Ten infantry and artillery battalions and a prolonged siege reduced Canudos to starvation and dysentery. Then the soldiers swept in. About fifteen thousand *Sertanejos* died in the butchery. The preacher's head was severed and shipped to the medical school in Salvador to study its "abnormalities."[23] The civilizers brought witnesses to the historic event to record their triumph. This included da Cunha, who had joined the troops as a reporter for a São Paulo newspaper. The scene left him distressed, and he would pour his mixed feelings into one of the great works of Brazilian literature, *Os Sertões* (1901), as an ode to progress and a lament about the violence it wrought. "Isolated in space and time, the [backlander], being an ethnic anachronism, could only do what he did do—that is, combat, and combat in a terrible fashion, the nation which, after having cast him off for three centuries almost, suddenly sought to raise him to our own state of

FIGURE 2.2. Canudos.

enlightenment at the point of a bayonet, revealing to him the brilliancy of our civilization in the blinding flash of cannons."[24]

On the campaign was a photographer from Salvador, Flávio de Barros, enlisted by the victors to document their feat. He took one of the few images of the *Sertanejo* survivors, their faces turned to the white man and his big machine.[25] Almost as famous as *Os Sertões,* which it would illustrate for generations of Brazilian readers, de Barros's is a portrait of the other side of conquest.

Da Cunha and de Barros were among the growing ranks of witnesses who represented the fate of strangers as they were being dominated. The global enclosure movement produced an urge to catalogue disappearing lifeways and a romance about fading people defeated and pushed aside by the inevitability of progress. Edward S. Curtis was a renowned American ethnographic photographer in his time. His most famous photograph, taken in 1904, was called *The Vanishing Race.* It pictured a column of Navaho riders disappearing into a blurred landscape to become an iconic image of "vanishing race" ideology, which combined ingredients of Manifest Destiny and social Darwinism to predict—across a spectrum from lament to triumph—the disappearance of Native peoples.

FIGURE 2.3. The Vanishing Race.

The photo exemplified the work of white photographers who performed the role of moral witnesses.[26]

To picture a disappearing world was one way to imagine the shift in world history as a tragedy. Global enclosure summoned new ways of thinking about the world as a single, encased unit. A French anarchist geographer named Élisée Reclus spent years wandering through Britain, the United States, and South America. He eventually settled down in Switzerland and would go on to chart with startling accuracy the human experience of the planet in terms of its rivers, its mountains, its deserts—how the physical map of the earth was a guide to the multitude of societies that were growing ever more dependent upon each other. For Reclus, a new age required a new scientific and humanistic imagination, a new cartography, a "Uniform Atlas" to represent the planet in a way that freed earth from conventional maps that carved it into illusory political patterns colored as nations and empires. "The globe," he insisted, "outdoes the map by nature of its truthfulness: it represents the planet in its true structure, it varies exactly according to the real contours, whereas maps, increasingly false as they are applied to greater parts of the planetary surface, can only deceive the viewer regarding the relative dimensions of different regions [while] on the curvature of an artificial globe it is impossible to err with regard to the relative area of the various terrestrial entities."[27]

Unification brought loss. If Reclus dreamed of a universal world, he mourned the passing of old worlds. As he scanned his creation, everywhere he saw how commoners and peasants were losing their lands, pulling up stakes to move, or being crowded out by debt—when they were not exterminated by invaders. He penned an extended letter in the form of a pamphlet called *To My Brother the Peasant,* which he published in 1893. It became an anarchist classic. Reclus pointed out that the spread of industry, trade, mechanization, urbanization—migration and imported foodstuffs—was bringing the curtain down on old worlds. The integration of strangers turned the most rooted class of the world into a relic of a past time: "No love is stranger than that of the peasant for the soil he plows and sows, from which he is born and to which he will return! Yet so many enemies surround him and covet the land that he loves."[28]

Risky World

Bringing distant parts together involved laying down infrastructures to draw lines, connect spaces, and devise rules to manage the fixity of land. They also aimed to manage the fluidity of money needed to build the infrastructure of integration. The gold standard, mentioned in the previous chapter, after a series of gold conferences in 1867, 1878, 1881, and 1892, evolved into a "standard."[29] An ornate system of interbank cooperation kept the payments system open to club members. At the center was the Bank of England, which Walter Bagehot called the "cornerstone" of economic security.[30]

As capital flowed from centers in Europe to clients worldwide, there was a problem. The observant Bagehot spotted it. Bagehot's "money market" was riddled with uncertainties, weak links, and dodgy characters. As he noted prophetically, the "essence" of deposit banking "is that a very large number of persons agree to trust a very few persons, or some one person." The money market could be risky, uncertain, prone to stampedes if the "large number of persons" panicked.[31] This happened with greater frequency and casualties. And because of the gold standard's disciplinary mechanism, panic could lead to harsh punishment and sharp contractions.

In such a tightly coupled, interdependent system, shocks quickly spread. Few economies could escape the booms and busts; the circulation of capital and rules of exchange locked them in. A default from a large borrower, like a railway failing on a dividend or a government being unable to honor a bond, could send investors clamoring to redeem their titles, pushing brokers and bankers to the edge. The Baring Crisis of 1890, provoked by a municipal bond failure in Argentina, nearly brought the mighty house of Baring Brothers & Co. to its knees, seized up the London money market for years, and sent financial tremors around the world. In response, the Japanese government began to withdraw large amounts of gold, which it had accumulated as part of the Chinese war indemnity, from the Bank of England's coffers. Some speculated aloud: were the Meiji panicking or seeking to weaken the British presence in Asia?[32] Alarmed British financiers rushed to call in their own loans from distant corners. As capital retreated to London, Mexico and Brazil got whiplashed. Even lending in India contracted sharply. Banished from the gold club, Argentina plunged into depression. "Business is almost at a standstill," noted the Buenos Aires paper *The Standard*. But not everyone paid a price: "Hundreds of the working classes are starving and soup kitchens are crowded by hungry applicants. Nevertheless, the display of carriages and Russian horses at Palermo Park last Thursday was really superb, quite equal to what one sees at the Bois de Boulogne of Paris. The people who own the carriages are evidently living in a fool's paradise, ignorant of the volcano on which we stand."[33]

The sense of risk revealed the perils of the global Gilded Age. Income disparities spiked; unemployment and farmer hardship spread.[34] By the fall of 1894, wheat prices in London and Chicago hit record lows.

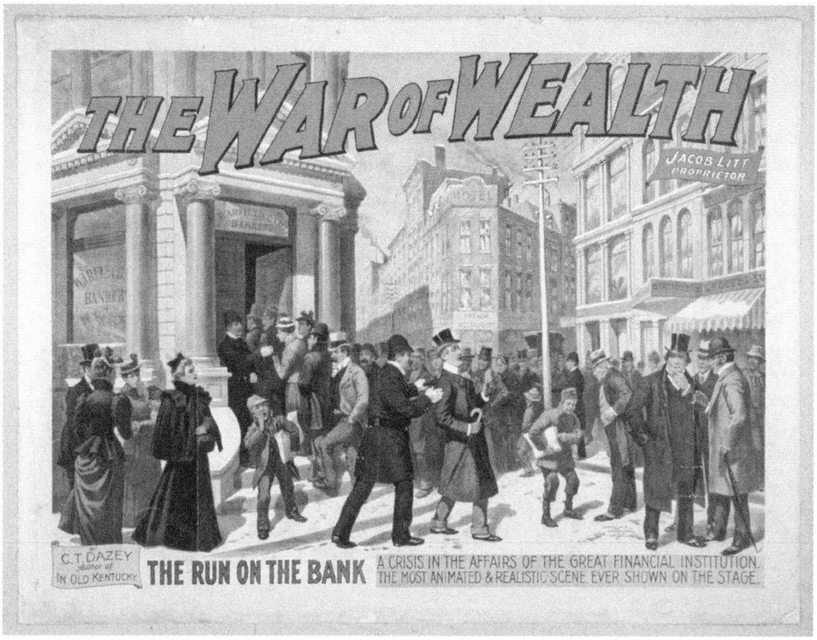

FIGURE 2.4. The War of Wealth.

Workers around the world locked arms in an unprecedented wave of strikes. The New Unionism took off in Europe. By 1894, almost a fifth of the American workforce was unemployed. Strikers paralyzed the nation's rail system from May to July that year; workers struck in factories in Detroit, Chicago, Cleveland; thirty people died in riots and police shootings. The Socialist Party of America was born. The former Senator from Nebraska William Jennings Bryan railed about how farmers and workers were being crucified on a "Cross of Gold," the title of his famous speech. Broadway shows dramatized the New York Stock Market crash of May 1893, shows like *The War of Wealth*, which featured a scene in which frantic investors stormed the stage to save their money.

The risky world and its unequal toll began to concern economists. Some began to wonder whether the long boom of the nineteenth century was coming to an end in a paroxysm of unfairness. Thorstein Veblen, son of hardscrabble Norwegian settlers in Minnesota and early American economist, coined terms like "conspicuous consumption" and "leisure class." He had an eye out for the ostentation of the baronial classes and reserved special attention for the tribulations of the humble farmer. To prosper, they plowed more land to send staples to far-away consumers. The more they grew, the more wheat went to market. As supplies of wheat rose, prices sank. So farmers borrowed money to fill the gap. And to pay off debts, they plowed more land and sent more wheat to market, further depressing prices. It was a spiral of interdependence (in technical terms it is part of something called the "cobweb problem").[35]

The uneven effects of interdependence were on the mind of the Gujarat-born savant-merchant Dadabhai Naoroji, who moved to London to become the first British Indian Member of Parliament. He also kept up his publicist work and statistical obsessions. It was not the New World homesteader that Naoroji worried about, but the Indian peasant. A collector of social facts and statistics to prove that Indians were held down by a venal imperial system, Naoroji wanted India to prosper by being a free part of the world economy. As his evidence mounted, he grew frustrated and eventually outraged by what he saw as the widening gap between splendor in England and squalor in India—and the tone deafness of raj rulers. The more he pored over his data about rice production, dhal consumption, and salt revenues in Madras, the angrier he got. Armed with statistical tables, his *Poverty and Un-British Rule in India* (1901) warned the British that they failed to honor their side of the liberal deal. "Let India have its present drain brought within reasonable limits, and India will be quite prepared for any free trade," he wrote.[36]

From Enclosure to Closure

The fear and outrage about the workings of the world market were compounded by growing apprehension that integration and enclosure had finally exhausted the world's resources. After fifty years of opening, the world seemed suddenly encased into a single biome.

Disease and famine played their part in tilting the emotional economy from exaltation to anxiety, optimism to pessimism. The Salween River flows from the Tibetan Plateau into the Andaman Sea. A narrow watershed, it has divided China from India for centuries. Its upper reaches have also been a borderland for the shifting frontier between infected and uninfected provinces of the bubonic plague since the fourteenth century. When a revolt broke out in the 1850s in the province of Yunnan, Chinese troops forded the Salween to suppress the insurgents. Unaware of the lurking bacteria *Yersinia pestis,* the soldiers picked up the disease and carried it back across the river. As troops went home or got redeployed by Qing authorities to put down the Taiping Rebellion and to drive out European gunships, the *pestis* spread across the Middle Kingdom. While the Qing struggled to put out the fires of sedition, they were helpless when it came to plague outbreaks. By the 1890s, the plague had reached the treaty ports. In 1894, European settlements in Canton and Hong Kong went into a panic at the sight of swelling buboes and erupting pus. In 1896, the pandemic reached Bombay—and would wipe out six million Indians. Then it struck Aden, Mogadishu, and Cairo, spreading fears that Rome and Marseilles would be next on the contagion's hit list. The *pestis* showed up in San Francisco in 1900. Fears of a new Black Death raced ahead of the pathogen. Authorities in major seaports began to close their hubs, leaving millions stranded and cargoes rotting on wharves.

Faced with the spreading hysteria, bacteriologists saw an opportunity. The crisis spawned scientific collaboration. Japanese and French scientists descended on Hong Kong to "discover" the mysterious *Pasteurella pestis* culprit behind the plague. International task forces set up in Hong Kong, Bombay, Sydney, San Francisco, Buenos Aires, and Paris. It was not just the people who had to be isolated. Recent bacteriological discoveries also taught public health authorities how to stop infected rodents, especially rats, from spreading the *pestis* to native species, like ground squirrels and other burrowing rodents. A worldwide campaign, supported by a global consortium of scientists and the new International Office of Public Hygiene (created in 1909), went on a crusade against the bubonic bacillus. They contained it and rolled it back by 1922. It became orthodoxy that the unity of the world's bacterial pool transcended political divides.[37]

The 1890s also brought new attention to the effects of climate on living habitats, adding fears of scarcity and shortage to panic about pestilence. The plague coincided with climate changes wrought by the shifting El Niño currents, which caused drought across the world's breadbaskets. The combination with the economic malaise and pictures of destitution was a toxic mix.[38] 1891 saw massive crop failure in Russia. The Imperial Free Economic Society of St. Petersburg went into emergency meetings. Liberals and radicals pointed their fingers at feudal landlords. Others blamed backward peasants. Eventually, the alarm subsided, but not before sowing the seeds of lasting anxiety.[39] Climatologists joined the search to explain environmental pressures. In a century of ballooning, measuring, and observing, along with meteorological professionalization with larger telescopes, more journals, and scientific sociability like in the Societé météorologique de France, founded in 1852, the atmosphere became a new common frontier.[40] The science of weather prediction also yielded more awareness of connected risk, hazards, and foreboding. In 1896, a Swedish chemist, Svante August Arrhenius, looked to the atmosphere for clues about the making of the Ice Age. He argued that the quantity of CO_2 might affect temperatures by functioning like glass in a greenhouse—and that anything that trapped carbon dioxide might raise temperatures. The conclusion: smoke-belching coal-fueled factories might explain heat waves, drought, and climate change for everyone on Earth.[41]

In the 1890s, relief could not come fast enough. It felt like the Four Horsemen of the Apocalypse were on a rampage. Shortages and crowding cities revived the ghost of Rev. Thomas Malthus and his pessimistic prophecies. Could the world be running up against its physical limits, growing populations consuming their surpluses and farmers pushing into less fertile land while migrants carried pestilence from port to port? The planet's biological and physical circuitry seemed not just subject to the same human-induced forces, but faster-moving news, germs, money, and commodities made it feel smaller, riskier, and inescapable.

The Birth of Geopolitics

It appeared even more as if enclosure was yielding a closed—and now overheating—system. "Closing" was the key word of a famous lecture by a then-obscure American historian. When Frederick Jackson Turner stood before his peers of the American Historical Association in 1893, he outlined the ways in which the open frontier had been the defining feature of the American character—a valve to release pent-up tensions, a forge for everyday democracy, a source of muscular individualism. Blessed with vast reserves of "vacant" land—here one can see the vanishing race ideology in full flight—America had been allowed to chart its own, almost providential, course. Turner declared that those days were over. All he had to do was read the words of the director of the 1890 census: the frontier, defined as territory beyond which population density was less than two people per square mile, was officially "closed." For Turner, without "free" land (as if the displacement of Native peoples were costless), America would hereafter become more and more European, replete with crowding and crises—and become less exceptional. "And now," Turner prophesized, "four centuries after the discovery of America, at the end of a hundred years of life under the Constitution, the frontier has gone, and with its going has closed the first period of American history."[42] He echoed a wider mood. The Minnesotan firebrand Ignatius Donnelly pronounced that "we have practically reached the limit of our available free land supply." The consequences were menacing: "Free-land has been the safety-valve of Europe and America. When the valve is closed, swarming mankind every day will increase the danger of explosion."[43] The avatar of new British imperialism, the mining empresario, and prime minister of the Cape Colony, Cecil Rhodes, declared in 1898 that "Little England is now hopeless."[44]

Anglo-Americans were not the only alarmists. Famine ravaged India. For Florence Nightingale, the celebrity humanitarian angel of the Victorian age, rampant starvation revealed the ugliness of the raj. Echoing a rising chorus of Indian and British critics of colonial governance, Nightingale concluded that "we [the British people] do not care for the Indian people."[45] In Russia, opening Siberia was one way to alleviate the tsar's fears of encirclement while releasing the pressure on peasant communities in the black earth provinces. The 1891 famine made the drive more urgent and redoubled fantasies of an eastern frontier for Russian Orthodoxy in Asia just as the western frontier had been for Protestant Americana. Famished peasants of inner Russia could also be moved to

Central Asia to colonize the Kazakh steppe.[46] Europeans looked upon America's abundant resources with envy. The French philologist and historian Ernest Renan fretted about the shortages and malaise and warned of the inevitability of socialism—unless a means of distraction, such as looking to strangers, could defuse the tensions. "A nation that does not colonize is condemned to end up with socialism, to experience war between rich and poor," he proclaimed.[47] French leaders had been eyeing North Africa as a frontier of their own for a long time. By 1896, Émile Zola was composing one of his last works, dedicated to the problem of closure and fertility, called *Fécondité*.[48] Third Republic ideologues were in a fit about scarce resources, declining fertility, and fears about the demise of "the French race." German nationalists, caught between expanding Russia and expanding France, also yearned for room to grow. In 1881, the *Westdeutscher Verein für Kolonisation und Export* (West German Association for Colonization and Export) was formed; in the 1890s, the association lobbied hard to go beyond partitioning Africa—to settling it. Kaiser Wilhelm II's *Weltpolitik* envisioned "a place in the sun" with no less than a project of overland integration of Asia and Europe with Germany as the hub and its railways, like the Berlin-Baghdad Express, as the spokes. By the middle of the decade, some were toying with ideas of annexing Germany's neighbors. The Leipzig Chamber of Commerce drafted plans to annex Poland. The *Alldeutscher Verband* (Pan-German League), formed in 1891, formulated elaborate schemes to integrate Eastern Europe, Mexico, and South America through German settlement to safeguard resources for the pan-German peoples.[49]

Alarm about closure and fear of shortages informed a way of viewing the interdependence of nations as rivals in a world of scarce resources and the rise of what became called "geopolitics." The military strategist Alfred Mahan in the United States; Friedrich Ratzel, the man who coined *Lebensraum* (living space), in Germany; the British imperial cartographer Halford Mackinder, who climbed Mount Kenya because he wanted to beat the Germans to it; the Swedish geographer Rudolf Kjellén—all imagined a spatial and biological destiny for humanity that was at once interdependent yet divvied into sovereignties. Mackinder proclaimed that centuries of expansion into the New World were now over; the "Columbian epoch" was no more. No longer could states presume that their citizens live in abundance and open frontiers. The world was interdependent, Mackinder noted, but its parts were struggling for space.[50]

Scrambling for territory and frontier grabbing did not defuse tensions, as many rulers hoped. Quite the opposite. They spiraled into more competition. In all, the number of conquered territories leaped from 300,000 square kilometers in the 1860s to 6 million in the 1870s, almost 9 million on the 1880s, and over 7 million in the 1890s, before settling down to 2.8 million in the first decade of the twentieth century, by which time most of the world was carved between conqueror and conquered.[51] Not since the early days of Iberian conquistadors in the sixteenth century had a handful of countries laid claim to so much of the planet. As he reflected on the partition of Africa, Joseph Conrad noted that Europeans "grabbed what they could get for the sake of what was to be got. It was just robbery with violence, aggravated murder on a great scale, and men going at it blind—as is very proper for those who tackle a darkness."[52]

Cut Up Like a Melon

If closure sharpened Europe's, Japan's, and America's sights on the lands of strangers, older empires, like the Ottoman and those of China and Spain, grew more anxious about falling behind. For the vintage dominators, encirclement made catching up more urgent than ever, lest they slip into the ranks of the dominated. As part of a "self-strengthening" drive, Chinese reformers went on campaign mode. One desperate reformer pleaded, "If China does not reform herself, then hereafter foreigners will meddle everywhere in the mining and railway affairs of the interior." The source of the anxiety was a sense that the world's resources were running out and compelling Japanese, U.S., and European powers to fasten their sights on China, its markets as an opportunity and its burgeoning population and scarce resources as a source of unstable danger. Business magnates like Sheng Xuanhuai hired German engineers to plan mining enterprises in Shandong in the 1890s. In the words of Yen

Fu, an alarmed foreign-trained scholar, engineer, and naval officer: "Since the products of the earth and the heavens are limited, but peoples' desires limitless, and daily multiplying, in the end, they will not be enough. Shortage leads to contestation, and human morality's greatest tragedy arises from this contestation." All he could see was foreboding, rising global demand and pressing shortages—and intensified rivalry, *sauve qui peut* on a global scale.[53]

It was Japan's defeat of China in 1894–95 that sparked a Pacific scramble, culminating in a debate among conquistadors over whether to partition China as they had Africa. One might say that the collision over China really began with Russia's expansion eastward, especially as the tsar's ministers fastened on access to the ice-free Pacific terminus of Port Arthur. This made Japanese rulers nervous: a weak China and vulnerable tributary Korea were prone to Russian incursion. Russian colonists had been moving into Manchuria. The Trans-Siberian Railway builders wanted year-round port access. Russian capitalists poured money into coal mining at Fushun, China, for access to coal was essential for the railway economy, and railways were indispensable for the Russian imaginary to break encirclement. And the scramble for carbon lay at the heart of the growing tensions between St. Petersburg and Tokyo. Harbin, like other borderland cities, grew from scratch as a railway hub and filled with Russian engineers, Chinese villagers from Shandong, German doctors, Korean laborers, and Japanese merchants. It was a polyglot world of muddled yet divided peoples who would get pushed around by the millions as frontiers of war and revolution would wash back and forth across north China.[54]

In a preemptive dash, the Meiji regime went on a spasm of expansion to block Russian expansion. It meant taking out weaker powers and incorporating new colonies in mainland northeast Asia. Starting with the stunning defeat of Qing armies and navies in 1894, here was upstart Japan delivering a decisive blow to the Middle Kingdom. This led to seizing smaller islands like Iwo Jima and the Kuril, and folding in Korea and Taiwan. Japanese traders went to the Philippines in search of markets and material for Japanese industry. The foreign minister, Enomoto Buyō, became an outspoken advocate of the need for settlement and colonization. The newspaper *Shokumin kyōkai* declared in early 1893 that "emigration is presently an urgent business for Japan. . . . As soon as the European powers started undertaking emigration projects, they eagerly planned national enrichment. Therefore, Japan must plan such an enterprise."[55]

Japan's campaign set off a chain reaction. It nurtured alternative visions of world order and pan-Asian solidarity capable of standing up to Europeans. It led some Meiji rulers to envision a Monroe Doctrine for Asia, which included Japanese say over the future of China. The Spanish, clinging to the Philippines, grew increasingly alarmed at the *espantajo japonés* (Japanese scarecrow). Russia and Japan were locked into a collision course that led to war in 1904. The British feared that their outpost in Hong Kong would soon be overwhelmed by rivals.[56]

Americans took note of the panic in the Pacific. William Alden Smith, a senator from Michigan, grumbled that Washington stood around while other powers were grabbing what they could. Henry Cabot Lodge, a recently elected senator from Massachusetts who cherished American exceptionalism as a counterpoint to grubby Old World imperialism, worried more about the high seas and U.S. reach far away, as he watched "great nations . . . rapidly absorbing for their future expansion and their present defense all the waste places of the earth."[57] He urged Alfred Thayer Mahan, the Naval War College professor and grand strategist, to turn his lecture notes about naval power into his landmark: *The Influence of Sea Power upon History, 1660–1783*. National greatness was forged on the high seas; it was there that the cause of free and open trade would be decided, according to Mahan, and thus determine the balance of world power. The sea was the old-new frontier in the making of geopolitics. Mahan captured the zeitgeist about landed closure, and the idea in turn influenced military strategy. One of his avid readers was the emperor of a nearly landlocked country squeezed between old rivals, Germany. Kaiser Wilhelm II "devoured" the book and named Admiral Alfred von Tirpitz as secretary of state for the navy in 1897, en route to a legendary arms race with Britain. Albion responded with the dreadnought, the most complex military invention in world history to date. Launched by the Royal Navy in 1906, the dreadnought was not just belted by foot-thick high-quality steel to thwart any projectile; it had ten massive rotating guns capable of hurling three-ton shells at targets ten miles away.[58] The American president, Theodore Roosevelt, wanted some for his own—only to be stymied by a stingy Congress. Wilhelm, however, prevailed, and budgeted for his spending spree on his navy—thus setting off an escalation in building of dreadnoughts, battlecruisers, and super-dreadnoughts at an eye-watering price.

Mahan's vision of geopolitics and the anxiety of closure did shape American self-conceptions on the world stage, though it was to the Pacific, and specifically to Japan and China, that the gaze turned. Washington eyed the Spanish Philippines with concern: what if Japan beat Spain and seized the archipelago? But America, argued the exceptionalists, needed noble reasons to justify overseas military excursions, unlike Old Worlders. Events in Cuba, another Spanish colony, could be manufactured for this purpose; Cuba's struggle for freedom gave the exceptionalists their moral card. As the Spanish army, led by General Valeriano Weyler—alias "The Butcher"—resorted to brutal tactics to suppress Cuban insurgents after 1895, the American press found their righteous cause. James Creelman, an American journalist whose reportage would have an outsized influence on inter-American affairs, wrote in the *New York World* in May 1896 about "blood on the roadsides, blood in the fields, blood on the doorsteps, blood, blood, blood." Under the banner of a "Battle for Humanity," American forces defeated the exhausted Spanish troops and made Cuba, Puerto Rico, and the Philippines theirs.[59]

Now China had all the great powers at its doorsteps. Qing reformers agonized. Kang Youwei, a Chinese intellectual, began to write about occupied Poland as an example of "lostness." "Polandization" became a catch-all for dismemberment. (In 1795, the Russian and Austrian empires swung the last axe to an independent Polish-Lithuanian Commonwealth). Alarmed at the widening gap between the modern West and an ancient kingdom, this Confucian modernizer was an important figure in mentoring a generation that would make catching up a centerpiece of their crusade to save China from ignominy. Among his most important disciples was Liang Qichao. Son of a teacher and farmer from Guangdong province, where commercial, financial, and missionary penetration into China was most intense, Liang steeped himself in Western texts, then traveled to Beijing in 1895 to sit for his exams. That year, Japan's victory ripped away the illusion that China could remain walled off. "The defeat in 1895, loss of Taiwan, and two hundred million taels in reparations awoke our nation from its four-thousand-year-long dream," he proclaimed.[60] Another intellectual, Yan Fu, worried that his country would now get "cut up like a melon."[61]

The crisis finally came when insurgents, known as Boxers, began to attack foreign missionaries across northern China in 1899. Embattled, the Qing government initially supported the uprising. As with the specter of atrocity in Cuba, the suffering of Christians overseas was a pretext for holy meddling. This prompted an Eight-Nation Alliance of Britain, France, Russia, Japan, Germany, Italy, Austria-Hungary, and the United States to "intervene" to protect threatened foreigners. Along with invading armies came reporters, like James Ricalton, an experimenter in stereoscopic photography. Famous for going to great lengths to get elevated for panoramic images (he would perch himself on elephants and camels, or build raised platforms for bird's-eye view shots), he followed the warrior frontier—shooting the shooting in the Greco-Turkish conflict, South Africa, and the Philippines. On July 5, 1900, he reached Tientsin (later Tianjin) in time to watch the siege and bombardment of the Boxer-held city. In his "illustrated travelogue," a genre for the popular nonfiction marketplace, his words dripped with disgust at the decay, filth, and disorder. Chinese cities, he wrote, were "redolent of every known and unknown odor and teeming with filthy myriads of human life." But he didn't flinch. As the shells rained down, he set up his gear amid "a holocaust of human life, lines of homeless, weeping human beings." Still, he did find room to portray Christian solidarity. Consider the shot in Figure 2.5 of American troops rescuing "native [converted] Christians" as "refugees" from Boxer fighters.[62]

In the end, the Allies did not partition China. Better to leave a hobbled and indebted Qing regime to manage domestic social unrest while paying an indemnity to the liberators in gold. Instead, the humanitarians added to the list of unequal treaties and concessions. In the year of the settlement known as the 1901 Boxer Protocol, Yen Fu penned a

FIGURE 2.5. Refugees in Tientsin.

prophetic essay on imperialism that charged the do-gooders with masquerading under humanitarian banners in order to subdue China while endorsing Chinese exclusion and violence back home. In Tientsin, the liberal Yen Fu was busy translating Adam Smith and John Stuart Mill, and poring over the news. As the editor of the newspaper *Guowen Bao*, he followed the anti-Chinese lynching in South Africa and suppression of Filipino freedom fighters with dismay. "Even though the independence of the Philippines has been all but crushed, and the independence of the Transvaal confronts imminent disaster, and while imperialism [*diguo zhuyi*] is on the ascent . . . the furious struggle between imperialism and Independence will surely be many times fiercer than [the struggle unleashed by] revolutions in Europe. . . . Are not Asia and Africa the battlegrounds of the twentieth century?"[63]

Earth Hunger

In the age of mass media, telegraphs, and news agencies, it was not hard to connect the dots from East Asia to South Africa to the Caribbean. One blistering editorial in *The Gold Coast Aborigines* in late August 1900 drew a direct analogy between the partition of Africa and the invasion of China, and the global divide between the liberators and not-so-liberated: "The insolent whites thought that China was dead, but they now find her very much alive. The same will be found true with the blacks." The editorial continued, arguing that "opening" rhetoric was a mask for a different, more insidious purpose. "The old slavery is dead, but a more subtle if not cruel slavery may take its place. The demand of the capitalist everywhere is for cheap and docile labour. . . . Hence the China crisis, hence the danger to the blacks in Africa." The work of the conquering Cecil Rhodes was creating a new style of imperialism, it argued. "But we may thank him," the editorial read, "for exposing his designs and so warning the Negro race of the evils in store for them if he and his like are to bear sway."[64]

As the world got sorted into a visible hierarchy, critics gathered force. After reading the poetry of José Rizal, the Filipino patriot shot by a Spanish firing squad, and depressed about the latest round of Chinese humiliations that left the Qing too crippled to rule but so indebted that its sole mission was to serve other empires, Liang Qichao penned a bitter diatribe "On the New Rules for Destroying Countries," cataloguing the fates of Poland, India, and Egypt at the hands of capitalists. "To those who claim," intoned Liang, "that opening mining, railroad, and concessionary rights to foreigners is not harmful to the sovereignty of the whole, I advise you to read the history of the Boer War." In the meantime, he dreamed of an alternative history. Liang penned a utopian novel set in the year 1962, *The Future of New China*, which begins during the fiftieth anniversary of Qing reform in Shanghai and envisions a celebration of the World Expo as Shanghai, the hypocolony, had become an entrepôt for a global China.[65]

The hierarchy of the world was geographic and racial. What dominated the urge to dominate, for many, was anxiety. "If we open a map," Liang urged his readers in 1899, "we see that the White race has already taken five of the six continents, excluding only Asia." The source of the scrambling was economic. "Europeans want to find customers in Africa for their industry and commerce," and so they carved it up. This was not enough; Africa was too poor. But since "the problem of overproduction still haunts the Europeans . . . they are ever more hard-pressed." They would do even more. "They turn their evil eyes to China with savage greed in their hearts," Liang concluded. "My fellow citizens! If we do not have the will for the struggle to survive, will we be in any way inferior to the Philippines and the Transvaal?"[66]

If Asian and African observers connected the dots, so did Europeans, often referring to the same economic arguments. John Hobson, who had been fretting about British underconsumption in the 1890s, cast his eyes across an international horizon. Until then, he had been an advocate of gunboat diplomacy and liberal imperialism, of opening China, expanding free trade, and deepening interdependence in the John Stuart Mill tradition; these were all part of the providential style of liberalism's "rational cosmic plan." The escalation of tensions in the 1890s, however, sowed the seeds of doubt; he grew increasingly uneasy about the ways in which the world market was being hijacked. The botched Jameson Raid against the South African Republic drew Hobson's eye to the hidden hand of Cecil Rhodes and stockjobbers. He began to publish articles about imperial ethics in *Progressive Review*. Sent by the *Manchester Guardian* to report on the South African War in the summer of 1899, he was alarmed at the violence and appalled at the official lack of concern about its economic and moral toll—and the thrall to a handful of mine owners and financial speculators who controlled the press in South Africa and their jingoistic allies in London. The war was justified as a necessity to block rival, notably German, influence on the gold-rich colony. The largest military mobilization since the Napoleonic Wars, it led to the death of thousands of civilians, many from starvation, and featured new weapons, like the Maxim gun and barbed wire, and adaptations of pandemic isolation strategies—like the "concentration camp"—for martial purposes. Capable of firing *continuously* as soon as the trigger was depressed and cease only when it was released, the Maxim's lethality multiplied the killing potential of a single round. The Battle of Omdurman of 1898 pit fifty-two Maxim gunner teams against waves of Dervish fighters, leaving less than fifty British dead and about twelve thousand Sudanese. One German war correspondent observed that "it was not a battle but an execution." (As lore would have it, it was not the Maxim gun that made the headlines but the archaic "gallantry" charge of the 21st Lancers.)[67]

The Maxim also wreaked havoc against the Matabele in southern Africa. "The white man come again with his guns," recalled one fighter, "that spat bullets as the heavens sometimes spit hail, and who were the naked Matabele to stand up against these guns?"[68] To Hobson, the "early flower of human cosmopolitanism" rooted in a liberal world of cooperative interdependent nations was ceding to increasingly aggressive competition and hypernationalism. Above all, it was the rise of a financier class, emboldened by steel and cable, that turned liberal powers into land-grabbing imperialists. As long as countries simply traded with each other, there was no need for any formal control or conquest—just occasional "intervention." The rise of the financier changed the equation, according to Hobson. Wars and costs of empire were borne by working and middle classes for the benefit of monied plutocrats. As for the colonies, Hobson concluded that they were becoming "a vast system of outdoor relief for the upper classes" of Europe.[69]

Often seen as a critic of empire, Hobson was far from it. What incensed him was the perversion of empire from its original liberal, freedom-expanding purpose. What he noted, while recycling the cultural assumptions of an earlier era about who was fit for sovereignty, was a fundamental break in the world system that empires had created. Upon his return from South Africa, Hobson issued his most famous tract, *Imperialism,* in 1902, a book which has heavily influenced social reformers and radicals ever since. A flawed but quite brilliant work—Hobson confused a cyclical downturn of the 1890s with structural decline, he exaggerated the influence of merchants and financiers on policymakers, and he missed all the other ways in which the powerful tied the powerless into a hierarchy without having to rely only on Maxim guns—there was a point worth underscoring: imperialism was a choice, not a necessity. It was a choice made by elites who would rather hoard their money and cause a shortage of demand at home. Rather than share with the working and middle classes to deepen a domestic market, they turned to foreigners, their markets, and their resources. Late nineteenth-century imperialism overturned the Cobdenite fantasies of free trade and replaced them with protection rackets, a "lust for racial domination," and a mass psychology of "jingoism." The difference now was that strangers had to be colonial subjects in order to be dependable. This agitated dependence on strangers, their lands, and their subordination Hobson called "earth hunger."[70] This fever, earth hunger, Hobson believed, was the toxic element of a postliberal brand of imperialism, one which, when unleashed, was an existential threat to liberalism and democracy itself; a gluttonous investorate, a gang of monopolists who hoarded the savings of good working people, was seizing the keys of a once-virtuous liberal empire and instead of being content with the civilizing effects of colonization and free trade, was seeking to dominate and extract from what Hobson regarded as "lower races" by whipping up the passions of nationalism and jingoism.

Removing the Blindfold

The escalating violence and atrocities committed in the name of the civilizing mission shook the grounds upon which the ethics of interdependence once stood. It was the privileged, the powerful, the liberators who led the charge to remove constraints against hideous treatment of strangers—and then tried to blame them for their fate. The circular, self-serving logic got harder and harder to bear; witnessing became more and more heated because invading the lands of strangers initiated modern, anti-colonial, guerrilla warfare. Guerrilla wars are by definition escalatory and vicious; the distinction between combatant and civilian dissolves, which means even the most well-meaning civilizer winds up warring against those whom they want to civilize and in short order finds themself behaving in ghastly ways. British, Dutch, German, and French invaders each found tortuous ways to justify their behavior; each increasingly screamed about the other's atrocities in a futile effort to crush the resistance—while borrowing each other's playbooks of torture, encampment, and scorched-earth counterinsurgency, all clad in a rhetoric of racial superiority and Christian destiny.[71]

No country was more riven by the gap between the euphoric rhetoric of enlightened integration and the harsh realities it produced than the United States. This was in part because no country wrapped its self-imagery in as providential a cloth as the United States.

One might say that the horrible outcome was only predictable in hindsight. But it wasn't. Moral witnesses made it horrible in real time. As American forces got bogged down in a pitiless war in the Philippines, the press turned bad for the liberators. Pictures of torture involving a

FIGURE 2.6a. "Watercure."

technique euphemistically called "watercure" began to show up in magazines back home. The one pictured in Figure 2.6a and b was staged. President Theodore Roosevelt assured a friend that it was "an old Filipino method of mild torture," adding, incredulously, that "the Filipinos had inflicted incredible tortures upon our own people."[72] For reporters on the scene from the *New York Evening Post* and *The Times*, it was a harrowing spectacle. Soon, there would be congressional hearings on torture practices inflicted upon the liberated.[73]

With the detention camps and stories of torture came massacres. One of the most notorious took place in March 1906 on the sides of the volcano Bud Dajo, when troops, many of them veterans of extermination campaigns against Native peoples of the American plains under the command of General Leonard Wood, slaughtered around one thousand Tausug Muslims. Massacres at Wounded Knee, Pine Ridge, and elsewhere were already on the résumés of many officers in the Philippines. Roosevelt cabled Wood, congratulating him on "the brilliant feat of arms" in "honor of the American flag." American newspapers filled with

FIGURE 2.6b.

chest-beating. But then the news of the atrocity followed. The *New York Times* headline of March 9 read:

"WOMEN AND CHILDREN KILLED IN MORO BATTLE. . . . President Wires Congratulations to the Troops."

Wood, gloating that he would take senators to the next campaign to counter the "fake outrage," dismissed the accusations.[74] But then

FIGURE 2.7. On Bud Dajo.

came the visuals. There were two or three photographers on hand. One photograph escaped the efforts of the U.S. military to destroy it. Smuggled out of the Philippines by an American teacher who sailed to Japan on furlough, it eventually reached stateside and was first published in Johnstown, Pennsylvania's *Weekly Democrat* on January 25.[75] It captured a gulley—the *Trench at Bud Dajo*—full of cadavers of civilians, including many women and some children, rimmed by American soldiers. On the defensive, Wood claimed that women dressed as men for combat. Then he said the rebels used women and children as shields. It shocked the American public and set in motion a furious debate about the morality of empire on the floor of Congress. Democrats denounced the "wanton butchery." An aging Mark Twain authored a blistering rebuke of the Proconsul Wood and hissed at the president's chest-thumping about "our uniformed assassins [that] had *not* upheld the honor of the American flag."

Twisted, tangled bodies, a mass of flesh and shredded clothes—one can almost smell the stench of decaying corpses. The violence was distilled in the poses of the conquering whites, all but one of whom turned to face the photographer while dead "natives" lay in a heap. The young African American intellectual W.E.B. Dubois took one look at this image and, horrified, wrote to the president of the Anti-Imperialist League that it was "the most illuminating thing I have ever seen. I want especially to have it framed and put upon the wall of my recitation room to impress upon the students what wars and especially wars of conquest really mean."[76]

Images like this turned the "White Man's Burden" into an emblem for all that was wrong about the white man's hubris. It was only a few years earlier that Rudyard Kipling penned a poem of this title urging Americans to assume their moral responsibility to uplift dark-skinned people by force, particularly in the Philippines (subtitle was "The United States and the Philippine Islands"). Kipling had moved the duty to civilize into a burden, the right to dominate into an obligation. Many countered. The British journalist E. D. Morel blasted the occupiers with an exposé of imperial cruelty in a scathing article called "The Black Man's Burden." There was also a Black Man's Burden Association, linking the fate of colonized people in the Philippines and Cuba to Black people in the United States. The African American clergyman H. T. Lawrence used the same title for some bitter stanzas for Kipling published in the *Cleveland Gazette* in April 1899.[77]

Pile on the Black Man's Burden.
'Tis nearest at your door;
Why heed long bleeding Cuba,
or dark Hawaii's shore?
Hail ye your fearless armies,
Which menace feeble folks
Who fight with clubs and arrows
and brook your rifle's smoke.
Pile on the Black Man's Burden
His wail with laughter drown
You've sealed the Red Man's problem,
And will take up the Brown,
In vain ye seek to end it,

With bullets, blood or death
Better by far defend it
With honor's holy breath.

Massacres were to nineteenth-century humanitarians what disappearances and prisoners of conscience became for human rights advocates from the 1970s, and fueled a moral response to distant injustice. What was distinctive about this outrage was that it was not just directed at distant authorities in Turkey or China. Earlier justifications for humanitarian "interventions" bathed in righteous fury at "despotic Orientals" for persecuting minorities (to some extent Jews, but the true wrath was reserved for the treatment of Christians). Now, the anger was directed at the flag bearers of civilization. For the growing ranks of critics, the urgency was to protect strangers from the liberators, not to liberate them.

To illustrate this arc, consider one episode involving truth-tellers and enslavers, shareholders and crusaders—and how it anticipated the way in which moral witnesses, humanitarian brokers, and authorities jostled in the global public sphere for the high ground in the debate over the material and ethical entitlements and obligations among strangers, in this case Europeans and Africans. Sir Harry Johnson, linguist, botanist, explorer (Mount Kilimanjaro was one of his expeditions) of Africa from 1879 to 1884—before the continent was carved up by European powers—had ventured up the Congo River to serve the cause of "gradually rais[ing] the millions of Central African Negroes to a condition of peaceable self-government." Two decades later, Johnson had gone from an earnest opener to a crusader for the rights of "native" Africans to be free of European despots.[78]

Like previous European conquests, this one started with virtuous claims and ended in scandals about latter-day conquistadors and their cruelty to Natives. The International Association of the Congo, founded by the Belgian King Leopold II, was formed in 1879 and recognized in the scramble over Africa by other European powers as the framework for uplifting and integrating Congolese into commercial benevolence. It was that or expose "natives" to "wicked Arabs" and their thirst for ivory and, worse, slaves.[79] What better way to justify the grabbing of territory than by defending Natives from enslavement? *Le Parisien* called this a "peaceful conquest."[80] Within a decade, Leopold had turned the region into his personal colony. His company used deception, quotas, forced labor, and hostage-taking on a mass scale overseen by the gendarmes of Leopold's Force Publique.[81]

By 1896, missionaries were sending reports about thugs and extortionists. "This rubber traffic," the American Baptist Joseph Clark confided to a friend, "is steeped in blood, and if the natives were to rise up and sweep every white person on the Upper Congo into eternity there would still be left a fearful balance to their credit." Inspectors began to note widespread depopulation. Journalists began to look at Leopold's account books and found huge discrepancies between his earnings and his "royal liberality." Missionaries had taken Kodaks to catalogue their work and create lantern shows for parishes to raise funds. Their Kodaks soon provided evidence of atrocity.[82]

One who sought to "pull off the blindfold" was the British consul in Congo, Roger Casement. Born in Dublin to Anglo-Irish parents, Casement would emerge as an archetype of this global age. An agent of empire, he would come to view the horrors of European colonization through new lenses. Teaming up with Edmund Dene Morel, the former clerk of a Liverpool shipping company who had probed into the Congo Free State's trade accounts to find evidence of abuse, Casement authored a devastating report in 1904. It catalogued atrocities in Congo and a new kind of African slavery on African soil to benefit a few Europeans, like the king of Belgium. It created a template for moral "truths" behind the workings of the world economy.

Casement's revelations of wickedness captured the imaginations of social reformers and human rights activists back home, who railed against British and Belgian tycoons for exploiting "natives" living in some rustic state of nature. There was a reason he had been chosen for the investigative task. Casement was seasoned at the Congo River trade, having gone to the tropics to work for the Congo Railway Company. While there, he had met Joseph Conrad in 1889 or 1890. The two shared a room for several weeks, enough time for Casement to rub off on the younger, impressionable Pole with writerly aspirations. The character of Charlie Marlow in *Heart of Darkness* owes much to what Conrad saw in his bunkmate. One can speculate on how much Conrad took from the horse's mouth. Whose words were these, Marlow's or Casement's? "The conquest of the earth, which mostly means the taking it away from those who have a different complexion or slightly flatter noses than ourselves, is not a pretty thing when you look into it too much. What redeems is the idea only. An idea at the back of it; not a sentimental pretense but an idea; and an unselfish belief in the idea—something you can set up, and bow down before, and offer a sacrifice to." The real Casement came to similar conclusions. His diary records over and over the Central African depopulation, the empty villages, and the severed hands, baskets of them in every market square. His outrage was fevered. At one marketplace, he saw 242 men sitting with their rubber "all guarded like convicts." "To call this 'trade,'" Casement scribbled furiously, "is the height of lying."[83]

His report reflected a dawning style, in gritty, punctual realism that contrasted with the steampunk escapism of Jules Verne or H. G. Wells, for an investigative age fired by an eyewitnessing spirit to close the gap between the homes of victims and the homes of reader-citizens far away, to solve Adam Smith's little finger problem so that strangers could *see* what they were doing to each other. Shortly after returning to London from Congo, Casement wrote to the American journalist and owner of the *New York Evening Post*, Poultney Bigelow, that "if he [an observer-reporter] wants to see how a people lives and how they are affected by the laws they must obey and the taxes they must pay he goes, if he goes for truth, to the homes of the people themselves."[84]

Morel, meanwhile, saw the opportunities to drum up support for an assault on King Leopold's personal claims, to stir public opinion in Britain and Belgium to revoke the concession to the king. Protests and gatherings were not just occasions for speechifying, but for lantern shows of mutilation. (Lantern shows involved projecting light from a small "magic lantern" through a transparent glass plate with a painting, or by the 1890s a photograph, attached to it onto a screen to enlarge the image—and eventually, the slides would be captioned, made to circulate more quickly across the projector lens, and become a "moving picture." Several decades later, my grandfather was still using the same medium, parish lantern lectures recast as slide shows from China with talking points for ministers to recite to churchgoers to enlist contributions to the mission.) Concerned citizens gathered in churches and chapels around Britain to hear testimonies and to see displays of photographs projected onto makeshift screens. Morel's "atrocity meetings" soon made their way into the press and relied on sources and images from activist missionaries in the field. Alice Seeley Harris was one of them. A "missionary wife" to John Harris, Alice Seeley Harris accompanied her husband to King Leopold II's Congo Free State in 1898. Soon, she was shooting the nightmare with her Kodak. "I use my camera to take photos of the nature, the strange insects, the interesting animals," she wrote to her sister from the Upper Congo in 1900. "The other use I'm making of my camera is this; we have seen several children and young people with a hand missing. Sometimes both hands." One trader told her it was a "native rite." "I will keep taking these photos as a kind of documenting process and then I will send them back to the Regions Beyond missionary headquarters in London to see what they make of them. In my heart I fear that this points to a far greater evil than we can yet understand."[85]

One day, a man called Nsala approached Seeley Harris. He was carrying a bundle of leaves. Opening the bundle, he revealed a child's hand and foot. He claimed they were his daughter's. Leopold's sentries had, evidently, eaten the rest of her. Appalled, Seeley Harris sat Nsala down and took the photo shown in Figure 2.8 with her Kodak.

She sent the image to colleagues in England (as my grandfather did from China to Canada), who got them to Morel as visual evidence for his lantern lectures. In *Nsala of Wala,* the man's left hand cupping his chin as he mourned the remains of his daughter, viewers saw an image of victimhood that made graphic the moral qualms over slavery and the demand for news about the venality of Leopold's empire. Soon, Seeley Harris abandoned the insects and the flora and used her Kodak to accumulate a thick atrocity album, the basis of a lantern show of some sixty slides divided into four parts—covering philanthropy and conversion of "natives" to the "cannibalism" and labor practices of the Congo

FIGURE 2.8. Nsala of Wala.

Free State. Hundreds of Seeley Harris lantern shows went on tour across parishes and town meetings in Europe and the United States. Photo-reportage of this kind became an exhibition—some would later say exploitation—of the pain of others, especially non-Western, non-white, people. Morel's Congo Reform Association spread across Europe, and after his visit and lantern lecture tour in the United States, it took root there. Morel called for a joint Anglo-American intervention "on behalf of the oppressed and persecuted peoples of the Congo, for whose present unhappy condition you, in America, and we, in England, have great moral responsibility from which we cannot escape."[86] Morel recruited Alice and John Harris to tour. Many didn't share the same humanitarian bravura about Anglo-Saxon moral superiority—but the images still packed a punch. As Mark Twain wrote in his 1905 satire of King Leopold, *King Leopold's Soliloquy*, "The Kodak has been a sole calamity to us. . . . [It is] the only witness I couldn't bribe."[87]

The Congo affair was a cause célèbre in an era of heightened publicity about wrongdoings in distant parts. Facilitated by the expansion of a global press, it also reflected the rising power of civic organizations mobilized to defend the rights of strangers, especially those forced to work for other strangers. Building on the campaign to end the African slave trade, antislavery crusaders and defenders of "native rights" like the Aborigines' Protection Society, the Congo campaign used the media to expose European hypocrisy and to uphold the humanitarian principles of empire wherever the flag was planted.[88]

Having created an interdependent, imperial order, Europeans now had to create movements and institutions to right its moral ballast. But it was not just a problem out there in some hinterland. Rivalrous interdependence made it a moral problem back home. Casement understood. He grew ever more despairing of the British Empire he served and the financiers it served. For Casement, so long as global integration was left to the devices of a clique of London financiers and unscrupulous hucksters in the periphery, it would only bring misery to the "natives" of the world and deny everyone their rightful share of the global pie. The market, Casement conceded, was here to stay. But at least the defenders of the Natives could promote a "gentler humanity" by exposing the nefarious collusions of Europeans and their local allies.[89]

International Counterpoints

The late nineteenth century saw escalating predatory behavior, land grabbing, and undisguised bullying to resolve the fears of scarcity, risk, and falling behind. This tilt mobilized new actors and norms of witnessing to restrain or to hold governments accountable. Escalating tensions therefore coincided with a drive to curb violence and the birth of civic agents and witnesses committed to holding states accountable to some wider, albeit still fuzzy, internationalism. The push to manage integration was yielding the first frameworks, institutions, and solidarities of cross-border collaboration to thwart or at least restrain the competition, the predation, and the land grabbing.

No longer did the liberal creed combine so easily material purpose with moral certainty as it did under the happy, if self-serving, mantle of the civilizing mission. If integrators were starting to doubt, colonial peoples were starting to despair. Global connection and cruelty were in the air when a thirty-two-year-old W.E.B. Du Bois sat down to compose his own worldview even before gazing upon Filipino atrocity photos.

He was well aware of the power of images. Du Bois sailed to Paris to collaborate on an Exposition des Nègres d'Amérique for the 1900 Exposition Universelle, a showcase of graphs, maps, tools, and charts from Atlanta University's sociology department, and most of all portraits of African Americans posing as calculus students and barristers. The gallery exemplified Du Bois's conviction that the visualizing experience could alter the view of African Americans as helpless, bereft of agency, in need of uplift by white strangers. It is no surprise then, when he crossed the Channel to join the First Pan-African Conference in London, that the news and images coming from beyond would also affect how he viewed a world order that was increasingly integrated and stratified at the same time. He followed the news of violence in China and South Africa in the London *Times*. As the conference closed, he composed a letter, a public epistle, in his "Address to the Nations of the World." It became part of the official closing statement of the London conference. It unveiled some words that would be a refrain about the condition of the excluded strangers upon whom white peoples had come to depend.

> In the metropolis of the modern world, in this the closing year of the nineteenth century, there has been assembled a congress of men and women of African blood, to deliberate solemnly upon the present situation and outlook of the darker races of mankind. The problem of the twentieth century is the problem of the color line, the question as to how far differences of race—which show themselves chiefly in the color of the skin and the texture of the hair—will hereafter be made the basis of denying to over half the world the right of sharing to utmost ability the opportunities and privileges of modern civilization.[90]

Though his was a plea on behalf of "over half the world" to share the world of which the half was an intrinsic and needed part, Du Bois noted a deeper dilemma. The nature of global enclosure meant that integrated strangers could not secede or break away once they were part of the interdependent order. Enclosing the world may have stoked anxiety among American, Russian, and Japanese expansionists. But it had an altogether different significance, more immediately perilous, for peoples at the receiving end of the expansionist drives. They were forced to be integrated but not on their own terms. The result was a double agony. As the *Times* reportage reminded Du Bois, there was no escape for China or Africa from assembly by European weapons and European capital. The world's non-whites were caught between the choice of assimilation or separation. But neither was truly available. The prevailing hierarchy prohibited assimilation. The path to separation, on the other hand, meant joining the columns of vanishing people, the disappeared, because they would not be dependent on terms defined by conquering strangers. The only path open to remain in the world for "over half the world" was integration without inclusion. The legacy was a long struggle for recognition in a world that was growing quickly accustomed to seeing the integrated-excluded as victims in need of rescue or as unfortunate but unavoidable casualties of making the modern world.

The result was an emotional jumble. There were increasing shrill justifications of civilization and peevish snorting from expansionists about noisy do-gooders. There was outrage. And there was despair. Casement himself traced the arc from being a booster to outraged witness, and finally to succumbing to despair as he watched British elites embrace the crusade against the venal Belgian emperor only to shrug when Casement returned some years later with another eyewitness exposé of imperial wrongdoing—this time from the Amazon, where British shareholders in the Peruvian Amazon Company's rubber business and exploitation of Putumayo Indigenous peoples violated anti-slavery laws. This indifference to the plight of strangers upon whom rubber consumers, with their rapidly expanding demand for tires, depended was also part of the emotional world economy. This open-eyed indifference drove Casement to renounce his imperial loyalty and to take up the cause of Irish independence during the First World War—and led him to the gallows in 1916.

The gamut of feelings about strangers that trade, investment, and migration made more important for prosperity and survival had thickened in intensity, widened in scope—and became ever more contentious. It did so because integration produced an underlying tension that civilizers agonized over or denied but that witnesses and critics recorded and published: integration favored the integrators more than it did the integrated, especially among those whose lifeways would be erased by enclosure. As long as power and voice were distributed unevenly and unfairly within and across empires, the distribution of rewards would flow accordingly. And as long as that was the case, the integrators had a self-interest in hoarding the returns and externalizing the costs. It was this vice that motivated chroniclers and witnesses. This is why, on the eve of the Great War, there was a spiral of calls for sympathy across borders *and* growing fear about competitive survival. What lessons would the world take from the carnage of the ensuing years? Would safeguards and restraints temper the hoarding and distribute the hazards more fairly? This was the challenge confronting the peacemakers as they sought to build the world anew on the rubble of world war.

3

The Axe and the Tree

Unmixing

As the ink dried on the 1919 Versailles Peace Treaty, conflicts broke out all over the world. In Beijing, Berlin, and Buenos Aires, crowds flooded the streets to protest capitalism, imperialism, or both. In many places, the First World War ended but killing went on. A lynching wave swept the United States. British troops slaughtered civilians in India. Polish armies fought Ukrainian nationalists. Civil war ravaged Russia while paramilitary squads tore through minority communities across Europe and the Americas. The violence exposed a truth about the new order. The peace was a pause. For many, the shooting, hanging, and bombing continued. The peace unsettled the sprawling, multicultural empires that had pulled the world together. It culminated in mass dehumanization and extermination of strangers worldwide.

The Great War cleared the way for more war and more news about a turbulent world. To cripple their Ottoman enemies, the British government of David Lloyd George, one of the Versailles signatories, promised concessions to many people: Arabs for self-determination, Jews for a homeland, Greeks for territory at Turkish expense. Though Versailles was supposed to end all wars, Greek forces advanced on their prize. Turks countered. Each side invoked principles of self-determination for themselves while accusing the other of atrocity. Ethnic cleansing drove 1.5 million Greeks from their Turkish homes; 355,00 Muslims fled the Balkans to Turkey.[1] A former wartime ambulance driver and aspiring novelist went to the Balkans to report for the *Toronto Star*. His name was Ernest Hemingway. The Greco-Turkish War helped to make his career as a writer about far-away places and shaped his terse realism. Hemingway watched Greek policemen pummel Muslim families. He saw a twenty-mile column of exhausted Greek refugees straggle out of Anatolia. One evening, Hemingway recounted the sight to his Croatian hotelier, Madame Marie. She responded witheringly: Greeks, Turks, Bulgars, they are "all the same." She shared a Turkish proverb about the wickedness of the blame game. When a tree is felled, "it is not only the fault of the axe but of the tree as well."[2] Observers like Hemingway monitored the degrading "transfer" of newly coined minorities, pawns in a drive, as Lord Curzon put it, to "unmix peoples" and sort them into homogeneous nations. They puzzled over the rights of humans versus the rights of states. Was it the rights of all humans or the rights of states that gave ballast to peace?[3]

They also puzzled over the spiral of scapegoating strangers, many of whom were neighbors a few years earlier. The feud over whether the axe or the tree was responsible for the fall was really a claim to justify retribution against the other. One avid reader of reportage about ethnic cleansing in the Aegean region, and apex blamer, was Adolf Hitler. A seething veteran of the Great War, Hitler admired Mustafa Kamal's crusade to purify the Turkish nation. It shaped his own fantasies of "unmixing" races and nations to make Germany great again.

Two decades later, on the eve of what would be called the Second World War, the American journalist Walter Lippmann observed that in an interdependent world, all wars are civil wars. "Modern wars are civil wars within one Great Society," he wrote.[4] Civil wars are a category of violence on their own—especially terrifying because each side fights for its survival knowing that to be defeated would invite awful reprisals, always starting with blame and often ending in extermination. The period from 1914 to 1945 was to the world what the Thirty Years' War was to Europe, a civil war on a global scale.[5] The Global Civil War left two hundred million dead. One-tenth of the world's 1939 population perished. Then, as now, nationalists did not want to put an end to relying on strangers. Rather: stoked by emotions of fear and resentment, they wanted to dominate strangers *because* they needed them in a conflict for what they saw as a battle over existence on Earth.

War Child

The Global Civil War shook human attachments to their foundations, starting with the idea of Europe as the cradle of civilization. Just as Europe had pulled the world together, it became the world's great destabilizer. In July 1914, the French socialist Jean Jaurès warned that a "contagious fury" might sweep Europe and destroy the order it had built. Then, a furious French nationalist shot him in a café while he was having dinner close to the offices of *L'Humanité* newspaper, which Jaurès edited.

Three days later, France was at war. Europe's civil war became global because butchery on this scale and duration required strangers, their resources, their recruits, their loyalties and disloyalties, to sustain it. Belligerents had to mount their armies and navies on the backs of imperial economies and the emotions intrinsic to how they worked. Sanctions and blockades—using the power to feed and to starve—weaponized the arteries of interdependence developed over the previous century.[6] In such a prolonged and stalemated war, the difference between winning and losing depended on cutting the lifelines to strangers and their lands. The Ottomans blocked the Straits to choke off Russia's grain and arms shipments. The British navy blockaded German ports and triggered food rationing. Everywhere but the Americas saw scarcity, rationing, and inflation. If food shortages were a problem by 1915, nothing prepared Europe for the shock of civil war and revolution in Russia, which tore the black earth granaries from the world food-trading system. By 1920, Russian and Ukrainian harvests were half of what they were before the war. Every egg, apple, and basket of wheat was fought over.[7]

Then there was the need for fuel, especially oil, for motorized divisions and navies. British and Japanese navies switched to oil-fired boilers from coal. By 1929, the entire Japanese navy relied on oil. Oil enabled deep-water fleets, including submarines, to sail farther and with fewer refueling stations, to extend blockades and tighten the screws of economic hardship. Without oil, one German official noted, "there is no militarily secure independence."[8]

The shift from coal to oil to power navies and merchant marines amplified the ways in which war stepped up global interdependence and intensified the violence across and within borders. In so doing, it globalized conflict and pushed the timeline of the Global Civil War to 1945. In October 1914, the Ottoman fleet bombarded ports of the Black Sea and torched the oil refineries and tanks of Novorossiysk, thus announcing the globalization of the oil war and making the Middle East the cockpit of energy interdependence. The tsar yearned to control the Dardanelles Straits, without which there was no escape for Black Sea oil. So Moscow mobilized Armenian battalions to fight Ottoman forces and sowed panic about the loyalty of Armenians and other Christians in Anatolia. The sultan threw down the jihad card, urging Muslims to rise up against Christian oppressors from Africa to Asia. His idea was to set off a political earthquake within British and French empires. Closer to home, the Ottoman army cleansed its ranks of Armenian soldiers, who were told to dig their own graves.[9]

The violence continued after 1918, with bombings, uprisings, and invasions. The stakes rose with the discovery (in 1927) of oil reserves in Baba Gurgur, near Kirkuk, and the immediate push by the Iraq Petroleum Company to build a pipeline to the Mediterranean port of Haifa, which was controlled by British authorities. France obsessed about Syria and Mosul to secure Mesopotamian oil. Allies seized the occasion to carve up the Middle East for themselves. At a planning meeting at Number 10 Downing Street, Sir Mark Sykes, London's desk man for the region, traced his finger across the map before the prime minister and his cabinet. "I should like to draw a line from the 'e' in Acre to the last 'k' in Kirkuk," he noted.[10] A fiercely anti-Turkish minister for munitions, Lloyd George, beamed, though Prime Minister Asquith worried about the dangers of fomenting Arab dissent against the sultan. A resolute antisemite, Sykes also believed that supporting Arab breakaway kingdoms would thwart Zionist ambitions for the Holy Land. From late 1915, he and his Parisian counterpart, François Georges-Picot (whose father founded the Comité de l'Asie Française, a lobby group for aggrandizement), schemed over their Catholicism and *mission historique* for the Orient. The Allies in unvarnished Orientalist terms assured to Woodrow Wilson in Washington that they would liberate "the people who now live beneath the murderous tyranny of the Turks."[11]

With God on their side and oil in their sights, British and French planners remapped the region, pushing Turkish power back to Anatolia, evicting any German presence, and dividing the region into League of Nations "mandates" for the occupying forces to "protect" former Ottoman subjects outside the Turkish heartland. Arab leaders woke up to the fact that their fates would not be decided in Cairo or Baghdad but in Paris. Egyptians demanded independence. Riots broke out in Cairo, Palestine, and Iraq. Australian and New Zealand troops who were about to go home were forced to stay as occupiers in the new mandates. Palestine saw feuds between neighboring Jews and Arabs. An Egyptian delegation rushed to Paris. It was too late. The day of his arrival in France, Wilson recognized Britain's "protectorate" in Ottoman lands; the Egyptian delegates never got a hearing. British negotiators were already mapping an oil pipeline from northern Iraq to the Mediterranean. The Hashemite Prince Faysal ibn Husayn, loyal to Sykes in the war, urged peacemakers to uphold promises of Arab self-determination. A democratic Syrian Congress formed in Damascus to support a constitutional monarchy. French authorities rounded on Faysal: disband and surrender or face our artillery. Aghast, to avoid more fighting, Faysal went into exile. The congress folded; the lights of democracy in greater Syria went out.[12] A few years later, a newly minted British Royal Air Force (RAF) unloaded gas-canister bombs over Iraqi civilians—Shia, Sunni, rural tribal leaders, and urbanites alike—to subdue them, prompting a furious debate back home over whether to "govern or go."[13] As the region's correspondent for the London *Times* noted, European powers were fomenting "one of the most serious existing dangers to the world peace's peace."[14]

If the Great War highlighted the precarity of interdependence, the peace treaties created new sources of resentment. Combined, they changed the emotional balance governing interdependence; earth hunger spread—and became more lethal. By the end of the war, the tally of damage summed between $125 billion and $186 billion directly and around the same indirectly. About one-tenth of the cost was left as debt. So just as world resources were indispensable for war, they were indispensable to pay it off. Even among the victors, borrowing eclipsed the entire stock of prewar foreign capital stock. The United States went from the world's biggest debtor to the world's creditor, lending $7 billion (over half to Britain alone) to fund the violence. The hunger for resources and financial toll from years of fruitless fighting ensured that "reparations" would become a thorny issue for peacemakers.[15]

Conflict and rivalry heightened the fears and anxieties of togetherness—and turned the empires of trade and investment and the occupying battalions of colonial peoples into global war machines. Once dread and resentment were in the waters of the emotional world economy, the work of making an inclusive order after the Great War was infinitely more difficult.

L'Ésprit International

Some men fancied themselves as having been born for this moment and purpose. Into this fevered conflict over strangers' money, canals, pipelines, and resources entered the American president, Woodrow Wilson. Promising relief and hope, he arrived to cheering crowds in London and Paris. He did not suffer from fear of being wrong; Wilson came brandishing a charter high on aspirations.[16] Some worried about lofty promises. Thomas Mann remarked skeptically that "we humans should not get too many big ideas about morality. If we manage to achieve a world peace, we will not have reached it along the path of morality. . . . Morality out of exhaustion is not a very edifying morality."[17] Others were more scabrous. Henry Brailsford called it a restoration of armed peace.[18]

Still, the exhaustion from war spurred efforts to remake the world with a tapestry of agreements, pledges, treaties, and accords, and a generation of careers were made of international lawyering, diplomacy, and humanitarian missionizing. The word "international" was plastered everywhere. There was the International Committee on Intellectual Cooperation, then an International Institute of Intellectual Cooperation, and Alfred Zimmern inaugurated the Geneva Institute of International Relations by declaring the enterprise's commitment to "the development of the international mind." The Carnegie Endowment for International Peace kicked off a European Center to promote "l'ésprit international." The same philanthropists created the Hague Academy of International Law associated with the International Court of Justice. Trained in classics, many of the protagonists imagined themselves as Greek or Roman civilizers bringing order to an unruly world. A "scientific peace" was supposed to provide new ballast for a new world order—and since science was supposedly international, clearing its way would dissolve the memories of hunger and smoldering grievance.[19]

Where the *ésprit international* leaned furthest was in the drive to contain the signature of national sovereignty: the right to wage war, not least because the Great War had become an economic one. It was one of the many paradoxes of the Global Civil War that the scale of the violence motivated audacious—if futile—efforts to eliminate it. The end of the Great War ushered in a prolonged effort to demilitarize the world, underscoring the use of weapons for blockading and sanctioning—and thus punishing civilian populations. The German Food Ministry called the blockade a biological weapon "to strike the bodies and lives of the entire civilian population—women, children, and the unarmed—and to lead to the extinction of the German race."[20] On this point, the victors agreed. The U.S. Food Administration printed a "hunger map of Europe" to spotlight the danger of a prolonged civilian calamity. There was a Naval Conference in Washington aimed at reducing the number of warships and submarines. Japan helped take the lead along with the American delegation. It led to a bevy of treaties to cap the arms race and to defuse tension. Unfortunately, when the U.S. Congress approved anti-Japanese immigration laws, observers in Tokyo wondered whether Washington's approach to cooperation rested on the equal regard for strangers.[21] Feminist internationalists, like the Women's International League for Peace and Freedom, formed in Amsterdam in 1915 to protest the Great War, mobilized millions of women to rally and protest the slow pace of peacemaking. Britain's Women's Peace Crusade came to represent over two million women voters in Britain and wielded enormous influence, especially on the fledgling British Labour Cabinet of Ramsay MacDonald.[22] The disarmament push culminated in extended negotiations in Geneva in the early 1930s. By 1934, weapons sales were in decline.[23]

With the disarmament drive went a drive to outlaw war of aggression. On August 27, 1928, in the Salle de l'Horloge near Quai d'Orsay, the General Treaty for Renunciation of War was signed to great fanfare. It remains in effect. Though many see the 1920s as the decade of American withdrawal from the world, the U.S. Senate ratified the treaty by a vote of 85–1. Known as the Kellogg-Briand Pact, a decade later it would be ridiculed as hopelessly out of touch with geopolitical reality. But the view from 1938 wasn't necessarily the view from 1928. Nor was it the view as the Global Civil War came to a close, when the victors wrestled with how to prosecute war crimes. Kellogg-Briand, it is often forgotten, framed the legal basis for prosecuting German and Japanese leaders at the tribunals of Nuremberg and Tokyo. In the late 1920s and early 1930s, it also drove efforts to disarm, even among those who would lead the arms race a few years later. The conference was further notable as a worldmaking media event: the opening was broadcast by radio live to anyone with access to a wireless. Japanese Prime Minister Osachi Hamaguchi, British Prime Minister Ramsay MacDonald, and President Herbert Hoover took turns applauding each other.[24]

A Peace of Equals?

In the end, the *ésprit international* ran afoul of competing principles and intractable tensions of interdependence. The most contradictory was the effort to dispel old imperial feuds and create peace by spreading the right to belong to a nation under the banner of self-determination—as if a community of nations would be less fractious than what came before. Spread internationalism *and* nationalism? How was *that* going to work? Woodrow Wilson's promise to make the world safe had a cornerstone, the League of Nations, an assembly of nations approved by the victors as guardians of the new order. But the "peace of equals" fudged what was meant by "equal"—and who was worthy of self-determination.

As Jan Smuts, the South African who now served the empire he once fought, made clear in his defense of the idea of the League: "Europe is being liquidated, and the League of Nations must be the heir to this great estate." The new peace, he felt, should preserve the best of empire, preserve a world hierarchy of races and civilizations, and restore the governing of the world to cooperative gentlemen and their salons. His pamphlet announced that "a gigantic task will thereby be imposed on the League as the successor of the Empires."[25] Wilson had a narrower club for the rulers in mind. The idealist announced, "We, Anglo-Saxons, have our peculiar contribution to make towards the good of humanity in accordance with our special talents. The League of Nations will, I confidently hope, be dominated by us Anglo-Saxons; it will be for the unquestionable benefit of the world."[26]

This was the peacemakers' crucible: rebuilding interdependence while preserving civilizational narratives and their determinants of who got to belong to a free nation. To this contradictory mess they added one more fatal ingredient: this was the moment for victors who, eager to blame strangers for their misfortunes, had no interest in giving up their colonies and set their sights on grabbing what they could from defeated Austrian, German, and Ottoman dominions. The Japanese joined the club, eyeing the German concession in China as their own. The foreign minister, Makino Nobuaki, and his ambassador to London, Chinda Sutemi, both educated in the United States and the latter a Methodist minister, agreed with the principle of civilizational hierarchies. They also believed that Japan now ranked, in Makino's words, among "the advanced cultures." To appease critics back home who harbored memories of unequal treaties since the 1850s, Japan's delegates proposed that the League covenant include a "racial equality clause." Wilson wasn't quite up to seeing Japan on par with Europe. He waved off the Japanese suggestion like it was a fly, leaving a bitter memory of exclusion from the circle of white, Christian rulers of the earth.[27]

Finally, the *ésprit international* as it rolled off the victors' tongues made little room for other kinds of internationalisms. Growing since the 1890s, a whole range of cross-border ideas and solidarities, often flowing through networks of writers and agitators, now proliferated when it looked like the old imperial order was over. There were surges in international feminism, socialism, and anarchism. There were also the burgeoning pan-African, pan-Asian, and pan-Islamic movements, which framed the war itself as a European, white man's fight; to the extent that it was about the world, it was a herald for a post-European era. Many of them indeed reinforced each other in a common search for a postimperial, peace-yearning imaginary, an imaginary that questioned the whole purpose of state sovereignty.[28] This was far from what the peacemakers had in mind. The costs of reconstruction were such that Europeans leaned even more on their empires to pay for it and on state sovereignty as the lever to extract the returns from interdependence while externalizing its costs.

In retrospect, the *ésprit international* didn't stand a chance. The peacemakers fastened on an idea of self-determination that conferred to nation-states the power to make and to deny rights—while delegating, arrogating, to the club of victors who got a nation-state. This sowed a fundamental flaw into the peace: as long as the rights to have rights were so unevenly distributed, those with power would always have an incentive to deprive strangers of these rights as means to exploit them. What is more, it would always motivate others to lay claim to that very power precisely because it gave them the means to exploit—or exterminate—strangers. It would take the horror of the next twenty-five years to nudge the *ésprit international* to see that it was doomed as long as the right to a say in the terms of interdependence was so grossly and self-servingly apportioned.

Peace of the Grave

Readers might object: surely this judgment enjoys the benefit of hindsight, knowing that the Great War would become a Global Civil War. The problem is, many *did* warn the peacemakers that they were drafting recipes for disaster. Many *did* convey the message to the club of peacemakers. With high hopes, Liang Qichao rushed to Paris to witness the worldmaking moment firsthand and to use his pen to influence the future. After a year, he came away chastened—and eventually returned to a very different China. "If we think we can rely on the protection of the League of Nations without standing up for ourselves, we are living in a fool's paradise," he wrote. Still, the League was his only hope for a universal peace and a guarantor of a "mutuality of states."[29] By then, Liang's star in China had fallen; once a radical, he was now seen as a conservative voice. Other stars were rising. In the summer of 1919, the young Mao Zedong observed that "Wilson in Paris was like an ant on a hot skillet. He didn't know what to do. He was surrounded by thieves like Clemenceau, Lloyd George, Makino, and Orlando." When Mao read the Reuters cable that Wilson conceded to Clemenceau's demand that Germany be barred from the League of Nations, he knew the pious American had been had. "When I saw the words 'finally agreed,' I felt sorry for him for a long time," Mao said. "Poor Wilson!"[30]

Poor Wilson. He was conceding to what he regarded as unseemly demands from his European allies. After offending the Japanese, he tried to appease them. Wilson gave Japan what he could not deny to Europeans, spoils wrenched from the vanquished: he gave them the German base of Qingdao, in China. This only worsened the blaming cycle. The Chinese delegation had traveled to Paris in the hopes of joining the club of nations. They learned that their country was being carved up. The news shocked Chinese students and witnesses in Paris, who sent news to Beijing. Students who were following events rallied in Tiananmen Square and marched upon the residence of the communications minister—Cao Rulin—who escaped as students ransacked his house. The upswelling spread to Shanghai, Hangzhou, Harbin, and other cities to form the May Fourth Movement. A symbolic awakening, it would permanently change Chinese politics and seal a memory of Western deceit. Liang Qichao, still in Paris, watched in dismay. Europeans, he lamented, "are like travelers in the desert and have lost their direction. . . . They once had a great dream about the omnipotence of science. Now their talk is filled with its bankruptcy."[31]

Another witness was W.E.B. Du Bois, who tried even harder to sway the peacemakers, starting with a president whom he supported. America's most important global thinker and a key voice in Pan-Africanism, Du Bois insisted that a "color line belts the world." It was inevitable that Du Bois would have to square off with America's other global thinker, the U.S. president. Both shared an affinity for idealism. Both believed in human improvability. Both had faith that government could solve problems.

Paris exposed the gulf between them. While Wilson ran seminars on his Fourteen Points on the USS *George Washington* bound for Europe, Du Bois was on the *Orizaba* explaining his thirteen-point plan, which included the contours of a "vast state in central Africa" where Blacks and whites would work together to give example for the new world. "I went to Paris," he noted, "because today the destinies of mankind center there."[32] February 19–21, the Pan-African Congress gathered at the Grand Hotel on the Boulevard des Capucines to underline the importance of African and African-descendant voices in the future of the world order. The final declaration argued that the world faced a choice: the assimilation of Africans into multiracial states with political and civil equality for all, or "the rise of a great black African state, founded in Peace and Goodwill" for all Africans and their descendants. Equality across the global color line was not a matter of "altruistic benevolence." It was a necessity, "the one road to world salvation."[33]

Like many other observers, Du Bois began to despair. "Thirty-two nations, peoples, and races" had gathered in Paris hoping to join the new global order. They had come "to see where they 'came in.'"[34] Du Bois sought an audience with his president in Paris. After explaining his plan to other journalists and some of Wilson's insiders like Walter Lippmann (who nodded but did nothing), he went straight to the American Commission and was turned away by an irritated guard.[35] Having witnessed the racism directed against Black troops in the U.S. Army in France, watched the Japanese equality clause be dismissed, and had his appeals for voice in the future of Africa go unheard, Du Bois returned to the United States dejected. Soon he became horrified. A murderous white mob tore through Knoxville, Tennessee, in late August until a thousand troopers subdued the rampage. Then it was Omaha's turn, then Phillips County, Arkansas. Over and over, Black sharecroppers, veterans, and storeowners had their heads put into nooses and were strung up on trees and lampposts until 76 African Americans had been lynched, entire neighborhoods razed. Another 250 more were killed in urban uprisings and a pogrom in the Arkansas Delta. Wilson, who had returned from Paris to stump for his treaty, stayed mum about the violence. The Red Summer of 1919 brought Du Bois to new lows. The founding editor of *The Crisis: A Record of the Darker Races* (whose monthly circulation surpassed *The New Republic* or *The Nation*) poured his despair into his editorials. "We do not believe in revolution," he intoned—"just the right to think, write, criticize, and to participate in American civic and political life like everyone else." As the corpses of Black sharecroppers were burned before jeering white onlookers, Du Bois spiraled into "apocalyptic bitterness." "Behold little Belgium and her pitiable plight," he wrote, reminding readers of the humanitarian outcry of 1914 that rallied allies to fight German aggression. "But," he added for his readers in a searing essay, "has the world forgotten Congo?" The new order simply meant that "it is the duty of white Europe to divide up the darker world and administer it for Europe's good."[36]

Disenchantment spread. In Sierra Leone, rice riots protested the high cost of food; rail and port workers went on strike against imperial owners.[37] Syndicalists and anarchists seized factories and occupied dockyards from Shanghai to Buenos Aires. The American ambassador to Argentina considered calling in warships to restore order. Instead, paramilitary squads did the dirty work, gunning down strikers and going on an antisemitic binge. A few months later, in April 1919, British forces clashed in Amritsar, Punjab. Crowds had gathered to protest the deportation of two nationalist leaders. The local army commander, Colonel Reginald "Rex" Dyer, tormented by fears of a mass uprising, ordered most exits from the main square to be blocked with tanks—and then instructed his troops to open fire on civilians scrambling for the few open gates, slaughtering up to four hundred and leaving one thousand wounded. Mass arrests, public floggings of school children, and more deportations were the order of the day—until it became clear that this spectacle horrified readers back home while the British government was playing virtuous peacemaker in Europe. British officers were likened to Germans in Belgium in the pages of *New India* and *Navajivan*. The Nobel Prize winner Sir Rabindranath Tagore asked the viceroy to take back his knighthood. The Indian nationalist and future prime minister Jawaharlal Nehru erupted: "Pax Britannica must be preserved even though the peace it gives is the peace of the grave."[38]

Recording History

The evolution of global reportage added to the sense of a fractured peace. Just as the Great War had sucked resources into the fight, so too newspapers and agencies mobilized to represent the fight. *The New York Times* called it the first "press agent's war."[39] The press agent's war brought news of far-away events closer to home, to shrink the world—and make it feel ever more closed, inescapable, and entangled. The German philosopher Walter Benjamin noted that the practices of creating and sharing information were creating the sense—some would say illusion—that the world was becoming verifiable, understandable as one, albeit feuding, world: "The camera . . . on the one hand, extends our comprehension of the necessities which rule our lives; on the other hand, it manages to assure us of an immense and unexpected field of action."[40]

While the cable companies and news agencies had wired the world together by 1914, the newspaper business thrived off the chronic sense of emergency. Not even the spread of the radio could dent sales of print. It would not be until the advent of television that there was true competition for the newspaper and magazine lords. This was the age that would give the world the popular glossy and pictorial "slicks"—*Paris Match, Der Spiegel, National Geographic, Time*—and the first lustrous magazine to cameo the picture *as* the story, *LIFE,* which did so much to report and represent the world's news with large format photos and adjective-heavy captions. Its founder, Henry Luce, born in China of American missionary parents, took inspiration from German and French splashy precursors. Walter Benjamin would complain about the barrage on the senses; there was so much information that it required constant explanation—with less and less storytelling. "Every morning brings us the news of the globe," he lamented, "and yet we are poor in noteworthy stories."[41]

It would be hard to exaggerate the density of international news flows after 1914. When the young African American scholar Ralph Bunche traveled to South Africa for field work in 1937, he was struck not just by the presence of jazz in Johannesburg—the popularity of saxophones, trumpets, and pianos, as well as the celebrity of African American boxers—but by the competition for news. He walked past a man on a soap box in Cape Town and was astonished to learn that the bellower was the famous Jamaican journalist Arthur McKinley, an agent for *Bantu World* and archrival of Marcus Garvey's Back to Africa campaign and *Black Man* magazine. Indeed, Pan-Africans had created the International African Service Bureau in London—led by George Padmore, C.L.R. James, Amy Ashwood Garvey, and others—to challenge their news rivals and in outrage over the European reporting of Italy's invasion of Ethiopia. They were also keen to get the pro-union message out to Black workers in the Cape.[42]

The scramble over public opinion thrust intellectuals, writers, photographers, and artists into ever more prominent roles. The scale of the propaganda war within and after the war revealed how much reporting and storytelling became a battleground in which writers and artists played the role of combatants as truth-seekers and witnesses. It was during the Global Civil War that the heroic photojournalist and the idea of photographic objectivity came into their own. Technologies set the photographer up as key in a new reportorial regime that prided itself on allowing the viewer to see history for themselves. Leica unveiled a fast-aperture, portable camera that carried a 35 mm roll of film. A photographer could take up to thirty-six shots a canister, rewind it, pull it out, and replace it with a fresh unexposed one. Fast. Quicker lenses, rapid film advancement, and "detective"-style shooters made handling easier, less obtrusive, and more intuitive, perfect for capturing action, making the motion the picture itself. The most important part, though, was the speed and accuracy, which could freeze-frame action, sometimes with just the right dose of evocative motion blur, and make it seem like real action. To this were added improvements in developing and printing in professional labs, often by the picture editor, which released the photographer to roam, a Leica draped around their neck, to concentrate on personal expression or journalistic reportage and send their

FIGURE 3.1. Armenian Genocide.

rolls back to the lab. The shooter could stay focused on the subject and keep moving.

Organizations from humanitarian relief to missionary stations, League of Nations staff to governments themselves, recruited photographers to catalogue and project images of field work back home. The moral witness no longer stood only outside the action, posing as the impartial observer. The Near East Relief program enlisted photographers to provide a visual chronicle of Turkish atrocity meted out against Armenians during and after the war. One German medic, Armin T. Wegner, defied Ottoman orders and stayed with Armenians in the refugee camp of Ras-el-Ain. Eventually, he smuggled out some of his negatives in his belt. Images like the one shown in Figure 3.1, featuring crowds of Armenian refugees, their worldly possessions and livestock huddled around makeshift tents as famine set in, would go on to a storied career as evidence of a genocidal campaign to wipe out Armenians.[43]

The photograph had become what the eye captured out there—snapped in all its blurred, grainy glory. By the late 1920s, consumers of news were learning to see photographically, isolating one moment from another, framing and "freezing" episodes and actions. These new forms of representation were the effect of mechanical and reproducible recording to produce gritty, spontaneous, candid "shots," a new aesthetic that echoed the Soviet utilitarian imagery of Dmitri Baltermants or the montages of German printers. The documentary gave way to a spirit of realism and the triumph of the heroic photographer raking the scene for—as Henri Cartier-Bresson put it—"the decisive moment." Pictures no longer illustrated the story; they were becoming the story, visual proof of the place of strangers in one's own world.

Making a World Economy

The advent of new recording practices coincided with the drive to reconstruct the world, a drive that would eventually falter in spectacularized, newsworthy, fashion. There was a world economy to rebuild. As Gustav Stresemann, a young deputy in the Reichstag for the National Liberal Party, noted, "Politics . . . [is] today first of all the politics of the world economy."[44] In some ways, the world of 1918 was not so different from that of 1914. There were still the manufacturing powerhouses and the primary exporters. The opening stage of the Global Civil War left most productive structures intact. It was the financial order that needed most help. Russia, Britain, France, Germany, and most other belligerents were battered, exhausted, and deep in debt. For perspective: the total borrowing from 1914 to 1918 was six and a half times all the national debt accumulated worldwide from the end of the eighteenth century to 1914. London, the nerve center of the world capital market, groaned under the weight of war debt. Among the victors, fully 88 percent of debt was guaranteed by the British Treasury, the rest by France.[45] Almost half of it was owed by the Russian government, which had just been toppled and was en route to a Bolshevik takeover. The Allies won the war. But they owed one country, the United States, a lot of money. Japan also emerged with massive balance of payments surpluses and a major creditor in Asia. To top things off, the method of financing did not extract from public savings but overwhelmingly from bank credit; banks granted loans to governments who honored the "promise to pay" by printing money—thus setting off an inflationary spiral that erupted after 1918.

There were also the direct cost of the war, damages to capital, shipping, and a long list of indirect losses totaling $338 billion. Europe had lost 8.6 million people, mainly able-bodied men.[46] Some vital parts, like Russia, had simply dropped out of the system. Others, like Italy and Romania, were broke. The system was jammed.

How to pay all this debt, lick inflation, and recover at the same time? How to do this when squeezing colonies like India (whose revenue transfers, "Home Charges," to London alone reached almost £150 million in 1919) while they were in revolt? If the peacemakers in Paris touted the virtues of self-determination for some, they struggled over the interdependence of the wider system and pinned their hopes on squeezing their colonies and gaining from the magical effects of German reparation payments, in effect rebuilding European interdependence by externalizing its costs onto colonies and the defeated, none of whom were at the table when the die was cast.[47]

One who foresaw trouble, starting with the pernicious effects of blaming the vanquished for causing the war, was John Maynard Keynes. The key to rebuilding interdependence was, he felt, economic recovery. Without it, any peace was doomed. With so much interlocking debt on the table, the parts were more interdependent than ever but faced incentives to make strangers pay for rebuilding. The only country capable of undoing it was the biggest creditor: the United States. Keynes drafted a plan that would repackage the debt to be sold, with Washington's blessings, to New York financiers. It got dismissed; Wilson did not want to strap the American economy any more to what he called Europe's "shaky financial structure." Keynes fumed. Instead of outlining a comprehensive recovery plan, treaty talks degenerated into how to "make Germany pay." To drill home the blame message, the German delegation was forced to travel by train through the most shattered moonscapes of France. When they reached Paris, posters covered the walls: "LET GERMANY PAY FIRST!"

Managing the world economy went the way of the new diplomacy—it required a semipermanent state of financial summitry to recycle

American loans to Germany so that Germany could honor obligations to the victors so that the victors' financial systems could stay afloat. The never-ending challenges meant never-ending meetings. Economists, bankers, and Treasury officials refined the art of what Patricia Clavin has called "diplomacy by conference."[48] International trade conferences convoked by the League—Brussels in 1920, Portorose in 1921 (much neglected though important because, for the first time, the "Great Powers" convened to listen to the "lesser" ones that filled the void of the Habsburg Empire), Genoa in 1922, two in Geneva in 1927—aimed to make the world economy a manageable unit and ended with ritual proclamations about the scourge of tariffs as a threat equal to, if not more menacing than, an arms race. It was an elaborate, if fragile, laundering operation to keep interdependence going at the expense of those who were not invited to the summits.

The interdependent economy of the Global Civil War lost the structures it had before 1914. Keynes gave some clues as to why. Before the signing ceremony in the Hall of Mirrors, the advisor to the British Treasury packed his bags in disgust and returned to England where he poured his dismay—some would say his personal venom—into one of the all-time best-selling economic treatises: *The Economic Consequences of the Peace*. Published in December 1919, just in time to affect the American debate over whether to ratify the treaty, it sold one hundred thousand copies in the first year and went into immediate translation in eleven other languages. It blasted what Keynes called a "Carthaginian peace" for imposing on Germany onerous payments while depriving it of the means to pay. Later, historians would poke holes in Keynes's estimates and his portrait of shortsighted victors. Meanwhile, American isolationists found justification for their rejection of the treaty. Disgruntled Germans pointed to *The Economic Consequences of the Peace* to justify their seething. Few voices did more to cast a pall over the peace than Keynes's treatise.[49]

But his general argument is worth underlining. Keynes's point about the Carthaginian peace was that it refused to recognize a disequilibrium at the core of interdependence. The victors had failed to see how the world had changed. The European world economy had benefited from centuries of New World resources after 1492. The Old World "staked out a claim in the natural wealth and virgin potentialities of the New" and for the ensuing four centuries reaped the harvests. Now those frontiers were closed. Interdependence produced closure. Echoing the neo-Malthusian *ésprit* that had been gathering steam since the 1890s, he predicted increasing shortages. "The forces of the nineteenth century"—the canals, the railways, the steam, telegraph, land grabbing, and settlement—"have run their course and are exhausted," he wrote.[50] Into this fatigued system, the victors in their vengeful myopia packed dynamite: they required that one of its vital parts, Germany, be saddled with massive and—according to Keynes, unpayable—debt. The result, he predicted, would be calamity. "Never in the lifetime of men now living has the universal element in the soul of man burnt so dimly," Keynes observed.[51]

Keynes was not alone in despairing about the inability of world leaders to appreciate the changing nature of interdependence. In Argentina, Alejandro Bunge pointed out that the primary exporting countries were doomed to lag if they did not industrialize. For others, development meant challenging the imperial-trade orthodoxy more directly. Nehru railed against British exploitation. "The only way to right [injustice and exploitation] is to do away with the domination of any one class over another," he told an audience in Lahore in 1920. "The exploitation of India and other countries," he complained in *Whither India?*, "brought so much wealth to England that some of it trickled down to the working class and their standard of living rose."[52] In September that year, delegates gathered in the Caspian port of Baku for the Congress of Peoples of the East. With Moscow's blessing, delegates demanded a new, postimperial world order, which included decolonizing the world economy.

Sun Yat-sen, the father of Chinese republicanism, echoed the complaints. Relegated to the fringes of a warlord polity that was about to slide into civil war, he was outraged by the humiliation of China by Paris peacemakers. Sun withdrew to Shanghai to think and to write. In a little studio at 26 rue Molière in the middle of the French Concession, he mapped out a global vision for China and a Chinese vision of a buoyant world.[53] In a stream of articles, mostly published in his party's organ, *Reconstruction* (*Jianshe*), he connected the problems of republican failure, national trauma, and worldwide economic injustice. China's weakness made it prey for predators; a weak China weakened the world economy. Like Keynes, he took the long view on interdependence. Sun gathered his thoughts in a 1920 manifesto, *The International Development of China,* arguing that his country was "a now prey of militaristic and capitalistic powers—a greater bone of contention than the Balkan Peninsula." Without a solution to "the China question," another war was inevitable; the key to the problem was economic prosperity of the backward part to rescue the struggling whole.[54]

Instead, the victors doubled down on a familiar division of labor with the gold standard at its core, a rigid order to stabilize a fragile system whose payments structure—the nervous system of modern capitalism—was awash in unsustainable debt; to qualify for aid and loans, postwar governments had to commit to currency stability and balanced budgets while struggling to pay creditors and meet welfare demands of citizens.[55] So much of the summitry focused on means to keep up international payments. Economic diplomats had one problem to contend with above all—keeping Germany afloat by recycling the Weimar Republic's debt which, by 1928, topped $30 billion, about one hundred percent of the country's GDP and half comprised of reparations obligations from 1919. Even the most extractive and embittered creditor could see this was totally unsustainable. Once again, summiteers were summoned. The American industrialist, Owen Young came up with a plan in 1929. *Time* magazine declared him "man of the year." But the underlying structures remained the same, even if the payment schedules were extended and the reparations sum was trimmed.[56] Most of the lending, in effect, came from one source. Loans to Germany were recycled to pay Britain and France, who could then honor their obligations to the United States. Capital flows sutured a new model of interdependence with a new money center, New York, which was also the hub of a speculative stock market craze. As it heated up, capital reversed its flows. Instead of supporting Old World debtors and primary exporters, it flooded back to Wall Street; net capital outflows from creditors plunged thirty five per cent between 1928 and 1929, exposing the financial nerves of indebted Central Europe.[57]

Bombshell

For a while, summitry, recycling, and muddling through appeared to work. In 1928, the League announced exuberantly that world trade had recovered to levels reached in 1914. The timing could not have been worse. The following year, the New York Stock Exchange crashed, which plunged the world into the worst global economic crisis in history. President Herbert Hoover called it "a depression."

Poor Hoover. In the first two years of his depression and the last of his presidency, over five thousand banks went under, ripping out the foundations of the New York money markets that had been juggling the world's lenders and borrowers. The financial core of a decentralized world economy imploded like a supernova. New York bankers called in their loans, sucking money from their shaky clients in Europe and producing a financial crisis for Germany and Austria, which only exacerbated things for the rest. As the situation got worse, Lionel Robbins, an economist from the London School of Economics, rebaptized the slump *the* Great Depression.[58]

The crash of 1929 revealed the limits of the truce in the Global Civil War. Hard-to-enforce treaties and round-the-clock summitry propped up interdependence. But once these devices crumbled, it was the powerful who were the first to defect from the system they designed; they, after all, had the least to pay and could more easily externalize the costs of a crumbling order. The crash of 1929 spurred protectionism. As countries hiked tariffs and resorted to competitive devaluations to favor exports and thwart imports, any country that stuck to the crumbling liberal order paid a price.[59] The U.S. Congress hurried to approve—in the teeth of Hoover's opposition—tariffs to protect national producers. Known as the Smoot-Hawley tariffs, their effect on trade was more symbolic than real. But in a fragile, edgy world and a supercharged affect economy, symbols mattered.[60]

It is tempting to see the crash of 1929 as setting off an inevitable spiral toward nationalism and predatory extraction. In fact, the crisis produced an effort to rescue the floundering liberal order. Major leaders took a last stab at restorative summitry after several years of currency turmoil once sterling was unmoored from gold in September 1931. A standard view, certainly among mainstream economists and Treasury officials in London, was that getting back to the stability of gold would thwart competitive devaluations, stabilize prices, and revive international trade. Restoring interdependence meant restoring the tried and true: the ballast of the gold standard. After much talking about talking, British Prime Minister Ramsay MacDonald opened the World Economic Conference in London in the late spring of 1933 by announcing that "self-sufficient nationalism in economics is the death-knell of advancing prosperity. . . . International cooperation is our best way to national recovery." King George V's welcome address was broadcast worldwide on the BBC.[61] Privately, few expected much. One British Cabinet member looked back on the meetings in the underventilated geological museum as "the largest bar the world has ever known."[62]

For six, sweltering weeks, delegates tried to steer the world market from the jaws of competitive interdependence. As the army of secretaries pumped out the minutes, diplomats, lawyers, bankers, and economists feuded over stable money—until they came up with a compromise. All they could deliver was the least appetizing "cooperative" solution—the rigidity of gold. At least it was familiar. Then came "the bombshell" telegram. The newly elected president of the United States, Franklin Delano Roosevelt, monitored the discussions from a distance. He was not a fan of the gold standard's rigidity. He wanted more flexibility. The orthodoxy on display in London gave him the pretext to tear the standard down. From his yacht off the coast of Cape Cod, he sent a message to London on July 2 that the American government would not abide by the proposal. The cable was a blistering rebuke: "I would regard it as a catastrophe amounting to a world tragedy if the Great Conference of Nations . . . should . . . allow itself to be diverted by the proposal of a purely artificial and temporary experiment affecting the monetary exchange of a few nations only." It was time, he dug in with some immortal words, to rid the world of "old fetishes of so-called international bankers." Currencies devalued and countries started to compete to depress them further to make their exports more appealing—setting off a competitive vortex that ended in worldwide deflation. The international payments system seized up.

The bombshell's financial effects cascaded; the remains of cooperation wrapped around the rigidity of gold gave way to escalating competition that spilled beyond the economy. Economic uncertainties set off me-firstism. Geostrategic thinking took off. After the Kellogg-Briand Pact, there had been hopes for a more advanced peace. That vaporized. It did not help that warmaking technologies adapted during the Great War pushed the violence into new frontiers, especially the skies, with new dehumanizing capabilities. "Air forces" could shower fear on those below. Strategists called this "terror bombing." British military commanders used wing-mounted loudspeakers, dropped bags of leaflets, and conducted "demonstration flights" over Iraq in the early 1920s to keep the peace. When that did not work, they resorted to aerial bombing to contain "general recalcitrance" and rout out rebels. Airplanes became ideal forms of control. With just a handful of bases and landing strips, and a few cooperative locals, the Royal Air Force could keep tabs on all of Mesopotamia. Indeed, the Middle East became tagged as "the Land of the RAF." It became a source of pride and conviction. Disarmament crusaders saw things otherwise and advocated the idea of demilitarizing the skies. British strategists got alarmed. In 1932, the High Commissioner in the Kingdom of Iraq declared that "bombing from the air is regarded almost as an act of God to which there is no effective reply but immediate submission."[63]

While financial authorities converged on London, the World Disarmament Conference opened in Geneva, the day after Hitler became Germany's chancellor. The goal was to ban weapons of aggression, like heavy tanks, and tools to inflict suffering on civilians, like submarines and airplanes. There was talk of eliminating offensive weapons altogether; the lame-duck American president, Herbert Hoover, even suggested that the United States might mothball its fighter planes, tanks, and one-third of its battleships. Franklin Roosevelt was more enthusiastic about Geneva than he was about the London summit. "If all nations will agree wholly to eliminate from possession and use the weapons which make possible a successful attack, defenses automatically will become impregnable and the frontiers and independence of every nation will become secure," he said in a message. But the *ésprit international* was vaporizing on many fronts at the same time. Germany and France could not agree to mothball their weapons, Poland and Czechoslovakia eyed their neighbors nervously, Japan had just marched into Manchuria, and Hitler promised to muscle up his military. After Roosevelt's bombshell cable to London, the Geneva gathering degenerated into acrimony. Germany withdrew altogether and embarked on rearmament in direct contravention of the Treaty of Versailles, triggering a new arms race.[64]

That was that. Hopes for a cooperative way out of the spiral faded. Dorothy Thompson had prophesized the collapse a year earlier: "The history of Europe since Locarno is a history of defeated internationalism, and no one loves a loser."[65]

Then came a new round of the blame game. Roosevelt blamed Europeans, the British and French blamed each other. Latin Americans, Chinese, and Indians pointed at imperial powers. It ended in volleys of complaints and accusations. Joseph Stalin, and the recently elected Hitler, gloated.

In the vacuum, the pressures to build walls around national markets and turn to predatory practices beyond them surged to the fore. It is customary, almost a liberal cliché, to point to Smoot-Hawley and tariffs as singularly destructive, setting off a cascade of trade wars, competitive devaluations, quotas, and exchange controls. They should be seen within a larger setting: protectionism at home was indivisibly linked to extraction abroad. It is likely that the assembly of policies and nationalist symbols had more effect on the *direction* of trade and interdependence than on the *volume*.[66] As the great and greater powers reformatted their economic orders into vertically structured blocs that resembled old mercantilist systems strapped to new industrial-age needs, trade within blocs grew as trade across blocs sank. This was not autarky. This wasn't about independence; this was remapping interdependence to reveal its ever-latent potential to re-create global hierarchy. In the pessimism and dismay, the country that had done most to open markets and pronounce the virtues of free trade in the nineteenth century, Great Britain, was one of the first to retreat to an imperial shell and its "sterling trading area." British conservatives had touted the virtues of imperial preference for years. Now, the sentiment was unleashed. The temptation to externalize the costs and hoard the gains of interdependence lay within reach. The method was direct dealmaking between the powerful and weak—with the powerful forcing weaker neighbors and partners to accept their terms or get shut out. As chancellor of the exchequer, Neville Chamberlain had proposed to slap a 10 percent duty on all imports, save those from dominions and colonies. "There is no article of your food, there is no raw material in your trade, there is no necessity of your lives, no luxury of your existence which cannot be produced somewhere or other in the British Empire," he intoned.[67] The government agreed to meet in the summer of 1932 in Ottawa. Under pressure by Canada and Australia and urged by proempire lobbyists at home, London promulgated a system of imperial preferences to promote trade within the empire at the expense of commerce with strangers beyond the rose-colored, "imperial" world. Back home, the Free Trade Union howled in opposition. In India, economic nationalists called it colonial economics.[68] Argentina, one of Britain's sources of meat and grains, was forced to negotiate an unfair trade agreement to keep access to its traditional market for beef exports. This deal became a potent symbol for later Argentine economic nationalists.

Others followed suit. Japan spread its "Co-Prosperity Sphere" in Asia (to the chagrin of nervous British colonial officers, who watched Tokyo latch manganese, tin, and iron concessions and began hoarding minerals). The French government under Albert Sarraut, a former colonial official of French Indochina and high priest of the *mission civilisatrice* of turning Vietnamese into "yellow-skinned Frenchmen," championed patriotic defense with a moat around the country's empire, echoing the same logic of imperial preference.[69] Just as Europeans doubled down on their colonies, the United States shifted to bilateralism to leverage its commanding size over strangers in smaller countries, though this was often advocated as a piecemeal strategy to restore neighbors' access to the American market after blanket protectionism of Smoot-Hawley.

Roosevelt was, by inclination, a multilateralist and a free trader. He blamed Republicans for "erecting an impregnable barbed wire entanglement around [America's] borders through the instrumentality of tariffs which have isolated [Americans] from all other human beings in all the rest of the world." What America needed was "the restoration of the trade of the world." Roosevelt's secretary of state, Cordell Hull, shared the same view. But as empires took refuge in trading syndicates with subordinate powers, Hull went bilateral and turned to neighbors to the south. The Reciprocal Trade Agreements Act of 1934 did not lower tariffs much; it did not abrogate Smoot-Hawley tariffs. What it did was shift commercial policymaking to the executive branch to negotiate bilateral trade deals. Within five years, eighteen countries signed pacts with the United States, almost all of them in the Western Hemisphere.[70] None reduced average duties on imports. Instead, they compelled dependent partners to agree to quotas or get cut out, and in return they had to throw their home markets open to American exporters.

More than anyone, it was Hitler who appreciated the opportunity afforded by the collapse of the international system to brace neighbors to the Third Reich's economic sphere. Buoyed by the anxiety-mongering, stranger-bashing, and Oswald Spengler–fermented press magnate Alfred Hugenberg, a forerunner of Rupert Murdoch's Fox News sensationalism, the Führer was given an opportunity to remap Germany's dependence and display the perishability of democracy in one fell swoop.[71] Hitler seized power in early 1933 with an eye to building a Reichsmark bloc of Bulgaria, Greece, Hungary, Turkey, Yugoslavia, and the Romanian old fields. One German military journal noted in 1934 that "the struggle of world politics is today more or less a struggle over oil."[72] One by one, East European and Balkan states negotiated deals that allowed them to swap their Reichsmark balances that couldn't be used elsewhere in return for military equipment from Krupp and Rheinmetall plants so they could rearm. This squeezed out French and especially Czech arms dealers; it also set the stage for a flurry of bilateral deals to swap wheat, oil, and other staples for German manufactures. Hjalmar Schacht, the conservative economist embittered by Allied reparations, became Hitler's minister of economics and exploited the vulnerability of smaller neighbors in Southeast Europe to negotiate preferential trade agreements, tripling German exports within the Reichsmark bloc. To Schacht, this was Germany's answer to the British economic moat around their empire.

It also realized some of Hitler's dreams. *Mein Kampf* pined for an empire for German-speaking peoples and their subalterns to meet the needs of the homeland, securing access to oil, rubber, foodstuffs, and iron ore. Hitler mapped it out in a memorandum in 1936 as a Four Year Plan, with lethal clockwork, culminating in bilateral deals. When that was not enough, the annexation of Austria enhanced his leverage with Central and Southeastern Europe to make Romania, Hungary, and Yugoslavia dependencies of a semiformalized empire. When that was not enough, steamrolling Poland and making plans to invade the Soviet Union enacted the grand plan to turn strangers into forced laborers, plunder their resources, and eventually exterminate them. Creating a ring of dependent vassal states was a way to reduce others' power to determine whether Germans would eat or starve. Survival meant "nutritional freedom," proclaimed one Nazi planner. By 1938, even the Soviet Union was lining up for arms deliveries from Germany in return for primary goods like wheat and oil, which set the stage for the ignominious Molotov-Ribbentrop Pact in August 1939, which secretly partitioned Poland between fascist Berlin and communist Moscow.[73]

The Fruits of Pessimism

The arms race and economic competition tapped into deeper-rooted structures of feeling. Pessimism tapped into thinking about population, resources, and the planet's capacity to sustain its people. From concern to anxiety, from anxiety to alarm, and from alarm to an extreme form of devouring, the Global Civil War descended into sarcophagy of stranger blaming and extermination.

While soldiers toiled in the mud and barbed wire of Flanders, Great War entomologists peered into their microscopes as they dissected insects. Worms were devouring the troops' precious grain supplies. Then there were the lice, which tormented the fighters and spread trench fever. The Cambridge graduate and poet, Siegfried Sassoon, after convalescing for six months, returned to the front in France in early 1917 to note in his diary that "the soldier is no longer a noble figure." He had become "a writhing insect among this ghastly folly of destruction."[74] Months later, Sassoon would be wounded again at Arras, by which time his early jingoism had turned to bitterness. When he penned an open letter denouncing the war, the government sent the decorated veteran to be treated for neurasthenia. It was at a war hospital that he wrote an ode to the human subject commanded to kill strangers to live. "Soldiers are citizens of death's grey land," it began.[75]

Sassoon's insect metaphor was apt in horrid ways; it was also literal. Seen from the air, the movement of armies made battlefields look like crawling ant heaps. Enemies treated each other like vermin, dousing each other with chlorine, a gas used to destroy as well as to delouse. For scientists like Jean-Henri Casimir Fabre, the father of modern entomology, or Raymond Pearl, head of the statistics division of the U.S. Food Administration, understanding bugs held the secret to saving lives, and maybe even ending the war. The specter of suffering spurred a search for new keys to global interdependence, to understand the delicate balance between cooperation and competitive self-destruction. It would lead to discoveries in biometry and the measurement of populations, and the formation of international scientific networks aimed to understand the earth's limits.[76]

It started with bugs. Observers of the small to explain the large, entomologists were lesser-known figures in a global search for new ways to envision human interdependence. The study of insects and soil was like so much of the Global Civil War. The obsession with fertility—of bodies and land—reflected a structure of feeling dominated by alarm and a shadow of mass death. Memories of wartime shortages and hunger loomed large. Then came disease and desiccation. While the North American plains got whipped into clouds of dust (generations of heavy tillage turned topsoils into baby powder, raised aloft into clouds by prevailing winds), Stalin looked upon the breadbasket of Ukraine as a means to strip food from peasants. "To catch up and overtake" the capitalist West, officials tore grains and livestock from farmers and spread mass starvation to support cities and industries.[77]

Legions of entomologists, demographers, and biologists from East and West converged on what the biologist Edward Murray East called the land's "carrying capacity." They wanted a bookkeeping system for the world, to gauge human and soil fertility and, since many of them were bona fide eugenicists, racial determinants. Out of this drive a new field of biometrics emerged, which, steeped in the anxiety of its time, only confirmed the reasons for despair. Biometricians believed that overpopulation and the need for land were what caused war in the first place. Peace did not solve the underlying problem rooted in scarce land and the over-reproduction not just of people, but of the wrong types of people. "Defective" people. The earth was not just closed; it was shrinking and shrinking fast, which meant species were condemned to compete over limited carrying capacity. Likening the planet to Noah's ark, Edward Murray East argued that "the vessel is somewhat elastic, it is true, but it is a closed vessel nevertheless." And as population grew, the vessel became cramped.[78]

The League of Nations became a brain trust for anxious biometricians pushing statesmen to think about human security beyond guns and missiles and in terms of lice and wheat stocks. French, British, Russian, and American scientists were in and out of Geneva in a frenzy of international brainstorming and doomsaying. It was in Geneva, at the World Population Conference in 1927, that Raymond Pearl revealed a model of the planet trapped by a "logistics curve," an idea he borrowed from French Malthusians. Population growth would eventually consume any surplus until societies reached their carrying capacity—and there they would stagnate and face the temptation to fight for the diminishing supply. The Soviet biologist Georgii Frantsevich Gause followed up with his "principle of competitive exclusion" to describe the ecological dynamics that swayed species. In his scheme, once humans reached their limits, cooperation was doomed; they would opt to duel their way to survival.[79]

For some, the problem of interdependence was that rich societies were locked into relations with poor, backward ones that produced more mouths and not enough food to fill them. John Lossing Buck, son of evangelists and a Cornell-trained agronomist, was a professor at the

University of Nanking. He lived in China for thirty years and become one of its most eminent agricultural economists. His *Chinese Farm Economy* (1930) and *Land Utilization in China* (1937) became classics in the study of peasant production. As concerned with saving peasant lives as Chinese souls, Buck traveled across twenty-two provinces, mainly by bicycle, surveying almost forty thousand farm families to produce a profile of farmers using rustic tools and exploited kin to overtill their soil. To Buck, what was happening to China's enormous population exemplified what goes wrong when poor land and overbreeding trap a society, becoming a scientific parable to explain the trap of backwardness.[80]

Buck the agronomist was far less famous than his wife, Pearl Sydenstricker, whom he married in 1917. After a few years, their marriage slipped into unhappiness. But Pearl Buck picked up on her husband's ethnographic style and fascination with farmers and the unglamorous life of the peasant wife and fused these in her novels. She also carried over something of her missionary streak. Writing to her sister about the plight of the Chinese, she said, "In the night, or a dozen times a day, I find myself thinking furiously about the peoples of the world, as if they were my personal responsibility."[81]

In 1931, she published *The Good Earth*, a portrait of the life of strangers in a strange land. A narrative of survival of the world's have-nots, it anticipated other bestsellers from George Orwell (think *Down and Out in Paris and London* or *The Road to Wigan Pier*), or Rómulo Gallegos (think *Doña Bárbara*), or John Steinbeck (think *The Grapes of Wrath*), and the visual documentary style of a Dorothea Lange (think *Migrant Mother*). Quasi-biblical, *The Good Earth* echoed the style of journalists and photographers like Robert Capa and Lange, and their commitment to simple, if downtrodden, soil-under-the-fingernails folk. Buck's skill was in turning distant strangers, like Wang Lung and his wife O-Lan, into household names at home. "I shall never sell the land!" Wang Lung declared. "Bit by bit I will dig up the fields and feed the earth itself to the children and when they die I will bury them in the land, and I and my wife and my old father, and even he will die on the land that has given us birth."[82]

In many ways, the Bucks were picking up on longstanding worries among Chinese intellectuals about the struggle for land and survival. Chen Changheng's *A Treatise on Chinese Population*, published in Chinese at the end of the Great War, echoed the Malthusian angst about China's plague of people. The U.S.-trained economist called for new studies and new measures to curb the reproduction of the wrong sort of citizens. Between 1927 and 1935, a whole generation of social scientists (*shehui kexue*) was summoned to conduct nine thousand surveys in the campaign to create social "facts" and reverse the country's long-term decline.[83]

The same story was being replayed worldwide about land being arid, farmers giving up, peasants starving—even if, as in the case of the Soviet Union, famines were planned. Around the world, observers rounded on the peasant village with fascination and unease. Global new dealers wanted more than make-work programs; they advocated dramatic population and settlement schemes. *The Polish Peasant in Europe and America*, a five-volume study completed by William Thomas and Florian Znaniecki (who became the first Polish chair of sociology at the University of Poznán) during the Great War, anticipated the problem of a social type—organic communities surrounded and imperiled by hostile forces in a fight for racial and cultural survival but choked in their collectivist, backward ways.[84] One French administrator in Indochina worried that it was premature to extend freedoms in such a "backward," agrarian society. Instead, the peasantry would "have to submit its economy to a firm discipline to avoid seeing it founder in chaos."[85] In October 1938, Nehru created a National Planning Committee in part to tackle the issue of population. Its leader, Radhakamal Mukerjee, pointed out that while the rural population of India had risen 25 percent since 1915, food supply had grown by only 10 percent. The result was a looming calamity—by Mukerjee's count, a shortfall of 42 billion calories.[86]

Population pessimism was not restricted to concerns about hunger and misery in poor countries; scarcity fears afflicted all countries. Around the world, immigration activists, birth control advocates, eugenicists, and demographers were scrambling to understand the limits of nature and the laws of human nature. The Population Association of

America was founded in 1931. The Rockefeller Foundation sponsored task forces around the world. The Scripps Foundation for Research in Population Problems opened shop at Miami University of Ohio, directed by a famous Malthusian, Warren Thompson, whose *Danger Spots in World Population* (1929) warned of imminent problems of survival. He correlated conflict with the spread of reproductive energies; fertility rates predicted future threats to world peace. By 1939, on the eve of Hitler's invasion of Poland, Thompson was regarded as something of a prophet.[87] In 1938, the Carnegie Corporation enlisted the Swedish economist Gunnar Myrdal to come to the United States to study "the Negro question" with this spirit in mind. Myrdal's 1938 Godkin Lectures about America echoed Chen Changheng's Malthusian fears about China—and touted "scientific" birth control to prevent miserable people from passing on their affliction.[88] Pearl Buck, while assuming the voice of the world's poorest farmers, became an active supporter of family planning back in the United States. Close friends with Margaret Sanger, she made birth control one of her crusades in the 1930s and 1940s, bringing to the fore a looming concern of the Global Civil War not just with the supply of but demand for food.

Catastrophists made Armageddon seem inevitable. Their anxiety made predation seem legitimate because it was necessary for survival. The discourse around the East European peasantry, where so much of the exterminationist alarm would focus, was steeped in racial pessimism and the fever to control and contain the threat of needy strangers.[89] True, some held out hope that new frontiers could be unlocked to release the pressure. But even in this case, opening new pioneering lands was about getting rid of needy, racially inferior strangers. Isaiah Bowman, founder of the American Geographical Society and eventually president of Johns Hopkins University, had cut his teeth in South American expeditions into virgin forests. During the Great War and at the Paris talks, he served the administration as its chief territorial specialist. In 1931, amid the hardship of the American dust bowl, he argued that pioneering could be reinvented on a scientific basis; overcoming the old, "spontaneous" model of skimming off the land required a new alliance of geographers, agronomists, and responsible farmers to unlock the vast potential of even the more arid hinterlands. He called this "second wave pioneering," and upheld the "science of settlement" and dry farming as a panacea for a world of scarcity and hunger.[90]

Up to a point. Some strangers were simply hopeless, he felt, like Jews. A devout antisemite, Bowman could not abide the idea of settling Jewish refugees—whom he regarded as a degraded form of depraved peasant. Deeply influenced by the concept of *Lebensraum*, Bowman as the president of Johns Hopkins imposed strict Jewish quotas and banned African Americans. When tasked by Franklin Roosevelt to help find homes for Hitler's pariahs after the Evian Conference (1938), Bowman claimed that the American frontier was "closed." He scouted geographers and humanitarians to find other places to send them: Madagascar, the Philippines, the Dominican Republic. Couched behind his neutral calls to study world resource limits, he sounded ever more ominous about demographic pressure, racial fear, and overcrowded land in a "nationalized world."[91]

Room to Grow

The specter of fecund bodies and infertile lands spread fear of irrevocable decline and increasing envy. In the past, earth hunger justified colonial scrambles for prosperity; the 1930s turned land grabbing into a means for survival, even if it implied not just colonizing but exterminating strangers—and thus blurred the lines between humanitarianism, survivalism, and ethnic cleansing.

Karl Haushofer, the son of a prominent political economist, had served in the Bavarian Royal Army. In 1908, he set sail for Japan via the Suez Canal, India, and Singapore to serve as military attaché to the German embassy and as an advisor to the Japanese government. He returned home two years later via the Trans-Siberian Railway, brimming with new ideas about global power, resources, scale, and boundaries—and having been impressed by Japan's plans for Manchuria. Haushofer resented Anglo-Saxons for their colonial outlets in the Americas and India. He upheld the example of Japanese expansionist energy and maintained intimate relations with Japanese military officials. Japan was

Germany's mirror on the other side of Eurasia—catching up, boxed in by vintage dynasties, bursting with martial energy. He railed against the traditional view of power associated with guns and soldiers as archaic. Instead, he argued for a modern regional form of territorial integration. This Eurasian vision, harnessed to social Darwinism, drew Haushofer into the world of geopolitics to create an influential magazine called *Zeitschrift für Geopolitik*, an organ for thinking about geopolitics and its alternatives. He faced an intractable problem: space was filling up with hungry people, rivalrous states, and desperation. Haushofer borrowed a term from the zoologist-turned-geographer-journalist Friedrich Ratzel, *Lebensraum*, referring to space for national expansion, and attached it to a concept of state power, national security, and world order. For the elder Ratzel, though he was steeped in evolutionary theories, the challenge of finding security in the world was not (yet) racialized in the way it would become in the hands of his descendants. But still, an interdependent world required a geography of states to manage and protect its citizens; the need for land for survival implied expansion of states. A spirit of geopolitics, all the rage in a shrunken, postwar Weimar Germany with slumping fertility rates and plentiful right-wing alarm about lapsing morals, framed Haushofer's vision.[92] His friend and Nazi leader Rudolf Hess introduced Haushofer to Adolf Hitler so that he could impress the Führer and other Nazi brass with this new variant of racialized geopolitics.[93]

Geo. By giving semantic authority to voices worried about depletion, about being cornered and constrained, the prefix "geo-" changed the language of land, territory, and earth. Geo; with this prefix in mind, Haushofer and others scanned the Eurasian scene where they found echoes of similar anxieties. Their gaze reached Japan. The Great Depression hit Japan hard. Dozens of banks failed while China's turmoil cut into food supplies, ever a source of anxiety for the archipelago nation. Manchuria, the region in northeastern Asia, became the flash point. Anxiety over oil and coal gripped Japan in the 1920s and intensified in the 1930s, and Manchuria was the source of 46 percent of Japan's iron and 64 percent of the country's coal. Moreover, it was vital for tungsten and produced half the world's soybeans.[94] The South Manchuria Railway was also a player in the drive to survey colonizing opportunities across the North China Plain with scientific curiosity, drawing Japan's spotlight even more to Manchuria.[95]

Moving into Manchuria and establishing a puppet regime put Japanese rulers on a collision course with worried internationalists. After the Mukden incident, a false flag event involving dynamite planted near a Japanese-owned railway that triggered Tokyo's forces to invade, the League of Nations sent a commission of inquiry and relayed the story of a trumped up pretext for aggression. The league assembly entertained a resolution denouncing the invasion. Dressed in black, Japan's dapper chief delegate, Yosuke Matsuoka took the podium. He defended Japan's right to make Manchuria theirs as a matter of life and death. Would the United States give up the Panama Canal? "Read your history," he urged, before walking out as the assembly voted 42:1 calling for Japanese troops to withdraw. "We are not coming back," Matsuoka said on his way out.[96] Privately, some Japanese officials worried that their government had gone too far. The finance minister, Takahashi Korekiyo, noted in 1935, "Our country is poor in natural resources and I doubt we can compete in an autarkic economic environment." Preferring peaceful trade between strangers, he grew more alarmed. Japan's finance minister worried openly that Japanese commanders would militarize Manchuria. Sure enough, on February 26, 1936, months after the Italian invasion of the Horn of Africa, Japanese soldiers burst into Takahashi's home and stabbed, slashed, and shot him while screaming "heavenly punishment," which ushered in assassinations and putsches until the government became a martial regime committed to coercive expansion across Asia.[97]

The urge to solve the food problem, to expand, to dominate strangers reached its maximal expression under National Socialism. Nazi slogans like "Nutrition is not a private matter!" and "Your body belongs to the Führer!" covered billboards and subway stations. *Lebensraum* was a precept in one of the most notorious diatribes in history. Though it sold poorly upon its release, *Mein Kampf* became a bestseller in Germany once the author became the chancellor. Hitler fumed about German elites who had made a vital error in the nineteenth century by opting for trade, horizontal interdependence, and the "internationalization of the German economic life."[98]

By turning their backs on native soils, Hitler wrote, elites rewarded the source of the nation's weakness: Jewish financiers. There was altogether too much *inter*dependence between strangers and too little control over them. An avid reader of Karl May's western novels, obsessed with planetary limits, and seething over Germany's vulnerability to Allied blockades during the Great War, he pored over agrarian manuals looking for evidence of inevitable soil decline and the threat of race degeneration as unwanted Jews and Slavs wafted into the homeland in the relentless struggle to survive in an enclosed, competitive world. He also scribbled frantic Malthusian doomsday notes. One page of his agitation was labeled "Das Hunger als Macht" ("Hunger as Power"). Hunger was capable of arousing the "the Goddess of Want" and "Want" was the "Greatest world power." Scrawled across the landscape of his deranged musings was "Jewish fraud."[99]

The solution was spatial; the model was in the New World. He admired American manufacturing ingenuity, like its automobile industry. Above all, he saw in America an elemental truth about soil and blood. "The relationship of surface area to the population of the American continent is vastly superior" to anything known in the Old World. And with the infinite capacity to expand came an infinitely growing domestic market—and "guaranteed . . . internal sales" of cars. In the second book, a set of rambling manuscripts later folded into *Mein Kampf,* Hitler spelled out the stark consequences for those who stood in the way of German survival. In a world that was now enclosed with no more new land and carved into rivalrous nations that quarreled over access to strangers' resources to survive, the future of any race meant that "the final decision in the struggle for the world market will lie with force."[100] It was time, Hitler concluded, to "turn our gaze toward the land in the east." "At last," he declared, "we break off the colonial and commercial policy of the pre-War period and shift to the soil policy of the future."[101]

War was a colonizing project and colonization was the point of war. Both cleared the way for cleansing coveted lands of unwanted strangers, to lay claim to what they had but Germans needed. In a rambling speech to the Reichstag at the end of 1938, after the failure of the Evian Conference to resolve the "Jewish problem" by accepting Hitler's unwanted and settling them elsewhere, Hitler extended his vision of interdependence: create more room to grow and create more markets—and thereby "export, or die." It did not take much imagination for his audience to figure out who was going to export and who was going to die.[102] The *Generalplan Ost*, drafted in July 1941, outlined the vision for *Lebensraum* after the envisioned conquest of the Soviet Union. It catalogued the way in which the war-state would depopulate villages and impose mass birth control, forced sterilization, abortions, and deportation to make room for German settlers. Areas like Byelorussia and Ukraine were to be "cleansed." The destruction of Jewry and the redemption of Germans were thus intimately connected. Jews, after all, were "useless eaters."[103]

Out of Abyssinia

If there was a turning point, a moment beyond which it became impossible to reverse territorial and human frenzy, to stop escalating outgroup dehumanizing, it was 1935. That was the year in which coercive interdependence turned lethal. The collapse of the international payments system, the impasse of disarmament, and the resurgence of earth hunger changed the balance and removed the guardrails against outright predation and a groundswell of resistance. "Fifteen years have elapsed since 'the war to end all wars,'" wrote two dismayed critics in 1934. "Yet the arms industry has moved forward with growing momentum as if the pacific resolutions of various peoples and governments had never existed."[104] Later in 1935, a Syrian preacher named Shaykh Izz al-Din al-Qassam, was shot in a gunfight with British forces in the Galilee Hills as the occupiers tried to keep the peace in the Holy Land. Al-Qassam had a large following in Haifa, especially among young Palestinians who yearned to be rid of mandate authorities. When his corpse was brought back to Haifa, demonstrators cried, "Revenge! Revenge!" Within months, the Great Arab Revolt was in full swing, calling for a free state from Aleppo to Yemen.[105]

The revolt made world news—inspiring other rebels as well as rivals wanting to take advantage of British overstretch. Benito Mussolini followed the news closely. He also followed reportage, along with Hitler's

Tokyo clique, of Japan's Manchurian land grabbing. He dreamed of a new Roman Empire and vengeance for the humiliation in Abyssinia in 1896. He also dreamed of reversing generations of Italian emigration, promoting native fertility, first through internal colonization—and then external colonization. "Overseas expansion" would eclipse overseas migration; America would be replaced by . . . Africa. By the 1930s, Mussolini was marching to a geostrategic beat about the need for soil and room—what he called *spazio vitale* (living space)—to release Italians from the threats from and thrall to untrustworthy strangers. Fueled by the geographic vistas of the fascist thinker Giuseppe Bottai, Mussolini yearned to bridge Italy to Libya, thereby controlling the Mediterranean, and overland to Ethiopia, thereby opening a gateway to the Indian Ocean. If nothing else, it was grandiose. Fantasies and furies intoxicated despots and their followers. Il Duce's plan to overrun independent Abyssinia in the 1930s was a decisive turning point in world history, fusing an old-style colonial land grab and the first fascist conquest of strangers. After Abyssinia, anxious predators rushed for their own share of a shrinking planet.[106]

Mussolini needed a pretext. It came in the form of yet another "incident"—a manufactured device for nationalists to bully neighbors. He also needed a moral justification to gild his plan. Humanitarian activists gave it to him on a platter. Antislavery campaigners had been calling for an Ethiopian intervention for years. But the niceties of League commitment to sovereignty were a constraint. The trick was to show how the African state contravened international norms and laws against slavery; Addis Ababa failed to conform to the "standard of civilization," a convenient metric that Europeans self-servingly defined for everyone else. Ethiopia was the subject of relentless reporting by Major Henry Darling, Sir John Harris, N. A. Dyce Sharp, and others associated with the Anti-Slavery and Aborigines' Protection Society about the persistence of "slave markets." Joseph Kessel, the French journalist, published an extended essay with photos in *The New York Times Magazine* in July 1930 about the trade in "black ivory." "Human beings—though perhaps one must say human beings in their most elementary stage of development—were there serving others just as animals are used," he

WITH THE SLAVE HUNTERS IN ABYSSINIA

An Arab Trader Shows How He Captures Human Chattels for the Markets of the Near East

FIGURE 3.2. With the Slave Hunters in Abyssinia.

wrote of the markets. Readers were treated with eyewitness observations and photos to drive home an argument about Arab inhumanity and the justification for European intervention.[107]

The British-based group teamed up with the Società antischiavista d'Italia and called for a "new crusade." They invoked images of chain gangs, whips, and violence pulled straight from the 1927 cinematic blockbuster *Uncle Tom's Cabin*. *The Times* of London, the new BBC, echoed the drumbeat about Ethiopia's shortcomings as a "civilized nation." By 1935, there was a veritable propaganda onslaught against the Emperor Haile Selassie. Selassie's protests sounded like a cover-up. Emboldened, Mussolini took the charges of mass slavery to the League of Nations. British and French delegates sat on their hands as the league condemned Selassie.[108]

With a humanitarian pretext under his arm, Mussolini invaded Abyssinia in October 1935. On hand was the German photographer for *Berliner Illustrirte Zeitung*, the pioneering precursor to *LIFE*, and The Associated Press, Alfred Eisenstaedt, who catalogued the lead-up to invasion for the world to see. In the ensuing six years, 760,000 Ethiopians, most of them civilians, would die from famine, disease, bombardment, or gas. In some places, forced labor was worse under the Italian heel. On December 6, 1935, six Italian planes bombed the ancient city of Gondar, killing four women and six children. Twelve more planes dropped their payload on Dessye, hitting an International Committee of the Red Cross (ICRC) dressing station and a Seventh-day Adventist mission, both marked clearly as medical installations. They followed up with another bombing run on a Swedish field hospital, then a British tent in the Korem Plain. An ICRC doctor, Marcel Junod, sent ground and aerial photographs of the incendiary bomb destruction, the large Red Cross tent markings in shreds, and scattered cadavers, to Geneva, pleading for intervention. The point of air bombardment was to shock and traumatize civilians. Incendiary and explosive shrapnel bombs to erase villages were part of the plan. In Geneva, the awful question was this: Did the cross on hospital tents turn them into targets rather than protect them?[109]

Abyssinia exposed the disfigured logic of the civilizing mission. The Ethiopian emperor fled to Britain, where he was warmly received by large crowds around Waterloo Station. By then, reportage of Italian atrocities replaced the antislavery storm the year before (though the Anti-Slavery Society doubled down on its righteous support for the Italian invasion). Public opinion split. Sir Oswald Mosley and his fascist Blackshirts gathered at Hyde Park to protest the Ethiopians' presence. By the summer, a worldwide solidarity movement condemned the invasion. On June 22, Lillian Rabin and Eloise Robinson—white and Black Americans—chained themselves to a signpost in front of the Italian consulate in New York wearing shirts announcing "HANDS OFF ETHIOPIA." The victims were no longer slaves needing rescue; now they were refugees, fleeing European invaders. Gandhi declared that "India cannot ignore Benito Mussolini's threat against the coloured people." He called for an Indian Red Cross delegation to travel to Ethiopia because Europeans lacked the moral will.[110] For the Cuban communist Blas Roca, defending Ethiopia "should now be a major center of our work among blacks, who feel a great sympathy with the Abyssinian people."[111]

Selassie went to Geneva, where the global color line was shining bright. On the afternoon of June 30, dressed in a dark cape and derby, he passed through large crowds of supporters, and entered the new league palace to address the delegates. He urged sanctions against the invaders. He wanted his country back. Before he was introduced, the assembly was reminded that the Italian campaign was "a sacred mission of civilization." Selassie took the podium and spoke in Amharic. Italians whistled and jeered. The hall lights had to be dimmed several times to restore order. Finally, in a low, soft voice, he outlined the history of the invasion and catalogued the war crimes. He explained that Ethiopia was a lesson for others—that bombing civilians posed a challenge to international morality and "collective security." "It is us today," he warned. "It will be you tomorrow." If sympathizers hoped the emperor would sway the assembly, they underestimated the contagion of predatory interdependence. Polish colonial advocates piped up. "We Poles, like the Italians, have the right to demand export markets as well as areas for settlement be opened for us, so that we may obtain raw materials necessary for the national economy under conditions similar to those enjoyed by colonial states," argued Warsaw's delegate. As he was petitioning Geneva for Poland's own room to grow, Stalin and Hitler had their eyes on carving Poland for their survival dreams.[112]

One reason why Abyssinia became a potent symbol was the eyewitness accounts of a South African reporter for the London *Times*, George Steer. Steer saw firsthand the effects of the bombings in Dessye. He reported his findings in *The Times* to outraged readers. The foreign minister, Sir Samuel Hoare, who had inherited his share of Foreign Office flops, was struggling to keep Mussolini out of any alliance with Hitler. As a sop, he gave Il Duce much of Ethiopia, dismissing it as "a corridor for camels." When news of the bombings hit *The Times*, the outcry forced Hoare to resign.[113]

Steer's story returns us to the role of the media in making meaning of the Global Civil War and the polarizing view of strangers. By 1935, reports from Manchuria and Ethiopia heightened the sense that a crowded, wanting world was collapsing into unrestrained competition and a lethal racial hierarchy. But media reporting also triggered a sense of horrified togetherness, solidarity even. Steer, the moral witness, played his role. As he was scrambling to finish his exposé about Mussolini (called *Caesar in Abyssinia*) in what would be a short, intense career in war reportage, Steer got sent to Spain. His introduction to *Caesar*, datelined "Burgos 1936," cited an Italian leaflet that had been dropped on Ethiopian civilians warning of a pitiless death. To this, Steer added his own warning for great power leaders: "Ethiopia is nearer to Europe than they think."[114]

Spain was the next front of the Global Civil War. Steer was among the many reporters for whom the Spanish Civil War held special significance in the struggle to convey the truth of a struggling republic.[115] As journalists gathered for dinner in the Torrontegui Hotel in the Basque capital of Bilbao on the night of April 26, 1937, someone came tearing in. The nearby town of Guernica was on fire. Steer jumped into a car with Christopher Holme of Reuters, Noel Monks from the *Daily Mail* and Mathieu Corman of *Çe Soir*. They drove through the night—and as they neared the town, the sky glowed with the burning. Made largely of wood, Guernica was a "royal carpet of live coals" as the journalists entered it.

"Operation Rügen" sent German and Italian planes to shower Basque towns with fragmentation and incendiary bombs. After waves of assaults from the air, Messerschmidts and Heinkels then strafed the roads choked with fleeing civilians. This was the "terror bombing" doctrine at work, contrived to shock the senses. As Steer spent the day interviewing horrified survivors, he found three aluminum tubes in the rubble. He took them back to the Torrontegui. Stamped with German imperial eagles and "Rheindorf factory, 1936," they served as vital evidence of German involvement. In the ensuing days, Steer interviewed refugees streaming into Bilbao by foot or on ox carts.

The first to break the news was Holme, for Reuters. When Steer's article appeared in *The Times* on April 28, it was long, detailed, and piercingly analytical. "The object of the bombardment was seemingly the demoralization of the civilian population and the destruction of the cradle of the Basque race," he wrote. By then, the nationalists had their own narrative. The same *Times* published a report from their other stringer, James Holburn, who echoed the Franquista denial; true, the

FIGURE 3.3. Image of bombed-out Guernica from the front page of *Le Petit Journal.*

town was burned to the ground, but in a classic retort, the fascists insisted that the reds did it themselves to summon the world's pity.

Meanwhile, the French papers also ran the stories, including Steer's. On May 28, Pablo Picasso read the story in *L'Humanité* and followed up with *Çe Soir* and *Le Petit Journal*, which quoted extensively from Steer's eyewitness account.

Months earlier, Picasso had agreed to prepare a work of art for Spain's fair at the Paris International Exhibition. But he was uninspired, uncertain how to represent his loyalty on the world stage. Then came the news of Guernica and the stories and photos of the terror bombing. His lover and photographer, Dora Maar, recorded Picasso in a controlled frenzy, painting his epic across an enormous sheet of muslin. Echoing the documentary photography he saw in Parisian papers, he worked in black, white, and a lot of gray. He mimicked the effect of crime photos lit by flash bulbs and made his creatures scream—like headlines. At the center of the work was the body of a twisted horse made of mashed-up newspaper. Picasso adapted his fracturing, Cubist style to exemplify the shattering of a little, Basque village. He also aimed to render the image more easily replicable, like a photograph, so it could be cheaply

FIGURE 3.4. *Guernica,* half done in Picasso's studio.

reproduced and disseminated. And that it was: *Guernica* would become the world's most recognizable image of war. When a German officer later asked him, "Did you do *Guernica*?" the painter shot back: "No, you did."[116]

The news of atrocities in Spain reached readers worldwide. The news brought shock, outrage, and the end of illusion. Throughout that winter, Virginia Woolf sat in her study looking at images like those that horrified Picasso, trying to hang on to what remained of the threads of her own illusions. She thought of the images as objective reckonings with subjective tremors. They "are simply statements of fact addressed to the eye." She repeated this several times in her 1938 essay *Three Guineas*. "But the eye is connected with the brain," she added, and "the brain with the nervous system. That system sends its messages in a flash through every past memory and present feeling." Body parts, bodies, a house blown in half, a bird cage swinging from a beam in the open air, the horror—what the viewer saw could be people, or "be the body of a pig." It was hard to say; the bodies were so mutilated. It was meant to be hard to say: terror bombing was—and remains—hard to articulate. On the other hand, noted Woolf, the images bonded the observer to the suffering of strangers: "When we look at those photographs some fusion takes place within us; however different the education, the traditions behind us, our sensations are the same; and they are violent." *Three Guineas* advised an unnamed educated gentleman on how to prevent war, noting that such a task required thinking differently. She floated the idea of creating a new college for young women, an institution devoted to teaching "the art of understanding other peoples' lives and minds" so that they may "influence," a key word in her prose, the dehumanizing propensities of men—an illusion. Two years later, the Nazi Blitz destroyed her London home, the Woolfs escaped to Sussex, and her illusion gave way to despair and suicide.[117]

As for Steer, appalled that his paper, *The Times*, defended appeasement, he quit and returned home to catalogue German war schemes in Africa. *The Daily Telegraph* got him to cover the Soviet invasion of Finland, where he saw more aerial bombing of civilians. He then joined British intelligence, served in the army in Ethiopia, and helped restore Haile Selassie to the throne. He died in Burma when his overloaded Jeep crashed on Christmas Day, 1944.

4

After Nagasaki

The Cloud

The sun had not yet risen on August 10, 1945, when a young military photographer called Yōsuke Yamahata slipped into Nagasaki. Smoke and dust were rising from the city's embers. Bodies were floating in slowly moving thick, brown, streams. Some were still alive as people plunged into the water in a futile effort to soothe their flaming skin. As he coughed and picked his way through the remains, afraid a second bomb might land, Yamahata took over a hundred shots of the blasted landscape. He returned home to Hakata and developed the pictures. His roommate, the writer Ashihei Hino, was so anguished by the images that he could not sleep. The rubble and humans were all jumbled together; charred limbs were hard to distinguish from burned beams; Yamahata's photos seemed at once over- and underexposed as he captured the sun's light filtered through a gauze of dust and smoke. Four days later, the Emperor Hirohito announced Japan's surrender.

Yamahata wondered what to do with his images. The witness showed them to his father, a prominent military propagandist, who encouraged him to find a publisher to illustrate Japan's victimhood. Some appeared in the August 21 issue of the magazine *Mainichi Shimbun*. The following month, General Douglas MacArthur banned all atomic-related news. It was not until 1952, after the censorship laws were lifted, that Yamahata's images spread—featured in *LIFE* and published in album-style books.[1]

FIGURE 4.1. Nagasaki.

Yamahata died of cancer in 1966 at the age of forty-eight, likely due to the radiation of his day in Nagasaki.

Writers also struggled to represent this new form of horror. Two short stories on the bombings, both written in 1945, were shelved for nearly three years before censors agreed to release them. When Hara Tamiki's "Summer Flower" ("Natsu no hana") and Yoko Ota's "City of Corpses" ("Shikabane no machi"), did finally appear, censors blotted out many lines in Japanese editions. In May 1946, the editors of *The New Yorker* magazine dispatched John Hersey to the scene of the first atomic blast. Born in Tianjin, China, in 1914, a missionary son, Hersey was already a well-known author. He slipped into Hiroshima and spent three weeks in the wreckage interviewing helpers and survivors. Unlike Yamahata, Hersey was too late to witness the dead. All he saw was rubble and survivors. The result was an issue of the magazine devoted to a single story, simply called *Hiroshima*. It was a sensation when it hit the stands a year after the blast. Later a mass circulation book, *Hiroshima* became one of the bestselling works of nonfiction of all time. The key was giving to the survivors, the *hibakusha*, voice. Following the trails of six of them, Hersey recounted the morning and its aftermath, how the initial silence gave way to sounds of crashing and crumbling, followed by moans and cries. "Please help! Get us out!" came voices from under the ruins. Hersey's narrative was so piercing because his protagonists were so basically human; their efforts to help themselves and other survivors made the unimaginable imaginable. In 1949, *Hiroshima* was released in Japan.[2]

Hiroshima and Nagasaki detonated the paradigm of interstate industrial warfare that had dominated capitalist interdependence; cities and giant munitions factories were good for target practice. Mass armies were useless in the face of such weapons. Indeed, total war of the industrial age was, quite simply, impossible without total annihilation.[3] So, how to prevent it? Franklin Roosevelt had envisioned America's nuclear monopoly as the lever for a muscular peace, one that would do for the world what the New Deal did for America—dissolve the sources fear and restore the bonds of togetherness. Hereafter, prosperity and peace in the world were to be indissoluble. The protection of both, inscribed in basic charters like that of the new United Nations, became a "groundnorm" for all other laws, rules, and norms.[4]

Along with a new groundnorm, another effect of victory was to create a new source of fear, annihilation. It positioned one country above all as guardian, creating an exception, an existential carve-out, to the idea of an assembly of free and equal nations. All nations would delegate their ability to build a nuclear bomb to a powerful international agency, forfeiting their sovereignty over this deadly new weapon under the benign eye of the monopolist. But: only America would retain its command over how to obliterate strangers, giving new meaning to superpowerdom. What Roosevelt envisioned, however, is precisely what Stalin feared: America's nuclear monopoly was the instrument to build a world order centered on the United States. The bombing of Nagasaki was the first strike of the Cold War.[5] The year that saw *Hiroshima* published in Japan, the Soviet military detonated its first atomic bomb, shattering the American nuclear monopoly and the illusion that only far-away strangers outside America were in danger.

By then, across Asia, all states occupied by American, British, French, Dutch, and Russian forces were at war once more. The struggle over decolonization spread to Africa and beyond. It ensured that dismantling empires to create the assembly of free nations militarized global politics in the nuclear age.

The groundnorm for interdependence was crippled at birth. Within a year, the United States nearly doubled its atomic arsenal. At the end of the decade each side aimed a staggering number of weapons at each other. The 1952 advent of the hydrogen bomb, a device that places a nuclear bomb inside itself to trigger a chain reaction of nuclear fusion, the near equivalent of one thousand Nagasaki bombs going off at the same time and location, elevated rivalry to a new level of potential extinction. President Dwight D. Eisenhower worried. The news of the hydrogen bomb might "scare the country to death."[6] Sure enough, to strike fear into Americans during the 1962 Cuban Missile Crisis, the Soviets tested a three-hundred-kiloton warhead—whose electromagnetic charge left Kazakhstan's grid in shreds. The same day, Soviet pilots airdropped an 8.2-megaton hydrogen bomb over the Novaya Zemlya test site. A week later, Soviet fighters pursued an American U-2 in their territory and American pilots with nuclear warheads rushed to escort the spy plane out of danger. The same day, a Soviet submarine surfaced for air near Cuba. Sailors climbed to the deck and watched American jets fly low overhead and strafe the water nearby. The Soviet commander ordered his nuclear torpedoes activated; his crew scrambled down the shaft. Realizing that the pilots had gone too far, an American officer signaled an apology to the last remaining Soviet crewman on deck—who relayed the message below. The alarm went off.[7]

The prospect of war pushed the planners, who had never truly gone into retirement after 1945, into high gear. Fear led to escalation. By 1967, the U.S. stockpile reached 31,255 nuclear bombs. The Soviets countered. Others joined the atomic race. In the deadly spiral, strategists coined a euphemism to justify it: deterrence. The escalation was an unfortunate necessity to prevent the adversary from hitting the launch button. If they did, they were committing suicide. Others called it a balance of terror. At least there was one agreement: the arms race made interdependence a matter of existence.

This delicate framework for interdependence was clear enough to Washington's adversary. The Red Army went on an appropriations binge, seizing factories and industrial equipment from East Germany to North Korea; everything that could be made movable in occupied Manchuria, like the massive Nippon Steel Company of Chung-jin, furnaces, ovens, chemicals, even office chairs, were uprooted, loaded on to trains or ships, and hauled to the USSR (the Union of Soviet Socialist Republics) for industrial-scale weapons manufacture. When a U.S. survey mission arrived in Manchuria and North Korea in early 1946, they found the region stripped bare of its industrial capacity to turn the Soviet Union into an economic fortress.[8]

Treating the planet like a laboratory for testing the limits of mass destruction made it more dangerous than ever to be alive, and put everyone at risk from decisions of unknown, unheard strangers and their unfathomable weapons dropped from unseeable bombers and eventually unmanned missiles. The news, just like the threat, was hard to contain. In 1954, the American military set off a hydrogen bomb on the Bikini Atoll islands in the western Pacific. They'd removed the local population and kept the press at a distance. But they could not control the winds or curb freedom to sail in international waters. They also vastly underestimated the power of the explosion. A Japanese fishing vessel, the *Daigo Fukuryu Maru* (*Lucky Dragon No. 5*), was trawling outside the blast zone downwind from the mushroom cloud. By the time the crew got back to Japan, it was vomiting and blistering. The country's worst nightmares stormed back: the *Lucky Dragon* rekindled memories suppressed by censors who wanted Japan to move on as a loyal ally in the fight against communism.[9]

The *Yomiuri* newspaper broke the news. Millions of readers followed the fate of the boat's radio operator, Aikichi Kuboyama, as he slowly died in hospital. The U.S. government had tried to protect the secrecy of its experiment: it pressed Japanese authorities to burn the ship as evidence. In the end, Washington expressed "regret" over the "incident"—choice words in the diplomacy of deflection—and hastened to pay $2 million to each survivor *ex gratia*. The uproar could not be contained. One Japanese international lawyer and former advisor to the wartime government, Kaoru Yasui, made the vessel an icon for the swelling antinuclear movement. Purged from his position at the University of Tokyo, Yasui mounted a crusade that harvested a staggering thirty-two million signatures for a call to stop testing and to keep Japan nuclear-free. He soon became Japan's leading ban-the-bomber and a regular figure in peace rallies worldwide. By 1958, mushroom clouds appeared on placards of demonstrations in London: the first mass demonstration outside Japan took place on Good Friday when ten thousand people withstood icy rain and wind to stand in silent vigil outside the barbed wire fence at Aldermaston, ground zero for Britain's nuclear weapons program.[10]

The atom bomb ended the Global Civil War, but its shadow permanently altered the meaning of interdependence. The nuclear menace underlined the need for new institutions, new alliances, new ideas to prevent history from repeating itself. In no moment of world history had one society ever commanded such military, material, and moral power over the rest as the United States wielded in 1945. The combination made one country the world's ballast under the specter of annihilation. But that country's monopoly also bred fears and resentments of those who did not—could not—trust it because it self-defined as an adversary. How could the United States safeguard the groundnorm of world peace and prosperity while pointing atomic daggers at strangers? The United States positioned itself as the source of hopes, fears, and eventually disenchantment with a nation-based order envisioned to replace empires as the wardens of interdependence.

Pax Americana

A nuclearized divide was not the only outcome of the ashes of Nagasaki. A drive to produce postimperial groundnorms, also with the United States as watchman, emerged as well. Here Roosevelt had another plan, to roll back Europe's and Japan's empires, which he thought had been the drivers of instability and rivalry for the last century. Emancipated societies of Africa and Asia would join a fraternity of nations and play by shared rules and norms torn from the playbooks of America's peace planners. Decolonization, it was hoped, would distribute interdependence beyond empires and their archaic standards of civilization—to be replaced by standards of "governance" and economic modernization that would piece the post-Nagasaki world back together as inclusive and free. That was the script, at least.[11]

The script, however, contained a tension over what kind of inclusion would replace the old extractive inclinations of empires. What *was* the American model? Was it the spread of democratic universalism, to help the world's strangers look ever more like Americans? Or was it, as the anthropologist Margaret Mead once noted, more like an "orchestration of cultural diversity" to make a symphony out of the world's many parts? If the atom bomb cast its shadow over the post-Nagasaki world, Japan's defeat triggered these core questions while the smoke was still clearing. Just as the commander of the U.S. forces in Japan, General MacArthur, looked out from the deck of the USS *Missouri* on the ruins of Tokyo, he announced that "today, freedom is on the offensive." Two weeks earlier, nationalist movement leader Sukarno proclaimed Indonesian independence. The same day MacArthur "freed" Japan, September 2, 1945, Ho Chi Minh announced the independence of Vietnam. Four days later the People's Republic of Korea formed its first free government. An anti-imperial cascade set in.[12]

The war left the United States in charge of a world whose old empires were decomposing into a world of many parts. It also left Washington over two thousand overseas military bases, martial and economic muscle of unprecedented historic scale, enough to remap the world by filling the gaps opened up by collapsing empires. The process had begun before the United States even entered the war. In the sweltering summer of 1941, the American president, Franklin Delano Roosevelt, escaped to cooler waters off the coast of Newfoundland to meet with the British prime minister, Winston Churchill. Aboard the USS *Augusta,* the two drafted a vision for a future without empire. They called it the Atlantic Charter. And while Churchill resisted, the cost of American support to save the British nation was the British Empire. In eight points and a modest four hundred words, there was a commitment to ban territorial aggrandizement, to uphold self-government by all peoples, to guarantee freedom to navigate the seas, and to cooperate in social and economic affairs to prevent disasters of the 1930s. They informed the framework, five months later, of the Allies' joint declaration of the intent to create a United Nations, this time with Joseph Stalin's blessing.

The charter, Roosevelt argued, was a Magna Carta for a new world for the whole world. This meant "disarmament of aggressors, self-determination of nations and peoples, and the four freedoms—freedom of speech, freedom of religion, freedom from want, and freedom from fear." Good riddance, he declared, to "the old term 'Western Civilization.'" It "no longer applies" and should give way to "a real world civilization."[13] The 1948 Universal Declaration of Human Rights echoed the late president. Article 3 is pithy: "Everyone has a right to life, liberty, and the security of person."[14]

Everyone. To become free was to become free of want, and freedom from want meant to develop. It was the third of Roosevelt's four freedoms announced in January 1941 in the annual address to Congress. "Translated into world terms," Roosevelt said, freedom from want means "economic understandings which will secure to every nation a healthy peacetime life for its inhabitants—everywhere in the world." When Winston Churchill resisted Roosevelt's call for open trade and defended imperial preferences, the American president countered: "Those Empire trade agreements are a case in point. It's because of them that the people of India and Africa, of all the colonial Near East and Far East, are still as backward as they are."[15]

Everywhere. All four of Roosevelt's freedoms ended with the incantation of "everywhere in the world," making sure that the universal significance would not be missed. The charter drafters added prose about its principles applying to "all men." There could be no just peace or prosperity without addressing the discrepancies between haves and have-nots. What is more, the charter affirmed that each individual had a relationship to the world order of which they were an interdependent part, and thereby might have access to a supranational legal system to uphold their dignity and rights.

The young South African law student and activist Nelson Mandela immediately saw the revolutionary potential for oppressed peoples. He would later claim in his autobiography that reading this passage of the charter about the necessity of human dignity for a peaceful world changed his life.[16] The international legal theorist Hersch Lauterpacht also saw in the recognition of universal rights and individuals' fundamental freedoms a transformational moment. He noted that there could be a goal to create an interdependent economy, but that "improvements in social conditions also cannot be fully achieved by the efforts of one state or a group of states." Just as states were willing to give up some economic sovereignty in the pursuit of prosperity, any advancement of human rights "implies a more drastic interference with the sovereignty of the state than the renunciation of war."[17]

The real-world civilization rested on American hegemony—a foundation with unique enabling properties.[18] That the United States should be the new order's guardian was, even to Soviets, beyond doubt. In 1945, the United States boasted over a third of the world's output, about 50 percent of industrial production, and 80 percent of hard currency reserves. In a world reduced to rubble, America could not help but be a screen upon which hopes and redemptions would be projected. Even the USSR had survived and won the war in part thanks to American loans. By definition, however, this was a condition that could not last; indeed, if the rebuilding were to be successful, it should not last. American power was programmed to wane—and as it did so, American power was destined to appear to fall if not to fail. With so many hopes pinned on America, it was almost foregone that they would boomerang back and turn into disenchantment about limits and hypocrisies of Pax Americana. The Global Civil War culminated with a dramatic redistribution of power. It shifted the burden of reconstruction to a United States willing to shoulder it as long as the multilateral and international order rewarded and recognized the hegemon. But as hegemony slipped, it would cast shade on the hegemon and tax its commitment to the order it had once stewarded.[19]

The buy-in also required self-identification from the hegemon's patriciate. The Atlantic Charter echoed a growing view among American elites that the world required its leadership, and that America had experience in democracy and development to share and could replace—so they thought—Europe's imperial ways. Edward Mead Earle, one of the behind-the-scenes *penseurs*, placed the American challenge against a panorama of world history. Humanity, armed with aircraft carriers and heavy bombers, had erased the prophylactic effect of distance and reached a threat limit that required a new understanding of strategy. "War," Earle wrote in 1941, "instead of an occasional and regrettable 'instrument of national policy,' [has become] to the totalitarian states both the supreme expression of human personality and the dominating consideration in all statecraft."[20] New totalitarianisms and new weapons threatened to annihilate civilization—and required that liberals think anew, beginning with the premise that isolation was over. He would urge a "grand strategy" of military, cultural, psychological, and technological forces to make total war obsolete. Any polity that defected from the new rules would face eviction from the family of nations and the bounty of their interdependence. This required a power and a coalition capable of enforcing these rules. From his perch in Princeton and in regular contact with magnates in Washington and New York think tanks, Earle created a model for stability with the United States as the fulcrum of a new world order.[21]

This required a new American self-imaginary. The war brought out clarion callers. Henry Luce, China booster and editor of *LIFE* magazine, had warned in 1941, as Earle was crafting his grand strategy, that Americans lived in a fog of "self-deceit." It drove Luce to distraction that his fellow citizens were content while knowing "that the sickness of the world is also our sickness." They were in denial of the degree to which America depended on the rest—and vice versa. "Our world of 2,000,000,000 human beings is for the first time in history one world, fundamentally indivisible," he wrote.[22] The result was a gentrified sense of historical duty, not just as citizens of the country but of the world. As George C. Marshall, the military commander and new secretary of state, in early 1947 put it in a speech to students at Princeton University, the war ended, but "the world is a very small place," while most "countries of the world find themselves exhausted economically, financially and physically." He urged his audience to study world history and develop "a sense of responsibility for world order and security" and "a sense of overwhelming importance of this country's acts, and failures to act, in relation to world order and security." He added: "These, in my opinion, are great musts for your generation."[23]

Torqued by decolonization and Cold War tensions, American-led interdependence ceded to a triumphant democratic universalism, overshadowing Margaret Mead's alternative of pluralistic inclusion. A confident, forward-looking America with its GIs and Ivy League experts, became its bulwark; making the world safe for interdependence required American supremacy and a grand narrative to fit. So it was that a world designed for nations in 1945, overseen by a United Nations headquartered in New York with a gleaming new building (construction began in 1947) designed by a galaxy of celebrity architects, had the United States as enforcer and financier. This gave the world order ballast that was missing in 1919. It was perhaps clearest in the domain of the world economy. Organizations like the International Bank for Reconstruction and Development (better known later as the World Bank) and the International Monetary Fund (IMF), and financing like Marshall aid and schemes to alleviate dollar shortages, stabilized a shattered international payments system.[24] International money doctors, "peacekeepers," aid agencies, and cultural trusts for the planet proliferated to make good on the general principles of the charter and its promises. The United Nations Educational, Scientific and Cultural Organization (UNESCO) called for a unified "History of Mankind," a sweeping narrative to service a "world civilization," a unity created out of cultural exchanges that would material ones, always with the assumption that encounters and interactions inevitably led to greater understanding, if not mutual identification under the keyword of the era: humanity.[25] To be associated with any of these organizations was to join a beehive of global experts from universities that had cast aside their ivory-tower seclusion to join the war effort and to serve (or govern) a postcolonial world. It was new and meant to seem new, to convey a sense of a fresh start.

American hegemony enabled international cooperation in a moment in which backsliding was not just a possibility; to many, it seemed inevitable. Even before the collapse of Nazi Germany, Churchill was girding for more fighting. He used terms like "iron curtain" and "third world war" in private telegrams. He even asked his chiefs of staff to draft plans for war against the USSR codenamed Operation Unthinkable. George Orwell's dystopian novel, *Nineteen Eighty-Four*, made it imaginable. For many, its protagonist, Winston Smith, an everyman laboring in the Ministry of Truth that spewed lies about the menace coming from fictive rivals of Eurasia and Eastasia, was a parable of the present. The grimy story of rationing and the despotism of "bureaucrats, scientists, and technicians" reflected a mood. Prophetic about the dark side of managerial surveillance, the novel portrayed the "last man in Europe" (the original title for the novel) as caught in a continuous and unbroken web of hardship, rationing, and war.[26]

Instead of gray bleakness, the world got reconstruction and promises of abundance and synthetics. But as the world's hegemon, the United States found itself also playing the role of enforcer. For those who strayed from the script, like the nationalist presidents in Guatemala and Iran in the early 1950s, the first seizing landed estates of the United Fruit Company and the second the Anglo-Iranian Oil Company, Central Intelligence Agency (CIA) covert action with local counterrevolutionary allies took down governments that were seen as crossing the permissible line. Even allies like Britain and France had run-ins with the hegemon. When they decided to seize the Suez Canal back from the Egyptian leader, Gamal Abdel Nasser, in November 1956, their pursuit of national interests menaced a wider geopolitical order. Nasser, grumbled British Prime Minister Anthony Eden, had his "thumb on our windpipe."[27] The windpipe was a metaphor for the conduit of precious petroleum inconveniently pooled under the sand in the Persian Gulf. Washington cared more about world peace than British oil supplies. Keen to keep the Arab world from slipping into a rising Soviet orbit, the Eisenhower administration turned on Paris and London. Washington didn't even have to unleash the CIA; let markets do the disciplining. Oil embargoes and a stampede on the French franc and especially the British pound (India, China, and others pulled their dollar deposits out of Britain) brought the adventurists to their knees—which accelerated the dissolution of their empires in Africa and

Asia.[28] The paradox was, of course, that in the collapse of European empires with American cheerleading, Washington found itself drawn into postcolonial vacuums. By the end of the 1950s, America was inching its way, without planning to, toward becoming a Eurasian power to replace Eurasian empires—from Persian Gulf to Indochina.

A Contradictory World of Nations

The post-Nagasaki world combined realism and idealism, national sovereignty and lofty universal proclamations, under an umbrella of rights. The combination gave clarity of purpose and produced a muddle at the same time. It cleared moral grounds for interdependence by universalizing rights but made state sovereignty the condition for enjoying them.

On one principle there was growing consensus: old empires, as the traditional guardians of interdependence, had to go. W.E.B. Du Bois, one of the silenced voices of 1919, wrote to the American delegates shaping the fledgling United Nations in 1945 that any universal declaration of rights had to include those without their own states. Yes, trials promised to put Nazi and Japanese warmongers on the stand; good. But over 250 million people still lived under imperial bootheels in Asia and Africa while swaths of people everywhere were unequal citizens at home. For Du Bois, peace meant not just restoring rights to the uprooted, but giving them to the many more who still lived in colonies as subjects of self-serving standards of civilization defined by some and applied to all.[29]

Du Bois was not alone in yearning for a new international ethics. Emerging from the savagery of the Global Civil War, Hannah Arendt, the German-Jewish refugee, declared that the atrocities demanded a new guidance system. There could be no going back to a world in which some had rights and others did not, not if the "never again" rhetoric was to mean anything. If people were to take equality, especially equality among strangers, seriously, they had to ensure that all humans had access to political membership and legality. They had a "right to have rights," as she put it immortally in *The Origins of Totalitarianism* (1951), a book she began to compose as she was fleeing fascism in Europe. She worried that the old civilizers were slow learners: "No paradox of contemporary politics is filled with more poignant irony than the discrepancy between the efforts of well-meaning idealists who stubbornly insist on regarding as inalienable those human rights, which are enjoyed only by the citizens of the most prosperous and civilized countries, and the situation of the rightless themselves."[30]

She was prescient. Nowhere was the "poignant irony" more evident than in the persistence of the internment camp, which "has become the routine solution for the problem of domicile of the 'displaced persons.'"

As if to prove Du Bois and Arendt right, old empires clung to their colonies. Yes, they dallied over giving some citizenship rights to subjects, but they were slow, piecemeal, and churlish. Old empires needed strangers for economic recovery and for recognition in the new world of great power politics. Colonies, many of whom sacrificed in the Global Civil War, wanted their say and their share. No sooner was France liberated from the Nazi yoke than the people of Damascus and Algiers demanded to be liberated from the French yoke. When anti-French demonstrations broke out in Syria, an incensed Charles De Gaulle sent troops, tanks, and gunships to suppress them. Weeks after celebrating VE (Victory in Europe) Day in Paris, General Fernand Oliva-Roget ordered the shelling of Syrian cities; French troops shot into civilian crowds, killing over one thousand. In Algeria, similar demonstrations in Sétif and Guelma led to a massacre of up to twenty thousand. VE Day in Europe was a kind of Independence Day in Algeria and set off a gruesome war of secession. The struggle for recognition and a share of interdependence's fruits yielded a wave of frustration and bitterness.[31]

Even more nettlesome: how to ensure that nations behaved properly with their own citizens? For international lawyers, the Second World War was a reminder that peoples did not have human rights as long as their own states could not be held to account. As reporters and photographers struggled with how to portray the news of Bergen-Belsen, Auschwitz, and Treblinka, the purpose of the fledgling peace changed. The idea of staging "war crime" tribunals was supposed to countersign the new moral start. Was that enough? The reportage of death camps and the scale of the Judeocide forced Washington to relent and, once the

United Nations was established, to endorse a commission to enshrine individuals' rights—and thus legal means to hold states accountable for what they did to their citizens, culminating in the Universal Declaration of Human Rights in 1948.[32]

The new world of nations was born with a contradiction at its core. Decolonization required creating sovereign nations, but peace, interdependence, and universal rights required weakening national sovereignty. The result was an unstable compromise. According to the Canadian John Humphrey, a key drafter of the declaration and the first director of the UN Division of Human Rights, who also played the shuttle diplomat between irascible, blowhard, Cold War–obsessed envoys in Geneva, the declaration was born compromised because it was the result of state envoys agreeing reluctantly to limit what their states could do. His Geneva diary entry after a long day of negotiating in August 1948 observed that "there is a great similarity between the actions of nations and those of children. I could develop this thought at length were it not for the temptation of reading. Moreover, I am tired."[33]

The emerging consensus about restoring state sovereignty drew the frustration of Hersch Lauterpacht. Born in an Orthodox Jewish family in a small town in Eastern Galicia, he emerged as one of the world's great mid-century legal thinkers. He joined the staff of the British War Crimes Executive, actively contributed to the International Military Tribunal at Nuremberg, and poured his years of thinking about peace founded upon international law into the task of outlining such a vision. As he did so, he also learned that his parents, sister, brother, and all their children, practically his whole family, perished at the hands of Nazi exterminators. "Daddy does not say much," his wife, Rachel, wrote to their son as the news came in. "He never displays much emotion."[34] Instead, he channeled his critique of state sovereignty into a code for a new human law to prevent states from legally wielding such power again. What he felt the world needed was not a covenant that made sovereign states the dispensers of peoples' rights, but a pledge to humans irrespective of their political memberships; there was a law that was superior to the "law of the State." Looking back, he blamed the horrors of the war on the terms of the peace in 1919, and the tragic position into which "minorities" had been consigned in the urge to create new nations without guaranteeing all humans their rights. Defending the rights of humans, Lauterpacht argued, "implies a more drastic interference with the sovereignty of the State than the renunciation of war and the acceptance of the principle of compulsory judicial settlement." In the end, he would be disappointed by the drafting of the Universal Declaration; it left too much to the hands of nation-states.[35] Still, he took some solace from the Nuremberg Trials. After watching the opening speech of the chief U.S. prosecutor, Robert H. Jackson (who had been reading Lauterpacht's work), he wrote to his wife, "I shook [him] by the hand for a long minute. . . . It was an unforgettable experience to see, for the first time in history, a sovereign State in the dock."[36]

Others worried that high-minded rhetoric obscured hypocrisy. The human rights of the dominated existed alongside the right—and might—to dominate. Some historians have looked upon the origins of the United Nations as a cunning effort to repackage imperial internationalism and global racial segregation in a new guise.[37] Jan Smuts, the premier of South Africa, had been one of the defenders of the new discourse on human rights. As the debate over a charter of human rights heated up in late 1946, many pointed to racial injustices. The Indian envoy to the United Nations, Vijaya Lakshmi Pandit, denounced South African racism; Smuts lashed back with accusations of cruelty about the Indian caste system. Du Bois was outraged not just about Smuts but about America's own rhetoricians. "Nothing so vividly illustrates the twisted contradiction of thought in the minds of white men," he blasted, than extolling rights abroad all while oppressing Blacks at home. This was the second time he watched white leaders, after taking the world to war, proclaim new virtues while subordinating Blacks. Du Bois singled out U.S. Secretary of State James F. Byrnes. A prominent South Carolina politico, Byrnes "arraigns Russia for lack of democracy while he represents South Carolina, where the majority of the people have never had a chance to vote." For Du Bois, what was necessary was a different narrative of world interdependence, one that did not imagine integration as led by the West, which tolerated the Rest as charity cases, but rather as an epic in which Africa and Asia played a vital part. Those from

Africa, he concluded, "have been read almost out of the bounds of humanity." A new world order needed a new, more inclusive narrative for itself.[38] One Nigerian nationalist, Nnamdi Azikiwe, lashed out in the pages of *West African Pilot*: "Are we fighting for the security of Europe," he asked, "whilst Africans continue to live under pre-war status?" Du Bois, fuming about European duplicity, Smuts's prancing on the global stage, and American cowering before Southern racism, snapped: "We have conquered Germany . . . but not their ideas."[39]

The Modern Refugee

Here was the agony. Decolonizers fought for entry into and recognition by the family of nations. They wanted to be part of international society that promised to open them to the bounty of trade and investment and welcome them to the narrative of humanity. But that required sovereignty. How to square the spread of national sovereignty with new universals of international society? The limits of compromise and the rhetoric of humanity were most evident in the challenge of how to handle the millions of peoples uprooted and dehumanized from war. Statelessness then and now has been a feature of state systems, not an exception, accident, or a misfortune. Modern refugeedom was designed *not* to challenge state powers to determine who was eligible for rights while at the same time insisting that all people had rights to flee their tormentors. In this sense, the modern refugee regime rhymed with the post-Nagasaki compromise of letting chosen states build annihilating weapons while creating treaties that, ostensibly, committed them to self-restraint.

The persistence of what Michael Walzer has called "necessitous strangers" demanded an ethical response unless the worldmakers were prepared to deny their own humanity.[40] At the end of the war, Europe had sixty million without homes; China, ninety million; South Asia, twenty million. The numbers were astronomical: fully 7.6 percent of the world's population was displaced.[41] As she was writing *The Origins of Totalitarianism*, Hannah Arendt had put her finger on a dilemma. World peace premised on universal rights made rights dependent on membership in nations and the guarantee that everyone could belong to one.

But nations had sovereign powers, which included the ability to exclude undesirables, create undesirables, or expel or exterminate them. As a refugee herself, thinking about the world's stateless people, the problem haunted her. A century of interdependence revealed what happened when nations faced incentives to hoard the benefits of interdependence for citizens while externalizing the costs onto strangers. History proved nations necessary *and* deficient for assuring the dignity of all humans.[42]

What was to be done? For many, finding new homes in old countries, repatriation, was one solution. But for many, there was no country to return to. Where there were no families to adopt the homeless, like the millions of Jewish survivors, camp life lasted as long as the war years themselves. That is, until Jews could be sent to their new homeland in Palestine—and in so doing, Europeans and Americans solved the problem of the unwanted in Europe by creating a stateless population among the Palestinians.[43]

Entangling the fates of stateless Jews and colonized Palestinians was an early sign that the architects of the post-Nagasaki world had learned partial lessons from the past. Recognized as humans according to the new internationalist rhetoric, the dispossessed still lacked rights to have rights. International society stopped short of means to confer them. The earlier practices of issuing transit papers and contingent residency rights, like Nansen passports given to white Russians driven from their homes after 1917 and important instruments of early anti-Communist internationalisms, conferred mobility rights and the right not to be deported, but little else. They were improvisations, workarounds, as long as states monopolized the determination of citizenship. The freedom of movement, the right to find shelter when persecuted by one's own government, was a sore point in the commission debates leading up to the Declaration of Human Rights. Eleanor Roosevelt, the commission's head, thought she'd been given a sleepy task in her subcommittee charge to define freedom of movement. Instead, she faced furious resistance. "A new type of political refugee is appearing," she wrote to her daughter. These are "people who have been against the present governments and if they stay at home or go home will probably be killed."[44] Who would protect their rights if their governments refused to?

It fell to the compromisers of 1945 to improvise a solution. Their makeshift has lasted to this day. It is now bursting. "Relief" and "protection" became the watchwords to keep alive those who did not have rights to have rights but without citizenship. The organizations created to fill the gap were never entrusted with powers to guarantee or supply rights. The United Nations High Commissioner for Refugees (UNHCR), founded in 1950 to fill the gap and to supervise the application of what would become the 1951 Convention Relating to the Status of Refugees, oversaw the welfare of people "outside the country of nationality" if they could prove "well-founded fear of being persecuted on the grounds of race, religion, nationality, membership of a particular social group or political opinion." True, this was a break from before 1939, when there existed specified protections for particular groups, not any individual who could show persecution. There was also a commitment to something called non-refoulement, which meant that states could not force refugees to return to states where they were unwanted and imperiled. But the new UNHCR could not intervene in sovereign states' ability to determine whose asylum claims were acceptable or not. Even these compromises were resisted: today, only three-quarters of the UN member states have accepted the convention. The United States never signed it (though it acceded to the follow-up 1967 Protocol Relating to the Status of Refugees, which admitted some obligations—they were useful Cold War weapons to wield against the Soviet Union). Between 1945 and 1985, the United States, for all the rhetoric of leadership and "never-againism," admitted scarcely two million refugees, mostly from the Communist bloc; among the most destitute in 1945, only 28,000 visas went to surviving Jews. The UNHCR took years to be accepted as a relief agency, and only if it did not challenge claims of sovereign states. Before 1955, the United States refused to fund it.[45]

Refugeedom revealed the limits of a world system when the workings of nation-states and the rhetoric of universal rights could not be aligned. Refugees fell out of international society. This had the paradoxical effect of fueling anti-colonial urgency: gaining sovereignty became even more essential for joining international society—without statehood there was no recognition, as secessionists in Bangladesh and Nigeria, and later, the decomposition of the Soviet Union and Yugoslavia would reveal. It also resurfaced the recurrent, barely repressible urge to retreat behind the moat of sovereignty, to deport en masse, to erect walls and electrified fences, to construct mass detention centers, to blunt questions of whether citizens had any obligation to welcome or protect necessitous strangers.[46]

Great Awakening

This new order placed the United States on a pedestal, one from which it was doomed to fall. By ridding the world of want, peace seemed almost tailor-made for American heroism and, eventually, a great fall from grace. On January 20, 1949, Harry S. Truman—on the heels of a surprise electoral result—addressed the public to outline a global approach to counter "the false philosophy" of communism. The war was over in Europe, but much of the rest of the planet hung in the balance. "We are moving on with other nations," Truman announced, "to build an even stronger structure of international order and justice. We shall have as our partners countries which, no longer solely concerned with the problem of national survival, are now working to improve the standards of living of all their people." The world needed a new form of United States leadership—and to that end his inaugural speech called for "a bold new program for making the benefits of our scientific advances and industrial progress available for the improvement and growth of underdeveloped areas." The Point Four Program (as it eventually became called) shifted foreign policy from strategic containment to economic prevention. What was essential for the have-nots was good for the haves in this formatted interdependence. "The old imperialism-exploitation for foreign profit has no place in our plans," Truman said. "What we envisage is a program of development based on the concepts of democratic fair-dealing. All countries, including our own, will greatly benefit from a constructive program for the better use of the world's human and natural resources." American dams, American science, technology, and ingenuity, could serve as a model for poorer countries to neutralize totalitarianism and clear a path for the have-nots as future haves by borrowing and importing the American way.[47]

The dream of development was not just an American hope. Sun Yat-sen argued that development in China was a condition for lasting world peace. Latin American leaders had petitioned through the 1930s for the creation of a lending institution to invest in countries suffering from capital shortages to import technologies. With the outbreak of the war in 1939, Latin American finance ministers met in Panama to create an Inter-American Financial and Economic Advisory Committee to inch the notion forward. Harry Dexter White of the U.S. Treasury even endorsed the concept at a meeting in Rio in January 1942. The 1943 Hot Springs conference took on food and agricultural issues, and the challenge of creating international institutions that could promote freedom from want. In India, the hope for development produced a sharper anti-colonial edge. Jawaharlal Nehru, leader of the country's nationalist movement, looked upon the Soviet model of five-year planning to accelerate the passage from a rural society to an industrial economy; he had served as a national planner to the Indian National Congress Party since the 1930s. As India seceded, Nehru entrusted a new National Planning Commission to the Cambridge-educated statistician and physicist Prasanta Mahalanobis with dreams of India becoming a manufacturing power bristling with its own heavy-metal plants. By coupling statistics with steel, Indian social scientists could effect a fundamental change in the global economic geography and halt centuries of hemorrhaging to the empire.[48] If British authorities once imagined themselves exporting modernity to the periphery, Indians now imagined themselves reversing the damage.

Gunnar Myrdal, the Swedish economist, called the turn to development and the focus on the have-nots as participants in the world economy "the Great Awakening," a moment that inaugurated "a new phase in the struggle for equality" as people became more aware of injustices at a new, international scale. At the core of the Great Awakening was the spread of developed countries' "inherited ideal of equality of opportunity" to the underdeveloped. Poorer lands were seeing themselves less as "backward countries" and more as deprived. The trouble was, out in the peripheries and colonies, getting to equal opportunity on a global scale meant "world revolution." The issue for Myrdal was whether it would be a peaceful revolution or a violent one.[49]

Development involved groping for models, metaphors, and narratives about economic change from misery to prosperity; these narratives outlined the pathway to full and equal membership in international society, to emerge from the shadows of "backwardness" by becoming modern. These were the glory years of social scientific self-confidence—years for muscular intellectuals to export the confidence in their models to their clients seeking membership, if not equality, in the world economy. One might argue that the creed of modernization theory was *the* great American intellectual export. The ultimate goals of development, noted wunderkind of the new confidence Walt W. Rostow to an audience, were "psychological and political."[50] Rostow's *The Stages of Economic Growth: A Non-Communist Manifesto* (1960), a book that quickly earned a kind of Talmudic status and went through twelve printings in its first five years, was a distillate of his understanding of the industrial revolution mixed with lessons about how to shake traditional societies from what he saw as their timeless lethargy. Tradition, he argued, inoculated societies from science and the rewards of its application, and condemned them to a perpetual cycle of diminishing returns. Rostow aimed to show the poor how to "enjoy the blessings and choices opened up by the march of compound interest."[51] At the peak of his influence—and bravura—*LIFE* magazine gave Rostow a spread along with other "action intellectuals" who were modeling the new world order. "A brotherhood of scholars," wrote the journalist Theodore White, "a new priesthood," was remaking America and the world.[52]

It is easy to scoff at American braggadocio. But the idea that one could master history and accelerate it soon dissolved into an impatience. Just as intellectuals thought they had found the clues to programming time into stages and sequences in order to accelerate it, leaders began to feel as if the clock was running out. Brazilian President

FIGURE 4.2. Brasilia.

Juscelino Kubitschek summoned the country to a pace of "fifty years' progress in five" (his campaign slogan), a drive to cover the country with a spiderweb of roads and cables—including deep into Amazonia. In 1958, construction of the "road of the jaguar" began to open a causeway into the forests from the coast. Unveiled to fanfare in 1960, the "caravan of integration" opened the *terras devolutas* (unsurveyed lands), to privatization; between 1959 and 1963, 13.4 million acres of land in the state of Pará were privatized. The scramble for the Amazon and its systematic deforestation was on. Frustration with the pace of reform at the transnational scale prompted Kubitschek in 1958 to call for Operation Pan-America to uplift the region as a whole. By luring foreign investors into domestic industries, opening highways to hinterlands, and erecting photogenic modernist icons in the wilderness of the plains of central Brazil for his new capital, Brasilia, Kubitschek was the emblem of "development*alism*" (the push having become an "-ism" of its own).[53] The Hungarian photographer Thomas Farkas captured crowds of awestruck civilians walking on top of the new congress building, a peoples' palace, at its inauguration on April 21, 1960.

Where the urge to compress time took off was in the Communist world; what the master-planners of capitalism dreamed up was nothing compared to the development utopias of party chiefs. In 1957, Comrade Nikita Khrushchev announced at a gathering of world party leaders at a congress to celebrate the fortieth anniversary of the October Revolution that the Soviet Union was committed to eclipsing American industrial output in fifteen years. Not to be outdone, and frustrated that China was still inching along after one Five-Year Plan, Mao Zedong made his proclamation of a Great Leap Forward to outdo British industrial output in fifteen years. In the euphoria, the missile scientist Qian Xuesen wrote "How High Will Grain Yields Be?" for *China Youth Daily* to convince doubters of the promise of "sputnik" expectations. Mao began to rethink his own fevered projections: surpassing Britain may take only two or three years, "especially in steel production." When it became clear that better carts were needed, "cartification" became the aim. Then came the urgency of ball bearings for home factories. "Every household a factory, every home ringing with a ding-dong sound" was the slogan. *People's Daily* celebrated national "bearingification" as a monumental breakthrough. Figure 4.3 shows a 1958 poster depicting a Chinese man racing past a paunchy Brit to mobilize Mao's subjects for the Great Leap Forward. Meanwhile, "degenerate peasants" blamed for slowing the pace were rounded up; reports of local food shortages were dismissed as "temporary crises." Thirty million people starved to death in three years in humanity's worst manufactured famine.[54]

Stoked by American Fordism, there was a compelling illusion that a new world could be created by weaving its parts together with expertise, planning, technologies, and the right dose of intervention to close the gap between strangers and make them more interdependent by making nations for each of them. With great fanfare, the newly elected president of the United States, John F. Kennedy, went to the United Nations General Assembly in September 1961 and proposed that the 1960s be called the "United Nations Development Decade" to signal development as the key to nation building. A few months later, the assembly voted euphorically to approve the proposal. It made "development" the key word to welcome newly decolonized nations into an enlarging United Nations.

FIGURE 4.3. The Great Leap Forward.

It was also a key word to repair a gash in the international fabric: a few weeks earlier, the UN general secretary, the Swedish Dag Hammarskjöld, died in a plane crash while on mission to negotiate Congo's independence from Belgium and to stem a civil war. Control over uranium ores and later rare earths hung in the balance.[55]

Jet Age

For all the concerns about nuclear war, and the foreboding that decolonization and development may not live up to their hopes, there was a sense that new technologies favored an integrating world by expanding its horizons. The mobility of images, news, and travel were hallmarks of this interdependent, intervisible, opening world which overlapped with the Great Awakening.

Behind the scenes, military strategists treated the skies—and eventually the solar system—as a frontier for bombers, missiles, and satellites. Aviation became a symbol for a new airborne class. Propellers gave way to jet engines; planes became larger, faster, and capable of longer hauls. Juan Trippe, founder of Pan American Airways, opened up transpacific travel, collaborated with Boeing to develop pressurized cabins, and gushed about how jets were the real instruments of world peace because they made it so easy for strangers to meet each other. In 1958, he ordered his first fleet of 707s; Pan Am's pilots and stewardesses could get travelers and businessmen across the Atlantic in seven hours. "In one fell swoop," he declared, "we have shrunken the earth." Pan Am's rival, Trans-World Airlines, opened its New York "flight center" in 1962. Designed by Eero Saarinen, with its famous wing-shaped rooves held aloft with massive Y-shaped piers, it conveyed the sense of taking flight even before boarding (it's now a securitized shopping mall known as Terminal 5 at JFK).[56] By 1960, a hundred million people were jet-setters.

It was not just the skies that filled with new traffic connecting strangers. Ancient byways of land and sea got a makeover. Highways (even "superhighways"), large trucks, and bus systems left the gentrified travel on trains, with their Pullmans and Oriental Expresses, in the dust. Countries got laced together by chains of "gas stations" and became increasingly dotted by franchises. Total (in France), Esso (Eastern States Standard Oil—eventually Exxon), and British Petroleum went from being drillers and refiners to distributors for commuters and travelers, with service stations as nodes for nations. Even sea lanes underwent a transformation. Steamers and packet boats gave way to freighters and elaborate docking systems, driving down the price of long-distance goods. Cranes replaced stevedores—accelerated handling—made inventories easier to keep, and extended the complexity of what would, by the 1980s, be called "supply chains." Pumping systems sucked cheap crude out of "tankers" from Venezuela and Saudi Arabia and conveyed it through steel pipes to refineries to be made into gasoline or home fuels. The recovery of Japan and Western Europe depended on expanded tanker sizes. In 1945, a typical large tanker carried twenty thousand deadweight tons of fuel; by the eve of the 1973 oil crisis, the largest supertanker topped three hundred thousand deadweight tons. Coal waned. In 1950, oil accounted for 21 percent of all energy from fossil fuels, surpassing coal in 1964; by 1972 it reached 46 percent, its global peak. Never in world history had one source of energy, fossil fuels, so utterly dominated and literally fueled the integration of the world's parts.[57]

While people and products took to the road, skies, and high seas in unprecedented numbers, there was a simultaneous making of an international image economy to reflect back a representation of an increasingly interdependent world—and its eventual disenchantments. By the late 1960s, even the planet itself would become the supermodel of the space age when Apollo astronauts turned their cameras to focus on the earth they left behind.[58]

The biggest leap in the image economy was the advent of television, specifically the production and regulation of (scarce) electromagnetic frequencies. It would not be until the 1980s that this scarcity got lifted and the broadcasting regime exploded on the way to the digital age. Before then, control of the airwaves and circulation of frequencies was largely the purview of governments, who conceded networking arrangements that dominated national broadcasting worldwide.[59] An oligopoly of private "networks" sold airtime to advertisers who were responsible for producing content that contoured the ways in which people envisioned each other. Shows, such as Procter & Gamble's early "soap operas," highlighted sponsors' products. Before *I Love Lucy* (1951), television broadcasts had been live. *Lucy* was the first filmed television show. Released from live audiences (while simulating them with laugh tracks and canned gasps), studio entertainment frontiers opened up.

They increased the value of "primetime" and its ad revenues, and enabled a prerecorded show to broadcast irrespective of time zone differences at the same peak viewing slots. When Lucille Ball gave birth to her second child, Desi Arnaz Jr., in Cedars of Lebanon Hospital in Los Angeles in 1953, it made headlines in Japan and Europe; an AP reporter was waiting outside the delivery room with Desi Arnaz Sr., the father, waiting to break the news.[60]

Recorded television could also become an export. As were TVs themselves, which were part of a consumer boom in mass-produced durables, washing machines, refrigerators—and electronics—that piggybacked on the rising number of electrically wired households, pioneered in America but very much part of the consumer boom as it fanned out to Europe, Latin America, and South Asia (the Soviets would have their own, albeit uncommercialized variant of the transformation of the household into a consuming unit). The post-Nagasaki economic miracles in Japan and Germany could be measured by how quickly they closed the gap in TV consumption—and eventually, in the 1970s, Japan would become *the* powerhouse of TV production. Japan, in fact, electrified its homes earlier than Britain (what Japan lacked, comparatively, was space in the home to import the bulky new machinery). By 1960, almost 90 percent of American homes had a TV. By 1970, that number jumped to 99 percent—and color TV was just around the corner. What Japanese firms like Sony and Toshiba learned to do was package smaller gadgetry so that the Sony Trinitron, rolled out in 1968, soon came to dominate the world market for color TVs.[61]

As television expanded and went global, the old print media reeled. Most Americans, by 1963, turned on the tube to get their news. The shock was slower to unfold elsewhere, but it was inevitable; by 1970, shantytowns in Brazil and South Africa were cluttered with antennae. Television drained advertising dollars away from print. Local newspapers went into long-term decline. So did big glossy news and entertainment magazines like *Time* and *Newsweek*; their edge as nation-building and world weeklies with national adaptations for the Canadian, Asian, and European markets took a hit as they had to compete with national broadcasters. New York City, a hub of world publishing, had four evening newspapers in 1950. By 1960, it had two. By 1970, there was only one left. Between 1969 and 1972, three of the most widely read newsmagazines in America (*The Saturday Evening Post, LIFE,* and *Look*) closed down.[62]

Competition from the tube-and-screen changed reportage and the identity of the old guard fourth estate in print media, just as the society of spectacles was coming to full fruition. Skilled machine operators who once controlled the pace of production lost power with the advent of cold type systems or phototypesetting. What is more, by the 1950s, print news as a mixture of text and graphic reportage from around the world reached its zenith. Striking images, dramatic shots, and quick words became the medium for a new kind of message about a connected and fast-paced world in need of news about itself. Henry Luce's *Time* magazine, with separate editions niched for different markets, was tailor-made for the age of organization man. Its slogan, "Take Time—It's Brief," aimed at the busy executive who wanted to get the world's news compressed into an hour's read, oftentimes digesting the news by flipping through the graphics and reading the captions. Photospreads and captions were the news. It became the world's largest circulating world newsmagazine. At its peak, it had tens of millions of weekly readers; it sat on newsstands in Spanish and brought world news to Asia through the Hong Kong–based *Time Asia.* A reader-viewer of *Time, LIFE,* or *Paris Match* could be excused for confusing the graphic ads with graphic news—and often enough the photographers who took both came from the same studios. We think now about the heralded global Magnum Photos agency as the model for photographic humanism, with shots by fearless photojournalists like Robert Capa (born in Hungary) or David Seymour (born in Poland and also known as Chim)—both of whom would die while covering anti-colonial wars. But Magnum's revenues came from *Ladies' Home Journal* and Madison Avenue ad agencies.[63]

A new generation of reporters came to the fore, a generation whose style and alignments picked at the sacred cows of Pax Americana—beginning with the faith in American leadership and exportable values to create an inclusive interdependence. It was the showcase of tropical development with the backing of American technologies for Cold War containment and Vietnam that became the screen upon which disenchantments with the post-Nagasaki order were projected.

Vietnam: a coda to Pax Americana, a war that consigned the United Nations to the sidelines of a conflict it could not prevent but paid for in the currency of gridlock and American resentment. The post-Nagasaki narrative about a fresh start for the world faded into the new spectacle of napalm. Reporting on the Vietnam War unfolded to make it less an episode of Yankee heroism and more and more a tale of hubris, peasant killing, and jungle burning for a purpose that the rest of the world, and eventually many Americans, began to disavow. The Associated Press had an active bureau in Saigon. The German photographer Horst Faas turned it into a new style media hub. He figured out how to send photographs by wire to editorial offices in North America and Europe using cylindrical wirephoto drums. On February 1, 1968, the seasoned photojournalist Eddie Adams came in, deposited a 35 mm roll taken from the streets, and turned around and went back out. Faas took the roll and retreated to the dark room. He picked out a few samples from the contact sheets, including the one shown in Figure 4.4, the execution of a Viet Cong assassin, Captain Nguyễn Văn Lém, as a bullet pierced his motion-blurred skull, and cabled it to New York where photo editors marketed it to clients. *The New York Times* grabbed it instantly. By then, news consumers were becoming accustomed to bad news from Indochina. This image did more: it was evidence of how reporters were truth-tellers of time frozen, pulling back the veil of official rhetoric about America safeguarding the world.

Saigon Execution, with its graphic semblance of unfiltered instantaneity, was an immediate expression of a crisis of Pax Americana. While it made the South Vietnamese puppet state look like a gang of thugs, 1968 saw a more general unraveling of the postwar fabric—on display in glossy magazines, the front page of world newspapers, and eventually beamed into kitchens and family rooms' televisions. (Adams, incidentally, was dismayed at the framing and reception of the photo he only saw later; the executed man was not a civilian, but an undercover assassin and had just been chased down after he had executed a Saigon policeman. What really went on that day in the streets of Saigon may never be

FIGURE 4.4. Saigon Execution.

known. But photographic uncertainty vaporized in the graphics of a soldier pointing a revolver at a tied civilian. Immediacy, not ambiguity or complexity, is what came through.) Photojournalists shuttled between Vietnam and Nigeria, Mexico and France, the United States and Czechoslovakia. Few epitomized the drive to chronicle the shortcomings of the post-Nagasaki promise more than Gilles Caron. Scarred by what he saw as a French soldier fighting in Alegria in the early 1960s, he would spend two months in prison for disobedience. He learned to wield a camera. Starting as a fashion and celebrity photographer, he turned his lens to the rising protests in Europe and beyond. By 1968, he was dragging his Nikon from Vietnam to the wreckage along the stately rue Saint Jacques in Paris to the bloodshed in Mexico. He would team up with the British photographer Don McCullin, who added more grit to the visuals. Together, they fused a new spirit of photojournalism. If Robert Capa's heroism was about doing what it takes to catalogue history without being partisan, Caron and McCullin went a step further. It was not enough to be daring to get the shot. Theirs was a commitment to the victims premised on a conviction that world empathy could be summoned by making the suffering of strangers visible. Caron, McCullin, and a new generation of photojournalists sided with have-nots to make the spectator a witness to their deprivation. In the international order, to be a bystander was not an option. The journalist was becoming part of the story.[64]

By the end of the 1960s, the news business was a global space populated with self-conscious actors with worldmaking aspirations and principles. It was embracing a purpose of making the world intervisible with immediacy, urgency, and increasing moral outrage. As the 1960s dissolved the confidence of the Atlantic Charter, advocacy journalism supercharged the emotional debates about the world's fractured togetherness.

Extinction

In 1962, a quiet, diminutive oceanographer who liked to paddle about on ocean shores and explore tidepools shocked the world. Her name was Rachel Carson. Her book, *Silent Spring,* originally serialized in *The New Yorker,* was a sensation with few precedents and stripped the patina from the surface of the post-Nagasaki cornucopian promises that technologies and free markets would deliver the world from want. Scientific reportage added to the activist reportage in reframing the needs and threats among strangers. Carson called attention to the unintended effects of scientific efforts to domesticate nature. The book opened with an epigram from E. B. White: "I am pessimistic about the human race because it is too ingenious for its own good." Carson took aim at one "genius" attempt in particular: the chemists' campaign to free the world of mosquitos. Their solution: DDT (dichlorodiphenyltrichloroethane). For Carson, here was a classic case of a solution to one planetary curse, including malaria, which risked everything. Science, coupled with American corporations that commodified it, was not a solution; it was the problem.

Raised in the Pennsylvania countryside near the Allegheny River, Carson came by her interest in nature honestly. She would earn a master's degree (and much later several honorary doctorates), do some teaching at Johns Hopkins and the University of Maryland, and join the U.S. Bureau of Fisheries. Her stories began when she took an interest in a Long Island trial in which residents sued federal and state authorities who wanted to douse their lands with DDT. Conversations with her agent, the publisher at Houghton Mifflin, and the editor of *The New Yorker*, the remarkable William Shawn who shepherded the magazine from 1952 to 1987, led to a series of articles and a more extended book about the effects of pesticides. As assistant editor, Shawn had been the man behind Hersey's account of the Hiroshima bombing. A year before the conversation with Carson, he had commissioned Hannah Arendt to report on the Eichmann trial in Jerusalem. Now, Shawn had a hunch that he had another explosive story on his hands.[65] As she labored on her story, Carson's health deteriorated. A tumor had been removed in early 1960. While doing her research and writing, Carson was in and out of radiation. Starting in June 1962, her first story went to press. The storm was instantaneous, so that by September, when the book finally appeared, there was already a furious reaction.[66]

"As man proceeds towards his announced goal of the conquest of nature," wrote Carson, "he has written a depressing record of destruction, directed not only against the earth he inhabits but against the life that shares it with him." The slaughter of buffalo for their hides and of egrets for their feathers were precursors to a more insidious and potentially cataclysmic "crusade against insects." Humans, armed with "the spray gun," had become exterminators. Robins, raccoons, domestic pets, and even farm animals were becoming the bystander casualties in the fight to distance humans from bugs. They disappeared. To get rid of mosquitoes and insects that infested farmers' fields, chemical companies devised toxins that could be sprayed innocently over fields and lawns and create a green utopia of a garden without pests. The manufacturers had failed to consider the role of bugs in the wider food chain; eradicating the nuisance fly denied some creature of their lunch. But what started as ignorance became wanton denial. Scientists, lured by corporate money and unsupervised by public authorities, failed to understand a basic feature of the natural world—the world is like our bodies, intricate and interdependent. "There is also an ecology of the world within our bodies," Carson argued. "In this unseen world minute causes produce mighty effects; the effect, moreover, is often seemingly unrelated to the cause, appearing in a part of the body remote from the area where the original injury was sustained." It is all about relationships. When one part is attacked, the whole suffers.[67]

There came a howl of outrage. Some were more tempered critics, like the Canadian Department of Agriculture official who nodded to the book's good effects of raising attention to "the adequacy of information on pesticide residues," but, he added, "many of the statements in the book were inaccurate, and many of the conclusions drawn were based on emotion rather than sound scientific logic." Many critics were unmeasured and furious. The pesticide manufacturer, Velsicol Chemical Corporation, threatened to sue Houghton Mifflin. The firm's letter warned that Carson's work would reduce U.S. food supply to "east-curtain parity." Velsicol was soon silenced when, in November 1963, massive fish kills were reported along the lower Mississippi. In the uproar, scientists traced the gory scene of catfish bleeding from the mouth and around the fins—by the millions—to massive pesticide emissions (endrin, "the most toxic of all the chlorinated hydrocarbons," according to Carson) from a waste treatment plant owned by . . . Velsicol; endrin was one of the prize pesticides from the firm's Chicago lab.[68]

At a White House press conference at the end of that summer, President Kennedy assured reporters that the Department of Agriculture and the Public Health Service were looking at pesticides more carefully thanks to Carson's book. But the debate was not just American. *Silent Spring* was immediately translated into twelve languages; a Dutch plant specialist, C. J. Briejèr, wrote to Carson that "the hurricane you unchained is now over us."[69] Less than a year after *Silent Spring*'s publication, British Parliament flared with arguments over DDT use in the English countryside. Naturalists, who'd noticed the disappearance of the peregrine falcon, kestrels, and sparrow hawks, were in uproar. In Sweden, sensational revelations that DDT was flowing through human breast milk into newborn mouths led to radical curbs on pesticides in 1969, the year of the first Earth Day.[70] By the late 1960s, sickness, fallout, and a rage over chemicals filled the news and airwaves. What was revolutionary was a new vision of the planet as a fragile, shared ecosystem in which actions or suffering of one part affected others.

Science was not producing a cornucopian promise but the destruction of Eden. Vanishing bald eagles (whose eggshells were too thin to resist the penetration of aerial DDT spraying), burning rivers in Cleveland, Ohio (like the Cuyahoga, alight in 1969 due to oil slicks—which was only one incident in a constant incendiary cycle thanks to dumped industrial waste), and napalmed jungles in Vietnam all joined the parade of images and stories less of consumer abundance and more of threat and extinction.

The Undoing

Along with science, the idea of development revealed fissures in the international architecture forged in the shadow of 1945. When the United Nations pronounced the 1960s as the "Development Decade," American foundations rushed to support work in the Third World. So did the American government. The idea was that the United Nations would broker an alliance of African, Asian, and Latin American leaders as decolonization gathered force. It is hard to imagine nowadays, but when President Kennedy addressed the UN General Assembly on September 20, 1963, he called for the organization to lead the causes of world disarmament and economic development.

Instead of closing the divides, the pursuit of development opened them; building an inclusive economy meant dismantling social hierarchies. As more and more voices from the Third World proclaimed, development meant economic decolonization. Months after Kennedy's final address, leaders of 119 countries, mainly from Latin America, Asia, and decolonizing Africa, gathered in Geneva with the UN general secretary, the soft-spoken Burmese diplomat U Thant. Delegates included two Argentines, the professional revolutionary Che Guevara, and the economist Raúl Prebisch, who called for deep reform of world trade to free the Third World from being only raw material exporters and in thrall to foreign extractive companies. The assembly demanded economic fairness and an honoring of the Bandung Conference, the 1955 summit of Asian and African leaders that called for a new inclusive world order. This time, the spotlight was on economic decolonization.

Thant, ever alert to the Bandung *ésprit,* denounced the "continued economic bondage." To make good on their words, the UN Conference on Trade and Development became a permanent body; Thant named Prebisch its first director—in the teeth of American resistance, an early warning sign of collisions to come.[71] The World Bank, originally designed for postwar recovery, became a full-throated development agency devoted to recycling member contributions to build dams, railways, factories, and ports around Asia, Africa, and Latin America. But by the time "Mr. TVA" (Tennessee Valley Authority) himself, David Lilienthal, joined the Lyndon B. Johnson administration to help rescue a floundering war effort in South Vietnam with nothing less than a Mekong Delta Development Authority, only a shrinking circle of insiders had any confidence that the scheme would pacify, never mind develop, war-torn Indochina. In a desperate effort to defuse the conflict in Vietnam, Thant enlisted the president of Ghana, who had just published *Neo-Colonialism: The Last Stage of Imperialism,* a book doomed to rub First Worlders the wrong way. Kwame Nkrumah's role was to shuttle between Hanoi and Beijing. While he was in the Chinese capital, a platoon of Ghanian soldiers backed by U.S. and British operators barged into the home of the Ghanaian army chief, General Charles Barwah; they demanded that he join their coup. When he refused, the rebels shot him while his wife and children watched, screaming. Nkrumah, president of Africa's first postcolonial state, never returned home.[72]

The patina of consensus around development quickly wore off. To many, its grand promising style started to ring hollow. The Argentine poet Jorge Luis Borges wrote thus in a poem called "The Moon," calling out the great planners for their follies:

> History tells us how in that past time
> When all things happened, real,
> Imaginary, and dubious, a man
> Conceived the unconscionable plan
>
> Of making an abridgement of the universe
> In a single book and with infinite zest
> He towered his screed up, lofty and
> Strenuous, polished it, spoke the final verse.

About to offer his thanks to fortune,
He lifted up his eyes and saw a burnished
Disc in the air and realized, stunned,
That somehow he had forgotten the moon.

The story I have told, although a tale,
Can represent the witching spell
So many of us use when at our craft
Of transmuting our life into words.[73]

Ambitious plans compressed into a single tome crowing about "the one true way" to the future all too often left out the basics, like the figurative night's moon. Borges captured the growing recognition of the fallibility of the urge to dream big, which can lead to missing crucial details. The effort to master the universe was a recipe for perfect imperfections; it could also yield to darker forms of what Borges called "strangeness."

The absurd could also be agonizing. Psychiatrist Frantz Fanon was among the chorus calling attention to the shortfalls of national freedom through development. He turned not to myth or imagination like Borges, but to the embodied mind of those subjected to the ambitious plans. A regular reader of *Présence Africaine* (a journal devoted to reporting on the African presence in French culture and a platform for ideas of negritude, a concept about which he would have deeply mixed feelings) from the late 1940s, Fanon had long been concerned with the place of African and African-descendent societies in the world of nations. And though he would align himself with nationalist freedom fighters in North Africa, he would grow increasingly despondent about the false promises of Third World nationalism. Formal national sovereignty and the grail pursuit of economic progress were turning into a torment. In 1952, he sounded his first alarms about the agonies of being Black in a world order designed by whites in *Black Skin, White Masks*.[74]

As the 1950s unfolded and Fanon's psychiatric work in field hospitals meant that he saw more and more patients traumatized by the violence in Algeria, he began to wrestle with the relationship between mental illness and political conflict. From his hospital in Blida, he could see the plumes of smoke over the mountains where French warplanes bombed Algerian National Liberation Front (FLN) strongholds. “Le caractère pathogène du conflit est privilégié,” he noted in a Tunisian medical journal in 1959.[75] “The pathogenic nature of the conflict is clear.” That year, he stepped out from behind his identity as doctor to become a voice for the Algerian Revolution while brooding over its limits. The conflict was no longer just a secessionist war turned savage. It was a conflict over the fractured soul of a dark-skinned Third World, a source of madness, because decolonization was not just about repudiating France, not just coping with the external violence and torture. It implied an unavoidable disappointment with the new freedom and the false promises of technocratic development. To be free yet alienated meant a new sickness, one that exceeded Fanon’s early faith in neuropsychiatry’s healing power. Not only did the urge to develop lead to disasters, with dams turning to droughts and people being pushed off the land, but the “cult of industry” could never keep up with the teeming numbers of people moving from countrysides to cities in search of jobs. Blacks were condemned to ask whites for recognition in impossible, and white, terms. The “African masses” suffered from “aliénation radicale,” rampant ulcers, upset menstrual cycles, hypersomnia, hysteria, and mental breakdown, he wrote.[76] Fanon invoked the acidic words of an unnamed “Senegalese patriot” disenchanted with the promises of the poet-president Léopold Sédar Senghor: “We asked for the Africanization of the top jobs and all Senghor does is Africanize the Europeans.” Fanon did not think much of the “narcissistic monologues” of the colonial bourgeois and their action intellectuals who rid colonies of their European masters while having assimilated the colonizer’s culture, and so authored a “self-hatred that characterizes racial conflict in segregated societies.”[77]

If Gunnar Myrdal once worried about whether the revolution would be peaceful, Fanon had no doubt. It would not; it could not. As he mulled over his psychiatric case notes of “obsessional neuroses” and the pathologies of the “occipital lobes” taken from patients in a shattered Algeria, he became convinced that true liberation required a violent cleansing, an idea that inspired one of the twentieth century’s most wrenching works, *Les Damnés de la terre* (*The Wretched of the Earth*).

Written in Fanon's dying months, from April to July 1961, the book's wrath aimed to slice through the mist of development's pretenses. He concluded:

> The Third World must start over a new history of man which takes account of not only the occasional prodigious theses maintained by Europe but also its crimes, the most heinous of which have been committed at the very heart of man, the pathological dismembering of his functions and the erosion of his unity, and in the context of the community, the fracture, the stratification and the bloody tensions fed by class, and finally, on the immense scale of humanity, the racial hatred, slavery, exploitation and, above all, the bloodless genocide whereby one and a half billion men have been written off.[78]

The Development Decade was barely a year old when *Les Damnés de la terre* hit the bookshelves. As if to embody its faltering dream, Fanon, while Algeria's envoy to Ghana, fell deathly ill of leukemia and passed away before ever seeing the book in print. But it echoed the disenchantment behind radical appeals in Algeria, Cuba, Ghana, and Congo—where the focus turned on the hegemon whose multinationals, technicians, and Green Berets could not help but identify it as another empire. In late 1964, Che Guevara, who turned development into a cosmic anticolonial struggle, traveled to Algeria to denounce "the bestiality of imperialism." He returned to Havana to pen his farewell letter to Fidel Castro and prepare for his suicide missions to fight the CIA and Marines in Congo and Bolivia. Dripping with nostalgia, Guevara reminded his *compañero* (partner) of the day they met in in a comrade's house, of the spirit of sacrifice to which they had taken a vow. "In a revolution," wrote Guevara, "one wins or dies." Now it was time to take his hopes elsewhere: "I carry to new battlefronts the faith that you taught me, the revolutionary spirit of my people, the feeling of fulfilling the most sacred of duties: to fight against imperialism wherever it may be. This is a source of strength, and more than heals the deepest of wounds."[79] That year, Edmundo Desnoes struck a less defiant, more resigned tone in his novel *Memorias del subdesarrollo* (*Memories of Underdevelopment*). Echoing Dostoevsky's prose of doubt and isolation, Desnoes's rendition of development uprooted his protagonist, Sergio, without giving him new ground. Far from living in Marxist certainties about phases and stages, Sergio wanders socialist Havana in a state of limbo. Underdevelopment has become a state of mind, disorientation. Revolutionary Cuba dedicated to transcending the past leaves Sergio sighing: "The truth is I feel washed out, sad with my new liberty-solitude."[80]

The Other Bomb

A fear began to seep through the Third World that development would never keep pace with the needs of necessitous strangers, especially where development was most needed. But if it was a source of disenchantment and discord for some, it was the road to disaster for others. Even more than the effects of DDT or the spread of military coups in the tropics, a more menacing threat was about a different kind of bomb: the explosion of population growth. In 1965, the United Nations Department of Economic and Social Affairs held a ten-day summit on world population in Belgrade. Its tone was anything but upbeat. The widening gap between haves and have-nots was pinned on the divide between societies with declining fertility and those with rising fertility. This, the conferees agreed, drove global inequalities. What was more perverse was that the culprit was development itself. As life was prolonged and mortality among the poor reduced, families at the bottom were swelling. With agriculture no longer able to support teeming families, people flowed from the countryside to cities and into shantytowns. Cities, once imagined as the nodes of modernization, seemed increasingly packed and overrun. Halfway through the UN Development Decade, reports were coming in that things might be getting worse, not better. The head of the United Nations' economic and social department, Philippe de Seynes, noted that while demography was possibly the eldest of the social sciences, it may not be up to contending with the fundamental contradiction of the modern world—"accelerated growth on an unprecedented scale with the expression of 'population explosion.'"[81]

Catastrophic thinking about a Malthusian calamity was nothing new. We have seen its influence in the 1890s and 1930s. What was new was the scale and its spillovers. Well-meaning humans trying to better the world were risking its survival.[82]

Bomb metaphors got repurposed and attached to a primitive fear of poor people gobbling up the world's scarcer resources. No sooner was the war over than the problem reared its head. In 1949, the United Nations staged a Scientific Conference on the Conservation and Utilization of Resources in Lake Success, New York. The idea was to create inventories of the world's capacities, including a count of minerals, fossil fuels, water, forests, agriculture, wildlife, and fish resources. What would happen when they all got tapped for a rebounding world population? There was an undertow of eugenic fears about the wrong kinds of "defective" people teeming in numbers. It was a French demographer, Alfred Sauvy, looking at the population growth curves in the 1950s—with one eye glancing sideways at the worsening conflict in Algeria—who coined the term "Third World" to warn that one part of the world was posing a demographic problem for the rest. Imagine if all those Muslims, warned one French report in 1952, came to France to "fill our empty spaces."[83] The fears were shared by Third World planners themselves. With the support of a postindependence state convinced of Malthusian truths peddled by UN demographers, five-year planners in India, Brazil, and American philanthropies embraced the euphemism of "family planning." Urged by insiders like Lady Dhanvanthi Rama Rau, the interventions went beyond education and propaganda—into a mass sterilization of women.[84]

Fears of a population explosion affecting the whole planet required thinking in interconnected ways about the planet as a whole. One route came from observing the populations not of humans but of fish. More and more evidence was surfacing that humans were plundering the seas. Stocks were being invisibly depleted. Fishermen pointed fingers at each other and attacked each other's trawlers. In a now-forgotten 1954 paper, "The Economic Theory of the Common-Property Resource: The Fishery," the Canadian economist Scott Gordon proposed a solution: maybe we should optimize, not maximize, our fishing habits. To explain his reasoning, he invoked the concept of a "common-pool resource." This is a type of property that cannot be fenced off or held in anyone's hands exclusively. It is vulnerable to congestion and depletion. Scott had suggestions for how to keep salmon and halibut stocks going. He also revolutionized economic analysis and created a new vocabulary for understanding limits by pointing out that much of what made the planet planetary, its water and air, did not have to be, indeed could not be managed by old enclosure and private property solutions. Cooperation and comanagement were alternatives for survival, especially where open-access but depletable resources were at stake.[85]

Tucked into Gordon's calculations about fish stocks and the vulnerability of common-pool resources was a powerful reframing of the population problem. Consumption that came with rising wealth and growing numbers did not create dilemmas just for specific societies, but for all societies. Assembling the concern about human reproduction with a new way of thinking about planetary limits as a fragile commons had implications for thinking about interdependence on a new scale and seeded doubts about postwar optimism.

The person who pulled the two sides of survival—the survival of humans and the survival of the planet—into one hyper-alarmist equation and metaphor was the outspoken eugenic biologist Garrett Hardin. Hardin had come under the spell of the Malthusian ecologist W. C. Allee at Stanford, who convinced Hardin, already a eugenicist worried about racial degradation, that the big threat was not the *supply* of food. The Green Revolution and application of pesticides that horrified Rachel Carson were helping on that front. Hardin was obsessed with *demand*. Cornucopian supply-side green revolutionaries had forgotten about the eaters. Hardin inverted the obsession and bequeathed the memorable and highly influential image of eaters consuming their way to scarcity, despoiling the world's resources and producing a "tragedy of the commons." He was fond of thought experiments, like what would happen to an unenclosed pasture or open sea if people could just take what they could while they could. Unrestrained, and faced with growing demand, grazers and fishermen would naturally extract what they could until there was nothing left. What to do about all that demand? Hardin did another thought experiment, this time to mock the optimists of the jet age who had faith in their "gadgetry" (a word Hardin used to belittle innovators). What if rockets could lob the planet's extra people into space to colonize other planets as Europeans had once colonized the Americas? "Neither physicists nor professional demographers have, so far as I know, recommended extra-terrestrial migration as a solution to the population problem, but the idea appears to be gaining ground among the laity even without scientific support," he mocked. He did some quick math about the carrying capacities of fleets of spaceships operating like Greyhound buses shipping the hungry to other planets, in an effort to lampoon the tech optimists.[86] Hardin became the ur-catastrophist and predicted, in a hugely influential and lurid essay called "The Tragedy of the Commons," a global calamity. "There is no technical solution" to the finitude of the planet, he wrote. "It is [in] the remorseless working of things" that the drama reveals "the futility of escape."[87]

Earthrise

In 1968, the planet started to look different. The National Aeronautics and Space Administration (NASA) launched the first crewed Apollo missions and came back with a stunning Ektachrome photo of Earth seen from outer space. Here we were, all compressed onto one little ball. It was the dawn of a whole Earth era. It was also almost an accident. Astronauts took their cameras with them as if they were tourists. One of them, William Anders, happened to peer out the porthole just as his craft was rising above the lunar horizon to catch Earth in the distance. He scrambled for his Hasselblad and got the shot before the ship pivoted away.[88]

This image, turned ninety degrees from the original shot to convey a hopeful colorful planet "rising" above its moon, got attached to an older metaphor that was gaining currency, Spaceship Earth. Adlai Stevenson stood before the United Nations General Assembly and talked about how we were all "passengers on a little spaceship, dependent on its vulnerable reserves of air and soil." *Spaceship Earth* was the title of the English economist and Baroness Barbara Ward's 1966 bestseller; the following year the architect, futurist, renewable energy designer, and popular systems theorist Buckminster Fuller wrote an *Operating Manual for*

FIGURE 4.5. Earthrise (original angle).

Spaceship Earth. He had been using the term Spaceship Earth extensively in lectures and writings through and popularized it. If the Apollo imagery gave the term an upbeat aura, Spaceship Earth was starting to take on a different meaning.[89] This orb needed care.

Biafra Babies

Back on Earth, the ebullient 1960s ended in angst. Barricades blocked the streets of Mexico City, Paris, and Prague. Martin Luther King Jr. and Bobby Kennedy died in the arms of weeping followers. Mao Zedong doubled down on his campaign to restore a true communist faith. Television screens around the world flickered with the images of burning villages in Vietnam. The world was coming unhinged.

As cities seethed and jungles burned, would we have enough food to feed the rebelling masses? And what about the rest? These were questions posed by the UK Freedom from Hunger Campaign. Deputized to find the answer, the journalist and BBC scriptwriter Arthur Hopcraft circled the Third World and declared that access to food was the world's new great divide. It was no longer the iron curtain. Nor was it democracy versus dictatorship. What partitioned Spaceship Earth was a caloric divide. For Hopcraft, the worst instance was the province of Bihar in India, still recovering from a famine. It was an appalling sight; he estimated that two-thirds of the population of fifty-three million was malnourished. Millions were beggars. With nothing to harvest, bony fingers, bulging eyes, and inert bodies were everywhere. The state of Bihar was a harbinger. The teeming poor of India, Africa, and South America lived with an unprecedented mass menace. "The threat is hunger, and they are born to it," Hopcraft declared. In Uganda, he met with a French doctor in charge of a mission hospital, Sister Myriem, who showed him people wasting away from hookworm, unmoving in their soiled sheets. At the end, Sister Myriem turned to Hopcraft and said that she was hoping to build a special thirty-bed children's ward. It would cost $42,000. "In her little voice, and in these surroundings, it sounded like a colossal sum," he said. Hopcraft could not hold back a dig against the West's nouveaux riches. This sum "would not, of course, pay some British pop entertainer's tax for a year," he snarled.[90]

Underdevelopment was slipping into spectacles of deprivation, and deprivation in some quarters into destitution. So long as development and self-determination held out hope, "Third World" had a positive, emancipatory spin. As the Development Decade seemed to go awry, "Third World" became synonymous with calamity. By 1964, peacekeeping operations in Congo were exhausted. Blue Helmets, UN peacekeepers, were scattered across Kashmir, Lebanon, Gaza, Sinai, and Yemen. Ralph Bunche, head of the Office of Special Political Affairs, oversaw thousands of peacekeepers with threadbare resources.

The UN budget was running dry when the world acquired a new icon. "Biafra babies." In 1967, civil war erupted in Nigeria. Oil wealth in the eastern Niger Delta was in the hands of the Igbo peoples, who resented the claims of northern elites for control. The Nigerian government, with the support of the United States and USSR, and Shell and British Petroleum, could ill afford to give up control; its generals aimed to crush Biafra secessionists (who had support from French interests eager for a stake in the Delta). Federal troops surrounded the rebels. Civilians were caught in a blockade. Mass starvation set in. The Organisation of African Unity declared it an "internal affair" and warned the United Nations to keep its distance and honor Nigeria's hard-won sovereignty, only for the institution to be blamed for inaction or meddling.

The rest of the world might not have paid much attention to another story of misfortune in what was turning into a frenetic year for journalists. But Catholic missionaries, French doctors, and new nongovernmental organizations like Oxfam turned the war into a cause célèbre and a mediatized global humanitarian calamity. In May, Britain's International Television Network crew arrived on the scene. *The Sun*'s Michael Leapman and the photojournalist Ronald Burton were there too. So were Gilles Caron and the filmmaker Raymond Depardon. Caron would make three separate trips to Biafra between coverage of the upheavals in Paris and other hot spots. On May 4, *Paris Match* spread his photos of the "ignored war" across its pages. Don McCullin flew in to join Caron from Saigon. Caron turned his Nikon at first on soldiers; this was, after all, a war. At the time there was a strong 'Nam quality to the insurgent-versus-army reportage. But the visual narrative quickly changed as Caron turned his lens away from fighters to civilians; Biafra became "a war without pity." In his July trip, Caron focused on children, refugees, hospitals, schools, and camps for the unwanted. Then came portraiture of starvation. Perhaps the most famous of Caron's shots was of a girl, her rib cage pressed against taught skin, her eyes downcast, and a right hand on her cheek, almost posing.[91]

If Rachel Carson was a handmaiden for environmental thinking, Gilles Caron was a handmaiden of humanitarian witnessing. The spectacle of far-away hunger was starting to feel close, human, recognizable. Physical,

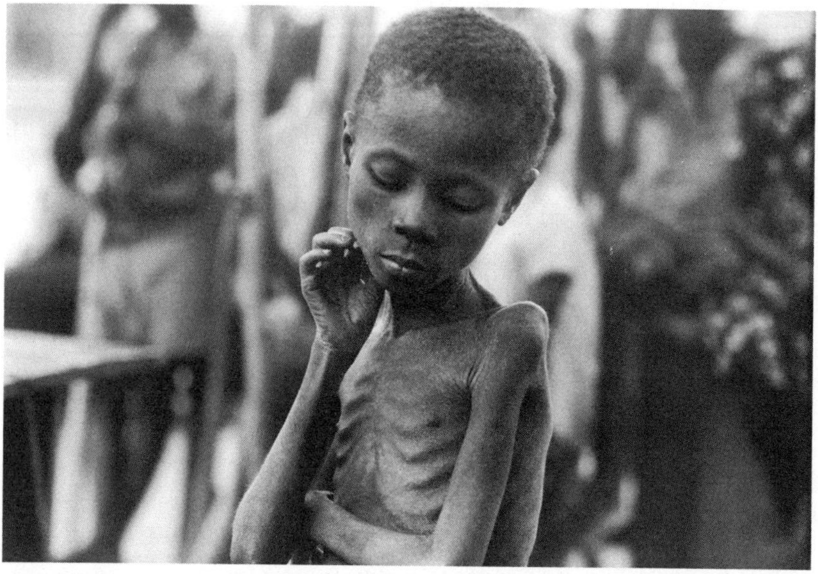

FIGURE 4.6. Biafra.

gritty, bodily images of extreme want pulled at the questions about the ethics of interdependence and informed a moral debate and new forms of action in the 1970s, which concern us in the next chapter. Biafra, the first of a train of "humanitarian crises" in which starvation was a becoming a permanent weapon of war, also brought to a close the unraveling consensus that national development, national liberation, and national defense were keys to the international new deal. Maybe the revolution the planet needed had nothing to do with gaining more sovereignty? Maybe it had to do with something more basic, like survival?

It would be too simple, however, to say that the end of the post-Nagasaki hope created new ways to imagine sympathy and togetherness. The presence of necessitous strangers could cut both ways: they posed the question of sympathy and attachment; they also created aversion, fear, and sheer indifference. Biafra was a humanitarian event and a turning point in humanitarian governance to replace the crumbling hopes and expectations of a free, self-determining country.

Biafra also triggered alarm about the menace of necessitous strangers. When the thirty-five-year-old Stanford biologist Paul Ehrlich published

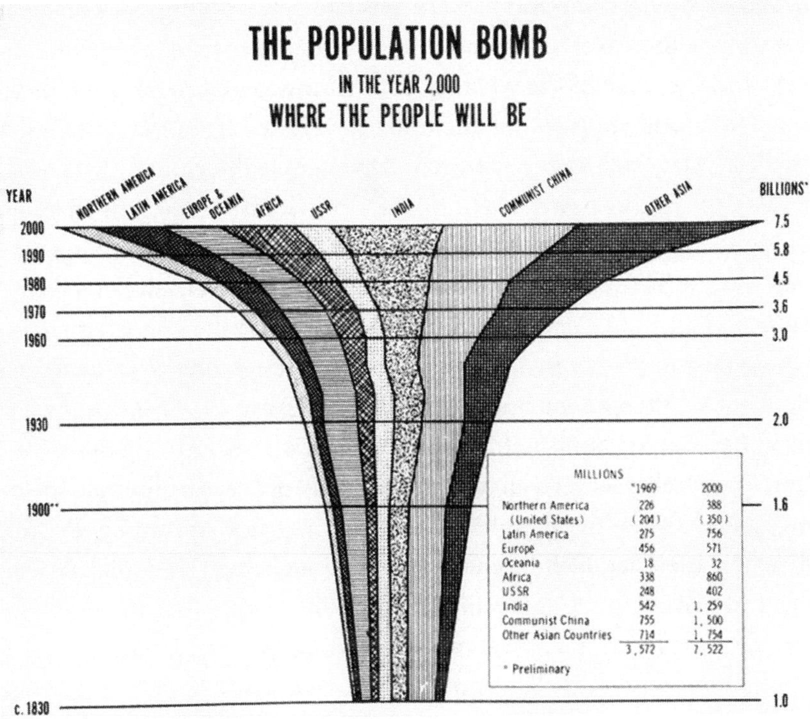

FIGURE 4.7. The Population Bomb.

The Population Bomb in 1968, he replaced the threat of nukes from the Cold War with the threat of people from the Third World, using the same metaphoric image of annihilation. *This* bomb was targeted not at any particular place on the planet; the planet was the target. In its first three years, the book went through twenty-two reprintings. In a brilliant marketing move, the book was titled to strike fear. The new bomb, and new stylized graphics of horror made to resemble a mushroom cloud, capped a decade of growing concern about the postcolonial world. The poster shown in Figure 4.7, for an environmental teach-in at the University of Michigan, exemplified the statistical imaginary of doom.

Ehrlich's prose oozed alarm. In an effort to "make the population crisis an issue in this year's election," Ehrlich juiced up the apocalyptic tone. "The battle to feed all of humanity is over," he wrote. "In the 1970s hundreds of millions of people will starve to death in spite of any crash programs embarked upon now. At this late date nothing can prevent a substantial increase in the world death rate." The nature of world markets and the scale of the want meant that it was no longer possible to segregate food supplies for the underdeveloped from the developed worlds. "Mass starvation" threatened to encircle the globe.

To explain this new scale of threat, Ehrlich introduced the formula of "doubling time"—how long does it take for people to double in number? Where he saw doubling time most vividly was in India. Indeed, he launched into *The Population Bomb* by describing the streets of Delhi, where he and his family had been passing through on the way back to the United States after a bucolic sabbatical in Australia. In a famous but lurid opening recounting his taxi drive from the airport, he described how "the streets seemed alive with people. People eating, people washing, people sleeping. People visiting, arguing and screaming. People thrusting their hands through the taxi window, begging. People defecating and urinating. People clinging to buses. People herding animals. People, people, people." In sum: "*too many people*."[92] In the absence of population control, Ehrlich's prophecy was a gruesome "death rate solution": a cleansing purge of starvation, plague, and global warfare caused by the scramble to control land and water. What Ehrlich did not know was that India was a site of the world's most systematic effort to "control" population. The scale of money poured into weaponizing states to conduct mass vasectomies, tubal ligations, and IUD (intrauterine device) insertions, much of it involuntary and much of it directed at India's most marginal "outcast" population, did not cross Ehrlich's mind.

By the late 1960s, the baton was passing from American action intellectuals to American celebrity prophets of doom. Ehrlich became a frequent guest on Johnny Carson's *The Tonight Show*; the biologist would appear there over twenty times. In early 1970, *Time* magazine initiated a new "Environment" section. Even President Richard M. Nixon piled on the bandwagon of alarm. In his state of the union speech to Congress a month after Ehrlich first wowed the king of late night TV, Nixon told legislators that the coming decade would challenge Americans to "make our peace with nature."[93] What was disturbing was that the change in mood was coming from the original factory of can-do optimism: the

United States. A beacon in 1945, America had become the target for, and source of, doubt and fear. Americans themselves were at the forefront of the rush to hit the alarm buttons.

This was a strange way to end recovery and reconstruction. Decolonization was irreversible. The number of UN member states more than doubled from 51 in 1945 to 117 two decades later. New nations sought their place under the sun. The world economy recovered; former enemies, Japan and Germany, became industrial powerhouses. If these were the goals of Pax Americana, they met with success.

Only it didn't feel that way. The Third World was winning its freedom, only to sink into frustration and despair and project disenchantments onto the United States, which played the role as oppressor du jour, torching Indochinese villages and toppling democracies in Latin America. Progress was becoming suspicious; the institutions and ideas devoted to promoting it were being pelted, literally and figuratively, for their hypocrisy. Instead of joy at expanding rights, more nations, and more prosperity, doubt and dismay seeped into the post-Nagasaki world.

5

Patient Earth and Deep Interdependence

Globalization

This chapter is about the moment in world history we learned to call globalization. Globalization deepened and broadened interdependence beyond anything imagined in 1945. In so doing, it broke the compressing logjam of the post-Nagasaki order and yielded an international division of labor that distributed power and voice. People became less and less dependent as cocitizens in nations and more and more codependent as strangers with practices that reflected the emergent order's need for ideas, actors, and institutions to manage mutual reliance on a new scale.

The result was contradictory. More interdependence created more wealth, less conflict, and greater social mobility than ever. And yet, it exposed people ever more to the choices and preferences of strangers far away; along with heightened opportunities went heightened risks. The cheerleaders of deep interdependence thrived on the rewards—and celebrated. But they could not, or refused to, hear warnings about the risks. Instead, they basked in a self-serving glory that was staged at global summits and trumpeted from the commanding heights of think tanks, pundit platforms, and elite universities—their unexamined certainties buoyed by a borderless market and patched by well-meaning global humanitarians who stepped in when governments' ability to protect people had been stripped bare.

The mediascape amplified possibility and hazard. Risks and rewards became ever more and instantaneously imaginable—indeed, they were framed as the image economy became a centerpiece of the economy. The scale and speed of circulating stories and pictures supercharged the affective spectrum and sharpened the juxtapositions. Skyscrapers built in Shanghai, a Louvre constructed in Abu Dhabi, doctors jetted to prevent deadly diseases from spreading from jungles, and torturers cashiered to international courts all became increasingly visible to the rest of the world. American and Chinese filmmakers competed to produce box office hits about global good guys and bad guys. But for every new Asian skyscraper, a factory closed in an old industrial heartland of Michigan or the Midlands. Airports were gateways for viruses. An occasional African despot wound up in court while war criminals in rich countries (of which there were plenty) got off scot-free. As long as the bounty from deep interdependence appeared to outpace the risks, as long as the burdens were shouldered by the misfortunate far away, as long as China in particular was a low-wage client and not a high-tech competitor, euphoria overshadowed doubt and despair. Seen from the commanding heights of banks, supply chain management firms, and yes, elite universities and the think tanks they populated, globalization looked as irreversible as it was transformative.

Naked Nations

The post-Nagasaki order was embattled by 1970. The pillars of Pax Americana were cracking. Television screens brought scenes of burning jungles and shattered GIs, student protestors, and coups d'état into living rooms worldwide. The upbeat imagery of a rising planet of the 1968 *Earthrise* shot gave way to the more ominous 1972 shot from Apollo 17—a lonely orb floating in the dark. It projected the image of a more precarious, fragile survival unit. Even the original negative had the world upside down. So as not to be too disturbing, publishers flipped it in print.

FIGURE 5.1. Blue Marble. Note the original had Antarctica on top.

Like the orb, the nation-state was also in trouble. Malaise set in everywhere. A growing chorus pointed to new concentrations of power that drained nations of their ability to protect citizens. One target was the multinational firm—oil giants like Standard Oil, food conglomerates like Nestlé, and chemical leviathans like DuPont. In 1971, Raymond Vernon, a Harvard economist, published a landmark study about the sprawl of multinational companies. It opened ominously: "Suddenly, it seems, the sovereign states are feeling naked." Nations and national economic strength "appear curiously drained of meaning." Multinational corporations, by contrast, "exude an aura of strength and flexibility." Vernon presented table after table to illustrate "the sense of nakedness and dependence" that flowed from the decline in nations.[1]

If an extraterrestrial had landed on earth in 1975, they would have witnessed feuding friends, spiking suspicions, and fears of scarcity that echoed the Malthusian anxiety of the ominous 1930s. In 1968, an Italian magnate and visionary summoned thirty scientists, statesmen, and intellectuals to form what would be called an "invisible college" known as the Club of Rome. They devised a "Project on the Predicament of Mankind" to probe the "world problematique." Four years later, it looked like the planet was on a course to self-destruction. In an Armageddon report called *The Limits to Growth,* an MIT-based team of scientists reported that the resources of the globe were being consumed at a faster rate than they could be supplied; we were running out. Using computational models to calculate feedback loops and interaction effects, the report predicted with gloomy confidence that "the limits to growth on this planet will be reached sometime within the next one hundred years." The effects would be an inevitable "adjustment" of a sharp drop in population and plunge in industrial capacity.[2] The dismal scientists plotted a dystopian future in a relentless parade of graphs with curves all sloping in the wrong way, like the one shown in Figure 5.2 that graphed upward-sloping scenarios of need for arable land and downward sloping supply, which predictably and conveniently intersect in the year 2000. After that, the question was no longer about development or prosperity. It was about survival.

Published a month before the United Nations Conference on the Human Environment in Stockholm, with a foreword by Secretary General U Thant, *The Limits to Growth* was so technical that it seemed doomed to obscurity. Not so: it was a bestseller in Germany and Great Britain. Thant declared that unilateralism, nationalism, and the Cold War splintered a finite world in need of a new scale of thinking and action. This report was proof that the Stockholm conference's slogan, "Only One Earth," had science behind the ecological summitry. *Die Zeit* pronounced that decades of hopefulness about leisure, longer lives, and prosperity were over. Welcome to the gloomy age. From Argentina to India, systems scientists scrambled to model the planet to chart and predict how and why humans might strangle it.[3]

The first reflex was to throw interdependence into reverse, reduce risks by throwing up barriers between strangers. It started with a drive to check the behemoth firms, even expropriate them. From copper mines in Chile to gas stations in Canada, the state muscled into the domain of multinationals to restore national economic sovereignty as a

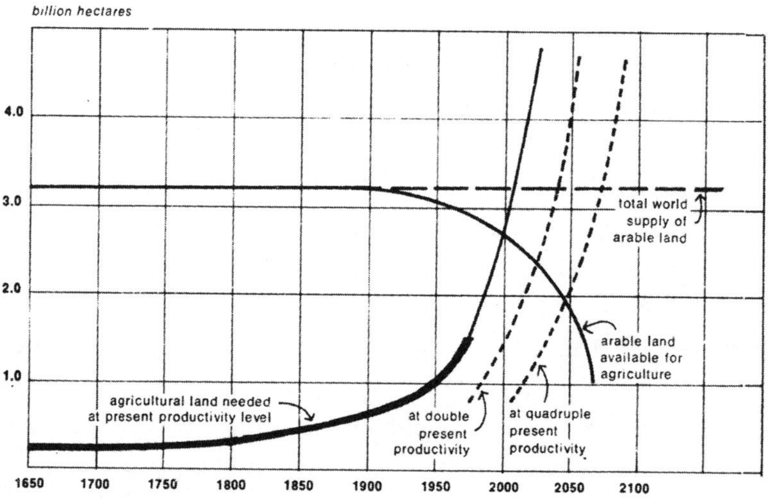

Total world supply of arable land is about 3.2 billion hectares. About 0.4 hectares per person of arable land are needed at present productivity. The curve of land needed thus reflects the population growth curve. The light line after 1970 shows the projected need for land, assuming that world population continues to grow at its present rate. Arable land available decreases because arable land is removed for urban-industrial use as population grows. The dotted curves show land needed if present productivity is doubled or quadrupled.

FIGURE 5.2. Limits to Growth.

way out of the malaise. Up went the flag of economic sovereignty and resource self-determination. Across the developing world in particular, governments targeted multinationals for price gouging and tax evasion. Anti-colonial voices of the 1960s turned from dismantling formal empires to tackling shadowy informal, economic ones. In April 1972, the Mexican president, Luis Echeverría, rose to address UN Conference on Trade and Development delegates in Santiago, Chile, and proclaimed the need for a revised division of labor premised on the "freedom to dispose of natural resources; the right of every nation to adopt the economic structure it considered most suitable and to treat private property as the public interest required." Taking inspiration from the Organization of the Petroleum Exporting Countries' (OPEC's) cartel, champions of a New International Economic Order (NIEO) called for new rules to check the power of multinationals by asserting the need for economic sovereignty—over resources, technology, and transfer payments. By 1974, the United Nations General Assembly adopted the NIEO as an action plan. It achieved little. Multinational behemoths were in retreat anyway. The same countries calling for economic redistribution were sinking into quagmires. The cost of oil was spiking. They turned to the new behemoths, foreign banks like Chase Manhattan and Citibank, for bailouts.[4]

Nor was the Third World the only defender of economic sovereignty. Most governments turned inward, tightened capital controls, and raised tariffs to defend workers from outside competitive pressures. A White House advisor said to a fretting president, "I believe we must ask—are we advocating our own economic interests as forcefully as we should?" These words came from the pen of Peter Peterson, former Bell & Howell CEO and Richard Nixon's secretary of commerce. The White House tightened the screws on Japan, making the return of occupied Okinawa conditional upon Japan restraining its textile exports in order to placate a segregationist senator of South Carolina, Strom Thurmond. Across the trading world, economic diplomats were embroiled in disputes over cars, citrus, tobacco, poultry, and lard. Richard Nixon "shocked" audiences who tuned in to watch him on TV during a steamy evening of August 15, 1971, announce the end of dollar convertibility to gold. Equally stunning were the 10 percent surcharge on all imports and the doubling of the average effective tariff on all dutiable goods. Nixon's goal: to bludgeon trading partners into buying more U.S. goods and to curb American appetites for imports. Allies were on notice.[5]

Where the impulse to retreat from needing strangers exposed the nerves of interdependence was in energy. Cheap fossil fuels had girded the post-Nagasaki recovery. Global energy consumption had tripled since 1949, as did supply and the diversity of its sources. By the end of the summer of 1973, Japan, Europe, and the United States were importing record barrels of oil, especially from the Persian Gulf. Oil prices were starting to climb. In a meeting between Richard Nixon and Soviet Premier Leonid Brezhnev in June, the Russian leader warned that the Middle East was a tinder box. Late one night, guards woke the American president for an impromptu huddle with the premier. An agitated Brezhnev warned that another war might jeopardize détente between superpowers. Nixon and his ever-confident secretary of state, Henry Kissinger, waved off the fears; oil exporters wouldn't *dare*. A few months later, Egyptian President Anwar Sadat flew to Riyadh to meet King Faisal of Saudi Arabia and told him of war plans against Israel. The wily king smiled and pledged a half billion dollars—and promised to use gulf oil as a warhead. "But give us time," he said. "We don't want to use our oil as a weapon in a battle which only goes on for two or three days, and then stops. We want to see a battle which goes on for long enough time for world public opinion to be mobilized."[6]

On cue, in October 1973, OPEC hiked the price of crude in response to America's support for Israel during the Yom Kippur War. It would not be the first or last time that rich, well-informed societies would take interdependence for granted and shrug off the voices calling for redistribution and inclusion. The price of oil tripled. Most Americans, oblivious that the country had gone from being the world's biggest exporter to a major importer, woke up to a new world. Europeans, more aware, hoped that their multinationals and military bases in the Middle East would keep the crude flowing. Muammar Qaddafi, the ruler of Libya, had warned that this dependence gave the Third World leverage. "We have the oil weapon and the financial weapon and we intend to use them both," he said. As oil prices soared, "gasoline fever" gripped the dependents. American long-haul truckers paralyzed interstate highways; one of them clogged the Delaware Memorial Bridge and froze traffic up and down the eastern seaboard. "Energy is our Vietnam," moaned a White House aide.[7] Behind closed doors, Kissinger groused to Arthur Schlesinger that "it is ridiculous that the civilized world is held up by 8 million savages. Can't we overthrow one of the sheikhs just to show that we can do it?"[8] By then, coups d'état were a staple of his statecraft.

The response was to push for "energy independence," lower thermostats, install wood stoves, drive slower, and lessen reliance on impudent foreigners and upstart "savages." But energy independence was easier to declare than to do. Even ur-realists had to square up to realities of interdependence. A year after the first OPEC spike, a fleet of twenty aircraft landed in Jeddah, Saudi Arabia. Nixon, Kissinger, hundreds of staff, additional planeloads of journalists (including TV glitterati like Walter Cronkite, Connie Chung, and Dan Rather), and armored limousines unloaded for the U.S. president to meet with King Faisal and set in motion decades of entanglement over global energy and regional security. Nixon acknowledged dependence to King Faisal. Over dinner, he joked that Air Force One would need Saudi fuel to get home. "We, of course, will pay the world price," he added.[9]

Calls for energy independence were a ruse. They also obscured the ways in which deepening reliance on others' resources energized another fact of deepening interdependence: more borrowing of strangers' money. Here too there were initial calls for and futile efforts at decoupling from strangers. Faced with balance of payments crises, strikes, and stagflation, governments hiked capital controls, restrained currency trading, and stiffened currency reserve requirements to curb capital flight. During one panic in the early 1970s, the West German government learned that the only way to dampen the alarm was to turn off all international telephone calls until the markets calmed.[10] But the drive to reduce dependence on capital flows went the way of calls for energy autonomy: nowhere. A surge of loanable capital made it cheap. Oil exporters received massive petrodollar surpluses they could not absorb. So they opened accounts in overseas commercial banks and funneled rents there. Petrodollars surged into the banking system just as countries from the Organisation for Economic Co-operation and Development (OECD) were slumping, producing a dollar glut. The London Inter-Bank Offered Rate (LIBOR, the inflation-adjusted rate charged on loans between financial institutions) plunged from an average of 4.1 percent from 1960 to 1971, to −0.8 percent from 1971 to 1980. Financiers looked at their spreadsheets and gazed at a vortex of losses as the supply of world capital soared.[11]

The decoupling reflexes were not working; they could not work. The familiar tools of national sovereignty and national security seemed to make things worse because they could not contend with the bisecting forces of waning American power and a postcolonial yearning for a more distributed and inclusive world.[12]

Between Carbon and Credit

Globalism did not spring from the brains of neoliberal visionaries.[13] Quite the opposite. Deep interdependence was based on the variables that seemed to cause the malaise: the helix of carbon-powered energy and easy credit. The result was a new international division of labor. As the new scale of economic life took hold and then consolidated, pundits found in ideas of market fundamentalism some narrative justification for deep interdependence.

Both carbon and credit required flow. The more they flowed, the more they reinforced each other's liquidity. Ease of credit allowed more consumption of carbon, and the surge in carbon supply injected liquidity into banks for more liquid distribution. Some corporate executives saw the carbon-credit helix coming—that big banks and big oil were allies. In 1967, Chase Manhattan magnates saw it. They pitched to monetary authorities the idea of abandoning gold convertibility to ease the glut of dollars that was prompting the urge to control capital. Sacrifice currency stability in favor of capital mobility, they urged. The condition was that captains of finance and of oil keep the price of capital and carbon stable to replace gold as the fixer. The American Bankers Association had a fit: *leave gold*? Unthinkable! Chase retracted the idea. But the solution was on the table, a solution that would allow the dollar to float in order to liberate capital to flow across borders and the pool of capital to grow thanks to injections from oil exporters.[14]

That is what happened. It took the shocks of the 1970s for fluidity of oil and credit to reconstruct the world economy. OPEC, instead of motivating energy autonomy, only scattered and deepened energy interdependence. High oil prices prompted the opening of new petroleum frontiers, diversifying fossil fuel sources. The "Arab" oil embargo blared across October 1973 headlines, burying momentous news that Soviet natural gas started to flow into the Eastern European pipeline system financed by West German banks; for their part, the Soviets, struggling to meet debt payments to the West, cut off domestic users that winter to ship to foreigners. For their part, European consumers, even fiercely anti-communist Bavarian conservatives, were only too relieved to welcome "red gas." In general, the surge in world oil prices set off a scramble for reserves in the North Sea, Western Canada, and above all in Soviet Siberia, which eventually came online and drove oil prices back down. Europeans swapped out their dependence on gulf oil for Siberian crude, with geopolitical implications that Vladimir Putin would later exploit. Russian "gasification" meant that, by the mid-2000s, half of state revenues came from levies on energy exports; from the start of its imperial dissolution, Moscow used its grip on the westward flow to submit Belarus, Moldova, Ukraine, and the Baltic republics.[15] The result was not scarcity but abundance. By 1986, as China and other fast industrializers were beginning their ascent, a barrel of oil cost ten dollars. Some Persian Gulf cargoes were unloading at losses of six dollars a barrel; OPEC's share of world oil output had slumped from over 50 percent to 29 percent.

The surge in rents from energy trading created a surge in capital. Oil exporters, unable to absorb their windfalls, deposited them in offshore accounts concentrated on London. It was there, helped by a friendly class of butler-bankers, that lenders and borrowers, savers and spenders deepened ties of mutual necessity. Currency trading centers opened shop, American and British legal reforms permitted transborder activity through remote hubs, a Eurodollar market emerged. Based in London, bankers avoided U.S. constraints on interest payments; by using American dollars, they ducked British restrictions on how much capital they could move.[16] Bank supervisors relaxed reserve requirements and erased the lines between commercial and investment banking. Interbank activity grew to absorb the torrent of petrodollars. Then came havens for avoiding not just regulators but taxmen, so that offshore nodes like Curaçao, off the coast of Venezuela and seasoned in the art of sheltering oil money and smuggling, became hot spots for shell companies incorporated to reduce their tax "exposure."[17] The British Virgin Islands, Panama, Hong Kong, and others became satellites in the orbital structures of global finance, many of them former or pseudo-colonies of the

United States, the Netherlands, and Britain, now repurposed for financialization.

The rising supply and fluidity of capital required more demand to reverse the bleeding returns on financial assets. But wealthy OECD countries were mired in stagnation from the oil price hikes and other shocks; there were no customers for capital among the rich countries. What better places to redirect the surplus than the struggling Third World and the Eastern bloc for bankers to peddle loans and fancy financial services?[18] The result was a cycle of debt-led growth. Pioneered by Latin American, South Korean, and Philippine dictators, and some Eastern European regimes, foreign debt became a solution for governments struggling for legitimacy at home but wanting to defer the bill on their spending ways.[19] After 1973, the global financial industry soared; within a decade, financial markets had grown 400 percent. In four short years, Latin America's foreign debt doubled to $331 billion by 1982—and continued to rise thereafter as debts piled up.[20]

The institutions that recycled surplus savings into debts became more proficient at binding lenders and borrowers. A coterie of large banks with extensive overseas operations formed a nucleus of international debtors and creditors. One innovation, the syndicated loan organized by a lead bank, bundled resources and negotiated with clients on behalf of a lending consortium to disperse the risks of default, share the spoils, and create powerful creditor blocs to lord over needy borrowers. For the top ten U.S. banks alone, the share of foreign earnings as a percentage of all gains rose dramatically from 1970 to 1982—from 17.5 percent to 54.7 percent.[21]

It became easier and easier to mobilize capital when an asset could be "leveraged" into not just one but two, three, or many instruments to back a loan; a massive amount of capital could flow from a single asset. Total credit market debt (public and private) in the United States doubled from 1970 to 1998. Then it soared and never looked back. By 2016, it had ballooned to $152 trillion—over 225 percent of world output. The new matrix not only deepened financial interdependence; it rebalanced power, releasing Asian exporters to send their wares to Western markets and making (mainly American) consumers increasingly dependent on (mainly Chinese) foreign savings. By the time American regulators scrambled to bail out its financial system in 2008, they relied above all on Chinese counterparts to mop up the sloppy mess of a world awash in dollars. In 1998, China held about $100 billion in foreign exchange reserves in its coffers; by the end of 2008, the figure topped $2 trillion. For all intents and purposes, the world had migrated to an Asian dollar standard rotating around an axle of Asian savings and American spending, Asian exporters and American importers.[22]

From the upper floors of their towers, financiers envisioned themselves as, in the words of the anthropologist Karen Ho, a "moneyed meritocracy."[23] The problem with this breed of meritocrats was that they felt especially entitled because they claimed to have earned their perks from pluck and wit. There was no room for humility or irony in their highly rewarded and self-regarded preference for mobility, fluidity, and liquidity. Global was more than a division of labor. It was a new scale for a new model elite.[24] In her ethnography of Wall Street at the height of its swagger in 2006, Ho observed the cult of shareholder value and hypercapitalist time bent to the pulse of a market as if it were a 24/7 living thing forever blinking from screens in Hong Kong, New York, New Delhi, and London. When she finished one of her training programs at Bankers Trust in 1996, she got the pitch to join the new highflier club—to "be global." "We act as a global problem solver for our clients," one of the J. P. Morgan recruitment brochures boasted, "moving ideas and insights seamlessly across time and space." Seamless: mobile, flowing, liquid.[25]

Asian Meridian

Shifts in carbon and credit markets were the first steps toward deep interdependence, the industrialization of Asia and parts of Latin America was the next—for it spread the addiction to fossil fuels to new frontiers to match the new frontiers of oil and gas supply, and blew manufacturing supply chains out of their homelands to yield a new international division of labor. The result: a new balance of capital to make Eurasia its exporter and the Americas a chronic importer.

New industrializers became new kinds of interdependent clients, fusing borrowed global capital with local cheap labor to seize the low-value links in growing manufacturing chains. In the nineteenth century, interdependence unbundled production and consumption. Commerce split the self-sufficient world of villages where neighbors took care of their needs. The locations of consumption and production diverged. Countries traded goods with each other, wine for cloth, machinery for wheat. For the next century and a half, this was more or less the international division of labor. The 1970s ushered in a new rearrangement: the new interdependence deconstructed industrial production itself into worldwide assembly operations. Instead of giant factories that metabolized natural resources into final products under one roof, the factories got broken up and scattered, with parts of a product moving from factory to factory inching closer to the final good. A growing share of manufacturing trade across borders was going on within industries and companies that straddled borders. The key was building factories in societies in low wage, environmentally lax sites where the steps in the process were more labor intensive or ecologically costly. The result was a global industrial revolution to eclipse the Euro-American one.[26]

It helps to underscore the improbability of the process. The recomposition of the world division of labor was gradual and often faltered; in retrospect it looks meteoric and miraculous. In the summer of 1975, as the West was mired in stagflation and it felt as if the world was spiraling into crisis, the entertainment empresario Don King, famed for organizing the legendary boxing match between Muhammad Ali and the world champion George Foreman in Zaire—the "Rumble in the Jungle" (a billion people watched Ali win on TV)—staged an event in his spread on the sixty-seventh floor of Rockefeller Center in Manhattan. Before a crowd of reporters and gawkers, a green-suited King, after a round of fist pumping with his guests, sat before a table covered with sports shoes, baseball mitts, and basketballs and announced to a puzzled audience that he was starting a new company dedicated to importing sporting goods from China. *China*? For *American* sneakers and gear? Why not? King swaggered as he called for consumers and capitalists of color of the world to unite; they had nothing to lose but the chains of white men's supply lines.[27]

King was a New York booster. But the textile tycoons were in Hong Kong. Hong Kong manufacturing, based on small firms and light technology, had carved a fabric niche from the 1950s. Factories of a dozen or so workers each specialized in cheap shirts, plastic flowers, or wigs. Outside investment was rare. Over time, the advent of flexible supply chains, the extension of Hong Kong educational and commercial networks, especially to North America, and the proliferation of banks brought capital into local manufacturing. Then, Hong Kong became the main wedges into China's incipient industrial restructuring for export, which started back in the late 1960s. It then intensified in the 1970s, and then jumped to a new track with one of the last pronouncements of Mao's right-hand man, Zhou Enlai, calling for Four Modernizations in 1975.

Family firms of Gordon Wu, Victor and William Fung, and others became Hong Kong magnates of manufacturing, shipping, and banking conglomerates. In early 1980, the partnership of Li & Fung took delegates of its largest client, an American clothing retailer called The Gap, to Shanghai and convinced the Americans to start buying their fabrics from an ultracheap manufacturer Shanghai Textile Import & Export Company; the deal was that Li & Fung would relocate its Hong Kong looms to neighboring Shenzhen mills run by Shanghai Textile to turn yarn into bolts of cloth that in turn had to be sent to Hong Kong to become apparel to ship to the United States under the shelter of the Multifiber Agreement (which gave the British entrepôt large export quotas while China had almost none). This was the beginning of a complex exchange between Chinese hinterlands and American shopping malls, spurring Chinese mills while closing those in North Carolina, and mediated by transpacific networks radiating out of the Pearl River Delta.[28]

China, via Hong Kong, opened for business. The industrialization of Asia became an engine of global growth, peaking after 2001 when China joined the club that monitored commercial interdependence, the World Trade Organization (WTO). A quarter century later and after much grumbling about a rules-based trading system that didn't punish rule bending, it came to be seen as a charter for constructing a new, some would say unfair, balance. Between 2003 and 2013, the world economy grew by an astonishing 30 percent. But China's economy grew by 250 percent, and India's by 100 percent, producing goods for distant markets. China's share of world exports leaped after 2001 from 10 percent to 30 percent.

Unbundling national industries into international circuits meant redistributing production to Asia. Paul Ehrlich, Gunnar Myrdal, and others who worried about the spread of Asian misery in the 1960s would have been shocked. If the United States accounted for 31 percent of world GDP in 1970, by 1994 it had shrunk to 24 percent; Japan leaped from 6 to 17 percent; China, still languishing at 3 percent as recently as 1995, jumped to 17 percent by 2020. This narrowed the wealth gap across countries. Conversely, the gap within societies widened, in some places sharply, fueling a backlash after 2008—a backlash that began as outrage against self-rewarding financiers and mutated into a full-blown assault on the gears of globalization they greased.[29]

One shuttered factory at a time, the domestic rifts of economic restructuring and the shattered post-1945 political coalitions were revealed. Meanwhile, a new rhetoric of innovation, acceleration, and mobility seized the headlines. In 1970, Pan American Airways sent a Boeing 747 Jumbo Jet on its first commercial flight. The futurologist Alvin Toffler predicted a breed of "new nomads." "Never in history," he mused, "has distance meant less."[30] If the jet age had come to fruition, it was the less glamorous container ships and pipelines that dominated the logistics of the new world economy. Purpose-built container ships in 1970 squeezed through the Panama Canal with one thousand twenty-foot containers. In 2006, Maersk launched the hulking E-Class, capable of carrying over fourteen thousand containers (the Triple-E now handles over twenty thousand). "Logistics," a military term popularized during the Vietnam War, became coinage of MBA training for how to manage inventories, flows, and distribution so that nothing would sit still. It was the munitions and logistics needs of the Vietnam War that gave Singapore and Hong Kong's cargo revolution the initial boost. Move, flow;

idleness was a value killer. Singapore, the capital of fluidity, had more container traffic than all the ports of France combined by 1986; a decade later it outstripped Japan.[31]

The logistics revolution scrambled divides between "origination" countries where strangers drew their staples and "destination" countries where products were sold. As more countries became manufacturers, the definition of a "final product" changed as bits and parts of a car or computer moved back and forth across borders along global assembly lines. What did "Made in Nation X" mean? American factories set up in northern Mexico and China's burgeoning SEZs, starting with the Shenzhen SEZ fusing imported technology with local workers. Tax-free, low-wage enclaves opened at home to link with Mexican and Chinese nodes. In the United States alone, there were 11 zones in 1965; by 2019, there were 1,068 filled with warehouses off the fiscal grid. It did not take long for those hubs to specialize in higher-value parts manufacture for global chains, assembling smartphones with LCD screens from Japan, chips from Taiwan, gyroscopes from Switzerland, and software from California. Zoning did not always work out. Newcastle, the gateway to the Zulu Kingdom in South Africa, was a model postapartheid development hub with vast new industrial parks to fill, perfect for Taiwanese textile manufacturers whose costs were rising back home to set up a new knitwear complex—or so businessmen like the Chinese investor, Eddie Liu, hoped. But he never could secure a ban on unions in a South Africa that was dismantling vestiges of white supremacy and needed popular Black support. Nor could he get taxes waived. Liu's hopes for a free trade and free labor zone dissolved; Newcastle's place in the global circuitry faded.[32]

In general, however, world value chains that reached beyond the old heartlands of the industrial revolution achieved what postcolonial countries had been striving for: a transformation on the backs of their own industrial revolution. Asia's share of world manufacturing, a mere 4 percent in 1970, reached 45 percent by 2019. Its share of merchandise trade leaped from 3 percent to 35 percent.[33]

Even what counted as "final" was commodified. The effluence from production chains became a commodity to be bought, sold and dumped on a world market for waste. Trafigura, a relative upstart in the superlucrative world of commodity trading, agreed to buy dirty coker gasoline from Mexico's Pemex for a song—only to learn that the most lucrative way to turn a profit was through caustic washing, a highly toxic process that yields noxious residue. Making coker gasoline sellable required offloading the horrid efflux. The trick was hiring an old tanker, the rusting *Probo Koala*, to carry the 528 cubic meters of caustic waste to a port and company that would relieve Trafigura of its unwanted waste but in a way that turned a profit at each link in the value chain. Based in the Ivory Coast, Compagnie Tommy took the contract for $20,000, found an open-air dump near Abidjan, and hired trucks to haul and dump the waste. The next day, tens of thousands of people became violently ill. When the legal dust settled, Trafigura had to pay the Ivory Coast government $198 million. The story revealed the degree to which cross-border flows included everything up and down every stage of production, merchandising, and their residuals were involved in making a global commodity.[34]

The result decentered the United States in the world economy and globalized the addiction to fossil fuels. In 1978, the entire Third World consumed less than half the petroleum the United States alone did; by 1994, the Third World surpassed the United States, and it exploded in demand thereafter—so that by 2006, developing markets needed as much as the rest combined. They stopped being called the "Third World." Once self-sufficient in oil in 1990, China became its biggest importer.[35] And with rising and spreading carbon addiction came rising and spreading sources of CO_2 emissions. Asia, Africa, and Latin America released four billion metric tons of carbon into the atmosphere in 1970; the figure is now ten billion. Fully half the fossil fuel–induced CO_2 emissions worldwide since 1750 have taken place since 1985; most of it came from Asia.[36]

The drive to decolonize the world economy meant industrializing the postcolonial world; in turn, industrialization spread carbon dependence. In doing so, Asia altered scales of production and circulation and put world gross output—which rose from $28.9 trillion in 1975 to $108 trillion by 2015—on steroids. The average earthling saw their wealth

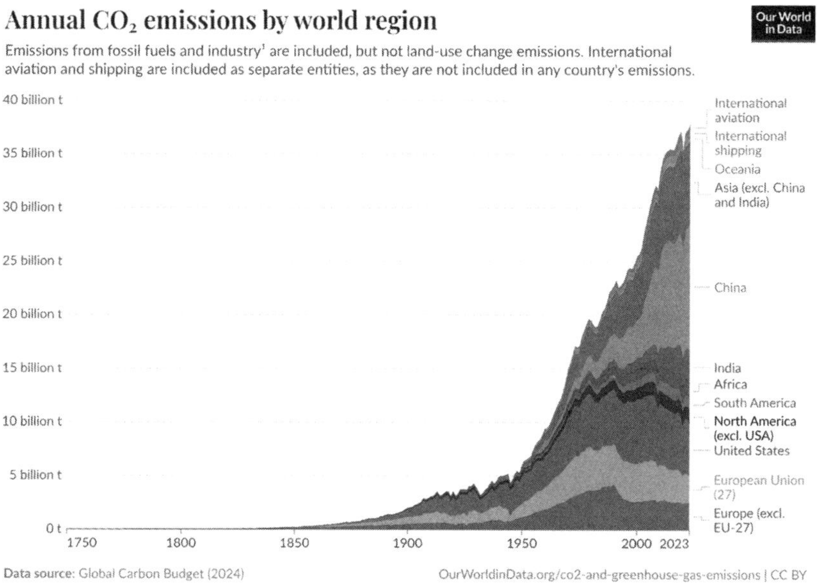

FIGURE 5.3. Annual CO_2 Emissions from Fossil Fuels by World Region.

double. The effect on social mobility was nothing less than astonishing, even if the gains were unevenly, often grotesquely, distributed. The result made Asia the lead protagonist of carbon emissions growth as well as its lead casualty.[37]

Inventing Globalization

Gloom dominated the 1970s, with a fragile orb, spreading shortages, and predictions of collapse. Pundits called it a crisis. As is so often the case, the doomsayers confused transformation with decline; the obsession with the malaise obscured the ways in which societies were becoming more interdependent and laying the grounds for a historic transformation.

In hindsight, from the other side of 1989, there is a tendency to read backwards, to see the transformation as inevitable. At the time, however, it was fevered, confusing, and violent. The rival blocs were in upheaval. The revolutions in Iran and Central America pulled apart Cold War alignments. Making the leap to uncontrolled markets and realigning the international division of labor meant deep social changes—and disquiet. There was also a global democratic upheaval from Poland to the Philippines. In the cockpit of power in Beijing, tens of thousands of students converged on the Tian'anmen Square calling for reform; hundreds went on a hunger strike. As a showdown neared, one of their heroes, the Soviet Premier Gorbachev, landed in the city on May 15, 1989, which put the party leadership in a spot. Gorbachev had to be whisked into the National People's Congress through a side door—and later told some of his staff that he was relieved not to be in Deng Xiaoping's shoes. "I do not want Red Square to look like Tian'anmen Square," he said. For his part, Deng already regarded Gorbachev as reckless. By making political opening a condition for economic reform, he'd "disturbed the dialectic." He turned to his son and declared that the Russian Communist was an "idiot." "He won't have the power to fix the economic problems and the people will remove him," he stated.[38] Two weeks after Gorbachev's return to Moscow to deal with his own headaches and as Deng observed the decomposition of the Soviet empire and vowed to prevent the same fate for China, the army moved into the square. The chilling, televised slaughter in Beijing in June reminded viewers who had the guns and tanks—and who did not.

Repression in China and the reminder of mailed-fist sovereignty, however, did not stand in the way of creating a new script about the end of an old order and the birth of something new. The general secretary of the United Nations and scion of a Cairene establishment, Boutros Boutros-Ghali, proclaimed a new role for a reborn United Nations for a new world order, one in which the traditional nation-state and the architecture of sovereignty were passé. Now was the time for a new internationalism, now was a postnational moment. "The time of absolute and exclusive sovereignty . . . has passed," he announced in a blueprint for UN peacemaking. "Its theory was never matched by reality." Yet it would be on his watch that the United Nations would be dragged into civil wars where sovereignty really did break down in Somalia, Angola, Yugoslavia, and Rwanda, which left the United Nations with a reputation for neglect and utterly overwhelmed by demands on its Blue

Helmets to stop fratricidal war. Between 1945 and 1989, the United Nations approved seventeen peacekeeping operations in total; between 1990 and 2006, *it approved twenty per year*. As the political order dissolved under the pressure of the transformation, a growing business in force for hire—contracted mercenaries—proliferated. The privatization of force took hold long before the misbegotten decision by allies to invade Iraq in 2003.[39]

The brutality of the transformation could not be dismissed. But it could be forgotten. Realities motivated a scramble for narratives of their emergence. Elections of Ronald Reagan and Margaret Thatcher, market reforms in East Asia, transitions to democracy in Latin America, and the end of apartheid in South Africa released new actors and validated ideas aimed to reinvent the tired, post-Nagasaki world. In the end, the breakup of the Soviet bloc was a fundamental turning point and capstone. It ushered in the last wave of decolonization, releasing Eastern Europe and Central Asia from an imperial yoke. The rewiring of the world economy was starting to be celebrated as a triumph of free-market foresight and corporate acumen. Investing in China, for instance, was not just good for China because it brought the bounty of the market, but it would also spread human rights and political liberty. To woo it into the WTO, President Bill Clinton and First Lady Hillary Clinton flew to Beijing to attend a state dinner at the Great Hall of the People overlooking Tian'anmen Square. The massacre of 1989 was all but forgotten, as were images of a Statue of Liberty paraded by students around the square, to be replaced by investment dreams gilded with a new rhetoric of liberty. Over shark fin soup and grilled beefsteak, the hosts, Jiang Zemin and his wife, Wang Yeping, and the Clintons, worked the banquet table. If China could stomach some Western preaching, foreign direct investment and Kentucky Fried Chicken would pour in. WTO members also had to agree to the bargain. At one point, Bill Clinton told a skeptical Congress on the eve of a decisive vote that China's entry into the WTO meant that "China is not simply agreeing to import more of our products; it is agreeing to import one of democracy's most cherished values, economic freedom. . . . It is likely to have a profound impact on human rights and political liberty." And with a nod to the emerging stakeholders in Silicon Valley, he added that "in the new century, liberty will spread by cell phone and cable modem."[40]

One of the most prominent cheerleaders was *The New York Times'* leading international correspondent, Thomas Friedman. His columns celebrated the promises of new technologies, new businesses, and new markets as the means to dissolve ancient enmities. His paean culminated in *The World Is Flat: A Brief History of the 21st Century* to announce the start of a new human era of togetherness, exchange, and unleashed entrepreneurial spirit on a recently leveled playing field. Here was a very short history of a century only five years into its existence. "I realized that this flattening had been taking place while I was sleeping, and I had missed it," he confessed. The work of a self-declared "compassionate flatist," the book merged anecdotes and opinion, travel and tech, to become a sensational bestseller, translated into dozens of languages, and lapped up by believers to make the word "globalization" a verbal rage.[41]

Readers could trace the word back to a 1983 article by Theodore Levitt in the *Harvard Business Review* (self-described as "the magazine for decision-makers") called "The Globalization of Markets." Levitt was, if anything, even more exalting than Friedman: "Gone are accustomed differences in national or regional preference. . . . The globalization of markets is at hand." New technologies of communications, travel, and trade "proletarianized" information, tourism, and commerce for the masses so that consumption would stitch the world together. He singled out the role of media and the arrival of a "Republic of Technology" that made all symbols universally available and the spread of mass consumption irreversible, so that McDonald's appeared on the Champs Elysées and in Ginza, Coca-Cola in Bahrain. "Nothing," he declared, "is exempt." The challenge was convincing business executives to get out of their foxholes and scale up for the big bang.[42]

Since deep interdependence distributed the source of its lifeblood, the triumphal spin also came from many parts. For decades, Latin American social scientists had been arguing that the pathway to development required uncoupling from the trading and financial systems engineered elsewhere. What became called "dependency theory" argued for extrication from world markets and sending multinationals packing. The 1980s flipped the script, to embracing dependence instead of resisting it. *More* dependency of what became branded "emerging markets" was the solution to debt and poverty traps. Hernando de Soto, the Swiss-raised Peruvian economist who extolled the virtues of Latin America's swollen informal sector and its bottom-up entrepreneurs selling lottery tickets and cigarettes on the streets of Lima, celebrated the emerging world—and became a global celebrity for advancing a new discourse of poverty-stricken entrepreneurship. To his credit, it was the poor who concerned de Soto; it was for the have-nots that he believed integration was most welcome, even if it was the haves who walked away with an inordinate share of the pie. Still, the point was clear: the pie was growing. Grow with it. Everyone should be a capitalist, regardless of creed or culture. The Rest needed to be more like the West and regard each other as possessive individualists in an ever more integrated, borderless market world. This was, he concluded, "the only game in town."[43]

The end of the Cold War shifted "the only game in town" from being a global condition to which one should resign themselves to being an apotheosis—at least from the vantage point of the so-called West. The fall of the Berlin Wall, the departitioning of Europe, and the swarm of privatizers, deregulators, and liberalizers into the former Soviet space gave Western liberals a sense of redemption after decades on the defensive. Few caught the zeitgeist more than the Washington-based *penseur* Francis Fukuyama. Once a conservative in the mold of Allan Bloom, Leo Strauss, and others who lamented liberals' slide into what they regarded as gutless, Gomorrahean relativism, Fukuyama did time in the hallways of the U.S. State Department and the RAND Corporation and came under the influence of grand strategy thinking. Owen Harries, coeditor of a neocon flagship journal, *The National Interest,* sought out Fukuyama for a piece connecting "history with the great traditions of political thought."[44]

Fukuyama published "The End of History?" in the summer of 1989.[45] By August, it was spotlighted in *Time* magazine and by influential columnists like George Will; it was the talk of Oxford and Cambridge common rooms (though I have to confess, since I was in one of them, that more people gabbed about the title than read the actual piece); the

French quarterly *Commentaire* featured a special edition to debate the article (at least the French did their reading). All this was before Peter Jennings of ABC and John Simpson of the BBC camped their crews in front of crowds tearing down the Berlin Wall in November—which gave "The End of History?" such prophetic qualities. In the essay, Fukuyama made the case, summoning Hegel's help, for the imminent desire of all humans for freedom and the ineluctable pressure against all forms of tyranny. Fukuyama never claimed that autocrats were destined to fall. It's just that they had a burden that democrats did not face: they had to suppress while democrats had to manage. And why the *end* of history? Fukuyama argued simply that democracy in its modern form no longer had any plausible rivals; history had played them out. The crises of the Eastern bloc manifested what a tradition of liberal philosophy, dating back to Mill, had been arguing about the underlying power of openness: in an open world, autocrats of the world had to expend so much energy to keep it closed. In that sense, they were more disposed to collapse than democracies. Fukuyama's tone reflected a dramatic shift in climate. Now, the West appeared to have won and the victory gave liberty some philosophical bona fides. For a while, at least. Not everyone was convinced. *Time* editor Strobe Talbott considered "The End of History?" as "The Beginning of Nonsense."[46] Many, however, seemed to be oblivious that there was a question mark at the end of the title; the essay's speculative qualities got buried in the triumphalism of the era. Fukuyama himself eventually clarified his thoughts and became decidedly gloomy about the post–Cold War world.

Meanwhile, events gave universalizers immediate reasons to gloat. Gloat they did, as well as preach, pontificate, and proselytize, so much so that they came to believe in the inevitability of free markets, open elections, and the need to export them worldwide—and not bother waiting for locals to tear down walls or push Party Central Committees to the margins. Social scientists brandished concepts like unipolarity, hegemony, and Empire with a capital *E* to describe a unified world unseen since the days of Marcus Aurelius. Pundits echoed them. By 2003, in a disastrous bookend to the jubilance of globalization, the United States led a "coalition of the willing" into a calamitous war and extended occupation of Iraq to bring democracy to the Middle East—under the pretext of ridding it of weapons of mass destruction and eliminating a world's despot. Why stop there? No sooner did Baghdad fall than the secretary of defense, Donald Rumsfeld, sent President George W. Bush a memo calling for "regime change" in North Korea. One of the architects of the whole saga, Paul Wolfowitz, had been arguing since the fall of the Soviet Union that U.S. foreign policy should use America's hegemony to take "preemptive" risks, exercising a right to intervene, invade, and occupy on behalf of a new world order.

Why wait for history to bend events to one's philosophy when one can use one's weapons to bend history?

In other corners of the world, the bravura from Washington and some European capitals did not so much ring untrue as merely hollow. From civil war–torn El Salvador to post-Communist Albania, "transitions" brought democracy. History looked like it had ended, but only if you didn't look too closely. Ambassadors of civil society swept in with NGOs while bankers and technocrats brandished market reforms. Seen from the eastern fringes of the Soviet empire, the end of the Cold War meant a flood of used Japanese cars and cheap Chinese tchochkes; Premier Gorbachev's vaunted "civilization" drained away, Russia languished, Asia took off.[47] At the other fringe of Eurasian socialist utopias, Lea Ypi remembered as a child the verbal gymnastics in post-Communist Albania: ritual dogmas of "fighting corruption" replaced "the anti-imperialist struggle," privatization substituted for collectivization, "transparency" replaced nauseous Party "self-criticism."[48] The end of history often meant lining up at embassies, forging documents, finding boats, and angling for Westerners to invite Resterners to conferences. The end of history and its moral compass were less something to celebrate than to accept.

The collapse of the USSR and the vice of the Washington consensus in "structurally adjusting" Latin America, Asia, Russia, and Africa gave the United States a momentary frisson unknown since the early post-1945 years that looked, according to its champions, like a permanent condition. The script to lace the world together with free trade agreements and open markets created an illusion that history was over with America back at the center.[49] In fact, something else, far more radical, was afoot. The multisided opening led to massive reordering that integrated Europe; distributed the source and exchange of ideas, products, music, art, and commodities worldwide; and hollowed out American manufacturing and attached American consumers to a dripline of Asian savings. The cumulative effects of the distributed attachments since the 1970s also transformed how strangers regarded each other, with consequences for thinking about strangers' obligations to each other.

Spectacles

The Sahel is a wide expanse of land separating the forests of Central Africa from the sands of the Sahara Desert. Stretching from Senegal in the west to Somalia in the east, over the centuries it has sustained empires, large cities, and extensive trade routes. It has also seen spells of drought. People had developed complex production, exchange, and migration systems to cope with weather patterns and the cycles of ocean currents. By the late 1960s, those coping mechanisms were in distress. Not a drop of rain fell between 1968 and 1972. Rivers and lakes evaporated. Pastoralists drove their herds farther and farther into shrinking pastures until humans and their animals died by the thousands wandering through the desert in search of missing oases. By 1974, Lake Chad was a puddle; the harbor piers of Timbuktu stood in caked sand. *The Wall Street Journal* predicted that up to thirty million people might die over the next year. "I never saw a drought so bad," one cattle herder said. "My father and grandfather never told me of so terrible a drought where so many people lost everything."[50]

While some blamed the skies, others noted that the real causes lay in changes in land use. This was no "natural" disaster. It was a human-made calamity born of the urge to expand the cotton and peanut frontiers northward in response to pressures to produce exports. Slash-and-burn clearing encroached on pasturelands. By the late 1960s, herds were converging on fewer wells and shrinking open fields of grass; herders were being accused of overgrazing even before the drought hit.[51] When rain finally returned, briefly, in 1972, it washed away the loosened topsoil; the organic matter and roots had been pulverized by monocrop tillage.

Then the drought came back, along with the wind, which lifted the powdered soil into clouds of dust. The drought would last until the mid-1980s, by which time the region had become a desert. Overcrowded, overgrazed, overexploited, over-everything, the Sahel became one more index of all that was wrong with development in the Third World. Pictures of a parched earth and wandering peoples anticipated the visual repertoire of climate change in our day.[52]

The Sahel was one of a growing number of examples of the ways in which the media, scientists, and activists posed basic questions about the effects of deepening interdependence on far-away places—and mobilized new practices of witnessing that questioned the relationship between wealth and indigence, production and precarity. Was there an ethical guidance system to square up to the way interdependence between strangers reconfigured their needs and disparities?

By the time news of the Sahel reached readers in New York and Paris, a revolution in media coverage, international scientific collaboration, and cross-border activism pushed moral questions into the public square. The French NGO Médecins Sans Frontières joined forces with the Brazilian photographer Sebastião Salgado in the Sahel. For eighteen months in 1984 and 1985, Salgado traveled back and forth across the stricken landscape. Now one of the world's most famous documentary photographers, Salgado was a twenty-six-year-old economics student concerned with poverty and inequality when the Brazilian dictatorship forced him to flee to France. One day, his wife, an architect, returned to their flat with a durable Pentax Spotmatic camera, a simple, 35 mm mechanical box with a screw-thread lens and no battery–perfect for excursion photography. Salgado found his tool to reveal extremes that, he felt, economics missed. He was no foreigner to drought; one of his first forays was to the backlands of northeast Brazil. For him, drought and hunger were "mostly a problem of distribution, not simply a natural disaster." When he reached the shores of Lake Faguibine and the prosperous way stations of Azouera in Mali, all he found was desert, with nomads, like the family in the image shown in Figure 5.4, with backs to Salgado, like the vanishing Native peoples a century earlier, walking into the blurred distance under 122-degree heat in search of food and shelter.[53]

FIGURE 5.4. Sahel.

Salgado's representations of the violence of the new landscape (some would say his aestheticization of despair) responded to moral ambiguities of an interdependence that drove societies to produce for someone else's consumption and unleash mass deprivation, which would be invisible without witnesses and their organizations. Deep interdependence coincided with—indeed spurred—the surge in visibility of connectedness and its emergencies.

To what effect? Did the ties that bound strangers together with the fibers of mutual self-interest produce mutual regard and sympathy in equal measure? Did practices of representing strangers to each other yield new normative bonds? Salgado and others were committed to reframing interdependence, changing the narrative, shifting the vision, aligning moral bearings with material ones, and solving the dilemma of distance even as container shipping and supply chains collapsed it materially. But many worried that the gap between interests and sympathies was not closing—and may even have been widening.

Some worried that the multiplication and hypercirculation of images of strangers' needs had the opposite effect, that of perverting mutuality into a one-sided portrait of need, as if distant strangers were the only ones who needed. In 1979, the government of Vietnam started to open Cambodia to reporters to convey news of how the Khmer Rouge regime had turned the country into killing fields. Gradually, international organizations like the International Committee of the Red Cross, a small, select Swiss humanitarian organization that had grown since the Nigerian civil war; the World Food Program; the British charitable relief agency Oxfam, which was growing by leaps and bounds; and others were allowed in. Jim Howard, the gruff socialist engineer for Oxfam, reported from Route 4, one of the key roads to destitute camps of refugees: "This was starvation at the worst Biafra level." From Tuol Sleng prison in Phnom Penh: "Quite horrific—like Auschwitz." His reports went to journalists. Predictions of a second Holocaust and two million dead by Christmas ricocheted around the world. NGOs launched unprecedented fundraising and public relations campaigns. President Jimmy Carter sent his wife, Rosalynn, to aid the drive and burnish the White House's humanitarian reputation. Dazed by jet lag and the horrors of refugee camps in Thailand, she had a visit that epitomized a problem with global witnessing. Trailing the First Lady was a pack of 150 reporters, camera crews, and photographers elbowing each other, refugees, and even her own Secret Service agents to get the money shot—hopefully of a stricken First Lady faced with an emaciated refugee. A Carter aide screamed at the United Nations High Commissioner for Refugees camp director, Mark Malloch Brown, "Create a photo opportunity! Create a photo opportunity!" until finally an aide separated one dying child from the arms of a Catholic priest so that Carter could hold the helpless infant. The press and her handlers got their shots.[54]

This spectacle of care and callousness provoked concern that not only was interdependence being recast as hyperdependence of one side (the ever-needy Third World) on the other (the ever-giving First World), but that it was commodifying need itself. A French theorist, Guy Debord, warned in the mid-1960s that life had been subordinated to a play of illusions: anesthetized viewers gazed blankly at a semblance of reality, its commodified form.[55] In his footsteps, a leading voice of

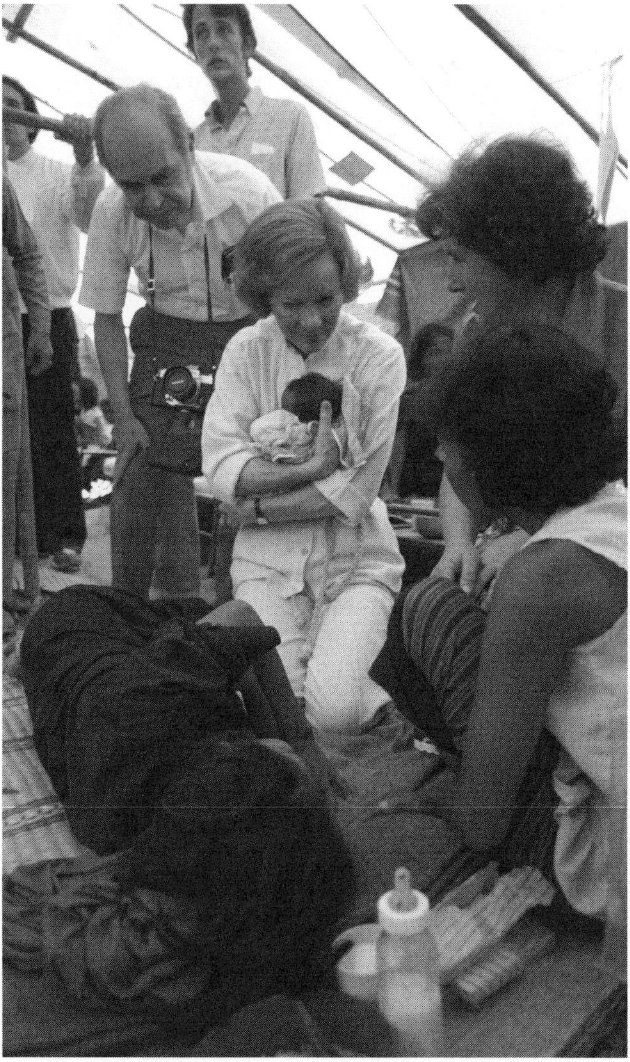

FIGURE 5.5. Cambodian Refugee Camp.

concern was the American writer Susan Sontag. Playwright, critic, and essayist, Sontag toggled between New York and Paris, American pop and French theory. She followed Vietnam reportage and went to Hanoi in a show of dissent. But, she wondered, did the images that so outraged her, of civilians bombed out of their huts in Vietnam and starving Biafran children, have the same effect on others? Or was the spectacle of suffering just a technicolor show, instantly reproducible, created by witnesses for some mass-entertainment drama? At stake was the survival of Adam Smith's impartial observer: a liberal myth in making markets moral, or as real-life moral agent? The parade of destitute Third World children looked like a carnival of pain marketed to the guilt-wracked and the overwhelmed. Her editors at *The New York Review of Books*, Bob Silvers and Barbara Epstein, urged her to pen her doubts. She did in a series of famous essays about commodified suffering as the green shoots of globalization were sprouting.[56]

Photos, Sontag felt, did little on their own to build attachments, giving instead merely the illusion, the image, of connection. They were "experience captured" for sale and circulation, and thus made it impossible to distinguish between the manufactured and the real. This was how a culture of consumption created a reality to make the past and present consumable. Photography had reduced tourism—thanks to Kodak's ever more "instant" powers—to the search for the photogenic moment to turn experiences into souvenirs. The pattern exploded when mobile phones became lens-based media with screens so that shots could be shared instantly, turning tourists into the subjects of their encounters for viewers to scroll and swipe their way through a self-replenishing catalogue of selfies.[57] It made the imaged world banal. What's more, any feeling of empathy or shock about the plight of strangers depended on the images being new. But the news business swamped the public square with an endless supply. "Unfortunately, the ante keeps getting raised—partly through the proliferation of such images of horror," she wrote. Instead of outrage, people felt anesthetized.[58] The result was "dissociative seeing," a habit of viewing but not really observing.

Dissociative seeing was supercharged by the press's relentless quest to capture and to commodify portraits of suffering strangers. This made others' pain more banal. Instead of promoting empathetic attachment, the industrialization of image making fostered detachment and ennui. Instead of being stirred, viewers became numbed. This position was staked out most cogently by Sontag, who posed fundamental questions about the practice of representing warfare. For Sontag, the mass circulation of photos of combat and civilian suffering created an "atrocity exhibition" that did more to sell the news than to end the war that sold the news.[59] With the advent of digitized media, the explosion in quantity and the accelerated speed of circulation of photos has heightened the debate and given rise to a sense of crisis around our fractured unity, unease, and skepticism about how to bear witness to what strangers do to each other and the extent to which human sympathies might keep pace with their material entanglements.

Sontag's critique has stuck; her message about media saturation and humanitarian fatigue would not go—and has not gone—away.[60] In effect, strangers became *more* intervisible to each other as they became *more* interdependent. Deepening the interdependence did nothing to resolve Adam Smith and David Hume's dilemma of distance; it highlighted the problem and burdened even more the impartial observer with the challenge of keeping sympathies aligned with self-interests. The dilemma was not just unsettled. That it was so graphic made it more unsettling. The effect set off a quest for a normative order to keep pace with its material structures.

Moral Globalization?

The capitalist only-game-in-town narrative provoked counterframings. These had two main taproots to yield a shared sense of togetherness of strangers that were not reduced to the transactions of an international division of labor and the merger of interests. The first was to imagine human security as a global concern, not a national one. The second was the ripening of earth science, which recast the planet as an enclosed and inescapable survival unit. Combined, they challenged an exclusively market-based framing for interdependence and forced a reckoning with the ethics and externalities of a conjoined world. Combined, they pushed imaginings of interdependence beyond the market parameters associated with globalization. Combined, they expanded the meaning of globalization.

Emphasis on human security emerged from an acknowledgement that human rights and needs were at risk around the world, and required norms and actions that went beyond ideas of national security and the national security state as manager of hazards. Nation-states were not just being stripped bare, as Raymond Vernon put it. They were increasingly being held accountable for the (mis)treatment of their citizens at home *and* for colluding and enabling the abusers across borders. Here, the 1970s legacy of the Vietnam War, the specter of napalmed villages in South Vietnam, the arrest of poets and scientists in the Soviet bloc, and death squads in Santiago and Buenos Aires, prompted lawyers and activists to reframe accountability of states on a new scale. To restore the moral credentials of the American state after Indochina, news of covert overthrows of democracies in Latin America, and the Watergate scandal, the U.S. Congress in 1975 adopted Section 502B of the Foreign Assistance Act. It bolstered human rights monitoring in the State Department and banned military assistance to governments guilty of failing basic decency stress tests. The fourth estate, already enlisting younger truth-seeking reporters who dispensed with some of the norms of objectivity to tell sympathetic stories of underdogs and victims, positioned itself as a moral guardian unconstrained by national passports and loyalties. What was new was the scale of solidarity, advocacy, and network building that mirrored the thickening communications systems and value chains that were globalizing the world economy. It was not just that gross violations were on the rise. New practices of mobilization around new norms—backed by foundations, risk-taking newspapers, and activist scholars—brought new actors and grassroots movements to the global stage to hold states accountable for what they were doing within and across borders.[61]

December 11–13, 1981, an American-trained battalion of Salvadorean soldiers marched through remote villages in the province of Morazán and slaughtered over a thousand peasants. They withdrew, thinking that no witness survived. But rumors spread of a terrible atrocity. Magnum's Susan Meiselas and Raymond Bonner of *The New York Times* grabbed their packs, Meiselas her Leica, and trekked into the hamlets from the Honduran side of the border. Alma Guillermoprieto of *The Washington Post* followed a few days later. Their reports confirmed what the Army and the U.S. embassy denied. There were fresh mass graves, bones, and skulls littered across the grass, and cornfields strewn with rotting corpses of children who had tried to escape. There was also a survivor who

FIGURE 5.6. El Salvador.

witnessed the slaughter, Rufina Amaya. In the mayhem, she had managed to crawl under a fence, hide in a patch of pine trees and maguey, and had watched as soldiers beheaded her husband and murdered her four screaming children. Meiselas photographed her days later, brow furrowed, in a fresh dress, eyes fixed on the earth in front of her.[62] Amaya's testimony took a while to come out, but the contours of what had happened soon made the front page of the *Washington Post* and *New York Times* a day before President Ronald Reagan was due to certify that the Salvadorean forces were "making progress" in their atrocious human rights record.[63] The indignation was immediate. El Salvador was one of rising numbers of cases of reporting about poverty and cruelty overseas that were entangled with and linked to policies made at home. Though witnessing and monitoring often blurred the line between detached news and *engagé* reportage, these new practices shaped what Kathryn Sikkink has called a justice cascade and, falteringly, unevenly, turned the moral compass of international relations.[64]

News about and atrocity images like Meiselas' fueled a transnational movement and calls to hold states accountable for violations against their citizens. But there was something else: the urge to hold states (like the United States) accountable for what they did to enable *other* states to behave atrociously. Jacobo Timerman, the Argentine journalist imprisoned and tortured by the junta, noted in 1984 that "a new phenomenon in recent years has been the emergence of several organizations—Americas Watch, Helsinki Watch, Amnesty International—that publish detailed accounts of human rights abuses. The victims are named; their murderers and torturers are named; their methods are examined; . . . the responsibility of the international community is assessed." The "machinery of justice" was often ponderously slow, not least because states were in the business of squelching truths at home, which required solidarities and attachments beyond borders to do what was so perilous to do within borders. The head of Americas Watch, Aryeh Neier, excoriated the Reagan administration for cozying up to dictator-clients, disregarding international law, and for blaming victims for the work of death squads because Reaganites pursued a callow vision of national security. He questioned whether "national security interests are so vitally affected by the [civil] war in El Salvador as to warrant suspension of efforts to promote human rights." To top it off, Neier blasted the Reagan government for sacrificing American rights (like the right to complain to Washington about misdeeds, like the right not be lied to by one's own government), as well as the rights of strangers, on the altar of a narrowed definition of "security."[65]

Here lay tracks for a normative order in which the rights of citizens were entangled across borders. The right to live in peace or be told the truth was affected by the deprivation of rights of strangers elsewhere. Human rights activists in Argentina and Czechoslovakia argued that their curbed rights were determined by security paranoia in Washington and Moscow just as the spectacle of superpower misdeeds overseas fueled claims to rights to know in Washington and Moscow—albeit hardly in equal measure; media repression in the USSR made American truth-managers look like pikers.

The drive for mutual accountability across borders eventually fused with the urgency to prevent war that had been so integral to atomic diplomacy. Under the umbrella of "détente," superpowers had agreed to restrain weapons testing and to open diplomatic channels. Westerners wanted peace and joint security in a fractured Europe. Easterners, with the Kremlin at the helm, wanted recognition for puppet regimes. The result of protracted negotiations, the Helsinki Final Act of 1975 struck a balance. It acknowledged peaceful coexistence of East and West. The East got the recognition that Moscow wanted in exchange for—and here was the kicker—respect for human rights of citizens on both sides. Leonid Brezhnev even canceled the ritual military parade in Red Square on May 9 because, he said, "there is no need to rattle the tanks and missiles along the square during the period of the intensive struggle for peace."[66] The Danish prime minister claimed that it assured "the interdependence of the entire family of man." The Lithuanian dissident Tomas Venclova was appalled, however, that the Final Act accepted Communist rule. He dismissed the document as "too boring" to read. Little did he know that the conceded freedom to move would dig at the foundations of totalitarianism. Organizations of lawyers, writers, and scientists sprouted; "Helsinki" became a watchword for cataloguing Soviet-style abuses, especially restrictions on rights to mobility. Then came backlash. Arrests almost wiped out Moscow's Helsinki Watch Group; Reagan declared war on Americas Watch and considered withdrawing from the Helsinki process. In the end, though, the doctrine of human rights was too useful a moral cudgel with which to browbeat a fissuring Eastern bloc, especially as unrest grew in Poland. To scrap the treaties would forfeit a Cold War weapon.[67]

Human rights diplomacy pushed arguments about cross border care away from charity for "necessitous strangers" to the idea that the rights of the needy should be attended to because they affected the security of all strangers. This overlapped with other humanitarian movements, like the effort to promote lifesaving and basic health as a universal ambition where nation-states failed, whose ethics shaped the growth of organizations like Médecins Sans Frontières as one of several looking out for humans' basic needs for food, water, vaccines.[68] From a practical standpoint, humanitarian and human rights often blurred; concerns about bodily autonomy, suffering, and hunger began to be seen in mutualized terms about rights and security. The spectacle of starvation and malnutrition mobilized an imaginative identification between observers and observed bound by sympathy and entangled with self-interest.[69] The convergence led philosopher-activists like Henry Shue to champion basic or subsistence rights, like freedom from want, which had been part of an internationalist imaginary of 1945 but were sidelined by Cold War *realpolitik* and the Third World drive to sovereignty. Shue's concern was for a "moral minimum" for what the world could tolerate in order to be human(e)ly tolerable. He and others saw a homology between the threat of nuclear war and the destabilizing and moral-affronting effects of desperation and abject want. By the 1980s, Shue's attention broadened from food and medical minima to wider bodily security concerns like torture and the threat of nuclear weapons to human survival. His classic, *Basic Rights*, was dedicated to two antitorture activists from the Philippines and Indonesia, Sister Mariani C. Dimaranan and Yap Thiam Hien. Yes, there was an element of traditional caring involved, as one might expect from a thinker who'd considered being a Presbyterian minister. Shue's impatience with "fact-free" philosophy and witnessing of congressional hearings about U.S. aid to Iran and Chile drove him to think about subsistence rights as a moral pillar for an alternative foreign policy because it was in the interests of Americans to live in a fairer world.[70]

The bundling of new ideas and practices of rights and security across border took a leap with the end of the Cold War. The decomposition of the USSR removed East-West rivalry from clogging work across geopolitical divides. The decomposition of states like Yugoslavia, Rwanda, and occupied East Timor spotlighted the *inaction* of powerful states who might have done something about mass murder. For a moment in world history, transnational advocacy dovetailed with the idea of an activist international regime, including the United Nations as more than a peacekeeper, but a peacemaker, to compensate for foot-dragging, naked nation-states. On May 25, 1993, the UN Security Council approved unanimously—unthinkable in the Cold War or now—a statute forming a Yugoslavia tribunal to prosecute violators of "international humanitarian law" who were not necessarily linked to acts of war. This step departed from the old Nuremberg principle that tethered prosecutions to crimes against peace and conformed to a tradition of victors' justice. Investigations, tribunals, and chasing down of criminals did not require that violators transgress laws of war; they could be prosecuted for crimes against humanity, and the signatories were obliged to cooperate. When Louise Arbour, the chief prosecutor at the Yugoslavia tribunal, visited Washington in 1997 to urge the military to arrest war criminals (many of them hiding in the French sector of Bosnia), she argued for a NATO "track and snatch" approach to criminals. Faced with grumbling about the global reach of law enforcement, she burst out, "Everyone has a good reason why someone else should do it. We must break this entitlement to impunity!"[71] This was a good statement of what David Scheffer, another protagonist in the new international justice zeitgeist, called "the tribunal era," which culminated in the Rome Statute in 1998 and creation of the International Criminal Court (ICC).[72]

In so many ways, this shift in norms and laws was momentous. But the justice cascade can also be exaggerated. Indeed, it was often in the interests of advocates to overproclaim their influence in order to wield it. Getting compliance with global morality that governed what states (and perhaps even more, nonstates) could get away with was always uphill. Precepts of national sovereignty endured; securing the cooperation of national authorities in chasing down criminals proved as indispensable as it was hard. Many states did not recognize the authority of the ICC or its doctrine; the club of countries that voted against the statute included Israel, Iraq, Libya, Yemen, Qatar, China, and the United States (though President Clinton eventually signed the treaty, it was never ratified by Congress).

The underlying problem stems from the gap opened up by deep interdependence, between interests and understandings of how humans rely upon each other and the institutions that are deemed legitimate to govern those ties. Put another way, moral expectations of cocitizens of a nation outshine the regard for distant, unelected authorities who oversee dependency between strangers. Sympathies across borders paled beside the commitments among citizens within borders.

Herein lay the dilemma: sympathies among strangers struggled to keep pace with deepening self-interest between them. In this end-of-history moment it was nation-states that democratized, not international foundations, humanitarian organizations, and UN agencies—many of which were exempt from the accountability rhetoric that was being applied to naked nations. While a global normative regime challenged the rhetoric of "national security," institutionalizing an ethics of interdependence was vulnerable to the counterpush defense of the sovereignty of the nation-state, especially when those states were summoned to defend citizens against the hazards interdependence.[73] The gap resulted in growing fatigue and ennui as advocates mobilized—using atrocity images and eyewitness reportage—a public opinion whose sense of sympathies lagged behind their self-interests. At its worst, the moral fantasy of a global village created a delusional trap that led its apostles to hector and hound on behalf of necessitous strangers who were bereft of agency and who could only be saved by outsiders.[74]

Programming Survival

Still, there was an undeniable shift in new scales of moral attachment clad in the rhetoric of mutual human needs. This scale of attachment received a boost when fears about human survival got stirred into the mix of human needs. This brings us back to the alternative origin story of the word "globalization" as more than a market phenomenon. An example of how human security became reframed as a condition for world peace and survival appeared in the report of the Independent Commission on International Development Issues. It stands out because, for the first time, human needs were seen as so entangled that survival demanded a fundamental reversal of a centerpiece of sovereignty: the ability, indeed the right, of states to wage war. Peace was no longer just a matter of reducing war to safeguard peoples but a means to better meet the moral minima of a dignified life for all. Known as *North-South: A Programme for Survival,* or informally as the *Brandt Report* for its chair, the former chancellor of the Federal Republic of Germany, the report was a manifesto for the survival of the species. It attached human security to the survival of all humans. It emerged out of two disenchantments: first with a patronizing "aid" as a bandage for the have-nots, and second with "donor" countries' fatigue with aid. Both came to a head in a World Bank annual meeting in Manila in 1977, which led to a call for a new "Global Compact." The report was the response, fusing the language of ecological survival and economic togetherness with alarm about the arms race. The future demanded melting the First, Second, Third World divides to create an integrated whole in order to make the world more secure and more equitable. International lenders recognized that there was a looming threat coming from the Third World calling for a remapping of the international division of labor and its rules and institutions. Barbara Ward, a foremost advocate of combining ecology and equity into a model that averted a more direct confrontation between First and Third Worlds, visited the World Bank president, Robert McNamara, at his home in Washington. They spent an evening kicking around alternatives. "Why don't you find something for Willy Brandt to do?" asked Ward. "He's out of power and is finding it difficult to adjust to that and is rattling around. Why don't we try to use him on this?"[75]

The brain trust around McNamara agreed: this would be the road to a Global Compact. Shared self-interest was its glue. Brandt himself noted at the launch in December 1977 that the only way out of the impasse was to "seek out the mutual interests within our own industrial communities, and with the non-industrialised developing world."[76]

The *North-South* report deserves to be flagged as a milestone in the history of thinking about interdependence. For starters, the report put the term "globalization" into circulation when it invoked the "globalization of dangers and challenges" and the need to premise an alternative order on "principles of mutual interest." It coupled the cause of redistribution to the Third World to another, disarmament—the beating of swords into ploughshares on a new scale. By then, the World Bank chief and former U.S. Defense Secretary McNamara was mourning his mistakes in Vietnam and concerned that war was worsening poverty and poverty driving war. This formulation did not sit well with the military rulers in Latin America, Asia, and Africa who were seizing power as development faltered in the Third World. One Pakistani general lashed out at Global Compact talk, saying, "All we would get would be another lecture on how we ought to behave."[77] Others were disgruntled at the Washington duopoly of the World Bank and IMF; they preferred that the United Nations be the umbrella for a Global Compact and that it organize around the coordinates of the New International Economic Order project—a nonstarter from the point of view of wary First Worlders.

How to thread this needle, fix a global vision when the world's parts were so divided? As so often happens in these turning points, multiple agendas and projects got bundled into one and harmonized, some might say obscured, in the language of interdependence—and its emergency. In the end, the two lead authors were the former British prime minister Ted Heath and the secretary general of the Commonwealth from Guyana Sonny Ramphal. Citing the resources funneled into weaponry, the commissioners argued that the world had to choose, rather apocalyptically, between "destruction or development." The money being spent on "arming ourselves to death" could flow not to aid but to investment to mitigate hunger and disease, and to reduce sources of international conflict, which the report insisted had roots in global maldistribution, as it created conditions for spreading warfare and arms sales, especially in the Third World. This is why development was a matter of human survival: poverty was a source of insecurity and insecurity a source of instability—and a magnet for opportunistic arms merchants. A reduction of indigence among strangers would reduce global friction and allow states to roll back their arms spending and invest in reducing poverty. By plowing the dividends from unpurchased hardware into a World Development Fund, the developed and developing could gain alike by expanding and integrating markets and reducing the risks of war. Here was a virtuous cycle premised on mutual—though not equivalent—self-interests. The commissioners avoided worn out one-world talk and language of partnership. Redistribution via disarmament was in the self-interest of the haves, not an act of charity or other-mindedness. "Are we to leave our successors a scorched planet of advancing deserts, impoverished landscapes and ailing environments?" the report asked.[78] The report proceeded to outline a "new interdependence" of a rising and industrializing Third World, energy needs, the emergence of transnational firms, and the ecological risks of mass hunger.

What the report contained in vision it lacked in timing. January 1980 was an unfortunate moment to unveil a new vision. In the end, the *North-South* report did not survive the resumption of Cold War tensions in the 1980s. A second oil price shock of 1979 drove a wedge into the First–Third World alliance, Soviets poured their exhausted military energies into a ruinous war in Afghanistan, and American military aid to counterrevolutionaries in Central America bogged the White House in crippling scandals. But above all, the burden of a debt crisis pushed Third Worlders into the arms of creditors and the IMF.[79] The notion of a peace dividend from disarmament to fund human security needs got swamped out by the claims of bankers. The newly elected government of Margaret Thatcher dismissed it as wishful rubbish. Even a sympathetic social democrat like Gunnar Myrdal saw that such "a massive transference of capital to developing countries" prescribed by the commissioners was "rather futile."[80]

Still, events kept fears about embodied threats—and alternative global norms—alive. A renewed arms race and escalating nuclear terror mobilized millions to streets and squares from Tokyo to Toronto. After American forces began to plan to locate nuclear-tipped cruise missiles in the RAF Greenham Common base, "Greenham women," pictured in Figure 5.7, set up a camp—which lasted nineteen years—to obstruct trucks and to draw public attention to the secret plan. On December 12, 1982, thirty thousand women held hands and surrounded the six-mile perimeter.

The following year, fear and alarm reached new heights. A Korean civilian airliner strayed over Soviet airspace by accident and was shot down, killing 269 people. A massive wargame conducted by the North Atlantic Treaty Organization (NATO) nearly turned into direct confrontation. Millions went to the streets to protest Cruise and Pershing II missile deployments. Four hundred thousand people rallied in Hyde Park, London, on October 22. The Hague saw over a million protestors. The English historian E. P. Thompson's pamphlet *Protest and Survive,* lacerated a government manual on how to cope with an atomic bomb, *Protect and Survive*. A Sunday supplement to

FIGURE 5.7. Greenham Common.

many U.S. newspapers called *Parade* carried a story by the renowned futurologist and astronomer who had worked closely with the U.S. military until the Vietnam War shattered his confidence that scientists could remain objective while being funded by the defense industry, Carl Sagan. Sagan went public with a new menace, "nuclear winter," portraying what would happen to the planet beyond irradiation—dust clouds would plunge the earth into freezing darkness for a long time. Three weeks later, the American broadcaster ABC aired a sensational made-for-TV movie, *The Day After*. It depicted the aftermath horrors of a nuclear explosion for the citizens of Lawrence, Kansas. Viewers, including Reagan, who watched it in Camp David, were left shocked. The postshow discussion featured Sagan, who described the superpowers as irresolute enemies in a room "awash in gasoline" while wielding thousands of matches. It was not a mushroom cloud over a distant city that petrified people; it was "nuclear winter" that made everyone suffer. In *Parade*, Sagan had warned that the effect of a nuclear war would reduce human populations to prehistoric levels, "or *Homo sapiens* might become extinct."[81]

Letters poured into *Parade* editors, fifty thousand of them, addressed to the leaders of the United States and USSR. One junior high school student from Eugene, Oregon, told Ronald Reagan that "my friends are scared. Sometimes they think—Will we wake up to see the world tomorrow?" Then he pleaded: "P.S. Please don't make a dumb move."[82] Insecurity—near and far—was a unifying condition that put the world at risk. If everyone were a stranger consuming each other's products, everyone could also become a victim of distant calamities. The promise of flat-earth prosperity overlapped and collided with imagery and reporting that produced an altogether different narrative of interdependence.

Patient Earth

While a normative order was emerging out of a new fusion of rights and risks that crossed borders, there was a collateral effect of deep interdependence that echoed the alarm about nuclearized war. Here too advocacy networks of scientists, activists, and media altered the normative language of integration—and highlighted the need for concerted, cooperative responses to its externalities. There was one difference: instead of linking interdependence to human rights and security, environmentalists grappled with a diffused challenge that could not be so easily identified with a human face either as victim or perpetrator. Growing awareness of the ecological spillovers of market integration revealed the complexity of interdependence—and made it more abstract, distributed, and the source of a massive collective action problem. So the world learned about the effects of its common carbon addiction and confronted images of a planet that was in greater need than ever and yet logjammed because the prosperity from interdependence made its beneficiaries protagonists in the mounting risks of calamity.[83]

The Stockholm United Nations Conference on the Human Environment in 1972 set a tone that echoed what economists and others were saying about national sovereignty. One journal pronounced, "The fact is that the classical nation state is largely irrelevant in the environmental crisis." *New Scientist* called for "a genuine supranational community."[84]

From the comforts of living rooms and cafés, Westerners had to confront how old divides from Resterners were dissolving into one risky and perilous common fate. Teams of scientists around the world were turning to what two young Yale physicists, John Harte and Robert H. Socolow, called "patient earth."[85] The planet, in their view, suffered from maladies that humans had inflicted upon it in the past, from the exhaustion of Mesoamerican forests that led to the collapse of the Mayan civilization to the North American dust bowl in the 1930s. The difference now: the calamities were on a new scale.

Not everyone agreed. To Third World ears, the ecological turn sounded suspiciously like old Western preaching, replacing civilizational talk with conservationist evangelizing. The Chinese delegate to Stockholm, now that Taiwan had been forced to cede its place at the United Nations to the People's Republic of China, used his maiden event to lambaste Western capitalism for all human troubles. The Indian prime minister, Indira Gandhi, gave a concluding speech—to several standing ovations—in which she demanded that poverty, not pollution, be the at the center of the human drama.[86]

Thereafter, environmental statecraft had to grapple with the divide between conservation and development. But it was a divide that did not necessarily nor always pit haves against have-nots. Plenty of voices from the Third World made the case for environmental caution and many from the First World argued for unfettered growth. There were efforts to mend the divide. Gro Harlem Brundtland, head of the UN World Commission on Environment and Development, issued a sequel to the *North-South* report and folded in an environmental dimension. Called *Our Common Future*, it tried to patch the heated divide between conservationists and development advocates. The skilled Norwegian politician had been tasked to thread the needle of meeting "the needs of the present without compromising the ability of future generations to meet their own needs." The compromise term was "sustainable development." The commission made the term famous. Some thought it was an oxymoron: the Third World was under pressure to pay off debts by pushing commodity frontiers into the Amazon and Sahel while being confronted with evidence and reportage about deforestation and desiccation. "The Earth is one but the world is not," *Our Common Future* famously conceded.[87]

Emerging from this entanglement was an "earth system," a term coined in 1983 to frame the interaction of atmospheric, biospheric, cryospheric, and geospheric forces to create a whole. Earth systems echoed human security thinking: scientists and activists thought about intractable connections between strangers in the same scales and with the same complexity and growing sense of urgency. Strangers were all in this together, no one lives outside the whole; escape—short of colonizing outer space—is a pipedream for science fiction. Especially after 2010, with evidence that climate change was disrupting food chains and causing massive human migration, earth system and human security system thinking would start to converge. The atmosphere, land uses, and geological and marine spheres, scientists argued, had to be seen as one complex, integrated "system" whose parts affected each other in ways that new forms of data collection and computational capacities could model. It was not enough to look at the clouds without thinking about glaciers, ocean currents without considering atmospheric layering, and the feedbacks between them.[88] International coalitions of scientists, often with the imprimatur of the United Nations, which was becoming a forum for a "new science of the earth," weighed in on discourse and policy and often aligned with local NGO's to track the effects of global warming.

One reason was the deluge of news and images. From African savannas to Amazonian forests, images and stories of the destruction of habitats raised alarm. Doomsday scenarios were no longer the stuff of imaginary mushroom clouds and Godzilla movies, something that *could* go wrong. Something *was* going wrong. While images of the Sahel drew the eye of the beholder to sand and taught skin, there was another lens-based transformation going on to reveal a different view of Earth. If 1972 brought the plight of the Sahel to global attention, the *Blue Marble* shot framed a colorful yet lonely planet hovering in the endless black. Viewers were witness to two scenes at once: delicate beauty in the stars and destitution on the ground, fragile Eden from above and the relentless advance of desert below. The images and the data related to them questioned the very model that was integrating the world while putting the planet at risk.

It was from the skies that environmental consequences of economic integration were becoming visible. Scientists filled journals, international watchdog units, and UN data gatherers with evidence of solar cycles, desertification, and as Wallace Broecker of the Lamont Geological Observatory called it, "climate surprises." When *Mariner 9* entered its orbit around Mars in 1971, there were hopes of close-ups of the Red Planet's craters and canyons. Instead, what came back from deep space telemetry was a portrait of a planet enveloped in a massive dust storm. Dust, it turned out, could have profound effects on atmospheric life; what happened in the air could change what happened on the ground. Dust, smoke, and CO_2 changed the atmospheric filtration system that buffered Earth from the sun. On June 26, 1974, *Time* magazine announced provocatively to the world that our "prolonged streak of exceptionally good climate has probably come to an end."[89] Peter Wadhams, one of the world's foremost ice scientists, observed thinning ice and began taking his own photos of ancient ice as its melt seeped away from polar caps and high-altitude glaciers. He began to worry that, if the situation remained unchecked, summer sea ice might disappear altogether. Were these the first signs of an Arctic death spiral?[90]

Meanwhile, satellites and spacecraft quietly went about their work eyeing the planet's surface with increasing precision. In 1972, NASA launched a satellite with two sensors dedicated to taking the first unclassified photos of the earth's resource management. Later called Landsat, the satellite's radio sent visual data to ground stations. By the 1980s, despite budget cuts, orbital image-making advances on French and Japanese satellites yielded troubling insights into water movements and climate.[91]

A new generation of shuttles and satellites—this time from the National Oceanic and Atmospheric Administration—was picking up data on what was happening on land. On September 28, 1987, images came back to Earth of over five thousand fires burning in the Amazon. The burning was so intense it could be seen from the atmosphere. Fire, noted Brazil's environment minister, Albert Setzer, "has a strange effect on people's minds. It attracts their attention." Brazil's president, José

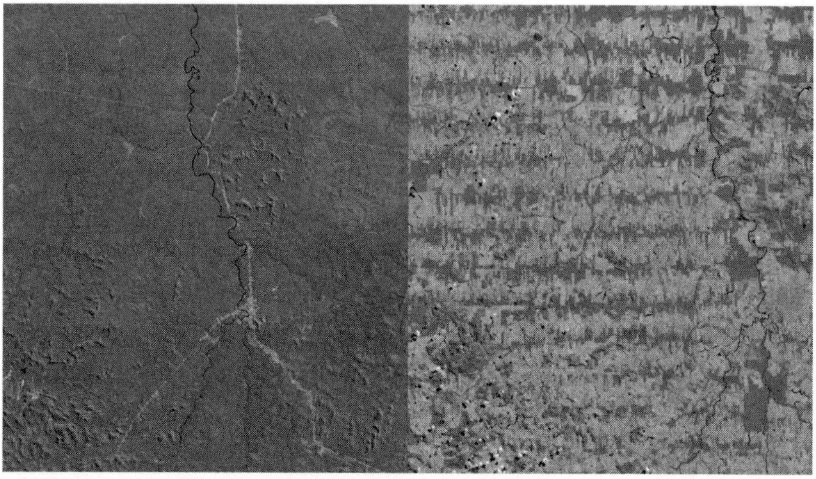

FIGURE 5.8. Amazon Burning. This image shows the effects of the north-south road artery cut through the Amazon by the military and branches of secondary roads. Settlers cleared around the main artery and then spread outward. Farmlands grew and began to merge. From the sky, a fishbone pattern appeared; the spot in the middle is a pop-up city.

Sarney, hardly an environmentalist, had to make a speech about the Amazon and pledged to ban burning.[92] Figure 5.8 shows two Landsat images from 1975 to 2021.

As the visual evidence of mass deforestation went viral, lawmakers worried about the consequences far away. The rubber-tapper activist in the Amazon, Chico Mendes, appeared before a U.S. Senate subcommittee and met officials at the Inter-American Development Bank (IDB), which had financed the roads into the forest. Leaders of wealthy nations grew more alarmed about distant tree burners and pushed their international financial institutions to "incentivize" conservation. To many, changing behavior with the market logic of rewards seemed utterly anemic. And yet, even that was enough to spiral into murder. Months after Mendes's testimony, a rancher's son pumped bullets into Mendes's chest. The Amazon was a battleground in the fate of the planet. His assassination was in the morning papers the following day in Paris and London.[93]

After satellites came drones. Fixed-wing, unmanned aircraft have been around for a long time. As always, war stimulated innovation and expanded surveying and spying applications. Military uses gave way to commercial ones. It took a while to create reliable and economical remotes. Getting cameras and sensors aboard that would not weigh down the tiny, unmanned craft or make them targets for antiaircraft fire was another challenge. They were also pricey. Eventually, firefighters, disaster relievers, and border patrols started to equip them with remote, aerial lenses. In 2006, the U.S. federal government issued commercial drone permits. Seven years later, Amazon, not *the* Amazon, announced plans to create a drone-based delivery system; demand for permits soared and went global.

The skies were not just the observatory from which to monitor the earth's surface; what was happening on the surface transformed the skies. *The New York Times* reported on 1974 findings from the New Hampshire Hubbard Brook Experimental Forest, supported with photos, that chronicled the ways in which rain was killing the local livestock. One prominent scientist and backpacker, Carl Schofield, was appalled, and began to report on the "extinction" of entire species in New York's backyard. Then came the stories of peeling paint and corroding bridges, replete with lurid and ominous pictures of the everyday effects of processes unleashed far away. Industrial smokestacks were belching filth into the clouds, which came back to earth as "acid rain"—sulfur dioxide and nitrogen oxide gluing to water molecules in the atmosphere hundreds of miles away and coming down as lethal drops. According to Michael Oppenheimer, who set aside his astrophysics research at Harvard to join the Environmental Defense Fund in the mid-1970s, this was one of the pivots in environmental thinking about the damage caused *through* skies by what humans were doing on earth. Acid rain was a concept shifter—for the visual effects of smelter emissions in one place on another far away required seeing through biospheric lenses that connected strangers and their landscapes.[94]

There was something basically discordant about the news. How could the planet prosper and face extinction at the same time? It made no sense; what to choose? There was so much more wealth—and risk. The first was easy to touch and feel. It was real. But those abstract images of a planet one could only see from afar—what did they really mean? To make things harder to unscramble, it was the conditions of prosperity, cheap carbon and cheap credit that fueled the risks. Moreover, in places showcased for their deforestation and biohomogenization, the reply was this: we want and need growth, and you want and need our stuff!

After Rio

The end of the Cold War removed geopolitical and ideological restraints to tackling the problem of globalization's externalities. For the next generation, ecological summitry struggled to reconcile the unreconcilable: deep interdependence and its bounty were driving the earth crisis while creating normative awareness of the common threats to human security. The G7 club of rich-country leaders met in Houston in 1990; there they urged their financial institutions to step up with market-friendly solutions to ecological problems. The newly unified German government pledged to support Amazonian conservation; the World Bank became a "trustee" with the Brazilian minister of the environment. By the time the Rio de Janeiro Earth Summit was mounted in 1992, Brazil's president, Fernando Collor de Mello, wanted to elevate the Amazon as a stage for his leadership. One hundred heads of state, 1,420 accredited NGO delegates, an additional eight thousand NGO representatives, and thousands more journalists convened. It was at Rio—with the backing of corporate interests and the International Chamber of Commerce, which were not opposed to environmental regulation but lobbied for it not to interfere with the free flow of trade (they conveniently espoused the virtues of self-regulation and the power of voluntary pledging)—that "sustainable development" became an all-but-official slogan for a post–Cold War, postimperial, civically engaged summit, one that bowed to environmentalists while touting business. It was a consummate effort to have it all ways, markets with morals, a green capitalism.[95]

Ripe for the new cable television age, the Rio event was a carnivalesque exhibition of protestors, street theater troupes mocking the jet-setters, and teams of CNN and BBC crews parked in front of the Sheraton. Inside, the event ended with nonbinding agreements and numeric pledges. Echoing the mantra of the post-1989 zeitgeist, they called for NGOs to mobilize as well as for more research from scientists for a joint "strategy" to meet the biophysical crisis, integrating activism and expertise.[96]

In retrospect, the next decade was as dispiriting as it was predictable. Having sidestepped the basic tensions and collective action problems inherent in a distributed capitalist system that relied on cheap fossil fuels and credit to power it, summiteers grappled with intractability while confronting more and more evidence that the risks of globalization were mounting. The Kyoto Summit five years after Rio, upon which so many hopes were pinned, was a failure. Monitoring was complex. Implementation was costly. Commitments were unenforceable and above all based on the illusion that fossil fuels would soon become uneconomical—when in fact the shale revolution would make carbon even cheaper! The obsession with replacing all fossil fuels with renewables meant there was little distinction between types of carbon; coal demand, the worst culprit, soared by 70 percent in the decade after 2000—and China and India accounted for 90 percent of it. And then, to cap things off in 2001, President George W. Bush promised to defend American sovereignty against treaties and reneged on the Kyoto Protocol. This gesture epitomized the cynicism that surrounded the problem; it was a toothless accord anyway. To twist the knife, three months later, when terrorists slammed civilian airplanes into office buildings and fields in the United States and turned jet fuel into bombs, Bush was only too happy to welcome the promises of allies to honor another treaty, Article 4 of NATO that pledged each member to come to the defense of the other if they were attacked. In the meantime, one by one countries went silent or failed to meet their own pledges. The letdown of Kyoto and the even more abject failure at the next summit in Copenhagen in 2009 opened a breach between what was known about the fragile earth system and the institutions created to manage it.[97]

Fragile Unity

The rewards of a market-based unity that relied on carbon and credit collided with the visible externalities that fueled alarm about human security and planetary survival. Deepening interdependence broke the stalemate of a tired post-Nagasaki order that depended on American centrality while dismantling the remnants of Europe's empires. It also challenged the powers of the nation-state to manage the hazards of relying on strangers—just as those risks were growing. Out of the rhetoric about global villages, flat earths, or one world emerged a spectrum of feelings about the need for strangers and the hazards of their behavior, from alarm to elation. In between, there were endorphin rushes from fast-fashion shopping for clothes made in Bangladesh or Morocco.

The earth was one, but the world was far from unified—deep interdependence distributed sources of legitimacy and power across more societies even as it wound them together in a common reliance on carbon and credit.

The result was an unprecedented tension, a tension born of integration with fragility. Deep interdependence spread mutual needs widely and under precepts that they should be governed by pluralistic and inclusive norms and institutions. More countries, more voices, more rights meant more of just about everything, including expectations and frustrations exhibited in ritual environmental grandstands at Rio de Janeiro, Kyoto, and Copenhagen, so much so that even a sympathizer would not be blamed for blurring the summitry, their declarations, and their acronyms into each other. The same with the annual meetings of the World Economic Forum where *Homo Davos* gathered for some Alpine networking. To say that the system was ailing from "collective action problems" barely begins to capture the difficulty. The world was more integrated and differentiated than ever, tackling ever more challenges together while seeming to fall ever shorter of the lofty promises. Globalization's apostles, however, could not admit how precarious and contested globalization had become until the conditions that had buoyed it—flows of cheap carbon and easy credit—plunged into crisis.

6

Great Displacements

A SHORT HISTORY OF THE TWENTY-FIRST CENTURY

Naked Interdependence

In late summer 2008, America's fourth-largest investment bank, Lehman Brothers, a Wall Street bastion since the global opening of the 1850s, filed for bankruptcy. Its failure brought on a near collapse of the world economy. Having made credit an elixir of deep interdependence, monetary authorities scrambled to salvage a system, not to change it. They pumped billions of dollars, euros, and yen into the economy and relied on technocratic tools and inscrutable interventions to prevent a meltdown. The People's Bank of China poured 12 percent of the country's GDP into a stimulus package. Public funds went to rescue big firms while millions lost their homes and jobs. Millions. According to the IMF, the ranks of the world's unemployed jumped from 30 million in 2007 to 210 million by the end of 2009, while debt became even more important for holding the world economy together.[1]

The global financial crisis and its handling became the watershed that separated an era of fluid globalization from an era of frictional interdependence. Rulers eyed each other with growing suspicion while the ruled watched their shared futures vaporize into blackening clouds of anxiety. Weather disasters, proliferating nuclear weapons, pandemics, a return to military aggression, smartphones as portable magnets of algorithmic addiction, wasteland scenes of civil war—the list of dangers was endless. What made 2008 decisive was that the moment opened people's eyes to the extent of use of a concept—leverage—to turn a single asset into multiplying means to lend, to borrow, and to remunerate the brokers of global interdependence who put it all at risk. Governments were then summoned to bail them out while strapping taxpayers and slashing public goods. Moneyed meritocrats in turn congratulated themselves for having "saved" the system they imperiled and rewarded themselves with eyewatering bonuses.

The rift laid bare injustices of deep interdependence and limits of the managerial class who dismissed critics as whiners. It broke the one-world, flat-earth, end-of-history narrative of endless opening and blissful fluidity—and gave way to a rising sense of risk, hazard, and threat, and the specter of zero-sum fears. Code words of liquidity gave way to codes of emergency. It no longer mattered that deep interdependence had buoyed hundreds of millions out of poverty. Looking back, all that lingered was dysphoria fueled by the surge in human displacement. Now was the time to raise walls, to add razor wire to the fencing, to protect citizens from outsiders with tariffs and visa restrictions, and to pour scarce funds into a new arms race scented with tear gas. Globalization sowed the seeds of a backlash and calls for a retreat behind the comforting barricades of the nation.

The rescue operation staved off a collapse, but it set off an outrage that took years to play out and drained legitimacy from the very groundnorms, institutions, and actors—tagged as "globalists"—that had made deep interdependence. Monetary authorities were seen as tools of jet-setting one-percenters they were supposed to regulate. One-percenters stopped looking like the job creators they called themselves. Vintage authorities of all sorts—regulators, heritage media, scientists, scholars—all tumbled in public regard. Brexiteers told Britons that they were sick of experts. Brazilian and American public health officials during the Covid-19 pandemic needed armed bodyguards. Reporters probing the possibility of a wet market origin story for the virus in Wuhan were dismissed as conspirators by mainstream media and those with business interests in China—until it became clearer that the cranks may have had a point. But who could really tell since the search for truths had been weaponized well before Covid-19 killed almost seven million people?

From resentment grew resistance. And from some darkened quarters of resistance grew a yearning for vengeance. The language of the nation became absorbed into the rhetoric of reaction; the palette of the flag became the rainbow of backlashing against a pluralist world of distributed burdens and benefits. In the depths of the Covid-19 mandated lockdowns and vaccinations, one Canadian veteran who had served in Bosnia, Afghanistan, and Iraq ruminated about his sacrifice and why he "had to go do what [he] did in all those different countries." As he did so, he said, "I discovered who the real enemy of this world is: the elites, the ones who are controlling what we hear, what we see, what we read, our education system, our monetary system."[2]

Disenchantment stoked a return to nation-states as the guardians to shelter people from the risks and hazards of interdependence whose management had been outsourced to nonstate, supranational actors; fear and anger tilted world politics away from cooperation toward competition and zero-sum rivalry—and more risk. Before the outbreak of the Covid-19 pandemic, teams of American doctors and scientists were stationed in China and worked together to stop scourges, like avian flu. In July 2019, the U.S. government under Donald J. Trump pulled them all out of the Chinese Center for Disease Control and Prevention and closed the Beijing office of the American Centers for Disease Control (CDC). By December, all that remained were two epidemiologists, an information technology specialist, and a few local employees working on seasonal influenza.[3] Washington accused China of stealing knowledge; China did not help matters when it became clear that there was a problem in Wuhan. "We must actively respond to international concerns," Xi Jinping told the politburo, "and tell a good story of China's fight against the outbreak."[4] On the eve of the coronavirus spilling into the nerves of air traffic, upholding the national good story was what mattered most. This was not a helpful response in a world that needed one—not a sign that China's leadership quite understood what it meant no longer to be catching up.

The spiral after 2008 cleared the grounds for a nativist and competitive surge that recycled anger at plutocrats and suspicion of strangers into support for strongmen who blamed newcomers, minorities, allies, and partners, and aimed to restore lordship over smaller and weaker neighbors. At the top of the blame heap was the United Nations and its affiliates, framed as a warehouse for global conspiracies and cover-ups masked by do-good rhetoric for strangers—and never for citizens who ponied up contributions.

We have seen this spiral of reaction against vulnerabilities to strangers before. Always latent in the dynamics of interdependence, the urge to hoard, not share, compete, not cooperate gained the upper hand in the 1930s. We know how that turned out. Many feared a repeat of the cycle. As nativists staked ground, public squares and bookstore displays filled with postmortems on liberal globalism and prophecies of civil war. The idea and practice of "sanctions," pushing a thumb down on the financial and trading windpipes, starting slowly after the Revolution in Iran in 1979, crept back into economic diplomacy and the securitization of interdependence. The world hovered between more shared risk and more rancorous response.[5]

The financial crisis and its aftermath revealed a contradiction. Deep interdependence was as inescapable as it was precarious: a tightly coupled world had few buffers to prevent a crisis in one corner from whiplashing another.[6] And yet, this declining system had no offramps, no way out. Deep interdependence was interlocking and the cost of delinking seemed punishing. In 1970, the Berlin-born economist Albert O. Hirschman penned a classic in the social sciences that anticipated many of the problems of contemporary capitalism. To depict how people respond to decline and disenchantment, Hirschman formulated a trilogy: people could double down on *loyalty* to the slumping organization, they could raise their *voices* and protest, and they had the option of *exiting* for another job, country, or brand. They could even mix their strategies. The threat of exit could, for instance, magnify the power of voice. Warning a boss that you might quit will get their attention (unless, of course, they want you out); telling a superpower that you are considering cozying up with their rival can get you on the schedule. But the reverse is also true. Having no way out reduces your leverage. Why would a boss listen if your only option is joining the millions who are already jobless? Why would a predator superpower pay any heed if, as American president Donald Trump liked to explain to needy allies, the other party has no cards to play?

What deep interdependence did was eliminate or severely restrict the exit options, which thereby weakened the power of voice and amplified the frustrations, especially among those who found themselves on lower rungs of, or slipping down, the world ladder. It was one of the ironies of the emergent era that so much disenchantment led to so much antiestablishment protest, and yet there was little room to move, to champion an alternative. Where was an indebted Chad, Argentina, or Greece to go? Countries on the borderlands of aggressive neighbors found themselves ever more compressed; the whole rim of the former Soviet Union and embittered Russia became a battleground for hackers, meddlers, and pawns.

If countries had nowhere to go, this was less true of their peoples. It was after 2008 that millions upon millions began to flood out of struggling states, only to get snared in a doom loop of statelessness. The drama showed the entrapping nature of interdependence; the deeper it became, the more hazardous it was for the leveraged and the more punishing were the few escape options.[7] Without exit or loyalty, where was voice to go? The impossibility of escapes or alternatives turned frustration into fury.

But a new Depression never came. Despite the punditry, fascism has not been on some ineluctable march. The world did not get a repeat of global war; there was no 1914 or 1939 moment. Though endism filled the airwaves, the end never quite came. Globalization was over. But interdependence, if anything, deepened.

In fact, nation-firsters did not aim to undo deep interdependence but to restructure it. They sought to hoard its rewards and externalize its costs, often using the very leverage wielded by the globalists they now excoriated for having abandoned forgotten heartlanders. Debt, commodities, advanced technologies, vaccines, data—they all sutured the world into one unit but became the instruments of a geoeconomic struggle over global stratification. The nativists' goal: to feast on catastrophism and replace the connected pluralism of the old age with hardened edges of a new hierarchy. One effect was to widen the gap between those who had access to strong states capable of bending interdependence in their favor and those who did not. Or who had no state at all.

One familiar narrative for this is crisis and collapse. Allusions to history's calamities, the sack of Rome, Mayan implosion, and epic upheavals spice up headlines. They sell news. But they also mislead. Old habits and social forces rarely collapse and disappear to make way for successors. That is not how most of history's crises unfolded, anyway. Most do not turn into apocalyptic "levelling" shocks.[8] Indeed, one reason why the blows of disastrous wars, economic upheaval, and a lethal pandemic did not roll out the carpet for the Four Horsemen of the Apocalypse was because the groundorms and institutions built by generations of interdependent strangers defused the tensions, contained the financial fallout, and delivered vaccines that were the dividend of scientific collaboration. Because they worked, they were taken for granted, increasingly fatigued, and overburdened.

Meanwhile, behind the crisis, the technologies and materialities of interdependence rapidly rewired themselves—though the old groundnorms and institutions increasingly lagged. That is the nature of the twenty-first century crisis. A quarter way into the new century, the specter is not collapse. It is prolonged exhaustion; even the most snarling of nativists do not want to forfeit the benefits of needing strangers, even if they could, while outsourcing and deferring the costs because they can. Rather, the goal is to blame and to bash the beleaguered international organizations and ideas while tolerating and using them so they can clean up the mess. If someone has to shoulder the externalized costs of interdependence, why not displace them to institutions created for and actors dedicated to looking out for strangers—especially as the hazards of climate change, migration pressures, and geopolitical tensions rise?

Hands Up!

The assault on authorities identified with the previous era had effects on the groundnorms and institutions that buoyed them. Antiestablishment populists railed against financial, governmental, and academic cabals, often rekindling myths of Jewish bankers gouging the commonweal, crying fake news, and questioning academic expertise. The French protest movement known as *gilets jaunes* (yellow vests) drew upon far-right as well as some far-left support and gripped Paris for months, leaving thousands injured, eleven dead, and Prime Minister Emmanuel Macron's ambition to reduce carbon emissions in tatters.[9] Gallup runs regular polls that track American public confidence in institutions; since 2001, the arrows point sharply downward, even for churches and the military. By 2024, only 27 percent of Americans trusted banks a "great deal or quite a lot." Only newspapers (18 percent), big business (16 percent), television news (12 percent), and Congress (8 percent) ranked lower. The only sector to inch up? Small business (68 percent), the sector that suffered the most from the financial crash.[10] One global barometer of twenty-eight countries reported in 2023 that the trends were, if anything, worse elsewhere. Across the board, the only sector mistrusted more than the media was: government. (Scientists, for what it's worth, still earn more respect worldwide than in the United States). The moment was ripe for conspiracy theorizing and alternative truths backed by the amplifying effects of new media technologies.[11]

Protests and occupations against technocrats and their clients had been familiar sights at anti-IMF rallies in Buenos Aires and Manila, where grievances about austerity, "structural adjustment," and the Washington consensus ran deep. But now, the rage and anger flowed from the peripheries to capitals like Washington, Athens, and Paris. Unemployment in North America and across Europe soared as banks called in loans and companies closed. In Europe, German bankers who had funneled money to dubious real estate investments in Florida told Greek and Ukrainian debtors to pay back what they owed to make up for their awful bets; the Greek economy plunged into depression.

Unemployment hit 25 percent; hundreds of thousands of citizens filled the public squares and streets to protest extreme austerity. In Ukraine, a desperate government turned to European banks for help, only to be told to "discipline" themselves, then turned to the IMF to get same message before turning to—yes—Moscow for relief, only to be tarred by the West for kowtowing to Vladimir Putin. In London, the chancellor of the exchequer, George Osborne, used the post-Lehmann hangover to impose medicinal austerity. Britain had been "living beyond its means," he declared. So he slashed government spending. Meet the moment by getting a job, he lectured Britons. And then he slashed corporate taxes to attract investors. "Today, we have paid the debts of a failed past," he said.[12] Meanwhile, eight million American homeowners surrendered to foreclosures. The other half struggled while the rich got much, much richer. The firms that made up the S&P 500 index spent $5.3 trillion, over half their profits, in the decade after the bailouts buying back stock and inflating the value of their shares. While most Americans waited for a recovery, the wealth of U.S. billionaires increased by over 80 percent. In 2013, five years after the crisis began, the French economist Thomas Piketty published a thick, technical tome about long economic cycles that played to the stereotype of the dismal scientist. Published by an academic press for specialists, *Capital in the Twenty-First Century* became a runaway bestseller; Piketty became a celebrity economist for the short twenty-first century.[13]

The disenchantment with globalization could have resolved in several directions. Some, like Piketty, called for more inclusion, more equity, and less liquidity. There were calls for new "global compacts" around climate change and migration, new levies on international finance to fund global public goods. The United Nations cast off its cape of diplomatic discretion and called for solidarity and activism. There were signs that the crisis and downfall of Neoliberal Man created room for interdependence in a new, more inclusive and more democratic, key.

There was an alternative: tear it all down, with an expletive for good measure. The American documentarist Michael Moore warned in October 2016 that the election of the apex sybarite, Donald Trump, to the White House (then dismissed as improbable by a vast majority of pundits and pollsters) would be "the biggest fuck-you ever recorded in human history."[14] People snickered. After all, protesting elites was a position associated with the left. Indeed, occupiers in Athens, New York, Buenos Aires, and Madrid called for redistribution and social justice in terms reminiscent of earlier countercultural movements, particularly among youth who had no direct memory of 1968 but for whom occupation, freedom of speech, and antihierarchical affiliation were organizing staples. Zuccotti Park, located in the heart of Wall Street in New York, became a campground for protestors chanting against corporate greed and official collusion until municipal authorities made conditions so miserable that occupiers began to disperse. The fury spread. Protestors chanted "Hands up! This is a robbery!" in Madrid's Puerta del Sol. Santiago, Kuala Lumpur, Frankfurt, Tel Aviv—the anger was contagious. When asked what inspired the organizers of Zuccotti Park, the answer was: the Arab Spring uprisings of the year before that toppled kleptocrats in the Middle East and North Africa. Worldwide, the antiestablishment mobilization seemed to favor a tide for democratic accountability and economic inclusion.[15] Figures like the socialist American politician Bernie Sanders became global celebrities. The Spanish Netflix series *La casa de papel* (*Money Heist*) became cult viewing. Though some of its antimonetarist technicalities flew over viewers' heads, the antisystem escapism did not. The quixotic series spawned clones in South Korea and elsewhere; Argentine babies were named after its Robin Hood heroes.

The crisis in fact flipped the script about how to contest the concentration of power. Within a decade, it was the global right and nativism that had the firm upper hand, not the traditional left. An emotional world economy saturated with anxiety, fear, and suspicion played to the strengths of the right rather than the left.

The global reaction echoed (if not appropriated) the left's anti-elite rhetoric but directed their ire against establishments they accused of turning their backs on national citizens in favor of distant strangers and commitment to a global administrative state. Antiglobalism became synonymous less with the anti-IMF left than the anticosmopolitan right because it could summon the idea of the holy nation and its state to defend its citizens from the claims of strangers. The tilt was the product of a growing frustration, fear, and despair about what might be done to help those left behind by deep interdependence; it also thrived off the escalating risks and turmoil. Global stopped looking as hot as McKinsey recruitment brochures made out; global evoked climate change, financial risk, and necessitous strangers on the march. Nativism sank roots in the aftermath of the 2008 financial upheaval, as the dependence on capital and carbon made people feel more vulnerable than fortunate. A chorus of blaming others and calling for ramparts and walls around the threatened nation grew steadily while protestors splintered and the institutions with which so-called liberals and globalists were identified—universities and heritage media above all—came under assault.

People Get Used to It

The aftershocks of 2008 revealed a complex and entangled crisis that assumed various local and regional forms. Their sum compounded the dysphoria and authorized the return to predatory politics, using *leverage* to restore and enforce hierarchy.

The new hierarchies would not have been possible without the long-term effects of carbon and credit interdependence, which exposed the asymmetry between relatively strong and relatively weak codependents. Fueled by a pessimistic turn, this asymmetry magnified the incentives for the more powerful to become more extractive. Of the many places where this turn to brazen extraction took hold, one was in the borderlands of the former Soviet Union. The financial crisis of 2008 pushed Ukraine to the brink. The economy shrank by 25 percent from 2009 to 2014. Creditors balked at relief for a struggling democracy. All those economics PhDs and MBAs made assumptions about markets and networks that neglected how fragile states—like Russia and Ukraine—might remember the open nerve that was Sevastopol, the warm-water port on the Black Sea and gateway to other gateways, the Mediterranean, Suez, and the Red Sea. Whoever controlled it had control over a commercial and military artery; in the dissolution of the Soviet Union, Sebastopol became Ukraine's, leaving Russian nationalists seething with resentment and vulnerability. As creditors pushed Ukraine to the brink, Moscow seized its moment. The Russian oil Goliath, Gazprom, halted gas shipments to Ukraine in the dead of winter 2009. Central and Southeastern European consumers shivered in the dark while Moscow squeezed Kyiv into submission and inked more deals to ship gas to addicted Westerners. The first Nord Stream pipeline linked Siberia to Germany's OPAL pipeline in May 2011 in the face of warnings from Ukraine, Poland, and the United States. By summer 2021, Washington finally gave up pressuring Germany to curb its reliance on Russian energy supplies; it was simply too abrasive to transatlantic relations—though it laid the grounds for Vladimir Putin's full onslaught six months later. The helix of dependency and aggression made petropower a central part of the arsenal of the new geopolitics.[16]

A lonely voice was George Soros, an avatar of postnational capitalism. He pleaded for the West to rescue Ukraine precisely because the forces of globalization were weaker than its champions thought, because he feared that a weakened neighbor would create incentives for a stronger yet grievous Russia to seize the advantage.[17] An IMF package in July 2015 was too little, too late, complained Soros. After years of angling for a friendly regime next door, the Russian government under Putin seized its next moment. He urged separatists and militiamen to stir resentments. Russian soldiers went on "vacation" to the Donbas. In 2014—a fateful year for the entangled history of geopolitics and geoscience, as carbon addiction pushed, in May, atmospheric concentrations of carbon dioxide beyond the barrier of four hundred parts per million for the first time in millions of years—the Russian ruler sent tanks into Crimea. A financially hobbled Ukraine could do little. Putin, chairman of the Board of Trustees of the Russian Geographical Society, staged a telegenic expedition to dive in a minisub to a Byzantine-era shipwreck near Sevastopol.[18] Russian separatists aimed a missile at a Malaysian airliner flying over Ukraine. Everyone died.

Turning global interdependence into a threat of annihilation took a turn for the worse, the spotlight again on a struggling Ukraine, in early 2022. In February 2022, General Sergei Shoigu (defense minister *and* president of the Russian Geographical Society, an "all-Russian NGO"), having stress tested Russia's new weaponry in Syria, sent columns of tanks to rumble on to Kyiv. Putin closed off the trading corridors through the Black Sea, causing fuel shortages and food price spikes around the world. He growled about using nuclear weapons for the first time since 1945. In so doing, Putin shattered a nuclear taboo because previously—under the logic of deterrence—states had promised not to use them first as a groundnorm for international membership and recognition. He then backed up the menace with an assault on Europe's largest nuclear power plant in Zaporizhzhia, threatening to initiate a meltdown. Putin cashed in the public secret about the nuclear taboo for blackmail statecraft. In doing so, he broke the guardrails against proliferation and extended a lease on North Korean missile tests and Iranian violations of UN arms control strictures. As globalization lost its shine, so too did peace-binding pacts. A reelected Donald Trump then dispensed with U.S. commitment to allies in torrents of social media posts, which set off a fright that Poland, Japan, Saudi Arabia, and South Korea would get nukes of their own. Putin announced the de facto death of the post-Nagasaki world and pushed the new one into a fog of insecurity.[19] The de jure demise was more mournful. On Thursday February 5, 2026, the New Start treaty between Washington and Moscow, a symbol of post-Cold War comity which capped operational missiles and warheads, committed the signatories to inspections and information exchange, and served as the lynchpin for the world's arms control regime, ended quietly. The notion that there might be new talks, after Trump declared a resumption of nuclear weapons testing in the middle of a war in Ukraine and at a time in which Russia was committed to balancing its weak soft power with a hard, titanium edge, was risible. The end of legal restrictions on nuclear arsenals meant that, to quote one dismayed observer, "we are now at the threshold of a new arms race."[20]

The war over Ukraine exposed global rifts. The invaded country became a screen upon which the awful contradictions of the society of spectacles got projected. The agony in Ukraine jolted a shortlived idyll of a democratic alliance, which drove up the mercury of mutual mistrust. But it also added to the sense of fatigue and frustration that so little could be done for suffering strangers, which soon drained the alliance's ability to defend itself. The photos from an invaded country horrified and inured at the same time. A century after hopes that the camera could bring the horrors of war home to debunk warmongering myths, as if furnishing a photo would make its subject incontrovertible, the practice of recording brutality was more equivocal—if no less urgent—than ever. Ukraine relied on Western aid while Western "values" were pinned to the fate of Ukraine. This was clear enough in the immediate aftermath of the invasion on February 24, 2022. Nine days later, *Der Spiegel* captured the zeitgeist with a photo from Maksim Levin's drone of a bombed apartment building. The subtitle of the feature article ran: "Where Europe's freedom is defended."

To fill the gap between the contradictions, one useful narrative, especially as the war slogged on, was the resilience story, a plotline about survival to make sense of the spectacle that many thought senseless. So how to make sense of it? The resilience story was one: brave Ukrainians defending the West. "Kharkiv Is Unbreakable" was the headline of one prominent *New York Times* story in the spring of 2024 as the question of U.S. military aid was in doubt and the looming presidential election campaign posed the possibility that a Republican triumph would slash it completely. The photos by the Pulitzer Prize–winning Tyler Hicks portrayed a battered Kharkiv. In Hicks's montage, dead Russians appear as props for soldiers and families. A little boy climbs on to the hulk of a rusted Russian tank to pose for his grandfather, himself a wounded soldier, taking a photo on his smartphone. By then, tanks had long since withdrawn from the battlefield as machinery of war; Kharkiv was being pounded by bombs launched from an invisible distance. It was a glide bomb that landed, intentionally, on the Planeta Mall, slaughtering shoppers and leaving the mall in ruins. One of the city's citizens lamented that "the most horrifying thing is that people get used to it."[21]

There is a tragic possibility that the images that have been so central to the war-crimes dossier against Putin inadvertently prolonged his version of hard bargaining. Within days of launching his assault on Ukraine, as it became clear that this was not going to be the cakewalk he expected, Putin agreed to talks with Ukrainian envoys to declare a ceasefire and truce. Whether it would have stuck is up for debate.[22] As negotiators were

FIGURE 6.1. "Where Europe's freedom is defended."

detailing a settlement, there came the horrific news and images of massacres in Irpin and Bucha. The image economy created a surge of international sympathy for invaded Ukraine. Volodymyr Zelensky visited stricken Bucha on April 4 as the photos of atrocity splashed across Western media. The next day, he appeared by videoconference before the United Nations Security Council, likened Russia to the Islamic State of Iraq and Syria (ISIS), and called for the country to be expelled from the

FIGURE 6.2. Kharkiv.

council. A few days later, the prime minister of Britain, Boris Johnson, ever seeking his own de Gaulle moment, paid a surprise visit to Kyiv and marched alongside Zelensky and his soldiers through the streets of a shelled capital. Citing the killing of civilians, Johnson promised "high-grade military equipment" (whatever that meant is still unclear) to Ukrainian forces. Johnson warned Zelensky that any deal with Putin "was going to be pretty sordid."[23] For Zelensky to agree to a truce in the face of the evidence of butchery was all but impossible. Instead, he upped the ante, pointed at the hideous visuals of Bucha, and called Russian aggression "genocidal." Now that he was a pariah soon to face a tribunal, the Russian leader had less interest in stalling or stopping. The truce unraveled; the war went on—for years.

Russian aggression, nursed by years, if not decades, of grievance, has singular features. But it echoes a wider urge to treat fragile interdependence and its weak links as an opportunity to hoard, to grab, to care less about the effects on strangers, and to walk away from international commitments designed to restrain predation since the Second World War.

Swipe

Adam Smith's impartial observer, the metaphoric figure in a godless world holding distanced strangers to account for their behavior, struggled to survive in a mediatized deluge of drama and fatigue. But if social media, deep fakery, and the explosion of personal recordings overwhelmed the vintage idea of documentary vision, the work of the observer was no less important. Indeed, the spiral of competition and grabbing made the observer's struggle to survive even more literal, not just figurative. The Committee to Protect Journalists, a nonprofit organization that monitors the freedom of reporters, catalogues the ways in which they have themselves become targets. In 2024, 103 were killed while working, another 361 imprisoned, and 67 went missing. A few years earlier, the Saudi government ordered a distinguished *Washington Post* journalist, Jamal Khashoggi, butchered in Istanbul. To be a reporter in Russia is to risk one's life. In the old days, the risk was getting caught in the crossfire, or stepping, as Robert Capa did, on a landmine by accident. But in the new escalation, as wars of humanity were waged over how they were represented, killing a reporter became less and less an accident. During Israel's invasion of Gaza, journalists were especially singled out. (Since Israel would not let foreign journalists into the Strip, reporting fell to Gazans—who were accused of being sympathetic to the terrorist organization Hamas.) Mohammed Mhawish, a university graduate with a degree in English and creative writing from Gaza City, dreamed of becoming a writer when Hamas butchered Israelis on October 7, 2023. In the ensuing Israeli assault, he gave up fiction to become a reporter for Al Jazeera. While feeling a duty to report what he witnessed, he grew weary of the relentless bombing—and eventually the feeling that he and his colleagues were the bull's-eye. "At some point, I had to abandon my press vest," he told *The New York Times*' Lydia Polgreen, "because it no longer provided me with the protection that I was seeking. In fact, it functioned as a target on my back."[24]

If the war over the narrative governing wars of humanity placed the impartial observer in crosshairs, there was a system shift in the practice of representation—and who engaged in it. The arrival of the digital age compounded the challenge of portraying the consequences of strangers' conduct toward other strangers. It raised the hazards of Sontag's lament about dissociative seeing—viewing more but witnessing less.

Visualizing practices merged images into a common portrait of decomposition and crisis, though they did not necessarily equip witnesses with the means to make sense of the collage. Indeed, the crisis of globalization coincided with, and was fueled by and fueled, a crisis of representation—an escalation of clashing images and beleaguered bewilderment. And yet, making sense of it as an expression of interdependence is as challenging as connecting Swiss financiers to civil war in Syria.

Technology expanded capacities to produce a supply of images that collapsed geographic distances. Portability, reproducibility, and manipulability of digital imagery, coupled with seamless and wireless connectivity, exploded the amount and velocity of circulating photos, changing what strangers we saw and how we saw them in our lives. The digital turn—the ability to capture light on photosensitive silicon cells to yield photoelements, or pixels—was a cornerstone for a new era of representation. If you zoom in super close on a digital photo, you can see tiny squares. Each is a single image. Increase the number of these pixels per photo and you create more detail density. The digital turn was so fast that Kodak, which had been tinkering with the technique, lost a step in the early 90s. A decade later it was no more. The speed of the changes yielded spectacular effects, vastly expanding the spectacle.

Digital recording for JPEG and MPEG standards in the 1990s coincided with the arrival of LCD (liquid crystal display) screens on cameras. Samsung, Sharp, and eventually Apple (in 2007) adapted small lenses and small screens and compressed them onto portable phones. It made everyone with a smartphone a documentarist. Darnella Frazier shook the world with her purple iPhone 11 on May 25, 2020, when she raised it to record a Minneapolis policeman, Derek Chauvin, staring blankly at her phone lens as he asphyxiated a Black man, George Floyd, crying out (seventeen times), "I can't breathe!" A nearby policeman quipped to onlookers, "This is why you don't do drugs, kids!" At first, the police blamed the victim. When Frazier posted her ten-minute recording of a blank-faced killer and his choking victim on Facebook and

Instagram, it reached millions and spawned a global anti-police uprising. But the icon of the uprising was not Frazier's horrific recording. It was another smartphone shot characteristic of the digital image economy, a selfie that Floyd had taken for his mother on his iPhone three years before, reproduced on walls and placards from Nairobi to London and painted as the mural on one of the relics of the Berlin Wall, shown in Figure 6.3.

Schools and online magazines began to instruct young documentarists on how to use their phones as research tools.[25] There's a commodification side to the self-recording style as well. Nowadays, Apple markets iPhones less as telephones and more as recording devices for content-creating consumer-citizens to produce and share what they witness and want to be seen as witnessing.[26]

To live in a visualized culture after the smartphone and social media has meant to plea for more tools for interpretation, more room for debate, more space for ambiguity, more pause to ask questions. And yet, the nature of Floyd's murder, or wars like Russia's invasion of Ukraine or Israel's occupation of Gaza, demands certainty, shining truths to bring the light of justice to bear on reprehensible behavior. For those upon whom horrible things have been forced, making room for questioning or pausing cannot help but appear to open the door for the perpetrators' self-defense; to admit uncertainty or ambiguity is just to be a quisling. To be clear, I am not making Russian and Israeli aggression equivalent—merely noting that both pump the fractured society of spectacles with an overdose of images that fuels tribal nativism of the aggressor and helpless revulsion for those who sympathize with the pulverized. Russian and Israeli leaders, for their part, respond by using their own arsenal of images to blame Ukrainians and Gazans as being the original aggressors, and add their supply of visual evidence to the oversaturated forum. The relentless stream of photos of bombed apartment buildings in Kharkiv and mass starvation in Gaza drains the sense of shock and reinforces the fatigue even as it thickens the file for prosecutors.

The images of drone swarms over Ukraine and the cinematic horror in Gaza reveal an appalling dilemma. A half century ago, Susan Sontag could take the position she did because the prevailing discourse of photography at the time still touted a dream of photographic objectivity;

FIGURE 6.3. George Floyd in Berlin.

bearing witness with a photo could demystify and clarify, reveal a truth. It could serve the function of Adam Smith's impartial spectator, bearing witness to restrain strangers from treating each other badly. That myth lives on. It drives an urge to mobilize images to bring peace and justice, like shining a lantern on the inhumanity of Russian or Israeli aggression. Sontag waved her arms: it's not working as it was hoped. Once the image became itself a commodity, its production and circulation could oversaturate—and become a manipulable weapon, like any other part of the fabric of interdependence. She was not disavowing the power and importance of image making. Rather, she called for critical reflection. And yet, dreams of objectivity, back-and-white lucidity, have not given way to Sontag's yearning for interpretation and contextualization, for slowing down to think. Instead, the image economy yielded to the instant, the scrollable, and the swipeable, to reflexes of glimpsing the dead, the half dead, the survivors, and moving on. Without pause or questioning, the same images may even prolong the agony. And the agony mobilizes the witnesses.

Part of the Equation

Market-based globalization laid the tracks for the new geopolitics of resources, territories, and bordered security. None of this would have been possible without earth hunger for carbon, notably oil and gas pipelines that linked Siberian wells to German living rooms. Vladimir Putin turned pipelines into parts of his arsenal. Nor was Russia the only beneficiary of hyperdependency on fossil fuels; the United States had gone from major importer to the world's biggest exporter thanks to the shale revolution. Washington deployed the dollar and natural gas to uphold its own vision of the world. China seized the opportunity to delink from American tankers to negotiate special rights to Siberian gas, securing its own lifelines. The world's biggest construction project was a pipeline that connected Siberia to the South China Sea, gloated Putin, though he added that "our Chinese friends drive a hard bargain."[27]

Chinese friends were not the only hard bargainers. Hard bargaining and extractive interdependence became ever more widespread as the scramble for resources, fear of scarcity, and concern about competition intensified. Nor was it just states that ramped up the struggle. Consider one dependence broker whose power thrived off risk: the commodity trading company. In the past, traders relied on capital reserves to buy stocks of food, fuel, and minerals at low prices and hoard them until prices peaked. A handful of firms had the savvy, risk appetite, and deep pockets to stay alive and prosper. The industrialization of Asia powered a commodity supercycle and poured fortunes into the coffers of firms brokering in old staples like grain and oil as well as the new ones associated with the energy transition, the "rare earths" that were rare only because the rich countries that needed them did not want the filth of separating the fine parts from mountains of sludge in which they are buried. Chinese leaders, from the 1980s, were willing to make the tradeoff and internalize the costs if it meant cornering a market.

Few private brokers thrived more than the Swiss-based Glencore, which had amassed vast reserves of wealth—a source of leverage to be wielded with dependent clients desperate to swap their commodities for capital. A shock came in 2010 when drought wiped out Russian grain harvests. Prices soared. So did Glencore profits.[28] Russia's most important customers, the Middle East and North Africa, saw bread prices spike. Bakers ran out of flour. When Russia banned exports to keep its own population from revolting, the Arab world went into paroxysms. Governments in a region seething with discontent about corruption and misrule scrambled to buy, with Glencore brokerage, what they could from Australia and North America. On December 17, 2010, a Tunisian fruit vendor named Tarek El-Tayeb Mohamed Bouazizi, fed up with police harassment in an impossible business, stepped into the street, poured gasoline over his body, and set himself on fire. Grainy images, taken by a witness on their phone, of Bouazizi staggering through a square aflame went up immediately on Facebook. It set off a democratic revolution in Tunisia, which cascaded across the region into the Arab Spring, bringing down governments in Egypt and Yemen, and Libya's strongman, Muammar Qaddafi. From a distance, the CEO of a giant grain dealer, Ian McIntosh, observed, "I wouldn't contend that [the Arab Spring] was caused by food, but food was certainly part of the equation."[29]

The spillovers of global drought also fostered conditions for the spread—the globalization—of a radical brand of Islam that seized on crumbling governments and exploited the desperation. In Chad, the kleptocratic government of Idriss Déby was on its heels by 2013, fighting jihadists from Mali and Nigeria while sinking in debt. His wars dug a hole in his treasury, so Déby turned to bankers in Paris and the World Bank in Washington, to no avail. Glencore, eager and able to turn risk into reward, came to his rescue in May with a cash outlay of $300 million backed by a prepayment of future oil supplies. By year's end, Déby's debts to Glencore had doubled. The following year, the dictator exchanged another $1.45 billion loan from Glencore in return for Chevron's stake in Chad's oilfields. Behind the scenes, Glencore leveraged investments from banks, the Public Employees Retirement System of Ohio, and the West Virginia Investment Management Board to fund Chad. But then came the shale shock. The surge in supplies of liquified natural gas sent oil prices plunging. Now Chad, dependent on dwindling oil revenues to pay debts, was utterly broke and surrounded by jihadists. Déby went back to Glencore, pleading for a restructured debt estimated at roughly 15 percent of the impoverished country's GDP. The price from Glencore was so punitive that even IMF officials called the spending cuts on schools and hospitals "dramatic."[30]

Wars of Humanity

The knot of extreme financial dependency, political fragility, and scramble to control world supply chains for basic goods tightened. Climate change only magnified the stakes and urgency. While a short-term spike in global food prices sparked the Arab Spring, a longer-term drought was sweeping across the region, taxing already mismanaged water systems. In northeastern parts of Syria, the situation grew especially bad. Farmers were abandoning their desiccated fields and moving to cities where local markets were increasingly bare. In July 2008, Abdullah bin Yahya, a UN Food and Agriculture Organization, quoted the Syrian Minister of Agriculture: "the economic and social fallout of the drought was 'beyond our capacity as a country to deal with.'" Even before the Arab Spring, bin Yahya worried about the spread of "social destruction" and a mass exodus.[31]

Syria's slow-burning crisis, a convergence of ecological and political pressures, finally erupted in early 2011. The dictatorship of Bashar al-Assad had relied on food and fuel subsidies and a bloated public service to stymie dissent. Debt and desertification undermined his brand of autocratic statecraft. In March 2011, rising food prices and cuts to public expenditures spawned prodemocracy rallies. Assad slammed down an iron fist. His opposition turned into an insurgency. By mid-2012, a civil war engulfed the country. The vacuum sucked in the same form of radical Islam that was besieging Chad. ISIS sent armies across Syria and Iraq in 2013. It exploited a region fractured by the calamity of the American invasion of Iraq and states crippled by austerity and sectarian divides. The messianic movement aimed to create a new caliphate. In Mosul, ISIS took down four Iraqi divisions in a single night's battle and fielded armies that reached as far as Nigeria. On November 12, 2015, jihadists left a Beirut neighborhood bathing in a pool of blood. The next day, seven suicide bombers killed hundreds of civilians in Paris.[32]

FIGURE 6.4. Aleppo.

In the course of this multipronged conflict between jihadists, a brutal government, and an opposition alliance hoped to replace Assad. Hasan Kattan, a law student at the University of Aleppo, went to demonstrations and used his iPhone to record protests—only to face riot police and unidentified secret agents hauling students into vans. Concerned about government lying about the opposition being jihadists and active on the relatively new platform Facebook, Kattan and friends met at a school in the free zone. How to fight back? The language barrier, they recognized, thwarted easy communication with the rest of the world. But the digital revolution created new opportunities to use visuals to get the story out. Kattan was one of several young men and women who created the Aleppo Media Center (AMC) to mount a democratic response to autocracy. Some travelled to Beirut for video and documentary training by humanitarian organizations to broadcast the atrocities, erasing distinctions between journalism, human rights monitoring, and anti-state activism. Using phones and laptops, and soon graduating to Canon 70Ds procured from Turkey and editing software when they got a bit of money by selling their images, they documented the war from the increasingly pulverized ground up. International reporters taught them how to focus, manage their exposure, edit. Linked to Agence France-Presse and the Britain-based Syrian Observatory for Human Rights, the AMC fed news outlets and booming social media platforms a flow of visuals of the destruction. By mid-2012, rebels controlled a good portion of the city, whereupon Assad, losing the media war, ordered barrels filled with oil and metal fragments rolled out of helicopters to land on apartment buildings below. Backed by a Moscow flush with oil and gas windfalls, Assad then besieged the city and turned to chemical attacks. AMC documentarists climbed to rooftops to record the savagery and to document the civilian response on the ground to being gassed and burned by their own government.[33]

In an interdependent world, all wars are civil wars of humanity; the mechanisms of mobility and visibility across borders turn local fratricidal conflicts into gashes in the global fabric. They cascade, extruding their effects and sucking in far-flung actors who are irrevocably transformed as they move across borders and become internationalized. Traders seeking opportunities, missionaries pursuing souls, journalists chasing a scoop, and humanitarians saving lives—all are part of the knot that binds societies together, a knot that tightens as the world becomes more interdependent. This was on display in the Middle East, pressured by the vice grip of climate change, desiccation, and the permanent security apparatuses of a "War on Terror." While it is tempting to depict the crisis in the Middle East as exceptional, it is a latter-day example of the unbounded nature of social life when markets, migrants, and the struggle for recognition lace the world into a single survival unit, a unity that was never unified.

It was early morning, September 2, 2015. A Turkish photojournalist, Nilüfer Demir, was patrolling a beach with her Nikon. Huddled in crowded dinghies, refugees had been crossing the Aegean Sea for years. That morning, Demir happened upon the corpses of several drowned boys. Waves lapped around one three-year-old's body, his face half down in the sand. The boy's name was Alan Kurdi. Demir raised her viewfinder. An emergency worker appeared. In tears, Demir continued shooting as the worker leaned over and cradled the boy in his arms.

The photo of Alan Kurdi was horrific. It was so recognizable: our children sleep like this. Many will object to publishing this photo as aestheticizing horror. But it soon became an icon of sympathy; three days later, ten thousand people rallied in Paris's Place de la République to denounce the Syrian government and plastered Demir's photo on leaflets and placards. Doubt has surrounded the publication of images such as this almost since modern media turned pictures into commodities and began to circulate them. By the 1960s, the debate about the society of spectacles turning the misfortunes of strangers into opportunities for lucre was in full flight. But they were also instruments of empathy. Indeed, while editorial boards around the world agonized over whether to print the portrait of Alan Kurdi, Nilüfer Demir's photos went viral online. Almost twenty million people saw Demir's photo within twelve hours, thanks to tweets that radiated from Turkey and were amplified from Beirut (via the *Newsweek* Middle East correspondent Martin Jay) and Geneva (via the Human Rights Watch Emergency Director Peter Bouckaert).[34]

The Middle East wars were the first to be waged fully on two fronts simultaneously: on the rubbled streets of Aleppo and on the new stage of social media, making it a war for survival and a struggle over how to represent it. The people of Aleppo climbed to the rooftops to post on Facebook (founded in 2004) images of Syrian jets dropping payloads on apartment buildings below. Human rights activists used a new platform, Twitter (founded in 2006), to denounce atrocities. The world watched in real time as a state pounded its civilians, sent millions to seek refuge from drought and violence, and raised the heat in a debate about the material and ethical conditions of globalization.

As the violence escalated, Iran and Hezbollah joined Assad's side; the war became increasingly regionalized, sectarian, and vicious, and left Syria depopulated as six to seven million departed and around six hundred thousand died. Human rights activism was no match for Assad's cruelty, Iranian messianism, Russia's arsenal, the misinformation barrage from troll farms in St. Petersburg, and the less visible ways in which fractured hyperdependency rewarded powerful actors who prospered from the trap of needing strangers.[35]

FIGURE 6.5. Je suis Syrien.

Assad's cruelty revealed the limits of the post–Cold War humanitarian ideals, of support for universal human rights and the obligation of states to help strangers persecuted by their own governments. That moral coding that was supposed to accompany market integration to give it some ethical content was put to the test. Images from the Middle East coursed into the veins of world politics at a time in which the faultlines of globalization opened new geopolitical rifts. The effects were at best equivocal—and hardly triumphal. The Hungarian government put up fences. German neo-Nazis bellowed in front of refugee centers. But there was also a surge of refugee sympathy and solidarity. Fearing images of dying refugees on European roadsides, the German premier, Angela Merkel, declared Germany's commitment to welcoming fugitives. Pope Francis greeted stragglers into the Vatican. The term "refugee" replaced the term "migrant" in global public discourse. Voters ousted the Canadian government that was blamed for denying Alan Kurdi's family asylum—and had forced it to seek a fatal route out of Syria. The sight of a child's face buried in the sand helped tip the scales against a heartless prime minister in a safe and wealthy country far away.[36]

Several months later, gunmen and suicide bombers attacked Paris cafés, bombed a nightclub, and tried to blow up the Stade de France. Planning the assault from Syria and staging it from Belgium, the Islamic State of Iraq and the Levant claimed responsibility. Some of the attackers had been part of the refugee influx a few months earlier. Within a week, the discourse about how to welcome necessitous strangers gave way to fear.[37] Suddenly, the word "refugee" was tainted. Necessitous strangers were quickly rebranded as "illegal migrants." A pall fell across the idea of sharing responsibility; the necessitous became suspicious.

The postnational "end of history" was supposed to end major conflict and shelter people under a new humanitarian mantle. Instead, states were collapsing, the international system was gasping to keep up, and the arms race came back to life. Military spending doubled in the two decades after 2000. Those holding it together were demeaned for doing too little too late with too few resources, like the United Nations' peacekeepers. Blue Helmets were supposed to be heroes of the post–Cold War narrative, not just keeping peace but building peace. After 1989, more people died from civil war than all other forms of mass violence put together. Perhaps worse, once a civil war erupted, it was hard to stop from recurring. Rates of recidivism rose as interdependence deepened. By 2010, a civil war had a 90 percent chance of breaking out again in the next ten years, whereas before 1989 only 30 percent of civil wars recurred. Civil wars became more common, more protracted, and harder to stop, and they spilled across borders to become regional conflagrations that drove millions of civilians into camps run by other beleaguered UN agencies and their humanitarian allies. The Sahel, Congo, and Mesopotamia, as well as gangster polities like Haiti, were melting pots of warriors and refugees.[38]

The spiral was exhausting. As the United Nations under-secretary-general for peacekeeping operations from 2000 to 2008, Jean-Marie Guéhenno observed after watching the backsliding in Afghanistan and Haiti, and the devastating calamity in Iraq, that the emblem of the 1945 order, the blue-helmeted UN peacekeeper, was a demoralized figure—yet was in ever more demand. By the time he stepped down, Guéhenno recalled, "The most painful lesson of Iraq is actually how little care, political as well as human, key member states showed for the organization they had created in 1945."[39] By 2011, a humiliated American army completed a withdrawal from a devastated Iraq, leaving behind thousands of dead civilians, a country ripped apart, and its archaeological treasures plundered; even the ancient past was a target for resource extraction. Ten years later, the same army pulled out of Afghanistan and left it in the hands of the same men from whom the United States claimed—in the zenith of its hubris—to have liberated the country after 9/11.

Once a moral ballast for globalization, humanitarians had become major actors in managing the costs of interdependence, trying to keep calamities from spreading; they were also gasping as the international guardrails cracked under the pressures of the new geopolitics. The nation-state returned with an edge, a purpose, to externalize the costs of interdependence on to outsiders and hoard the rewards for insiders. Human security, an idea the sought to balance market globalization with moral globalization, slipped into the hands of national-security brokers who clawed back their claims to sovereignty to serve their visions of internal and international hierarchy. Security was renationalized as more strangers were dehumanized. The reversion and degradation of norms was on display where the international system after 1945 had founded a new nation to prevent genocide. The world watched in horror and indifference as an Israeli military—conceived to defend a state that had vowed in its moment of creation to uphold universal human rights in 1948—pulverized the principles and the peoples they pledged to; the state of Israel and the Universal Declaration of Human Rights were born months apart. Provoked by a hideous attack when its vaunted security system failed on October 7, 2023, the Israeli government under Benjamin Netanyahu vowed to make neighbors pay any price for an atrocity they did not organize. Two years of mourning the Israeli captives and two years of razing Gaza left 89 percent of its schools and 94 percent of its hospitals in ruins. To manage millions of homeless, Netanyahu proposed to herd civilians into a so-called humanitarian city pressed up against the Egyptian border. As the accountability systems for human security turned to ash and children died in front of cameras from starvation, *The Economist* sighed: "Something has gone very wrong in Gaza."[40] But wherever war unfolded, in Sudan, Myanmar, Ukraine, and elsewhere, legacy containment, peace brokerage, and human security ceded to state violence meted out against neighbors—and increasingly to internal dissenters.

Burning Words

A new pattern emerged from globalization and the reactions to its injustices; it was darker, more precarious, but no less interdependent. Private magnates in Switzerland were becoming public creditors in Africa. Japan quaked when China suspended shipments of rare earth in 2010—which put the world on notice that outsourcing the ecologically expensive extraction to China introduced a new degree of interdependence and vulnerability. China became Russia's biggest creditor and market; Russia became China's main source of energy, elbowing aside Saudi Arabia; the Gulf was more dependent than ever on Western consumers. And together, they shared an enmity toward a West that had spent the post–Cold War years preaching about the virtues of its values. Western social scientists coined a term for the new age: "weaponized interdependence." Seen from Beijing, Moscow, and Riyadh, or indeed parts of Latin America or Africa that had struggled to adjust to rules imposed on them, interdependence had *always* been weaponized; it's just that *Homo Davos* couldn't see it through the lenses of their Alpine self-confidence.[41]

Homo Davos may have missed the warning signs, but it was not for lack of evidence. The changes in visualizing practices, documented with satellite images of retreating glaciers and the increasingly ubiquitous drone shot, reinforced the sense of a historic watershed. Two of the guidance systems that had emerged in the slipstream of globalization, earth systems and human security, lost none of their visualized urgency but lost what they had gained politically. Both had reframed interdependence as about more than just market integration and widened it to include mutual needs of sustainability and security. The first evolved from the growing recognition that climate change affected all, the second from the growing recognition that human calamities and tensions in one corner of the earth spilled over into others. Both were buoyed by transnational solidarity movements and scientific alliances. Both treated the risks as inescapably part of the human condition. Both pushed the frontiers of global institutions, rules, and norms toward more sharing the burden of interdependence and cooperation. After 2008, the slipstream of globalization turned into stiff headwinds. By 2015, gatherings of policymakers, pundits, and advocates that once filled the world's convention centers turned into summitry exhaustion as the problems they were supposed to solve piled up.

The world's globalized unity appeared to be crumbling, like the buildings of Aleppo, which supercharged the anxieties and eventually the reactive response to pull up the drawbridges, keeping the costs at bay while trying to reap and hoard the rewards. And yet, the image economy acquired the scalar power of height, thanks to satellites and drones, combined with the precision of digital recording, just in time for the gathering recognition of climate change and its inescapable consequences. In 2020, fires raged across California, torching the cabin of my old friend, a poet and historian. Her books and manuscripts went up in plumes of smoke. "The words burned right off," she texted me. What Amy Robinson saw and recorded has become an awful commonplace even if the particularity of her loss can barely be fathomed.[42] She sent me the picture shown in Figure 6.6 of her manuscripts, taken by and transmitted from her phone to mine.

FIGURE 6.6. California Burning.

How to picture what's disappearing, going up in flames or melting away? Long before drones and digital recorders, photographers catalogued vanishing species, Sumatran tigers, humans in Patagonia or North Dakota—vanishing because the landscapes that sustained them were being seized and enclosed. Vanishing landscapes and their peoples felt—and were made to feel—remote and distant. Digital, portable, and instantly postable imagery set the stage to document the collapse of distance in a new geological era called the Anthropocene. The notion that we live in an age in which one species has conquered the earth and determines the conditions of life of all other species is tangled with—and facilitated by—practices of shooting and viewing of the digital era. Popularized by the Dutch atmospheric chemist Paul J. Crutzen and the American biologist Eugene F. Stoermer, the word "Anthropocene" grafted onto a visual revolution that bridged the gaps that separated strangers from each other; it was no longer required to imagine in genres like science fiction. Evidence of extraction and its externalities was carried around in our pockets.[43]

There was even an urge to shoot extinction itself, though the urge revealed the difficulty of making sense of interdependence in a polarized age of image wars. No creature was more spectacularized than the polar bear, the subject of activists and climate deniers alike. The rush to document the Arctic's largest land mammal as a symbol of the climate crisis would lead to a scandal over how to represent it. Cristina Mittermeier, founder of the League of Conservation Photographers, and Paul Nicklen, an outdoor photographer famous for his life-risking style and astonishing Arctic imagery, are the pictures of celebrity photography. When Nicklen's photos are exhibited at the UN headquarters, it's an event. They are among *National Geographic*'s most-hyped image makers. In the summer of 2017, they spotted a visual quarry on the shores of Baffin Island: a dying polar bear "lying on the ground, like an abandoned rug," recalled Mittermeier. She raised her viewfinder. Nicklen turned on his video camera. The crew around them wept.

The video footage reached 2.5 billion viewers. I watched it on *The New York Times*' website, trembling in my kitchen in New Jersey. *National Geographic* picked up Mittermeier's still shots and added the caption: "This is what climate change looks like." (Nicklen, it's worth adding, had captioned his Instagram post with "This is what starvation looks like.") For climate activists, the image and caption confirmed their view of how to view global warming; this was what it was *supposed* to look like. For skeptics and some bear experts, the causal connection from the photo was less clear. Maybe it was just a really old bear? The internet exploded with predictable hyperbole. "We had lost control of the narrative," noted Mittermeier. *National Geographic* was forced to retract the caption and apologize for its overreach. The magazine also denied our request to reproduce the troublesome image here. So much for being able to tell complex stories.[44]

The photo album of a changing planet nonetheless shaped a narrative about a new form of togetherness. Atomic and demographic fears of an earlier era had lumped humans together on a lonely planet; the new togetherness was changing, in real time, the protective tissue of that orb. Even slow-moving, imperceptible rhythms of planetary change became sensational news. The graphic turn captured slowly vanishing prehistoric ice. In the summer, the surface of Greenland—now in the crosshairs of White House expansion dreams—looks strangely lunar, pockmarked with cryoconite holes where ice melt gathers. In recent years, the holes have been getting wider and deeper. At eye level they are hardly panoramic. An elevated view changes the spectacle completely. In October 2015, *The New York Times* published drone footage from NASA and the U.S. Geological Survey Landsat of trickles pooling into a river. As the river carved its route through the ice, the drone rose above the horizon, pursued the flow into a canyon, and then plunged with the water into a giant sinkhole to disappear into an invisible torrent under the icecap—which cascades into a massive invisible lake that flows to the sea under the ice—invisible but made visible thanks to a drone and its camera. Of course, it's the ineluctable melt that whets the yearning among twenty first century landgrabbers with their El Dorado dreams of precious metals for the chip wars just waiting to be liberated from the cover of an ancient glacier.

This kind of imagery became a commonplace to science reporting about the invisible effects of climate change. It fits a narrative. Watching the runoff disappear traces a story about vanishing—about how, thanks to this flow, by 2030 the Arctic will be a seasonally ice-free zone. All the "old ice"—the remnants of the Pleistocene Epoch—will have been liquified.[45] The urgency to film it prompted *Wired* magazine to launch an Arctic photo contest. The condition was that the submissions had to be "large"—800 to 1,200 pixels or more. Ice had become hot. Cracks were in. Magnum Photos, the ur-network for Leica-toting war and street photographers discussed in earlier chapters, exhibited a series from Paolo Pellegrin, known for his front-line portraits from Afghanistan and Libya, shadowing a NASA expedition in the Antarctic. From his perch in a P-3 turboprop plane, he focused on the crevices of a sheet breaking

FIGURE 6.7. Antarctic Cracks.

up. "I knew I was looking at something exceedingly beautiful," he noted. "Like a Sistine Chapel of nature—a beauty that is hard to grasp but which also contains something which is not well."[46] There it is: the nineteenth-century natural sublime with the twenty-first-century ominous.

While many worried that destruction and vanishing were being aestheticized and commodified, the resulting glaciers sheared off and drifted away to melt into the ocean. Camille Seaman, one of the *Wired* contest winners, captured the floating relics "heading to their end." Their shapes convey moods and personalities, melancholic, comedic, but always lonely. Paradoxically, since travel in polar regions has become more accessible because of the melt, tourists now throng to witness and to pose in selfies as parts of a vanishing world.

These simultaneous scenes of geopolitical and geological rifts and risks are not what was promised for a one-world, posthistory successor to a violent twentieth century. The twenty-first century was off to an unpromising start. Threat and menace activated the national security limbic systems. Once activated, the sense of dread went viral.

Take It Back

One effect of the dread has been to revive the language of "the West," now as an imperiled and besieged thing. In fact, "the West" has always been a vital category for the apocalyptic mind and its fears of civilizational decline. It came back to life thanks to new internal fractures, external threats, a mercantilist China, a resentful Russia, and nuclearized actors who disavowed globalization and despised the cultures and values that it hailed while deploying its technologies with grim elation.

In the pantheon of threats, none was more alarming than scenes—spread across social media—of necessitous strangers marching or floating in search of new homes. Right-wing pundits, reactionaries in the literal sense, bloviated about "invasions," oblivious to the history of "western" invasions of Asia, Latin America, and Africa at the dawn of capitalist interdependence. Éric Zemmour, the French far-right nativist and media pundit who parades as a historian, echoed widespread paranoia about the ethnonation overrun by migrants, a "great replacement." The term was coined by Renaud Camus as *Le Grand Remplacement* (The Great Replacement)—he warned of "genocide by substitution"—and popularized by Zemmour, who went on TV and filled newspapers with Cassandra warnings of *citoyens* overwhelmed by dark-skinned, Muslim strangers. His discourse soon pervaded white-nationalist militancy across the Euro-American landscape and got picked up by American media celebrities like Tucker Carlson, whose caravan of aggrieved includes Hitler apologists and the Nazi-curious.[47] It enjoys special appeal, as authors Ivan Krastev and Stephen Holmes have shown, in regions of the post-Communist world, notably in East-Central Europe, where the mass exodus of citizens seeking escape from austerity and hounded by Western liberals' preaching about civil society and democracy vacated towns and cities that were beginning to be repopulated by strangers. There, the backlash and the rise of right-wing illiberalism have been fierce. But all over the place, those with antennae for feeling abandoned and forgotten by the cult of fluidity and elitist managerial expertise went into fits about slumping fertility and population shrinkage; the "migrant crisis" represented a threat of long-term racial transformation or extinction.[48]

Defenders of Western civilization dusted off a declinist trope: we are bringing this on ourselves, like the corrupted circles who drained the Roman Empire of its virility. In the aftermath of 2008, it was cosmopolitan elites—"globalists"—who were responsible because they prized their borderless fantasies and preferred the company of fellow globetrotters to their neighbors and, to make themselves feel better, cared more for necessitous strangers far away than the unemployed and displaced back in the white, Christian heartlands of the West. Zemmour calls this "suicide": it is Western elites who are doing this to Western nations.

The new zeitgeist ushered in paranoia about existential dread, extinction, eclipse of "Judeo-Christian civilization," and the beginning of the end. It picked up on, echoed, and appropriated prophecies of climate disasters and channeled them for ulterior purposes—in effect, hammering on the futility of cooperation (how can one trust competitors?) and consensus (how can one trust the scientists who, after all, gave us the technologies of doom?). Prophecies of a Malthusian apocalypse and moral slumps replaced the cornucopian fantasies of limitless fluidity, networked entrepreneurship, and digital liberation. This was fodder for populists and autocrats, illiberals like Viktor Orbán and Recep Tayyip Erdoğan, Chinese nationalists, and American conspiracy peddlers like Steve Bannon, who made common cause out of a dream of restoring muscular ethnonations.[49] Even Hillary Clinton, in her futile effort in 2016 to prevent the United States from sliding into perdition, denounced a Trans-Pacific Partnership that she helped to negotiate for selling out American workers—even though half of American exports go to countries with which the United States has a direct, congressionally approved trade deal, even though protectionism punishes the bottom half of the population and opens more loopholes for the one percent.[50]

While the panic of Westerners and some of their histrionic leaders grabbed headlines, the reaction was not just Western. Nativist victories in one corner validated and motivated pop-ups elsewhere. All over the planet, nativists went on the warpath, used the same media, recycled the same tropes—and even borrowed each other's spinmeisters and mimicked each other. On June 29, 2014, the Iraqi militant Abu Bakr al-Baghdadi climbed the Grand al-Nuri Mosque on the west bank of the Tigris and from his perch proclaimed a caliphate and himself the first caliph to purify the Sunni nation. "The time has come for the community of Muhammad to wake up from its sleep, remove the garments of dishonor, and shake off the dust of humiliation and disgrace," he said.[51] Wake-up calls to restore the myth of the holy nation despoiled by strangers, infidels, and interlopers resounded around the world in multiple vernaculars. Narendra Modi, the Hindu nationalist, rose up through the ranks of Gujarat's far right to become prime minister of India in 2014 and promised to use his absolute majority to defend the Indian Hindu majority against Muslims and their cunning plans to subvert the holy nation. Oversexualized Muslim men were claimed to practice polygamy. "Love Jihad" became a conspiracy theory that Muslims were out to seduce Hindu women (and to justify beating, raping, and killing the seducers). "Romeo Jihad" was another. These ideas circulated across the WhatsApp airwaves like porn. They spilled over to Myanmar, which also had a democratic transition, this time from military rule in 2014. There, it was right-wing Buddhist nationalists and their electorate who lashed out against Muslim minorities, especially the Rohingya in Rakhine province; a democratically elected government, led by a Nobel Peace Prize–winning Aung San Suu Kyi, launched a campaign of ethnic cleansing that drove millions of Muslims into camps in Bangladesh.[52]

Nativists worldwide howled at the prospect of welcoming strangers and crafted new ways to estrange minorities at home. Katie Hopkins of the British tabloid *The Sun* called migrants "cockroaches." "Show me bodies floating in the water," she snarled, "I still don't care."[53] On New Year's Eve 2015, in Cologne, Germany, the central square filled with revelers. Scores of women were assaulted and groped by unidentified men, many of them recently arrived migrants. Three hundred seventy-nine women filed separate charges of abuse. In the ensuing days, right-wing protestors flooded the streets to decry the Merkel government's welcoming policy; left-wing protestors rallied against sexism, homophobia, and for good measure, capitalism. Cologne police were sent on horses, with dogs and water cannon, to keep the demonstrators, most notably the reactionary PEGIDA (Patriotic Europeans Against the Islamization

FIGURE 6.8. Breaking Point.

of the West, which started in Saxony and folded into the Alternative for Germany party) movement. The group called upon authorities to cleanse the country of Muslims. Merkel promised to toughen asylum laws.[54]

Dread and the toxin of decline created its own traps. The maelstrom upended one of the countries that was least affected by the migrant flow but chronically anxious about decline, Britain. A trickle of migrants managed to make it through the tunnel from France by hiding in trucks or freight cars. In the second half of 2015, Eurochannel officials intercepted thirty-seven thousand migrants. Dinghies were too rickety for the English Channel. The port of Calais, and especially the migrant camp known as "The Jungle" on its outskirts, backed up with people seeking passage. By August, thousands of British vacationers trying to cross the Channel had to make new plans. Nigel Farage, leader of the far-right nationalists and head of the UK Independence Party, called the scenes "lawless, scary" and warned of an "invasion." French nativists gathered in November calling for "reimmigration" and boasting placards saying "Diversity Is White Genocide."[55]

It was in this heated context that a British prime minister capable of elevating his banality to new heights, David Cameron, proposed a referendum to decide the matter of Britain's place in Europe—confident that his "Remain in Europe" side would win. It did not.[56] A slim majority of Britons voted to break away from the European Union. Brexiteers shamelessly used images of migrants as *the* reason to leave, even though Britain had one of the lowest per capita resettlement rates in Europe. Farage posed in front of a billboard of migrants crossing the Balkans. *This,* he gestured, this is why we must *break free* from Europe and *take back control of our borders*. The prized word "independence" in his rhetoric was no coincidence.[57]

As the votes came in on June 23, 2016, the BBC published results from Sunderland, a city in the north of England. The largest employer was the Japanese automaker Nissan. The Sunderland plant sent vehicles across Europe duty-free and made cylinder heads for France's Renault and other parts for the continent, which was one of the incentives for the Japanese firm to locate in the otherwise downtrodden city. Nissan's CEO flat out declared a "preference" for remaining in Europe. No matter. Sunderland voted overwhelmingly to leave. In the aftermath, Peter Goodman, a *New York Times* columnist, huddled with some locals to figure out why. He got a stew of reasons: resentment about welfare checks to Polish immigrants, dislike for "Brussels," and fears of Muslim terrorists beelining to Albion. The most common affect was rage. As one taxi driver put it, "No one really understood what Brexit was, or what would happen if we voted for it. We just knew that people in London had been fucking with us for as long as we could remember. Thatcher fucked us. Then Cameron and Osborne fucked us." Brexit gave voters an opportunity: "It was our chance to fuck them back."[58] There was little doubt that Brexiteers' strongest card, after its fuck-you to the ruling clique, was another fuck-you: to immigrants.[59]

Nativism has been one way to manage interdependence. Indeed, nativism represents a strategy to verticalize the bonds of need; it uses the language of independence—but actually, it is all about control. "Taking back control," building beautiful walls, excluding peoples, and grabbing lands are ways to assert, and not to negotiate, the terms of exchange with strangers, picking and choosing the rewards while displacing costs to the wall's, the channel's, or the razor-wire fence's other side. There was a second feature: forcing strangers, their goods, their cultures, their presence out was a strategy to reassert a form of majoritarian rule at home as a moral claim to restore the ethno-nation—often clad in anti-woke euphemisms about diversity or inclusion.

The two sides are linked. Reacting by asserting control over neighbors, rivals, and allies is what has authorized nativists to internalize the gains from interdependence; hardening the line between citizens and noncitizens is what has enabled nativists and their coalitions to claim to better the lives of homelanders. In this sense, majoritarian democracy is not just compatible with beggar-thy-neighbor policies abroad and exclusionary policies at home; it reaps the benefits of integration and pushes the costs onto strangers. Increasingly, the friend-enemy distinction enabled nation-firsters to claim to do well for their countries, and specifically for a bloc of peoples who wanted what the rest of the world offered but without the burdens. The distinction made it more challenging to manage dependence across borders while threatening pluralism within borders. Kindness was for wimps, or worse, for traitors.

The end of globalization revealed an irascible, fevered world rife with predictions about alienation and loss. Doom sells to alarmists. It also serves a purpose in the management of global interdependence. Doomsaying is cardinal for reburnishing a view of a world dominated by dominators to restore an overdue hierarchy for the strong to manage the weak. In this sense, declinist reactions have been around for as long as modern interdependence has, notably in response to moments in which the estranged claim and gain entry into an order to make it more horizontal and inclusive. Indeed, fears of Armageddon, either as a dramatic collapse or a slow-burning demise, comprise one emotional response to interdependence since its dawn. They have gained traction especially when fears of limits, scarcity, and risk coincide with and feed off the integration of the estranged, especially smaller countries and postcolonial societies who want to claim a place at the recognitional table.

It is not a coincidence that a more pluralistic world and the diffusion of power have triggered counterforces that sought to remake an international club of the strong, an alliance of bullies, until those bullies have nothing left to carve up and turn on each other. They have resurfaced over and over, these dreams of recovering lost omnipotence that feast on terrors of shortages and hostility to strangers to justify a model of integration managed by the mighty.[60] And in their justifications, the counterforces pick and choose from the debris of an imperial past what they do not want to face in the future. To restore "greatness," one has to erase the messiness of interdependence and narrow its ethical challenges to what we owe only to ourselves and never to others.

New Realism or Old Doomism?

Ours are not end-times. It's just the end of globalization, its authorities, its treaties, its compromises. As it was heralded after the fall of the Berlin Wall and the opening "emerging markets," globalization is done, leaving behind a trail of problems without a whiff of melancholy.

But interdependence is not done. For starters, the climate crisis and the shattering of the nuclear taboo mean that survival really does depend on the actions and outlooks of strangers. There is more. Climate change, population politics, and the remilitarization of international affairs are coiled together because spreading fear of strangers is the emotional condition for a self-reinforcing fusion of zero sum-ism and rivalrous responses to shared challenges. As climate change places the burdens inordinately on poorer societies clustered closer to the equator, the pressure to emigrate has been rising. As affluent societies watch their populations age and shrink, they need the migrants they do not want while erecting walls, visas, and tariffs that create the illusion of sovereignty. As the arteries of interdependence become weaponized, so do national budgets. The fact is, globalization *did* yield a peace dividend; world expenditures on real weapons halved from 4.3 per cent of global GDP in 1985 to a historic low of 2.1 per cent in 2018.[61] It has been creeping up ever since, especially after Russia's full-scale invasion of Ukraine and the second Trump administration's saber rattling. Population shifts may be the least of humanity's concerns.

If the risks that make us interdependent are greater than ever, the gains remain ever present. Even dire predictions of trade wars and violent delinking have been overblown, despite Trump's commitment to fortress America, Putin's promise of technological sovereignty, and Xi's drive for made-in-China self-reliance. Trade in goods as a share of world commerce may have peaked, a trend under way even before the tariff contest began, but goods have also shrunk as a share of all purchases. Trade in services, including health, education, and (cyber)security, has been growing in absolute terms and as a share of the world's economy. The percentage of service trade doubled as a share of overall commerce from 11.5 percent to 23 percent of world commerce since Lehman Brothers imploded; the value of service trade rose from $4 trillion to surpass $8 trillion. Between the global financial crisis and 2024, exports of total goods and services as a share of global GDP has remained constant at around 31 percent. Medical procedures in Turkey, tourism in Spain, cloud-based warehousing—over 60 percent of world foreign direct investment is now in services, not industry or agriculture. Some doomsayers predicted "slowbalization," a retreat from market based integration. They needed to take the longer view. The hazards notwithstanding, a new stage in economic interdependence, dominated by global value chains in information and services, has outpaced the unbundling of manufacturing supply chains into sprawling webs connecting just-in-time factories—which implies a deeper mode of mutual dependence.[62]

Even old value chains have rewired. Trump's election and Brexit in 2016 looked like declarations of independence. They were far from it. The British economy has been slumping ever since it uncoupled from the European Union. Trump's commercial belligerence with China came at a time in which imports from China had crested already and entered a wobbly phase. His trade czar, Robert Lighthizer, had a vault of grievances about Chinese commercial practices. He leaned on an old crutch of tradecraft and raised average tariffs on Chinese imports from 12 percent to 21 percent; China responded by hiking their levies. So Chinese exporters relocated to Vietnam, the Philippines, and Mexico, which all saw their trade with the United States grow. *The New Yorker*'s

Peter Hessler was living in China throughout the war of words. When he toured Chinese factories to see how they were coping with the trade wars, they were doing fine. Exporters contrived ways to blur "Made in China" labels for the glut of goods being sold on Amazon. Product pages for Chinese vendors used gibberish brand names like Zocavias and Zocanias to obscure the fact that they were parts of consortia based in Sichuan Province. Li Dewei, an enterprising manufacturer in Chengdu, seized on Trump's stimulus checks aimed to keep American consumer-citizens anesthetized. "We check the statistics every day," he told Hessler. "After the American government started issuing the money, the next day we saw an increase in sales." MAGA buyers were getting their red baseball caps, "North Dakota for Trump" flags, and T-shirts with Trump's face superimposed on Rambo's M60-toting made-to-kill torso from factories in Shaoxing.[63] By the time Trump was reelected in 2024, he had to declare a trade war against everyone because world value chains were so ornate and distributed. April 2, 2025 was "Liberation Day." The stock market crashed the following day.

Liberation and sovereignty were euphemisms for predation and extraction. Doomism, and the technologies of representation that make it viral, is a powerful instrument for a new brand of segmented and hierarchical interdependence. Indeed, while the reaction defends ethnic majorityhood and the home market, its advocates are not above manipulating strangers to destabilize rivals whom they accuse of caring more for strangers than homelanders. To jab at U.S. President Joseph Biden and poke Democrats in the eye, the Republican governors of Texas and Florida bused migrants to liberal cities like New York and Washington. In the autumn of 2021, the president of Belarus, Alexander Lukashenko, manufactured a refugee crisis, in large part to generate images to churn the European Union into another fit over border security and invasion. The photographs of desperate migrants were meant to tear at the rival feelings about welcoming and excluding in Western Europe.

Capitalizing on desperation in the Middle East, Lukashenko flew thousands of refugees to Belarus, bused them to the Polish border, and left them to starve. His guards pointed into the woods and Western Europe beyond. *Go that way*, they said. As families straggled forward,

FIGURE 6.9. Poland-Belarus Border. Note how migrants had been told to use their children as shields to heighten the image of Polish guards as the cruel excluders.

they ran into barbed wire barricades, Polish machine guns, and hundreds of reporters and their cameras on-site to record the spectacle of asylum seekers being driven back by Western gendarmes. The optics were meant to embarrass and to stir discord in the European Union, and force it to ease sanctions against Lukashenko's regime.[64]

The images of necessitous strangers provided ammunition in the battle between and within states over sovereign power to determine who can enter and who must stay out. They struck exposed nerves in divided societies.

Exposing nerves and raising fears were responses to crumpling states and pressures on survival systems. Above all, the fear was the effect, as Lukashenko and the Texas governor knew very well, of how this crisis was framed—framed as a failure of other peoples' governments, not how debt and carbon externalized costs onto others. Even less did they acknowledge a wider global compromise of the post-Nagasaki order, which redoubled the regulatory system that governed human migration.

It gave people rights to move (and made that right a weapon that could be used selectively to scold Soviet bloc countries for preventing dissidents from leaving) but did not require states to accept the movers.

As pressures mounted in states to protect citizens from the hazards of interdependence, states responded to the incentive to externalize costs of mutual reliance onto noncitizens at the very same time that migrants whose own states failed to shelter them responded to incentives (or coercion) to uproot. It was the migrant regime and its intrinsic compromise of state and individual rights that went into crisis after 2008. Especially the asylum system, that last gasp for necessitous strangers to seek shelter when it is denied at home, which was cardinal to the ethics of the post-Nagasaki settlement, blew to pieces.

The post-1945 rules and norms for managing people stripped of political community were ill-prepared for two shocks. The first was the scale of implosions from the Sahel to South Asia, caused largely by invasions and climate change, which led to indebted state collapses. There were similar implosions in Haiti, Venezuela, and Central America, mainly the result of autocratic rule and abysmal public policies. The second was the ways in which rich countries raised the barriers to entry, which forced regular migrants to resort to an overwhelmed asylum system to get protection. It became increasingly impossible for a citizen of a poor country to move to a rich one within the law. The combination exposed a lurking problem. The regime gave people "rights" to flee war and persecution, though it equivocated on whether spreading deserts, climate catastrophes, or the insidious cruelty of authoritarian neglect were premise enough to call the displaced "refugees." Either way, people packed their bags in rising numbers. However: if people enjoyed rights to leave, states retained the right to decide who got entry—and make them ever more restricted. When states decomposed and economies melted down, more and more people got caught between their rights to escape misery and oppression and states' rights to select who got admission.

Here, also, the lure of doomism needs perspective. This is a humanitarian crisis and a terrible waste of human life. But does it threaten civilization? The rhetoric of a global migrant crisis is riddled with false

TABLE 6.1.

Year	Number of Migrants (millions)	Migrants as % of World Population
1970	84.5	2.3
1980	102	2.2
1990	153	2.3
2000	174	2.8
2010	221	3.2
2019	271	3.5

Source: International Office of Migration, *World Migration Report 2020* (IOM, 2021), 39.

alarms and misconceptions. Start with the pervasive imagery—used across the political spectrum—of masses of necessitous strangers clamoring to escape oppression and destitution and bringing their dependency with them. Table 6.1 shows the numbers of all migrants crossing borders since 1970 until the eve of the Covid-19 pandemic.

Absolute numbers of migrants have risen substantially. But so has the world's population. Despite the alarms about a "great invasion," the migrant share of the population has only risen by 1.2 percentage points in the past half century and does not show a steepening trendline—though, to be clear, hundreds of millions would move if given the chance. Leave aside the considerable research on the net contribution from migration to host societies, which shows that migrants promote more growth, more innovation, and greater cultural and cognitive opening. Yet it is also true that welcoming strangers, even when they bring their talents and labor power, implies costs of adjustment, like education and public health. While the benefits are diffused, the costs land on particular communities, which often splinter over the burdens. As the United States, by far the largest destination for world migrants, watches the share of foreign born residents rise to the level it was in 1910 (14.7 per cent) and has stabilized after the post–Covid 19 spasm, there is little doubt that some communities shoulder the costs of integration more than others.[65] It is the quarrel on the home front over the distribution of rewards and expenses that fuels the backlashing.[66] The urge to deport and repurify the nation reflects real strains of the new interdependence. But they redistribute the burdens of interdependence rather than reduce them. Indeed, that is often the point. One way to dampen furor and backlashing at home *is* to blame outsiders and to externalize the costs.

This is not a mortal blow to interdependence; it redistributes its rewards to those who have rights to have rights at the expense of those who do not. It is an ethical failure of the international system compounded by the intrinsic difficulty of making sense of the splintered realities of our reality.

Even this failure has been far from complete. The initial response to the efflux of necessitous strangers from the Middle East and North Africa in 2014–2015 was not a reflex of fear and rejection. In hindsight, German premier Angela Merkel's decision—prompted in part by the surge of images of families struggling to cross the Mediterranean—to welcome around one million of them is often seen as impetuous and a trigger for nativists. But she was far from flying solo. Even the islands that were soon overrun by camps saw local citizens rush to the shorelines to help families clamoring to get off their crowded and deluged dinghies. Moral witnesses rushed to the frontiers of cruelty and abandonment. The late Yannis Behrakis, a Greek photojournalist working for Reuters, noted how locals of the island of Kos were apprehensive at first: who were these strangers, and were they going to stay, take our jobs, want our food? As were the refugees: would we be arrested? But the daily spectacles on the shorelines dissolved some mistrust and fear as hands reached out to hands. "At the beginning of a situation like this there is always some mistrust among both migrants and locals."[67] In one of his last essays, Behrakis noted that "the least challenging part of the assignment was taking pictures. The difficulty was the emotional involvement in the story. It was disappointing to see the same thing happening again and again." In the end, the scale and repetition eventually overwhelmed the initial tide of sympathy and spiked a reaction. In the meantime, Behrakis and others contributed to a steady flow of stories and images that stirred an emotional mix that refused to cede to pure fear or indifference. The experience of witnessing kept stirring his own emotions. One early morning on the shores of Kos, he happened on an elderly Palestinian woman gazing out at the sea. Not wanting to disturb

FIGURE 6.10. Facing the Light.

her serenity, he used a telephoto lens to shoot at a distance her smiling into the sunrise.

Later, as he approached, Behrakis noticed that she was blind. This redoubled the emotion of the moment; "as a photographer, light means everything."[68] The pathos in Behrakis's portrait and the compassion of his photography defy the simplistic narrative about the determination of rich countries to hoard and exclude—even if sympathy often crashes against the shoals of splintered societies and their fears.

The urge to externalize costs of interdependence points to a second feature of the global migrant crisis that needs to be underscored, especially as it relates to the most necessitous of strangers; it also spotlights the side effects of closing off access to migrant channels to affluent societies. In absolute and relative terms, the *refugee* crisis is overhyped as a threat to stability to the so-called West; it's simply neither equivalent nor analogous to the threat of nuclear annihilation, the inexorable effects of climate change, or a future pandemic—despite nativist fears. On the eve of the Covid-19 pandemic, the world population of internally displaced people had reached forty-one million, refugees twenty-six million, and stateless five million. That's 0.009 percent of the world's people, the highest total number on record, but the rate of growth had been slowing since 2012, and its share of the world's population has declined. Covid-19 slammed the flow shut. There was a surge in the wake of the pandemic. Then the flow subsided; by the end of 2024, the total number of people forced to flee their homes had reached 123 million, of which around 52 million were refugees. The rest live in fear and famine at "home."

More importantly, "Western" doomism demands a global perspective, one which includes regions once colonized—invaded—or under the thumb of the "West" at its imperial zenith, regions that historically have shouldered the externalities of deep interdependence. It is among Resterners that the costs of interdependence have been most externalized, though it is among Westerners that one hears the most alarm. For all the hysteria about swarms of necessitous strangers "invading" ethnonations, the vast majority of those who have fled since 2008 have gone to neighboring states within the Global South; almost all of them remain there. It's in the borderlands of state collapses in Syria, Venezuela, Sudan that the real burden rests—not the English Channel or the Rio Grande. While Westerners fret about a "global crisis," it is the Resterners who assume the responsibility. Colombia took in most Venezuelans, Turkey took most Syrians, Chad took from Sudan, Bangladesh took Rohingya people. When American and allied forces withdrew from Afghanistan after failing to liberate the country, millions had to flee Taliban rule. Pakistan took almost 1.5 million Afghans. The United States took 100,000. I have personally watched busloads of frightened and hungry Sudanese refugees carried by UN vehicles to mixed settlements—not camps—in northern Uganda, where the homeless are given homes, schools, plots of land, and support from local NGOs, churches, and mosques.[69]

And yet, the framing of necessitous strangers as a threat to rich countries that take relatively few of them has been a cudgel for absurd and immoral policies like sending asylum seekers from England to Rwanda, or deporting legal Haitians from Springfield, Ohio, because right-wing trolls spread rumors that they eat neighborhood pets, or arresting

Palestinian organizers with green cards in New York because they exercised their rights. All the while, hubs like Dubai and Singapore have been opening to professional talent from African and Asia, which has been increasingly excluded from a West afflicted with invasion fears; resource-strained communities in northern Uganda accommodate necessitous strangers and do not fret about being "replaced."[70]

Doomism has led to dehumanizing practices of offshoring the costs of managing human mobility. To release the ethical pressure, wealthy states franchise to others the task of holding millions in formal and informal camps in the borderlands. Europe struck a controversial bilateral deal in 2016 with Turkey to dampen nativist reaction. Erdoğan leveraged European hysteria to extract €6 billion in "aid" and visa-free travel to the European Union for some of his citizens. Informal deals are made with warlords in Libya to prevent dinghies from launching for Italy and to hold migrants in atrocious conditions. Egypt has made it clear that criticisms of its human rights record would be met by opening the valve for migrants to set sail from its shores.[71] The Trump and Biden administrations have pleaded to Central American and Mexican governments to hold migrants from reaching the half-fenced, drone-monitored, and increasingly vigilante-armed border. When Trump returned to power in early 2025, he emptied prisons and packed airplanes and sent them to El Salvador to populate massive "antiterrorism" jails built by American private corporations to absorb the unwanted in the United States. American and European pundits talked about nearshoring assembly plants; their governments outsourced the unwanted.

If decisions to leave home, to exit, in search of a better home reflect one way to redistribute the costs of unequal interdependence when other ways are sealed off or out of reach, the pushback from nation-firsters was a strategy to keep those costs beyond the borders of their nation while reaping the rewards.

In this setting, international cooperation is often reduced to containing the human flow with bilateral deals while relying on organizations like the United Nations High Commissioner for Refugees, peacekeepers, climate monitors, and NGOs to cover basic human needs on shrinking budgets. As fearmongers framed the post-Lehmann world as a threatening, warring, bottomless well of necessitous strangers and greedy cheaters, a vast metaphoric Sahel scrambling for the exits, the fabric of cooperation struggled against fear, despair, confusion, and indifference to keep some sense of balance and distribution of gains and costs of interdependence.

Where does this leave us? If the international institutions and people we need to safeguard our mutual needs—the nuclear watchers, the scientists who monitor diseases and gases that are oblivious of national borders, the witnesses who make sense of interdependence and serve as the closest thing we still have to Adam Smith's impartial observer—are on their heels, citizens turn to their nations. If they have them. Yet nation-firsters not only have few compelling answers to shared challenges that don't involve externalizing the costs and hoarding the benefits of interdependence, but their responses run into the claims of nation-firsters from other nations with the same inclinations. Hence the standoff between China and the United States once China flipped from being low-wage, environment-devouring client to high-tech competitor. But headline alarms about tensions between global superpowers echo at regional levels as well—in the Persian Gulf, South Asia, and Northeast Asia, to name some. This in turn produces more weak links and hazards in the chains of interdependence, which mobilizes more efforts to coordinate and cooperate, and even new solidarities of shared interests and affections to manage the risks that competitive nation-states escalate. This is not an irreversible spiral, though it is true that when predators are in the water, rather like sharks, it's hard to coordinate a common strategy. It's an impasse.

Our fractured unity is not locked into swinging either way, to transcend divides or to retreat behind them. It is in the nature of interdependence to pull both ways. If we are to uncover new pathways toward greater civility and public kindness, it helps to understand the source and persistence of the rancor. This means an honest reckoning with globalization and its managerial class's failures to heed the voices for whom the cult of fluidity and global citizenship sounded like someone else's creed even if they enjoyed cheap products, new music, and the talents that came from afar. Even more glaring was the neglect of the many for whom globality and fluidity meant great and involuntary displacements.

The key is also reckoning with a longer view of the contradictions of interdependence and to stop presuming that there is only one road forward, like independence or immersion, or that one system should be followed by another, from globalization to its-yet-to-be branded successor. History does not unfold in such neat stages or models. There have always been alternatives and rivals, just as transitions have often been prolonged, muddied, and full of risks. This reckoning begins with the admission that what we share also divides. People who need each other are condemned to harbor multiple feelings for each other, not least among those we know, but especially among those we don't.

CODA

Top of the Mast

TO SEE the present as a crossroads of alternatives for the future invites us to consider how we got here by navigating through junctions past. Creating that roadmap of the conflicted feelings churned by strangers' need for each other is what motivates this book, a voyage that begins in the middle of the eighteenth century when, as markets, money and migrants sutured the world into an unstable whole, some philosophers wondered about the power of self-interest and the limits of sympathy across distances. Could compassion for strangers keep pace with our need for them—and what mixture of fear and affection, indifference and excitement, would govern the fractured unity of the world?

Centuries later, the same question confronts us, though the needs and stakes are so much higher than anything that Adam Smith and David Hume imagined. In closing this book, another philosopher of the world casts his shadow over the modern world, one who was writing in a moment not of eighteenth-century opening but mid-twentieth-century closing. His name was Walter Benjamin. A Jewish refugee fleeing Germany and interned temporarily in France, Benjamin was forced to march with a few possessions to a "camp," worried about money, about his article on Beaudelaire, about his sister. He wrote on the fly as Nazi armies prepared to invade western Europe. He wrote about his dreams, including dreams about reading. "Last night," he wrote to friends in New York, "lying in the straw, I had a dream so beautiful that I cannot resist the temptation to share it with you." His transcription described a Benjamin walking through a forest to a terrace and finding three or four ladies, one of them holding one of his own texts and another on a bed, asking the wanderer to observe the pattern of her blanket while his eyes were "looking somewhere else" so that he could not distinguish what had been revealed.[1] Benjamin was recording his dreams as an escapee, a wanderer without direction, his eyes searching without seeing. Eventually, he returned to Paris from the makeshift camp hoping, who knows why, that a Nazi invasion might not happen. He returned to his beloved Bibliothèque nacionale. He bought a gas mask, just in case. On the last fumes of hope, Benjamin penned *Theses on the Philosophy of History* (or *On the Concept of History*). It would be his final major work.

Composed after Hitler and Stalin carved up Poland, after Franco's triumph over Republicans in Spain, after Japan's slaughter of civilians in Shanghai, as France and Britain braced for the crescendo of the Global Civil War, *Theses on the Philosophy of History* returned to messianic themes Benjamin had abandoned but to which he now returned to think about what a restoration might look like *after* the end of times. The ninth of his essays introduced readers to the "Angelus Novus" ("New Angel"). The image came from a monoprint that Paul Klee had sold to him two decades earlier. In Benjamin's mind, Klee's angel, with open eyes, spread wings, and gaping mouth, had become the angel of history. In a dreamlike style that featured more and more in Benjamin's writing, Angelus Novus faces the wreckage of the past trying to make it whole, trying to awaken the dead while history keeps throwing more wreckage at his feet. Meanwhile, behind him, the storm of the future (called "Paradise") gathers force. Paradise seizes and wraps the angel's wings. They cannot close; Angelus Novus can no longer fly. The wind sucks the angel into the future with his back to it as the mountain of rubble grows toward the sky. "What we call progress," noted Benjamin, "is *this* storm."[2]

As German armored divisions finally rolled toward France, Benjamin was forced to flee once more. He took one of the last trains for refugees heading south, with a few toiletries, his gas mask, and the memoirs of Cardinal de Retz. Benjamin sent a letter to Hannah Arendt noting that Retz's portrait of La Rochefoucauld's idleness reminded him of himself. Wracked by fear of reinternment, desperate for an exit visa in a crowded

Marseille hotel, Benjamin finally panicked and made a run for Spain before despair overwhelmed him and he committed suicide in a Pyrenean inn.

Set against the backcloth of personal hopelessness, the image of an angel trapped by a history it cannot control has gained currency in our darkening times, when it feels like a storm is coming while we look back and all we see is wreckage.

But ours are not end-times, at least not yet. Hannah Arendt, who arrived in Marseille too late to find her friend alive would later write an essay about him. In it, she quotes from another letter, this one from Benjamin to their mutual friend, Gershom Scholem. Written in 1931, just before Hitler's rise, the letter is also dreamlike. It says this about people in desperate need, what we have called in this book, borrowing from Michael Walzer, necessitous strangers: a necessitous stranger is "one who keeps afloat on a shipwreck by climbing to the top of a mast that is already crumbling. But from there he has a chance to give a signal leading to his rescue." After recalling Benjamin's gestures, his voice and his manners, his old-fashioned tastes, Arendt puzzled: why did Benjamin so love Paris in a way he did not love his Germany? Perhaps its boulevards and arcades, its writers and posers, were just the stage and actors to imagine new ways to think about home and hope? Paris, she noted, "offered itself to all homeless people as a second home."[3] In Paris "*a stranger feels at home because he can inhabit the city the way he lives in his own four walls*" (emphasis added).[4]

In the awful summer of 1940, one might say that losing Paris to the Nazis meant that Benjamin had lost his second home, the top of his mast; whatever distress signals he might have issued from that top were caught by the fascist storm; there was no more safe harbor.

Nowadays, tens of millions of people have climbed to the tops of their masts; all they want is a home in the world, their metaphoric Paris. For that, they *need*. They live in extreme conditions that define the edge of our ethics as humans. But extremes reveal aspects of the norm: we have all learned to *need* even if we do not recognize it. The past two-hundred-plus years have piled up an assembly of institutions, laws, actors, and norms which has, at least since Nagasaki, thus far prevented a world calamity. What the past has piled up at the feet of Angelus Novus is not all wreckage.

It has been the recognition of mutual need, its rewards and its risks, that produced this assembly, this architecture for the world. The architecture has proven relatively effective because it has been tasked with containing the costs of interdependence or absorbing them from the beneficiaries who prefer to displace the burdens onto others. Underscore the word "relatively." This is far from an absolutely effective way to deal with the benefits and costs of interdependence. The architecture includes city-scaled refugee camps. It catalogues the effects of our carbon addiction. It includes mass containment of necessitous Gazans to live in tents erected on rubbled tombs that were once their homes, to be fed and treated in "humanitarian" relief hubs, only to be shot in the swarm for survival. It includes euphemized "Terrorism Confinement Centers" like El Salvador's megaprison which now holds forty thousand detainees, increasing numbers of them forcibly deported from the United States. These are the edge-worlds that shade the difference between interdependence as a predatory hierarchy from something more inclusive and dignified. And yet, there has been no Third World War, Covid-19 and other pandemics have been contained, most migrants find new homes in strange lands and make them better. The architecture, for all its unevenness and unfairness, works, even if it has been bent into awful compromises and hypocrisy. It works because it shoulders a burden that nations and citizens prefer not to. It works because it has managed to uphold a pluralistic, integrated, intervisible world that, despite its differences, has avoided calamities that destroyed earlier orders and gave history its earlier end-times.

Walter Benjamin's Angelus Novus is not a prophecy—yet. He is a reminder.

However: being effective at managing the distribution of costs has produced two side effects. The first is this: shouldering the rising costs of interdependence leads to fatigue and drains legitimacy. Drainage means that contributors and sponsors forget the point and lose their understanding of the whole.

This crux produces a second side effect: the same architecture has been more effective at tackling immediate risks, where the returns are felt directly by those who bear the costs and reap the rewards, than the looming, longer-term, more complex ones that are deeply sedimented into the bedrock of interdependence, whose returns are more diffused and the costs displaced to other peoples and future generations.

As a result: the more interdependent and pluralistic the world becomes, the harder it is to pull its heterogeneous but integrated parts together in pursuit of common goals like accelerating an energy transition, reducing human insecurity, or containing an arms race all of whose rewards are less tangible or reaped by people far away in another place and time. Distributing the costs invites free riding, hoarding, and blaming, which reminds us of the Turkish proverb that Madame Marie once told a young Ernest Hemingway: in looking for what caused a tree to fall, it is tempting to fault the axe as well as the tree.

This is the peril of our postglobalization moment. The exhaustion of the institutions, actors, and rules that have been effective at shorter-term management in the nuclear age comes at a time in which the slow-burn, but maturing, challenges require capacities they do not have and that nations refuse to endow. The exhaustion amplifies the hazards of living together. In the mind-bending gap between the perceived rewards and real risks, and the real rewards and perceived risks, an antiglobal reaction feels like a way to address the anxiety. It decries pluralism as treason and promises to restore nation-first omnipotence as a means to protect and to reward homelanders. By hoarding, casting off the restraints of treaties, dismantling the guardrails against inter-state competition, and releasing a new arms race, they prompt others to follow suit. On the other side, one-worlders in their universities, think tanks, and NGOs speak in the universal tongue of rescuing and protecting strangers, as if referring to self-interest were ethically reprobate. By extolling the virtues of sharing and of self-sacrifice, even among those less able to pay for it, do-gooders have difficulty reckoning with the realities of risk in a competitive world. In the gap, more and more people search for their mast.

Which road will interdependence take? Will it follow the declension predicted by doomsayers, of more competition, more snarling, more rivalry, more exclusion, and more predation, a nasty, Hobbesian route cleared in the 1930s? Will this peril give new purpose to the fatigued architecture built up since Nagasaki, once envisioned to contain predation and to cope with the externalities of integration? Recent history has shown that the tide could go either way. The resurgence of snarling nation-firsters has coincided with solidarities, cooperation, and sharing—partly in response to *sauve qui peut* populism that blames strangers and stranger-lovers for society's problems. What is important to underscore is that the structures of interdependence have recycled over and again the contradictory pressures of competition and cooperation.

Note the conjunction: *and*. To acknowledge the contradiction and the intrinsic tension of sharing the planet is to see that interdependence implies living both ways at once because interdependence yields rising returns and poses inescapable costs.

The contradiction means there is never a stable equipoise. Compromises and settlements, yes. But a harmony of benefits and costs, hoarding and sharing? No. This is where the temptation of apocalyptic analysis and doomsday prophecies have run short: they conflate the challenges of our internal, fracturing tension over the need for strangers with a terminal crisis. This was true of the 1890s, 1930s, 1970s, and has resurfaced since the global financial crisis of 2008. Instead of seeing the history of the present as a moment of growing pains, the narrative becomes one of demise, decline of civilization, end of the West, final days of capitalism, death to liberalism—the list grows as headlines snatch the glimpses of our dwindling and splintered attention spans. In these moments of uncertainty over the path forward there is a risk of overperceiving hazards and reaching for the panic button, of hoping that nation-firsters can solve the problem of taking control with assertions of the right to dominate strangers because nation-first needs what strangers have and nation-first does not want to feel burdened by the cost. To sustain this, they rely on the shelters of their information bubbles and representational loops to avoid seeing that if everyone behaved and felt as they do, they too would be searching for their masts.

Is this a failure of imagination? Some say so. Some have argued that it requires the shock of being forced to envision a world without humans or life on a roasting planet to wake up, to "think like a planet," as David Wallace-Wells put it in a disturbing, if symptomatic, book. If we would wake up and break the cycle of apathy—having become too acclimated—we might see that "the threat from climate change is more total than the bomb."[5] This refrain echoes the loud doomism from the other end of the ideological spectrum. The scale of the need and the depth of the problem are so vast, like the struggle against capitalism, that they require a kind of cognitive rewiring, a new consciousness, a whole new matrix as the way out of the doom loop. With such a massive and abstract task ahead, no wonder despair makes sense. One is left to wonder: if we can't repair or upgrade something as banal as our electrical grids, where do we start to "think like a planet"?

These either-or apocalyptic narratives are too dramatic, too simple, and collapse into doomist traps that threaten to become self-fulfilling by magnifying the benefits of hoarding the gains of interdependence while externalizing its costs. Catastrophists recycle familiar terrorizing framings and end-time prophecies that have a distinguished track record of stoking fear, suspicion, and loathing. Modern history is overpopulated with examples of alarms that authorize the dehumanization of strangers who are blamed for being the source of what is wrong with the world.

There is an alternative. What gets driven out is a narrative that acknowledges the learning, admits the complexity, and bows to the ambiguity of what it means and what it feels like to share a planet over which one exerts, at best, only partial control because it is shared. It begins with a premise that recognizing interdependence means acknowledging the many ways in which self-interest and sympathies bind strangers together while differentiating and dividing them. That process yields asymmetries and unfairness, hierarchies of civilization, empires and dominators, as well as efforts and ideas, peaceful and violent, to undo them. It also yields deep pluralism, integration that resists the kind of universalism or totalizing visions that have dominated earlier global thinking and summitry cycles.[6]

The alternative admits a global history. The fact is, there has been a sea change in the imagination of togetherness that has been composed of the braided material and moral ties between people who have not known nor will ever know each other, though they gaze back at each other in mysterious and familiar ways in postcards and magazines, on TikTok and in their newsfeeds. The ideas, activism, solidarities, institutions—for all their shortcomings—have produced energies and counterpressures to balance the global distribution of rewards and costs of living together. The sea change began with the long struggle to dismantle the very empires that kicked off the cycle of integration (armed with their universalizing, emancipating missions) in the nineteenth century—whose dismantling dominated the twentieth in a global civil war and efforts to avoid a new, nuclearized clash.

To collapse into doomism means erasing that history. It means ignoring a pantheon of voices who have summoned alternative solidarities and imaginaries, José Martí and Liang Qichao, W.E.B Du Bois and the Women's International League for Peace and Freedom, Rachel Carson, Kaoru Yasui, Hannah Arendt, the postcolonial members of the Brandt Commission, Barbara Ward, Nelson Mandela, and the many scientists and philosophers, photographers and peaceniks, economists and beleaguered international managers and officials who have argued for integration with inclusion, for sharing the burdens and blessings of living together on a divided planet. The *cursus vitae* (course of life) of world thinking and expression, the Global Mind, does not read like a failure of imagination or an inability to envision a whole, unless one wants to read world history with one eye. Which many doomists do. If there is a failure, it is more deeply embedded in the difficulty of squaring up to a structure that is more complex and distributed, and that forces us to reckon with the conflicting emotional and material ties, the fluid mixture of self-interest and sympathy, that bind the world's strangers together while producing the fissures and torn feelings that are intrinsic to the Global Mind.

This history is unfinished. Since interdependence means living with risk and ceding control, the urge to form cartels of the entitled, clubs for the invited, and to dominate the Rest, will always be part of sharing the planet. Meanwhile, the same images that elicited anxiety and exhaustion also mobilized sympathy, solidarity, and renewed vows to work together—if not always out of compassion, at least out of necessity. The struggles and the compromises over the rewards and obligations of interdependence have mobilized the great arguments that have shaped the modern world and occupied the making and unmaking of the Global Mind. As long as we live together, as long as togetherness divides us, those disputes will unfold, take new shape, and find new expressions. It is the hope of this book that the quality and appeal of our understanding will determine which arguments prevail, so that, at the edge of human ethics that define the rest of our moral fabric, fewer people have to climb to the top of a mast to signal that their need has turned to desperation.

ACKNOWLEDGMENTS

THIS BOOK has been many years in the making. It folds ideas I have been puzzling over since my encounters with Harold Innis's writings on empire and communications while coming of age in Toronto, through a lifelong concern about the structures of Latin American dependency, and more recently in search of an alternative approach to world history, one that pays as much attention to fractures and closures as it does to integrations and openings. Though there is a half century behind it, this book is also a response to a more immediate drama that opened with the global financial crisis of 2008 and the ensuing waves of human displacement and backlash. We are mired in their legacies and searching for fresh ways to understand a shared past for an alternative future. This book, I hope, contributes to that urgent need.

Projects of this scope take long to write and therefore accumulate many debts. I will only be able to acknowledge a fraction here—and apologize to the many I have left out. The book began as a paper delivered at Boston University and their Sawyer Seminar on a new history of the twentieth century. Thank you to Brooke Blower for getting this voyage started. What began as a tangle of ideas about the twentieth century as a development century turned into this book, prompted by Brooke and her colleagues a dozen years ago.

To grasp the global is to confront forces that have driven us apart as much as those that have pulled us together. One key is to reckon with the contradictions of interdependence between strangers. I did not understand this when the voyage began; the voyage revealed the story. Many colleagues have shared advice along the way and helped me understand what it means to need. Thank you to Helga Nowotny for urging me to reread Norbert Elias; to Paul Warde on earth systems thinking; to Susan Stewart for recommendations on W. H. Auden (who, alas, did not survive the final editorial cuts, but the shadow of "Spain 1937" looms over the narrative of the 1930s); Gordon Chang who introduced me to early photography of Korea; Ciara Breathnach for catching a mystery figure in one of the photos; Marni Sandweiss for her inspirational approach to imagery; Ludi Jordanova for thoughts on the eighteenth century and the framing; Charlie Argon for snagging mistakes in chapter 3; Maxine Berg for help with Adam Smith and slavery; Amy Robinson for prompting me to read *Three Guineas* and sharing her story of fire; Dan Rodgers, Arcadio Díaz-Quiñones, Thomas Piketty, and Emma Rothschild for dialogues that helped me think anew; and to Howard Adelman for a lifetime of discussion about Hegel and the need for recognition. My fellow Fung Fellows in Princeton who argued with me for years about interdependence, Rita Kesselring, Kristin Surak, Guillaume Calafat, Tolga Demiryol, Onur Ulas, Joseph Prestel, Sophia Kalantzakos, Ayça Çubukçu, Sebastiaan Bouwman, Claire Vergerio, Pascale Siegrist, and Meng-Hsuan Chou, became cherished codependents. I can only hope that there was some reciprocity. Thanks to Steve Kotkin and to Nicole Bergman for the opportunity to run the Fung Global Fellows Program at the Princeton Institute for International and Regional Studies.

The making of this book overlapped with the making of the Global History Lab, which started in Princeton in 2012 as an open online course. The idea was to teach a course about the history of the world with the world in it. Especially as we leaned into emergency higher education in Afghanistan, Uganda, Lebanon, Ukraine, Russia, and elsewhere, I learned how challenging, rewarding, and urgent integration is. To internalize the world's borders and inequalities is not a neutral act—and it taught us all that divides have their global history. Among the lessons I learned is that working "without borders" or "without walls" is fabulous nonsense; borders and walls are sewn into the world's fabric. To think we can act or dream without them is to miss an opportunity to think seriously about them. Like this book, the lab began as conversations with Debbie Prentice, Jeff Himpele, and Clayton Marsh. I am grateful for fifteen years' support from colleagues at the McGraw Center for Teaching and Learning at Princeton and recently at the Centre for Research in the Arts, Social Sciences and Humanities (CRASSH) in Cambridge, and from the dozens of PhD students and colleagues over the years who have taught alongside me from Ho Chi Minh City to Buenos Aires, as well as to Princeton University and the Open Society Foundations for their generosity, and to Bill Jordan, Lenny Benardo, Jonathan Becker, Mark Malloch Brown, and Alex Soros. Above all, I want to thank the thousands of students who accompanied me. This book took longer to write as a result of our struggles to connect. But every page bears the imprint of lessons I learned from and with students of the world.

Draft ideas were lectures at Oxford, the New School, Yale, Harvard, Chicago, Boston University, Madrid, Athens, Paris, Tokyo, Hong Kong, Madrid, São Paulo, and beyond. So many colleagues contributed to the arguments that I cannot begin to catalogue them. However, I want to underscore special debts to Alessandro Stanziani for an important month at the École des Hautes Études en Sciences Sociales in Paris, where I presented drafts of three chapters that events forced me to rewrite. I am grateful to Silvia Sebastiani and Antoine Lilti for pushing me back into the eighteenth century to appreciate "the dilemma of distance" and to Fabien Locher who urged me to rethink the evolutionary origins of modern catastrophism. Shalini Randeria, director of the Institute for Human Sciences in Vienna, gave me a month of seclusion to write chapter 4 and I piloted an early chapter 5 to her wonderful colleagues there.

Chance encounters and exchanges often have outsized effects. But some were not by chance but rather by contract. I am grateful to the research assistance of Alyssa Wang, Kaspar Pucek, Rob Konkel, Kim Worthington, Nick Horvath, and Allyson Kim. Elisa Prosperetti and Kate Reed provided outstanding research on the global history of media. My editors at Princeton University Press, Brigitta van Rheinberg and Priya Nelson, stood by patiently as I rewrote and rethought; Priya's forbearance kept this project from derailing. Thank you also to Emma Wagh for last-mile help, to Nicole DiMella for help on images, to Sherry Gerstein and Holly LaFon for amazing editing help, and to Don Fehr, my agent.

Many of the ideas here have been the result of years of conversation with friends in the Global History Collaborative formed in my Princeton dining room so many years ago. To Masashi Haneda in Tokyo, Sebastian Conrad and Andreas Eckert in Berlin, and Alessandro Stanziani in Paris, I am so grateful.

Finally, as any world historian should know, the ability to go global depends on those at home. To Debbie, Sam, Jojo, and Sadie, thank you for your love and companionship, and to Debbie especially for the many, many conversations that sharpened the ideas and led to ditching others, and for reading a penultimate draft when you had more pressing and important tasks. As I completed this manuscript, two of my muses, my parents, passed away. I regret that it took so long for their counsel and support to materialize into a book they never got to see but that they profoundly influenced, beginning with the epigraph—after my father urged me to read Emmanuel Levinas.[1] To my siblings, the grief of recent years helped me to appreciate ever more what it means to share life with you.

Jeremy Adelman
Trim Tree Island
Ontario

NOTES

Introduction

1. Mark Leonard, *The Age of Unpeace: How Connectivity Causes Conflict* (Bantam Press, 2021), 16.

2. Paul Seabright, *The Company of Strangers: A Natural History of Economic Life* (Princeton University Press, 2004), 27.

3. Norbert Elias, *The Civilizing Process* (Blackwell, 2000), 29.

4. Elias, *Civilizing Process*, 370.

5. Psychologists call this a self-reference effect. Information about the self is more easily coded into memory than information about strangers. Anthony G. Greenwald, "The Totalitarian Ego: Fabrication and Revision of Personal History," *American Psychologist*, 35:7 (July 1980), 603–618; Michael Ross and Fiore Sicoly, "Egocentric Biases in Availability and Attribution," *Journal of Personality and Social Psychology*, 37:3 (1979), 322–36.

6. Albert O. Hirschman, *National Power and the Structure of Foreign Trade* (University of California Press, 1945), and in the same tradition, Robert O. Keohane and Joseph Nye, *Power and Interdependence* (Harper Collins, 1989). For more detail, see Jeremy Adelman, *Worldly Philosopher: The Odyssey of Albert O. Hirschman* (Princeton University Press, 2013).

7. Paul Gilroy, *Postcolonial Melancholia* (Columbia University Press, 2006).

8. Claire Jones, Sam Fleming, and James Politi, "'We Have to Rebuild Our Country': Donald Trump and His Team Pursue Economic Shock Therapy," *Financial Times*, March 12, 2025, https://www.ft.com/content/40ab6b86-7c26-4579-bde3-ebed640fa04f.

9. "Special Address by the Prime Minister of Canada, Mark Carney, 20 January, 2026, https://www.weforum.org/stories/2026/01/davos-2026-special-address-by-mark-carney-prime-minister-of-canada/. Accessed February 1, 2026.

10. Miri Rubin, *Cities of Strangers: Making Lives in Medieval Europe* (Cambridge University Press, 2020), on how strangers became neighbors.

11. Silvia Sebastiani, "What Constituted Historical Evidence of the New World? Closeness and Distance in William Robertson and Francisco Javier Clavijero," *Modern Intellectual History*, 11:3 (August 2014), 677–95.

12. David Hume, "Of Refinement in the Arts," from *Political Discourses (1752,1777)*, quoted in Margaret Schabas and Carl Wennerlind, *A Philosopher's Economist: Hume and the Rise of Capitalism* (University of Chicago Press, 2020), 114, 127. This essay went through various titles and editions.

13. David Hume, *An Enquiry Concerning the Principles of Morals* (1777), section 3, part 1, https://davidhume.org/texts/m/3. Amartya Sen has developed this connection in "The

Boundaries of Justice," *The New Republic*, December 13, 2011, https://newrepublic.com/article/98552/hume-rawls-boundaries-justice.

14. Adam Smith, *The Theory of Moral Sentiments* (Liberty Classics, 1976), part 3, chap. 1, 203–4.

15. Smith, *Theory of Moral Sentiments*, part 3, chap. 3, 233.

16. And yet, Hume hoped, there was reason to stock faith in "calm judgements concerning the characters of men." When the passions got restrained and the sympathies got aroused by exchanges across distance, the problem of distance might dissolve. "Besides, that we ourselves often change our situation in this particular, we every day meet with persons, who are in a different situation from ourselves, and who could never converse with us on any reasonable terms, were we to remain constantly in that situation and point of view, which is peculiar to us," he wrote. In other words, the propensity in commercial society for people to move, to trade, to encounter others, enables people to see differently and to see difference. "The intercourse of sentiments, therefore, in society and conversation, makes us form some general inalterable standard, by which we may approve or disapprove of characters and manners." Hume, *A Treatise of Human Nature*, B3.3.3 can be found in https://davidhume.org/texts/t/3/full, accessed February 1, 2026; Fonna Forman-Barzilai, *Adam Smith and the Circles of Sympathy: Cosmopolitanism and Moral Theory* (Cambridge University Press, 2010), 5.

17. Albert O. Hirschman, *The Passions and the Interests: Political Arguments for Capitalism before Its Triumph* (Princeton University Press, 1977).

18. Mark Donoghue, "Adam Smith on 'The Wretched Spirit of Monopoly' in the East Indies Trade," *History of Economic Thought*, 47:3 (September 2025), 377–93.

19. T. M. Devine, "Did Slavery Make Scotia Great? A Question Revisited," in T. M. Devine (ed.), *Recovering Scotland's Slavery Past: the Caribbean Connection* (Edinburgh University Press, 2015), 225–45; Stephen Mullen, *The Glasgow Sugar Aristocracy: Scotland and Caribbean Slavery 1775–1838* (Royal Historical Society, 2022); Maxine Berg and Pat Hudson, *Slavery, Capitalism and the Industrial Revolution* (Polity Press, 2023), 106–118.

20. Adam Smith, *An Inquiry into the Nature and Causes of the Wealth of Nations*, Book III:ii (Oxford University Press, 1976), 1:328. I am grateful to Maxine Berg for drawing my attention to this treatment.

21. Thomas Haskell, "Capitalism and the Origins of Humanitarian Sensibility," *American Historical Review*, 90:2 (April 1985), 339–61; for an excellent study of commercial abolitionism, see Bronwen Everill, *Not Made by Slaves: Ethical Capitalism in the Age of Abolition* (Harvard University Press, 2020).

22. The circulation of news, narratives, and reproducible pictures amplified the affective world economy. What the media did was focus and frame, crafting the material conditions of what Raymond Williams called "structures of feeling" that governed the culture or mood of a period. Focusing drew attention to characters, plots, subjects; in photographic terms, focus highlighted some subjects at the expense of others, sharpening here while blurring there, directing the eye. At the same time, framing drew lines around subjects and excluded others. If focusing sharpened and blurred, framing selected and blocked. The effect was to manufacture an image in a way that structured the meaning of the event that it was portraying. By the 1970s, the role of media's representation of strangers became a source of heated debate—and requires attention to the changing practices of image production and circulation. Raymond Williams,

Marxism and Literature (Oxford University Press, 1977), 128. The term was originally coined in earlier work on film criticism, but he widens and clarifies its application here.

23. Jürgen Habermas, *The Structural Transformation of the Public Sphere: An Inquiry into a Category of Bourgeois Society* (MIT Press, 1989), 13.

24. Frederick Douglass, "Lecture on Pictures" (December 3, 1861), in John Stauffer, Zoe Trodd, and Celeste-Marie Bernier, *Picturing Frederick Douglass: An Illustrated Biography of the Nineteenth Century's Most Photographed American* (W. W. Norton, 2015), 127, 141.

25. Pierre Bourdieu, *Photography: A Middle-Brow Art* (Polity, 1990).

26. Nathan Jurgenson, *The Social Photo: On Photography and Social Media* (Verso, 2019), 21.

Chapter One

1. Zahid R. Chaudhary, *Afterimage of Empire: Photography in Nineteenth-Century India* (University of Minnesota Press, 2012), 23, 50.

2. Alessandro Stanziani, *Capital terre: Une histoire longue du monde d'après (XII*^{e}*–XXI*^{e} *siècle)* (Payot, 2021), 89–92; Nicola Perugini and Neve Gordon, *The Human Right to Dominate* (Oxford University Press, 2015).

3. Charles S. Maier, *Once Within Borders: Territories of Power, Wealth, and Belonging Since 1500* (Harvard University Press, 2016).

4. See Douglass North's classic, "Ocean Freight Rates and Economic Development, 1750–1913," *Journal of Economic History*, 18:4 (December 1958): 537–55; Jan de Vries, "The Limits of Globalization in the Early Modern World," *Economic History Review*, 63:3 (August 2010): 710–33; Jeremy Adelman, "Mimesis and Rivalry: European Empires and Global Regimes," *Journal of Global History*, 10:1 (March 2015): 77–98.

5. Jürgen Osterhammel, *The Transformation of the World: A Global History of the Nineteenth Century* (Princeton University Press, 20014), 788–92.

6. The owners of abundant factors—land in the Americas, capital in Europe—acquired more political influence and means to exercise it; policies reflected their preferences. In Europe, domestic interests tilted to favor cheaper imports like timber, sugar, cotton, and above all, wheat. In turn, New World consumers wanted European manufactures and New World governments and tycoons wanted Old World loans. The realignment of interests and coalitions was hardly smooth. In some cases, it was violent. Civil wars in the United States and the River Plate region, for instance, were waged over rival models of integration into the wider world. Step-by-step, a bandwagon effect kicked in; accelerating with the Anglo-French Treaty of Commerce of 1860, the era of free trade rose above the horizon. Across the Atlantic world, countries dismantled protectionist barriers. When the creed pushed beyond the Atlantic, the dismantling was less and less voluntary and more and more imposed by Euro-Americans. David Todd, *Free Trade and Its Enemies in France, 1814–1851* (Cambridge University Press, 2015), 4–9; John V. C. Nye, *War, Wine, and Taxes: the Political Economy of Anglo-French Trade, 1689–1900* (Princeton University Press, 2007), 3–4; Jeremy Adelman, *Sovereignty and Revolution in the Iberian Atlantic* (Princeton University Press, 2006), 349–55.

7. Juan Bautista Alberdi, "Acción de la Europa en América," in *Obras completas*, t. 3 (La Tribuna, 1886), 80.

8. Markus Lampe, "Effects of Bilateralism and the MFN Clause on International Trade: Evidence from the Cobden-Chevalier Network, 1860–1875," *Journal of Economic History*, 69:4 (December 2009): 1012–24.

9. Patrick K. O'Brien, "Intercontinental Trade and the Development of the Third World Since the Industrial Revolution," *Journal of World History*, 8:1 (January 1997): 75–79; North, "Ocean Freight Rates," 537–55; A. G. Kenwood and A. L. Lougheed, *Growth of the International Economy, 1820–2000* (Routledge, 1992), 78.

10. Christopher Meissner, Dennis Novy and David Jacks, "Globalization and the Costs of International Trade from 1870 to the Present," Working Paper (Center for Economic Policy, August 16, 2008, https://cepr.org/voxeu/columns/globalisation-and-costs-international-trade-1870-present.

11. Walter Bagehot, *Lombard Street: A Description of the Money Market* (New York, 1873), 2–3.

12. Joseph Sassoon, *The Sassoons: The Great Global Merchants and the Making of an Empire* (Pantheon, 2022), 30–48; Mircea Raianu, *Tata: The Global Corporation That Built Indian Capitalism* (Harvard University Press, 2021), 18–23.

13. Charles A. Jones, *International Business in the Nineteenth Century: The Rise and Fall of a Cosmopolitan Bourgeoisie* (Wheatsheaf Books, 1987).

14. Geoffrey Jones, *British Multinational Banking, 1830–1990* (Clarendon Press, 1993), 23–34; Robert Bickers, *The Scramble for China: Foreign Devils in the Qing Empire, 1832–1914* (Penguin, 2011), 287–88.

15. Angela Radish, "The Latin Monetary Union and the Emergence of the International Gold Standard," in *Monetary Regimes in Transition*, ed. Michael Bordo and Forrest Capie (Cambridge University Press, 1993), 68–85. On gold, see the classical study by Barry Eichengreen, *Globalizing Capital: A History of the International Monetary System*, 2nd ed. (Princeton University Press, 2008), 15–24.

16. Osterhammel, *Transformation of the World*, 710–42.

17. Mae Ngai, *The Chinese Question: The Gold Rushes and Global Politics* (W. W. Norton, 2021), 19; Peter Guardino, *The Death March: A History of the Mexican-American War* (Harvard University Press, 2017). On Chileans and the gold rush, see Abraham Nasatir, "Chileans in California During the Gold Rush Period and the Establishment of the Chilean Consulate," *California Historical Quarterly*, 53:1 (Spring 1974): 52–70.

18. Christopher Andrew, *The Secret World: A History of Intelligence* (Yale University Press, 2018), 402.

19. Ben Wilson, *Heyday: The 1850s and the Dawn of the Global Age* (Basic Books, 2016), 175–76; Orlando Figes, *The Crimean War: A History* (Henry Holt, 2010), 313.

20. Yrjö Kaukiainen, "Shrinking the World: Improvements in the Speed of Information Transmission, c. 1820–1870," *European Review of Economic History*, 5:1 (April 2001), 1–28; Lisa Gitelman and Thomas S. Mullaney, "Nineteenth-Century Media Technologies," in *Information: A Historical Companion*, ed. Ann Blair, Paul Duguid, Anja-Silvia Goeing, and Anthony Grafton (Princeton University Press, 2020), 176–77.

21. Jeremy Black, *The Power of Knowledge: How Information and Technology Made the Modern World* (Yale University Press, 2014), 306.

22. Dana Schwartz, "Objective Representation: Photographs as Facts" in *Picturing the Past: Media, History, and Photography*, ed. Bonnie Brennen and Hanno Hardt (The University of Illinois Press, 1999), 166.

23. Edyta Bojanowska, *A World of Empires: The Russian Voyage of the Frigate Pallada* (Harvard University Press, 2018).

24. Michael R. Auslin, *Negotiating with Imperialism: The Unequal Treaties and the Culture of Japanese Diplomacy* (Harvard University Press, 2004).

25. Figes, *Crimean War*, 70–71, 152; Fabian Klose, *In the Cause of Humanity: A History of Humanitarian Intervention in the Long Nineteenth Century* (Cambridge University Press, 2022).

26. Erika Rappaport, *A Thirst for Empire: How Tea Shaped the Modern World* (Princeton University Press, 2019), 65.

27. Gerrit Gong, *The Standard of "Civilization" in International Society* (Clarendon Press; Oxford University Press 1984); Duncan Bell, *Reordering the World: Essays on Liberalism and Empire* (Princeton University Press, 2016), esp. chap. 2. For an alternative to civilizational historiography, see Josephine Quinn, *How the World Made the West: A 4,000 Year History* (Bloomsbury, 2024), 3–4. Quinn argues that the singular "civilization" gave way to a pluralist vision in the nineteenth century of a "West" counterposed to other civilizations. I agree and disagree. There *was* an urge to pluralize cultural spheres. But the effort reflected a more underlying impulse to stratify these spheres to highlight the superiority and manifest destiny of the West to bring the Rest into its fold.

28. Simon Morgan, "The Anti-Corn Law League and British Anti-Slavery in Transatlantic Perspective, 1838–1846," *Historical Journal*, 52:1 (March 2009), 87–107.

29. David W. Blight, *Frederick Douglass: Prophet of Freedom* (Simon & Schuster, 2018), 168–69.

30. Anthony G. Hopkins, "Property Rights and Empire Building: Britain's Annexation of Lagos, 1861," *Journal of Economic History*, 40:4 (December 1980), 777–98; Hopkins, *Capitalism in the Colonies: African Merchants in Lagos, 1851–1931* (Princeton University Press, 2024), 50, 86–87.

31. Henri Brunschwig, *Mythes et réalités de l'Impérialisme colonial français, 1871–1914* (Armand Colin, 1960); Matthew Burrows, "'*Mission Civilisatrice*': French Cultural Policy in the Middle East, 1860–1914," *Historical Journal*, 29:1 (March 1986), 109–35.

32. David Howell, *Geographies of Identity in Nineteenth-Century Japan* (University of California Press, 2005).

33. Mark Bassin, *Imperial Visions: Nationalist Integration and Geographical Expansion in the Russian Far East, 1840–1865* (Cambridge University Press, 1999).

34. J. S. Mill, *Principles of Political Economy With Some of Their Applications to Social Philosophy*, Book III:17, 7th edition (Longmans, Green, Reader and Dyer, 1871), II:8.

35. Mill, *Principles*, 3.

36. Mill, *Principles*, 13.

37. Mill, *Principles*, 18. Casper Sylvest, *British Liberal Internationalism, 1880-1930* (Manchester: Manchester University Press, 2009), 37fn51

38. John Stuart Mill, *On Liberty* (J. M. Dent, 1972), 128; see also Bell, *Reordering the World*, 300–302.

39. Mill, *On Liberty*, 129.

40. Mill, *On Liberty*, 42

41. John Stuart Mill, "A Few Words on Non-Intervention," in *The Collected Works of John Stuart Mill*, ed. John M. Robson, vol. 21, *Essays on Equality, Law, and Education* (University of Toronto Press, 1984), https://oll.libertyfund.org/title/mill-the-collected-works-of-john-stuart-mill-volume-xxi-essays-on-equality-law-and-education#lf0223-21_head_040. For Mill on empire, see Jennifer Pitts, *A Turn to Empire: The Rise of Imperial Liberalism in Britain and France* (Princeton University Press, 2005), 138–43.

42. Among the beneficiaries of the opium trade were Gujarati merchants like Jamsetji Nusserwanji Tata, pioneer industrialist and founder of the modern Tata dynasty. Like many Parsis, he found a way to do well under the raj. He seized the opportunity of the U.S. Civil War's halt on cotton shipments and the spike in the fiber's prices to dive into the cotton trade. When the war ended, and the market for cotton glutted, the Tatas took a beating, but then the family quickly recovered when Jamsetji Tata secured a lucrative contract to provision the British expedition to Abyssinia in 1867. Empire was good for local magnates. Tata sent relatives to Hong Kong and Shanghai to help manage the opium shipments and to send back silks and tea in return. It was not just the British who had an interest in opening China; it was an entire empire. By the 1870s, India was sending more textiles to China than Lancashire and Manchester. It all started, though, with opium. Sunil Khilnani, *Incarnations: A History of India in Fifty Lives* (Farrar, Straus and Giroux, 2016), 196–98.

43. Stephen R. Platt, *Autumn in the Heavenly Kingdom: China, the West, and the Epic Story of the Taiping Civil War* (Vintage, 2012), 104–9.

44. Platt, *Autumn*, 337, 165

45. Stephen R. Platt, *Imperial Twilight: The Opium War and the End of China's Last Golden Age* (Knopf Doubleday, 2018), 183; David Harris, "Imperial Ideology and Felice Beato's Photographs of the Second Opium War in China," in *Of Battle and Beauty: Felice Beato's Photographs of China* (Santa Barbara Museum of Art, 1999), 18; Catherine Pinguet, *Felice Beato (1832–1909): Aux origines de la photographie de guerre* (CNRS Editions, 2014).

46. Julia Lovell, *The Opium War: Drugs, Dreams and the Making of Modern China* (Overlook, 2015), 265.

47. Isobel Crombie, "China, 1860: A Photographic Album by Felice Beato," *History of Photography*, 11:1 (January 1987), 34; Lovell, *The Opium War*, 265.

48. Wong Hong Suen, "Picturing Burma: Felice Beato's Photographs of Burma, 1886–1905," *History of Photography*, 32:1 (2008), 1–26.

49. Karl Marx, *The German Ideology* (International Publishers, 1981), 47.

50. Karl Marx, "History of the Opium Trade," in *Karl Marx: Dispatches for the New York Tribune*, ed. James Ledbetter (Penguin, 2007), 30.

51. Karl Marx and Friedrich Engels, *Manifesto of the Communist Party* (Verso, 1998), 39–40.

52. Karl Marx, "The British and Chinese Treaty" in Ledbetter, *Dispatches*, 36–41.

53. Harold Laski, introduction to *Communist Manifesto: Socialist Landmark* (Allen and Unwin, 1948), 22.

54. Laski, introduction, 38.

55. Theodore Child, "Literary Paris," *Harper's Magazine*, September 1892, 492, https://archive.org/details/sim_harpers-magazine_1892-09_85_508/page/492/mode/2up.

56. Mary Louise Pratt, *Imperial Eyes: Travel Writing and Transculturation* (Routledge, 2008).

57. Cemil Aydin, *The Politics of Anti-Westernism in Asia: Visions of World Order in Pan-Islamic and Pan-Asian Thought* (Columbia University Press, 2007), 61–62.

58. Halil Halid, *The Crescent Versus the Cross* (Luzac and Co., 1907), 4–5.

59. Thomas Havens, *Nishi Amane and Modern Japanese Thought* (Princeton University Press, 1970.

60. C. A. Bayly, *Recovering Liberties: Indian Thought in the Age of Liberalism and Empire* (Cambridge University Press, 2012), 49, 107, 173.

61. Cited in Carlos Marichal, *A Century of Debt Crises in Latin America* (Princeton University Press, 1989), 56.

62. José Martí, "The Brooklyn Bridge," *Selected Writings*, ed. and trans. Esther Allen (Penguin, 2002).

Chapter Two

1. Avishai Margalit, *The Ethics of Memory* (Harvard University Press, 2009), chap. 5.

2. Cited in Hugh Rockoff, *America's Economic Way of War: The US Economy from the Spanish Civil War to the Persian Gulf War* (Cambridge University Press, 2012), 54.

3. Marcus M. Wilkerson, *Public Opinion and the Spanish-American War: A Study in War Propaganda* (Louisiana State University Press, 1932); Louis A. Pérez, *The War of 1898: The United States and Cuba in History and Historiography* (University of North Carolina Press, 1998).

4. Oliver Boyd-Barrett and Terhi Rantanen, "The Globalization of News" in *The Globalization of News*, ed. Oliver Boyd-Barrett and Terhi Rantanen (Sage Publications, 1998), 7; Tomoko Akami, *Japan's News Propaganda and Reuters' News Empire in Northeastern Asia, 1870–1934* (Republic of Letters, 2012), 12, 66.

5. Siobhan Angus, "Mining the History of Photography," in *Capitalism and the Camera: Essays on Photography and Extraction*, ed. Kevin Coleman and Daniel James (Verso, 2021), 57–61; Ricardo Salvatore, *Disciplinary Conquests: U.S. Scholars in South America, 1900–1945* (Duke University Press, 2016), 80–81.

6. Robert W. Desmond. *The Information Process: World News Reporting to the Twentieth Century* (University of Iowa Press, 1978), 215; Dana Schwartz, "Objective Representation," 168.

7. John Steel and Marcel Broersma, "Redefining Journalism During the Period of the Mass Press 1880–1920: An Introduction," *Media History*, 21:3 (2015), 237; Anthony Smith, *The Newspaper: An International History* (Thames & Hudson Ltd., 1979),152.

8. Jacob Riis, *How the Other Half Lives* (Scribner's, 1890), 5–6. Jack London followed with his own, *The People of the Abyss*, a chronicle of despair in East London, with his own (albeit less remarkable) photos.

9. Jeffrey Meyers, *Joseph Conrad: A Bibliography* (Scribner's, 1991), 92.

10. Joseph Conrad, *Heart of Darkness* (Penguin, 2011), 89; for more, see Maya Jasanoff, *The Dawn Watch: Joseph Conrad in a Global World* (Penguin Books, 2017), 222–25.

11. Isabel Hofmeyr, *Gandhi's Printing Press: Experiments in Slow Reading* (Harvard University Press, 2013).

12. Ronald Findlay and Kevin H. O'Rourke, *Power and Plenty: Trade, War, and the World Economy in the Second Millennium* (Princeton University Press, 2009), 411–24; Paul Bairoch,

"European Foreign Trade in the XIX Century," *Journal of European Economic History*, (Spring 1973), 8.

13. Bairoch, "European Foreign Trade," 13; François Crouzet, *The Victorian Economy* (Methuen, 1982), 342; W. Arthur Lewis, *Growth and Fluctuations, 1870–1913* (Allen & Unwin, 1978), 17, 115.

14. Dirk Bönker, *Militarism in the Global Age: Naval Ambitions in Germany and the United States Before World War I* (Cornell University Press, 2012), 26.

15. W. Arthur Lewis, "The Export Stimulus," in *Tropical Development, 1880–1913*, ed. W. Arthur Lewis (Allen & Unwin, 1970), 14–22.

16. Adam McKeown, "Global Migration, 1846–1940," *Journal of World History*, 15:2 (May 2004), 156.

17. John C. Weaver, *The Great Land Rush and the Making of the Modern World, 1650–1900* (McGill-Queens University Press, 2003), 88; Charles S. Maier, *Once Within Borders: Territories of Power, Wealth, and Belonging Since 1500* (Harvard University Press, 2016), 228–30.

18. Helen C. Farnsworth, "World Wheat Stocks, 1890–1914 and 1922–39," *Wheat Studies*, 16:2 (October 1939), 59.

19. Kevin H. O'Rourke and Jeffrey G. Williamson, "Around the European Periphery 1870–1913: Globalization, Schooling and Growth," *European Review of Economic History*, 1:2 (August 1997), 153–190.

20. John A. Hobson, *The Industrial System: An Inquiry into Earned and Unearned Income* (London 1909), 320; P. J. Cain, *Hobson and Imperialism: Radicalism, New Liberalism, and Finance, 1887–1938* (Oxford University Press, 2002), 76–80.

21. Tariq Omar Ali, *A Local History of Global Capital: Jute and Peasant Life in the Bengal Delta* (Princeton University Press, 2018).

22. Emilio Kourí, *A Pueblo Divided: Business, Property, and Community in Papantla, Mexico* (Stanford University Press, 2004), 29.

23. Robert Levine, *Vale of Tears: Revisiting the Canudos Massacre* (University of California Press, 1992).

24. Euclides da Cunha, *Rebellion in the Backlands* (University of Chicago Press, 1944), 162, 280.

25. Cícero F. de Almeida, *Canudos: Imagens da guerra; Os últimos dias da Guerra de Canudos pelo fotógrafo expedicionário Flávio de Barros* (Museu da República/Lacerda, 1997).

26. Rick Halpern, "Photography and the New American Empire," *Frames*, April 28, 2021, https://readframes.com/photography-and-the-new-american-empire-by-rick-halpern/; Martha Sandweiss, *Print the Legend: Photography and the American West* (Yale University Press, 2002), 215–19.

27. Federico Ferretti, "Pioneers in the History of Cartography: The Geneva Map Collection of Élisée Reclus and Charles Perron," *Journal of Historical Geography*, 43 (2014), 85–95; S. Alavoine-Muller, "Un globe terrestre pour l'Exposition universelle de 1900: L'utopie géographique d'Élisée Reclus," *L'Espace géographique*, 31 (2003), 156–70; Élisée Reclus, *Projet de construction d'un globe terrestre à l'échelle du cent-millième* (Edition de la Société nouvelle, 1895).

28. Élisée Reclus, *Anarchy, Geography, Modernity: Selected Writings* (PM Press, 2013), 115.

29. Barry Eichengreen, *Globalizing Capital: A History of the International Monetary System* (Princeton University Press, 2008), 15–19.

30. Walter Bagehot, *Lombard Street: A Description of the Money Market* (Henry King, 1873), 17; Martin Daunton, "Britain and Globalisation Since 1850: I. Creating a Global Order, 1850–1914," *Transactions of the Royal Historical Society*, 16 (2006): 1–38; Marcello de Cecco, *Money and Empire: The International Gold Standard, 1890–1914* (Blackwell, 1974).

31. Bagehot, *Lombard Street*, 37.

32. Jean Jacques Van-Helten, "Empire and High Finance: South Africa and the International Gold Standard 1890–1914," *Journal of African History*, 23:4 (1982), 535.

33. Carlos Marichal, *A Century of Debt Crises in Latin America: From Independence to the Great Depression* (Princeton University Press, 1989), 157.

34. Edward Anderson, "Globalization and Wage Inequalities, 1870–1970," *European Review of Economic History*, 5:1 (April 2001), 91–118.

35. Thorstein Veblen, "The Food Supply and the Price of Wheat," *Journal of Political Economy*, 1 (June 1893), 365–79.

36. Dadabhai Naoroji, *Poverty and Un-British Rule in India* (Swan Sonnenschein & Co., 1901), 1.

37. Mary Sutphen, "Not What, but Where: Bubonic Plague and the Reception of Germ Theories in Hong Kong and Calcutta," *Journal of the History of Medicine*, 52:1 (January 1997), 81–113; William H. McNeill, *Plagues and Peoples* (Anchor Books, 1976), 135–139.

38. Mike Davis, *Late Victorian Holocausts: El Niño Famines and the Making of the Third World* (Verso, 2001), 133, 277.

39. James Y. Simms, "The Crop Failure of 1891: Soil Exhaustion, Technological Backwardness, and Russia's 'Agrarian Crisis,'" *Slavic Review*, 41:2 (Summer 1982), 236–50; Simms, "The Crisis in Russian Agriculture at the End of the Nineteenth Century: A Different View," *Slavic Review*, 36:3 (September 1977), 377–98.

40. Fabien Locher, *Le savant et la tempête: Étudier l'atmosphère et prévoir le temps au XIXe siècle* (Presses Universitaires de Rennes, 2008), 70, 169–89.

41. Donald Worster, *Shrinking the Earth: The Rise and Decline of American Abundance* (Oxford University Press, 2016), 98–100; David Sepkoski, *Catastrophic Thinking: Extinction and the Value of Diversity from Darwin to the Anthropocene* (University of Chicago Press, 2020), 93–94.

42. Frederick Jackson Turner, "The Significance of the Frontier in American History," in *The Frontier in American History* (Holt, Rinehart and Winston, 1920), 1–38.

43. Thomas Robertson, *The Malthusian Moment: Global Population Growth and the Birth of American Environmentalism* (Rutgers University Press, 2012), 5.

44. Gregory Claeys, *Imperial Sceptics: British Critics of Empire, 1850–1920* (Cambridge University Press, 2010), 3.

45. Quoted in Sunil Amrith, *The Burning Earth: A History* (W. W. Norton, 2024), 130.

46. Mark Bassin, "Turner, Solov'ev, and the 'Frontier Hypothesis': The Nationalist Signification of Open Spaces," *Journal of Modern History*, 65:3 (September 1993), 473–511; Bassin, *Imperial Visions: Nationalist Imagination and Geographical Expansion in the Russian Far East, 1840–1865* (Cambridge University Press, 1999).

47. Eric Hobsbawm, *The Age of Empire, 1875–1914* (Abacus, 1987), 70.

48. Jennifer E. Sessions, *By Sword and Plow: France and the Conquest of Algeria* (Cornell University Press, 2011); Margaret Cook Andersen, *Regeneration Through Empire: French Pronatalists and Colonial Settlement in the Third Republic* (University of Nebraska Press, 2015), 25–51.

49. John Short, *Magic Lantern Empire: Colonialism and Society in Germany* (Cornell University Press, 2012); Sven Beckert, "American Danger: United States Empire, Eurafrica, and the Territorialization of Industrial Capitalism, 1870–1950," *American Historical Review*, 122:4 (October 2017), 1152, 1160–61; Sean McMeekin, *The Berlin-Baghdad Express: The Ottoman Empire and Germany's Bid for World Power* (Harvard University Press, 2010), 12–16; Duncan Bell, *Dreamworlds of Race: Empire and the Utopian Destiny of Anglo-America* (Princeton University Press, 2020).

50. Gerry Kearns, *Geopolitics and Empire: The Legacy of Halford Mackinder* (Oxford University Press, 2009), 63–75.

51. Oona A. Hathaway and Scott J. Shapiro, *The Internationalists: How a Radical Plan to Outlaw War Remade the World* (Simon & Schuster, 2017), 317.

52. John Short, *Magic Lantern Empire: Colonialism and Society in Germany* (Cornell University Press, 2012); H. Pogge von Strandmann, "Domestic Origins of Germany's Colonial Expansion," *Past and Present*, 42 (February 1969); Paul Kennedy, "German Colonial Expansion: Has the 'Manipulated Social Imperialism' Been Ante-Dated?," *Past and Present*, 54 (1972); Conrad, *Heart of Darkness*, 7.

53. Shellen Xiao Wu, *Empires of Coal: Fueling China's Entry into the Modern World Order, 1860–1920* (Stanford, 2015), 54–64, 139, 175.

54. Mark Gamsa, *Harbin: A Cross-Cultural Biography* (University of Toronto Press, 2020), 4–5; Victor Seow, *Carbon Technocracy: Energy Regimes in Modern East Asia* (University of Chicago Press, 2021), 21.

55. Michael Auslin, "Japanese Statecraft, Geopolitics and the Origins of the War, 1792–1895," in *The Russo-Japanese War in Global Perspective: World War Zero*, ed. John Steinberg, Bruce Menning, David Schimmelpenninck van der Oye, David Wolff, and Shinji Yokote (Brill, 2005), 17–18.

56. Cemil Aydin, *The Politics of Anti-Westernism in Asia: Visions of World Order in Pan-Islamic and Pan-Asian Thought* (Columbia University Press, 2007), 54–55; Josefa M. Saniel, *Japan and the Philippines, 1868–1898* (University of the Philippines, 1962), 77–79; Bickers, *The Scramble for China*, 326–33.

57. Stephen Kinzer, *The True Flag: Theodore Roosevelt, Mark Twain, and the Birth of American Empire* (Henry Holt, 2017), 25.

58. Christopher Clark, *Sleepwalkers: How Europe Went to War in 1914* (Penguin, 2012), 147–48; Patrick J. Kelly, *Tirpitz and the Imperial German Navy* (Indiana University press, 2011), 128–33.

59. John Lawrence Tone, *War and Genocide in Cuba, 1895–1898* (University of North Carolina Press, 2006), 218; Fabian Klose, *In the Cause of Humanity: A History of Humanitarian Intervention in the Long Nineteenth Century* (Cambridge University Press, 2022), 234.

60. Rebecca E. Karl, *Staging the World: Chinese Nationalism at the Turn of the Century* (Duke University Press, 2002), 33–39; Orville Schell and John Delury, *Wealth and Power: China's Long March to the Twenty-First Century* (Random House, 2013), 95; Pankaj Mishra, *From the Ruins of Empire: The Intellectuals Who Remade Asia* (Farrar, Straus and Giroux, 2012), 142–43.

61. Benjamin Schwartz, *In Search of Wealth and Power: Yen Fu and the West* (Harvard University Press, 1964), 33–42.

62. James Ricalton, *James Ricalton's Photographs of China During the Boxer Rebellion: His Illustrated Travelogue of 1900* (Edwin Mellen Press, 1990), 39–41.

63. Karl, *Staging the World*, 84; Schwartz, *In Search of Wealth and Power.*

64. Ayodele J. Langley, *Pan-Africanism and Nationalism in West Africa, 1900–1945* (Oxford University Press, 1973), 30.

65. Karl, *Staging the World*, 84; Ruth Rogaski, *Hygienic Modernity: Meanings of Health and Disease in Treaty-Port China* (University of California Press, 2004), 21.

66. Liang Qichao, "The General Trend of Struggles of Citizenries in Recent Times and the Future of China," in *Thoughts from the Ice-Drinker's Studio: Essays on China and the World*, ed. Peter Zarrow (Penguin, 2023), 30–31, 34.

67. John Ellis, *The Social History of the Machine Gun* (Croom Helm, 1976), 86.

68. Terence Ranger, *Revolt in Southern Rhodesia, 1896–7* (Heinemann, 1967), 121.

69. In his first articles and pamphlets, the odor of suspicion about Jewish bankers is hard to dismiss. Invoking the fear of the "Jew-imperialist" did more to liken the liberal reformer with snarling right-wing anti-Dreyfusards in France. J. A. Hobson, *The War in South Africa: Its Causes and Effects* (James Nisbet, 1900), 190–91; Trevor Lloyd, "Africa and Hobson's Imperialism," *Past and Present*, 55 (May 1972), 130–53.

70. John A. Hobson, *Imperialism: A Study* (James Nisbet, 1902), 13, 345; Claeys, *Imperial Sceptics*, 237–40. On Hobson's observations on emotions, Cain, *Hobson and Imperialism*, 99–103. On earth "productivism," see Stanziani, *Capital terre*, 95–96.

71. Tom Menger, *The Colonial Way of War: Violence and Colonial Warfare in the British, German, and Dutch Empires, 1890–1914* (Cambridge University Press, 2025); Aidan Forth and Jonas Kreienbaum, "A Shared Malady: Concentration Camps in the British, Spanish, American and German Empires," *Journal of Modern European History*, 14:2 (2016), 245–67.

72. Theodore Roosevelt, "Private Letter from Roosevelt to Speck von Sternberg," in *The Letters of Theodore Roosevelt*, ed. Elting Morison, vol. 3, *The Square Deal: 1901–1903* (Harvard University Press, 1951), 297–98.

73. Paul Kramer, *Blood of Government: Race, Empire, the United States and the Philippines* (University of North Carolina Press, 2006), 142, 219.

74. Kim A. Wagner, *Massacre in the Clouds: An American Atrocity and the Erasure of History* (Public Affairs, 2024), 181.

75. Olivier Charbonneau, *Civilizational Imperatives: Americans, Moros, and the Colonial World* (Cornell University Press, 2020), 106–7; see also Wagner, *Massacre in the Clouds*, 224–31.

76. James R. Arnold, *The Moro War: How America Battled a Muslim Insurgency in the Philippine Jungle, 1902–1913* (Bloomsbury, 2011), 176.

77. H. T. Johnson, "The Black Man's Burden," National Humanities Center, https://nationalhumanitiescenter.org/pds/gilded/empire/text7/johnson.pdf, originally published in *The Christian Recorder*, March 1899.

78. Sir Harry Johnston, Introductory Chapter to *Red Rubber: The Story of the Rubber Slave Trade Flourishing on the Congo in the Year of Grace, 1906*, by E. D. Morel (Nassau Print, 1906), ix; Robert Harms, *Land of Tears: The Exploration and Exploitation of Equatorial Africa* (Basic Books, 2019).

79. Neil Faulkner, *Empire and Jihad: The Anglo-Arab Wars of 1870–1920* (Yale University Press, 2021); Morel, *Red Rubber*, 27.

80. Harms, *Land of Tears*, 167; Brian Inglis, *Roger Casement* (Harcourt Jovanovich, 1973), 22.

81. Adam Hochschild, *King Leopold's Ghost: A Story of Greed, Terror, and Heroism in Colonial Africa* (Houghton Mifflin, 1998), 159.

82. Morel, *Red Rubber*, 54, 149.

83. Séamas Ó Síocháin and Michael O'Sullivan, *Eyes of Another Race: Roger Casement's Congo Report and 1903 Diary* (University College Dublin Press, 2003), 262.

84. Síocháin and O'Sullivan, *Eyes of Another Race*, 13.

85. Judy Pollard Smith, *Don't Call Me Lady: The Journey of Lady Alice Seeley Harris* (Abbott Press, 2014), 39; Heather D. Curtis, "Picturing Pain: Evangelicals and the Politics of Pictorial Humanitarianism in an Imperial Age," in *Humanitarian Photography: A History*, ed. Heide Fehrenbach and David Rodogno (Cambridge University Press, 2015), 22–45.

86. Charlie Laderman, *Sharing the Burden: The Armenian Question, Humanitarian Intervention, and Anglo-American Visions of Global Order* (Oxford University Press, 2019), 71.

87. Mark Twain, *King Leopold's Soliloquy: A Defense of His Congo Rule* (International Publishers, 1970), 73; Mark Anthony Sealy, "Decolonizing the Camera: Photography in Racial Time," (PhD thesis, Durham University, 2015), 18–20; Christina Twomey, "The Incorruptible Kodak: Photography, Human Rights and the Congo Campaign," *The Violence of the Image: Photography and International Conflict*, ed. Liam Kennedy and Caitlin Patrick (I. B. Taurus, 2014), 9–33; on the moment more generally, Kevin Grant, "The Limits of Exposure: Atrocity Photographs in the Congo Reform Campaign," in Fehrenbach and Rodogno, *Humanitarian Photography*, 64–88.

88. For more, see Andrew Porter, "Trusteeship, Anti-Slavery, and Humanitarianism," in *The Oxford Handbook of the British Empire*, ed. Andrew Porter and Wm Roger Louis, vol. 3, *The Nineteenth Century* (Oxford University Press, 1999), 198–221.

89. Jordan Goodman, *The Devil and Mr. Casement: One Man's Struggle for Human Rights in South America's Heart of Darkness* (Verso, 2009), 126.

90. W.E.B. Du Bois, "To the Nations of the World," in *The Oxford W.E.B. Du Bois Reader*, ed. Eric J. Sundquist (Oxford University Press, 1996), 625.

Chapter Three

1. David Fromkin, *A Peace to End All Peace: Creating the Modern Middle East, 1914–1922* (Henry Holt, 1989), 469, 546; Norman M. Naimark, *Fires of Hatred: Ethnic Cleansing in Twentieth-Century Europe* (Harvard University Press, 2001), 40, 52.

2. Ernest Hemingway, *Toronto Star Daily*, November 14, 1922, in *Dateline: Toronto: Hemingway's Complete Toronto Star Dispatches 1920–1924*, ed. William White (Charles Scribner's Sons, 1985), 249.

3. Rogers Brubaker, "Aftermaths of Empire and the Unmixing of Peoples," *Ethnic and Racial Studies*, 18:2 (April, 1995), 189–218; D. A. Moses, "Human Rights, Population 'Transfer,' and the Foundation of the Postwar Order," in *The Problem of Genocide: Permanent Security and the Language of Transgression*, ed. A. Dirk Moses (Cambridge University Press, 2021), 332–63.

4. From Walter Lippmann, *An Inquiry into the Principles of the Good Society* (Little, Brown and Co., 1938), 159. Civil wars are conventionally defined as conflicts within sovereign borders. See Stathis N. Kalyvas, *The Logic of Violence in Civil War* (Cambridge University Press, 2006), 5. But when those borders are blurred by interdependence, the unit and scale of violence escalate.

5. Robert Gewarth, *The Vanquished: Why the First World War Failed to End* (Penguin Press, 2017).

6. Nicholas Mulder, *The Economic Weapon: The Rise of Sanctions as a Tool of Modern War* (Yale University Press, 2022), 89; Gerd Hardach, *The First World War, 1914–1918* (Allen Lane, 1977), 30–31.

7. Laura Engelstein, *Russia in Flames: War, Revolution, Civil War, 1914–1921* (Oxford University Press, 2017), 622–23.

8. Anand Toprani, *Oil and the Great Powers: Britain and Germany, 1914–1945* (Oxford University Press, 2019), 3.

9. Ronald Suny, *"They Can Live in the Desert but Nowhere Else": A History of the Armenian Genocide* (Princeton University Press, 2017). The current estimates of the number of slaughtered or dead Armenians were around nine hundred thousand. By 1922, as Greek Christian survivors took refuge in the Balkans, 90 percent of Anatolian Armenians had perished.

10. James Barr, *A Line in the Sand: Britain, France, and the Struggle That Shaped the Middle East* (Simon & Schuster, 2011), 12.

11. Fromkin, *Peace to End All Peace*, 254.

12. Elizabeth F. Thompson, *How the West Stole Democracy from the Arabs: The Syrian of 1920 and the Destruction of Its Historic Liberal-Islamic Alliance* (Atlantic Monthly Press, 2020).

13. Eugene Rogan, *The Fall of the Ottomans: The Great War in the Middle East* (Basic Books, 2015), 399; Barr, *Line in the Sand*, 104–8.

14. Fromkin, *Peace to End All Peace*, 482–97.

15. Hardach, *First World War*, 247–48; Nicholas Mulder, "War Finance," in *1914–1918 Online: International Encyclopedia of the First World War*, ed. Ute Daniel, Peter Gatrell, Oliver Janz, Heather Jones, Jennifer Keene, Alan Kramer, and Bill Nasson (Freie Universität, 2018), https://encyclopedia.1914-1918-online.net/article/war_finance.

16. Isabel V. Hull, *A Scrap of Paper: Breaking and Making International Law During the Great War* (Cornell University Press, 2014).

17. Jörn Leonhard, *Pandora's Box: A History of the First World War* (Harvard University Press, 2018), 718.

18. The term was originally coined here: Henry Brailsford, *The War of Steel and Gold: A Study of the Armed Peace* (G. Bell & Sons, 1914).

19. Daniel Laqua, "Transnational Intellectual Cooperation, the League of Nations, and the Problem of Order," *Journal of Global History*, 6:2 (July 2011), 223–47; David Ekbladh, *Plowshares into Swords: Weaponized Knowledge, Liberal Order, and the League of Nations* (University of Chicago Press, 2022).

20. Tara Zahra, *Against the World: Anti-Globalism and Mass Politics Between the Two Wars* (W. W. Norton, 2023), 48–49.

21. Tomoko Akami, *Internationalizing the Pacific: The United States, Japan, and the Institute of Pacific Relations in War and Peace, 1919–1945* (Routledge, 2002), 37.

22. Catia Confortini, *Intelligent Compassion: The Women's International League for Peace and Freedom and Feminist Peace* (Oxford University Press, 2012); Glenda Sluga, "Women, Feminisms and Twentieth Century-Internationalisms," in *Internationalisms: A Twentieth-Century History*, ed Glenda Sluga and Patricia Clavin (Cambridge University Press, 2017).

23. Jonathan A. Grant, *Between Depression and Disarmament: The International Armaments Business, 1919–1933* (Cambridge University Press, 2018), 143, 157.

24. Hathaway and Shapiro, *The Internationalists*; Daniel Gorman, *The Emergence of International Society in the 1920s* (Cambridge University Press, 2012), 283–301; Adam Tooze, *The Deluge: The Great War, America, and the Remaking of the Global Order, 1916–1931* (Viking, 2014), 490–92.

25. J. C. Smuts, *The League of Nations: A Practical Suggestion* (Hodder and Stoughton, 1918), 11, 25.

26. Kenneth B. Pyle, *Japan Rising: The Resurgence of Japanese Power and Purpose* (Public Affairs, 2007), 157; Thomas J. Kock, *To End All Wars: Woodrow Wilson and the Quest for a New World Order* (Princeton University Press, 1992), 124–44; Erez Manela, *The Wilsonian Moment: Self-Determination and the International Origins of Anticolonial Nationalism* (Oxford University Press, 2007), 17–21.

27. Tomoko Akami, *Internationalizing the Pacific: The United States, Japan, and the Institute of Pacific Relations in War and Peace, 1919–1945* (Routledge, 2002), 25.

28. The literature on this phenomenon is now vast. But for how World War I affected the Islamic world internationalism, see Faisal Devji, "Escaping the Global Event: Pan-Islam and the First World War," *Modern Intellectual History*, 21:3 (2004), 503–23.

29. Liang Qichao, "The Self-Awakening of the Chinese People," in *Thoughts from the Ice-Drinker's Studio: Essays on China and the World*, ed. Peter Zarrow (Penguin Books, 2023), 178.

30. Quoted in Manela, *The Wilsonian Moment*, 137.

31. Quoted in Vera Schwarcz, *The Chinese Enlightenment: Intellectual and the Legacy of the May Fourth Movement of 1919* (University of California Press, 1986), 12; Rana Mitter, *A Bitter Revolution: China's Struggle with the Modern World* (Oxford University Press, 2004), 4–6.

32. David Levering Lewis, *W.E.B. Du Bois: Biography of a Race* (Henry Holt, 1993), 564.

33. J. Ayodele Langley, *Pan-Africanism and Nationalism in West Africa, 1900–1945* (Oxford University Press, 1973), 63–69, 376–77.

34. Cited in Carole Fink, *Defending the Rights of Others* (Cambridge University Press, 2008) 133.

35. Chad L. Williams, *The Wounded World: W.E.B Du Bois and the First World War* (Farrar, Straus and Giroux, 2023), 14.

36. The essay titled "The Souls of White Folk" was published in an essay collection published in early 1920. See the Du Bois anthology, *Darkwater: Voices from Within the Veil* (Schocken, 1969), 42. See also Williams, *Wounded World*, 210–11.

37. Langley, *Pan-Africanism and Nationalism*, 200–205.

38. Jawaharlal Nehru, *The Essential Writings of Jawaharlal Nehru* (Oxford University Press, 2003), 203.

39. Michael Schudson, *Discovering the News: Social History of American Newspapers* (Basic Books, 1978), 142.

40. Walter Benjamin, "The Work of Art in the Age of Mechanical Reproduction," in *Photography in Print: Writings from 1816 to the Present*, ed. Vicki Goldberg (University of New Mexico Press, 1988) 332.

41. Walter Benjamin, *Illuminations: Essays and Reflections* (Schocken, 1969), 89.

42. Ralph J. Bunche, *An African American in South Africa: The Travel Notes of Ralph J. Bunche, 28 September 1937–1 January 1938* (Ohio University Press, 1992), 55.

43. Peter Balakian, "Photography, Visual Culture, and the Armenian Genocide," in Fehrenbach and Rodogno, *Humanitarian Photography*, 90–99; Davide Rodogno, *Night on Earth: A History of International Humanitarianism in the Near East, 1918–1930* (Cambridge University Press, 2022), 90.

44. Adam Tooze, *The Wages of Destruction: The Making and Breaking of the Nazi Economy* (Penguin, 2007), 3.

45. Derek H. Aldcroft, *From Versailles to Wall Street, 1919–1929* (Allen Lane, 1977), 30.

46. Hardach, *First World War*, chaps. 9–10 for a summary.

47. Aldcroft, *From Versailles to Wall Street*, 75; Rajat Ray, *Industrialization of India* (Oxford University Press, 1979), 11–13.

48. Patricia Clavin, *Securing the World Economy: The Reinvention of the League of Nations, 1920–1946* (Oxford University Press, 2013), 17; Gorman, *Emergence of International Society*, 262–65.

49. For a good recent summary, see Patricia Clavin, Giancarlo Corsetti, Maurice Obstfeld, Adam Tooze, and Catherine Piner, eds., *Keynes's Economic Consequences of the Peace After 100 Years: Polemics and Policy* (Cambridge University Press, 2023), and Adam Tooze, *The Deluge*, 295.

50. John Maynard Keynes, *The Economic Consequences of the Peace* (Penguin, 1971), 12, 22; Anna Carabelli and Mario Cedrini, "Keynes and the Complexity of International Economic Relations in the Aftermath of World War I," *Journal of Economic Issues*, 44:4 (December 2010), 1009–27.

51. Keynes, *Economic Consequences of the Peace*, 207.

52. Jawaharlal Nehru, "Whither India? 1933," in *India's Freedom* (Unwin, 1962), 21.

53. Marie-Claire Bergère, *Sun Yat-sen* (Stanford University Press, 1994), 227.

54. Sun Yat-sen, *The International Development of China* (London, 1922). Eric Helleiner, *The Neomercantilists: A Global Intellectual History* (Cornell University Press, 2021), 247–50.

55. Barry Eichengreen, *Globalizing Capital: A History of the International Monetary System* (Princeton University Press, 2008), 44; Jamie Martin, *The Meddlers: Sovereignty, Empire, and the Birth of Global Governance* (Harvard University Press, 2022), 65.

56. For details on the Dawes and Young Plans, see "The Dawes Plan, the Young Plan, German Reparations, and Inter-Allied Debts," State Department, Office of the Historian, https://history.state.gov/milestones/1921-1936/dawes. This public service from the federal government has been discontinued by the Trump administration.

57. Aldcroft, *From Versailles to Wall Street*, 262–63.

58. Noah Mendel, "When Did the Great Depression Receive Its Name?" *History News Network*, February 15, 2009, https://historynewsnetwork.org/article/61931.

59. Harold James, *The End of Globalization: Lessons from the Great Depression* (Harvard University Press, 2001), 108–9, 119–21.

60. David A. Lake, *Power, Protection, and Free Trade: International Sources of Commercial Strategy, 1887–1939* (Cornell University Press, 1988), 207.

61. James, *End of Globalization*, 129; Patricia Clavin, *The Failure of Economic Diplomacy: Britain, Germany, France and the United States, 1931–1936* (Macmillan, 1996), 3–4.

62. Clavin, *Failure of Economic Diplomacy*, 4; Patricia Clavin, *Securing the World Economy: The Reinvention of the League of Nations, 1920–1946* (Oxford University Press, 2013).

63. Cited in Priya Satia, "The Defense of Inhumanity: Air Control and the British Idea of Arabia," *American Historical Review*, 111:1 (February 2006), 40.

64. Edward W. Bennett, *German Rearmament and the West, 1932–1933* (Princeton University Press, 2015); Kiran Klaus Patel, *The New Deal: A Global History* (Princeton University Press, 2016), 122–25.

65. Zahra, *Against the World*, 225.

66. Kevin O'Rourke, "Two Great Trade Collapses: The Interwar Period and Great Recession Compared," *IMF Economic Review*, 66:3 (2018), 418–39.

67. James, *End of Globalization*, 125.

68. Norman Miners, "Industrial Development in the Colonial Empire and the Imperial Economic Conference at Ottawa 1932," *The Journal of Imperial and Commonwealth History*, 30:2 (May 2002), 53–76.

69. Jacques Marseille, *Empire colonial et capitalisme français: Histoire d'un divorce* (Seuil, 1989), 186–89.

70. Douglas A. Irwin, "From Smoot-Hawley to Reciprocal Trade Agreements: Changing the Course of U.S. Trade Policy in the 1930s," in *The Defining Moment: The Great Depression and the American Economy in the Twentieth Century*, eds. Michael Bordo, Claudia Goldin, and Eugene N. White (University of Chicago Press, 1998); Frederick B. Pike, *FDR's Good Neighbor Policy* (University of Texas Press, 1995), 325–44.

71. Johann Chapoutot, *Les Irresponsables: Qui a porté Hitler au pouvoir?* (Gallimard, 2025), 92–102.

72. Toprani, *Oil and the Great Powers*, 3, 190.

73. Tooze, *Wages of Destruction*, 220, 246–47; James, *End of Globalization*, 142–43; Mulder, *Economic Weapon*, 190; Jonathan A. Grant, *Between Depression and Disarmament: the International Armaments Business, 1919-1939* (Cambridge University Press, 2018), 181, 188, 213; Zahra, *Against the World*, 259.

74. February 1917 diary entries can be found at the Cambridge University Digital Library, https://cudl.lib.cam.ac.uk/view/MS-ADD-09852-00001-00008/1, accessed 22 January 2026.

75. https://www.poetryfoundation.org/poems/43169/dreamers, accessed 22 January 2026.

76. Sharon E. Kingsland, *Modeling Nature: Episodes in the History of Population Ecology* (University of Chicago Press, 1985), 42–46, 50–65.

77. David R. Shearer, *Industry, State, and Society in Stalin's Russia, 1926–1934* (Cornell University Press, 1996), 77–85.

78. Thomas Robertson, *The Malthusian Moment: Global Population Growth and the Birth of American Environmentalism* (Rutgers University Press, 2012), 6–21.

79. Kingsland, *Modeling Nature*, 50–65, 76.

80. John Lossing Buck, *Land Utilization in China* (University of Chicago Press, 1937).

81. Cited in David Hollinger, *Protestants Abroad: How Missionaries Tried to Change the World but Changed America* (Princeton University Press, 2017), 41.

82. Pearl Buck, *The Good Earth* (Simon & Schuster, 2004), 8.

83. Tong Lam, *A Passion for Facts: Social Surveys and the Construction of the Chinese Nation-State, 1900–1949* (University of California Press, 2011), 3, 44.

84. Tara Zahra, *The Great Departure: Mass Migration from Eastern Europe and the Making of the Free World* (W. W. Norton, 2017), 82–84.

85. Jean de la Roche, "French Indo-China's Prospective Economic Regime," Institute of Pacific Relations, 9th Conference, Hot Springs, VA, January 1945, cited in Adelman, "Inequality, Development, and Global Distributive Justice," in *Debating Worlds: Narratives of Global Modernity and World Order*, ed. Daniel Deudney, G. John Ikenberry, and Karoline Postel-Vinay (Oxford University Press, 2023), 224.

86. Nicholas Cullather, *The Hungry World: America's Cold War Battle Against Poverty in Asia* (Harvard University Press, 2010), 32.

87. Cullather, *Hungry World,* 32–35.

88. Gunnar Myrdal, *Population: A Problem for Democracy* (Harvard University Press, 1940), 20.

89. Zahra, *Great Departure,* 110, 143–180.

90. Isaiah Bowman, *The Pioneer Fringe* (American Geographical Society, 1931), 8.

91. Isaiah Bowman, *Limits of Land Settlement: A Report on Present-Day Possibilities* (Council on Foreign Relations, 1937), 1; Zahra, *Great Departure,* 161–63.

92. David Thomas Murphy, *The Heroic Earth: Geopolitical Thought in Weimar Germany, 1918–1933* (The Kent State University Press, 1997), 8–9.

93. Christian W. Spang, "Karl Haushofer Re-Examined: Geopolitics as a Factor in Japanese-German Rapprochement in the Interwar Years," in *Japanese-German Relations, 1895–1945,* ed. Christian Spang and Rolf-Harald Wippich (Routledge, 2006), 139–58.

94. Victor Seow, *Carbon Technocracy: Energy Regimes in Modern East Asia* (University of Chicago Press, 2021), 150–173; Chad Denton, "More Valuable than Gold: Korean Tungsten and the Japanese War Economy, 1910 to 1945," *Seoul Journal of Korean Studies,* 26:2 (2013), 364.

95. Thomas David DuBois, "Local Religion and the Imperial Imaginary: The Development of Japanese Ethnography in Occupied Manchuria," *American Historical Review,* 111:1 (February 2006), 52–74.

96. Stewart Brown, "Japan Stuns the World, withdraws from League," UP, 24 February, 1993, UPI Archives, https://www.upi.com/Archives/1933/02/24/Japan-stuns-world-withdraws-from-league/2231840119817/ accessed 22 January 2026.

97. S.C.M. Paine, *The Wars for Asia: 1911–1949* (Cambridge University Press, 2012), 1[illegible]

98. Adolf Hitler, *Mein Kampf* (Houghton Mifflin, 1999), 235; Corinna Treitel, *Eating Nature in Modern Germany: Food, Agriculture, and Environment, 1870–2000* (Cambridge University Press, 2017), 2.

99. See Robert J. Mayhew, *Malthus: The Life and Legacies of an Untimely Prophet* (Harvard University Press, 2014), 179.

100. Tooze, *Wages of Destruction,* 10.

101. Hitler, *Mein Kampf,* 654.

102. Timothy Snyder, *Black Earth: The Holocaust as History and Warning* (Tim Duggan Books, 2016), 30–35; "Herr Hitler's Speech in the Reichstag," *Bulletin of International News,* 16:3 (February 11, 1939), 5.

103. Eric Weitz, *A Century of Genocide: Utopias of Race and Nation* (Princeton University Press, 2003), 126.

104. H. C. Engelbrecht and F. C. Hanighen, *Merchants of Death: A Study of the International Armaments Industry* (Dodd, Mead & Co., 1934), 256.

105. Barr, *Line in the Sand,* 169.

106. Zahra, *Against the World,* 216–17.

107. Joseph Kessel, "With the Slave Hunters in Abyssinia," *New York Times Magazine*, July 13, 1930.

108. Amalia Ribi Forclaz, *Humanitarian Imperialism: The Politics of Anti-Slavery Activism, 1880–1940* (Oxford University Press, 2015), 57–59, 150–60; Bronwen Everill, "The Italo-Abyssinian Crisis and the Shift from Slave to Refugee," *Slavery and Abolition*, 35:2 (May 2014), 351–52.

109. Aline Zuber, "The Cross in the Crosshairs: A Photographic Record of the Bombing of Red Cross Field Hospitals During the Second Italo-Ethiopian War," *Cross-files*, January 4, 2022, https://blogs.icrc.org/cross-files/the-cross-in-the-crosshairs-a-photographic-record-of-the-bombing-of-red-cross-field-hospitals-during-the-second-italo-ethiopian-war/.

110. Joseph Fronczak, "Local People's Global Politics: A Transnational History of the Hands Off Ethiopia Movement of 1935," *Diplomatic History*, 39:2 (2015), 245, 257; Everill, "Italo-Abyssinian Crisis," 354–55.

111. Cited in Tony Wood, "Another Country: Cuban Communism and Black Self-Determination, 1932–36," *Hispanic American Historical Review*, 102:4 (2022), 669.

112. Zahra, *Great Departure*, 125.

113. J. A. Cross, *Sir Samuel Hoare: A Political Biography* (Jonathan Cape, 1977), 217–20.

114. Nicholas Rankin, *Telegram from Guernica: The Extraordinary Life of George Steer: Reporter, Adventurer, and Soldier* (Faber & Faber, 2003), 82.

115. Paul Preston, *We Saw Spain Die: Foreign Correspondents in the Spanish Civil War* (Skyhorse Publisher, 2009).

116. Quoted in Rankin, *Telegram from Guernica*, 204.

117. Virgina Woolf, *Three Guineas* (Harcourt, 1938), 10–11.

Chapter Four

1. Rupert Jenkins, *Nagasaki Journey: The Photographs of Yosuke Yamahata, August 10, 1945* (Pomegranate Artbooks, 1995), 19; on reconciling defeat and bombing in Japan, see John W. Dower, *Embracing Defeat: Japan in the Wake of World War II* (W. W. Norton, 1999).

2. John Hersey, *Hiroshima* (Hosei daigaku shuppan kyoku, 1949). The work was originally published in 1946. Hersey, *Hiroshima* (A. A. Knopf, 1946), 26.

3. Rupert Smith, *The Utility of Force: The Art of War in the Modern World* (Penguin Books, 2005), 146.

4. The concept of groundnorm comes from Hans Kelsen, *General Theory of Law and State* (Harvard University Press, 1949).

5. Campbell Craig and Sergey Radchenko, *The Atomic Bomb and the Origins of the Cold War* (Yale University Press, 2008), 87–89, 169.

6. Spencer R. Weart, *The Rise of Nuclear Fear* (Harvard University Press, 2012), 80–84.

7. The events of the Cuban Missile Crisis have been extensively documented. On the role of the UN mediation, see Thant Myint-U, *Peacemaker: U Thant and the Forgotten Quest for a Just World* (W. W. Norton, 2025), 60.

8. Ronald H. Spector, *In the Ruins of Empire: The Japanese Surrender and the Battle for Postwar Asia* (Random House, 2007), 144–45.

9. Monica Braw, *The Atomic Bomb Suppressed: American Censorship in Occupied Japan* (M. E. Sharpe, 1991).

10. William Marotti, "Japan 1968: The Performance of Violence and the Theatre of Protest," *American Historical Review*, 114:1 (February 2009), 97–135. Mushroom clouds also triggered scientists, like the oceanographer Roger Revelle, chair of the National Academy of Sciences' Committee on the Biological Effects of Atomic Radiation, to study the atmospheric effects of emissions, which led to growing concern about carbon. Joshua P. Howe, *Behind the Curve: Science and the Politics of Global Warming* (University of Washington Press, 2014), 18, 35–36.

11. Martin Thomas, *The End of Empires and a World Remade: A Global History of Decolonization* (Princeton University Press, 2024), 31–32. Thomas is quite right to accent the script, though he treats it as the preamble to globalization, which I consider not just a postcolonial but a post–Pax Americana stage of interdependence.

12. On Mead, see Peter Mandler, *Return from the Natives: How Margaret Mead Won the Second World War and Lost the Cold War* (Yale University Press, 2013), 175; more generally on the postwar salvos, Daniel Immerwahr, *How to Hide an Empire: A Short History of the Greater United States* (Vintage, 2019), 230.

13. Elizabeth Borgwardt, *A New Deal for the World: America's Vision for Human Rights* (Harvard University Press, 2005); Mary Ann Glendon, *A World Made New: Eleanor Roosevelt and the Universal Declaration of Human Rights* (Random House, 2001), 3–5.

14. UN General Assembly, Resolution 217A (III), Universal Declaration of Human Rights, A/RES/217(III) (December 10, 1948), https://www.un.org/en/about-us/universal-declaration-of-human-rights.

15. Eric Helleiner, *Forgotten Foundations of Bretton Woods: International Development and the Making of the Postwar Order* (Cornell University Press, 2014); Borgwardt, *New Deal*, 24–25, 118–21.

16. Nelson Mandela, *Long Walk to Freedom: The Autobiography of Nelson Mandela* (Abacus, 1994), 110.

17. Borgwardt, *New Deal*, 29; Mark Philip Bradley, *The World Reimagined: Americans and Human Rights in the Twentieth Century* (Cambridge University Press, 2016), 57–63.

18. Hegemony is not the same as domination. Power, at least in countries with autonomous civil societies, rests as much on cultural consent and manufacturing common sense that obscures class divides. When, according to Antonio Gramsci, the "mask of consent" slips, then force comes into play. This is why, for Gramsci, intellectuals, broadly defined, have an outsized role in worldmaking in advanced capitalism. See Antonio Gramsci, *Selections from the Prison Notebooks*, ed. and trans. Quintin Hoare and Geoffrey Nowell Smith (International Books, 1971), 9–10.

19. Michael Adams, *The Best War Ever: America and World War II* (Johns Hopkins University Press, 2004); Alan Milward, *War, Economy and Society 1939–1945* (University of California Press, 1974), 331–39; Fred Block, *The Origins of the International Economic Disorder: A Study of United States International Monetary Policy from World War II to the Present* (University of California Press, 1977), who charts the mutation of self-interest in internationalism that was stress tested first with the loan to Britain, 33–38.

20. Edward Mead Earle, *Against This Torrent* (Princeton University Press, 1941), 7.

21. David Ekbladh, "Present at the Creation: Edward Mead Earle and the Depression-Era Origins of Security Studies," *International Security*, 36:3 (September 2011), 107–41.

22. Henry R. Luce, *The American Century* (Farrar & Rinehart, 1941), 5, 29.

23. George C. Marshall, "Speech at Princeton University," speech, The George C. Marshall Foundation, February 22, 1947,https://www.marshallfoundation.org/library/digital-archive/6-026-speech-princeton-university-february-22-1947/; Stephen Wertheim, *Tomorrow, the World: The Birth of United States Global Supremacy* (Harvard University Press, 2020), 22; Bruce Kuklick, *Blind Oracles: Intellectuals and War from Kennan to Kissinger* (Princeton University Press, 2006).

24. Barry Eichengreen, *Globalizing Capital: A History of the International Monetary System* (Princeton University Press, 2008), 91.

25. Glenda Sluga, "UNESCO and the (One) World of Julian Huxley," *Journal of World History*, 21:3 (September, 2010), 393–418.

26. Richard Dannatt and Allen Packwood, *Churchill's D-Day* (Diversion Books, 2024), 299. See the fictionalized rendering of Orwell's life as he was writing *1984* (the last novel he would publish while alive) in Dennis Glover, *The Last Man in Europe* (Overlook, 2017).

27. Alex von Tunzelmann, *Blood and Sand: Suez, Hungary, and the Crisis That Shook the World* (Simon & Schuster, 2017), 19.

28. Tunzelmann, *Blood and Sand*, 324–29.

29. Cited in Lucy Mayblin, *Asylum After Empire: Colonial Legacies in the Politics of Asylum Seeking* (Rowman & Littlefield, 2017), 141; Peter Gatrell, *The Unsettling of Europe: How Migration Reshaped a Continent* (Basic Books, 2019), 10–12; Glendon, *World Made New*, 10.

30. Hannah Arendt, *The Origins of Totalitarianism* (Harcourt, 1968), 279. The line on the right to have rights appears on p. 296 of the updated 1968 edition.

31. Julian Jackson, *De Gaulle* (Harvard University Press, 2018), 359–61; Martin Thomas, *The French Empire at War, 1940–1945* (Manchester University Press, 2007); Barr, *A Line in the Sand*, 306. For an index of the spectrum, see Gyan Prakash and Jeremy Adelman, eds., *Inventing the Third World: In Search of Freedom for the Postwar Global South* (Bloomsbury, 2023).

32. Glendon, *World Made New*, 9; Samuel Moyn, *The Last Utopia: Human Rights in History* (Harvard University Press, 2010), 42–43.

33. A. J. Hobbins, ed., *On the Edge of Greatness: The Diaries of John Humphrey, First Director of the United Nations Division of Human Rights*, 4 vols. (McGill University Libraries, 1994), 1:29.

34. Elihu Lauterpacht, *The Life of Sir Hersch Lauterpacht, QC, FBA, LLD* (Cambridge University Press, 2010), 266.

35. Hersch Lauterpacht, *An International Bill of the Rights of Man* (Columbia University Press, 1945), vi, 69.

36. Lauterpacht, *Life of Sir Hersch Lauterpacht*, 277–78.

37. Mark Mazower, *No Enchanted Palace: The End of Empire and the Ideological Origins of the United Nations (Princeton University Press, 2009)*, 61–65.

38. W. K. Hancock, *Smuts: The Fields of Force, 1919–1950* (Cambridge University Press, 1968), 469–73; W.E.B Du Bois, *The World and Africa: An Inquiry into the Part Which Africa Has Played in World History* (International Publishers, 1965), 43, 80, 255.

39. Both cited in Caroline Elkins, *Legacy of Violence: A History of the British Empire* (Knopf, 2022) 345–46.

40. Mira Siegelberg, *Statelessness: A Modern History* (Harvard University Press, 2020), 62–63; Michael Walzer, *Spheres of Justice: A Defense of Pluralism and Equality* (Basic Books, 1983),

48; T. Alexander Aleinikoff and Leah Zamore, *The Arc of Protection: Reforming the International Refugee Regime* (Stanford University Press, 2019), 33.

41. Peter Gatrell, *The Making of the Modern Refugee* (Oxford University Press, 2015), 3.

42. Arendt, *Origins of Totalitarianism*, 294; Arendt, "Understanding and Politics," *Partisan Review*, 20:4 (July–August 1953), 377–92; Jeremy Adelman, "Pariah: Can Hannah Arendt Help Us Rethink Our Global Refugee Crisis?," *Wilson Quarterly*, Spring 2016, https://www.wilsonquarterly.com/quarterly/looking-back-moving-forward/pariah-can-hannah-arendt-help-us-rethink-our-global-refugee-crisis/. This platform, part of the Woodrow Wilson International Center for Scholars was shuttered by the Trump administration and access to all its resources closed. The article is available by contacting the author directly.

43. David Nasaw, *The Last Million: Europe's Displaced Persons from World War to Cold War* (Penguin, 2020).

44. Glendon, *World Made New*, 29.

45. Gatrell, *Making of the Modern Refugee*, 6–8; Gil Loescher and John A. Scanlan, *Calculated Kindness: Refugees and America's Half-Open Door* (Free Press, 1986), 6, 40–41; Aleinikoff and Zamore, *Arc of Protection*, 42.

46. Emma Haddad, *The Refugee in International Society* (Cambridge University Press, 2008), 83.

47. Stephen Macekura, "The Point Four Program and U.S. International Development Policy," *Political Science Quarterly*, 128:1 (2013), 127–60; David Ekbladh, *The Great American Mission: Modernization and the Construction of an American World Order* (Princeton University Press, 2011), esp. 63–71, 162, 213; Sebastian Conrad, "'The Colonial Ties Are Liquidated': Modernization Theory, Post-War Japan and the Global Cold War," *Past and Present*, 216 (August 2012), 181–214.

48. Nikhil Menon, *Planning Democracy: Modern India's Quest for Development* (Cambridge University Press, 2022); Stephen Clarkson, *The Soviet Theory of Development: India and the Third World in Marxist-Leninist Scholarship* (University of Toronto Press, 1978). More generally, see Eric Helleiner, "The Development Mandate of International Institutions: Where Did It Come From?" *Studies in Comparative International Development*, 44.3 (2009), 189–211.

49. Gunnar Myrdal, *Rich Lands and Poor* (Harper & Bros., 1957), 7, 128–29.

50. Cited in David C. Engerman, "West Meets East: The Center for International Studies and Indian Economic Development," in *Staging Growth: Modernization, Development, and the Global Cold War*, ed. David C. Engerman, Nils Gilman, Mark Haefele, and Michael E. Latham (University of Massachusetts Press, 2003), 199.

51. W. W. Rostow, *The Stages of Economic Growth: A Non-Communist Manifesto* (Cambridge University Press, 1960), 6.

52. Theodore H. White, "In the Halls of Power," *LIFE*, June 9, 1967. Rostow became national security advisor to President Lyndon Johnson from 1966 to 1969 and oversaw the escalation of war in Indochina.

53. Susanna Hecht and Alexander Cockburn, *The Fate of the Forest: Developers, Destroyers, and Defenders of the Amazon* (Verso, 1989), 100–101.

54. Yang Jisheng, *Tombstone: The Great Chinese Famine, 1958–1962* (Farrar, Straus and Giroux, 2008), xviii–xxi, 77.

55. Alanna O'Malley, *The Diplomacy of Decolonisation: America, Britain, and the United Nations During the Congo Crisis 1960–1964* (Manchester University Press, 2018), 74–75, 118.

56. Alastair Gordon, *Naked Airport: A Cultural History of the World's Most Revolutionary Structure* (University of Chicago Press, 2004), 173.

57. Vaclav Smil, *Energy and Civilization: A History* (MIT Press, 2018), 274, 278.

58. D. J. Clark, "Digitized News-Image Markets and the Politics of Place: A Critical Exploration of Contemporary Changes to the Global Single Market and the Impact on Public Understanding of Place," in *International News in the Digital Age*, ed. Judith Clarke and Michael Bromley (Routledge, 2011), 147.

59. William Boddy, *Fifties Television: The Industry and Its Critics* (University of Illinois Press, 1990).

60. Todd S. Purdum, *Desi Arnaz: The Man Who Invented Television* (Simon & Schuster, 2025).

61. Raymond G. Stokes, *Ruins to Riches: The Economic Resurgence of Germany and Japan After 1945* (Cambridge University Press, 2024), 101, 131.

62. Sig Mickelson, *The Decade That Shaped Television News* (Praeger, 1998), xvii; David Croteau and William Hoynes, *The Business of Media: Corporate Media and the Public Interest* (Sage, 2005), 60.

63. Nadya Bair, *The Decisive Network: Magnum Photos and the Postwar Image Market* (University of California Press, 2020).

64. Michel Poivert, *Gilles Caron: Le conflit intérieur* (Musée de L'Elysée de Lausanne, 2013).

65. Frank Graham, *Since Silent Spring* (Houghton Mifflin, 1970), 18–19.

66. Joni Seager, *Carson's Silent Spring* (Bloomsbury, 2014), 9–21.

67. Seager, *Carson's Silent Spring*, 189.

68. Graham, *Since Silent Spring*, xi, 48–49.

69. Seager, *Carson's Silent Spring*, 189.

70. Jeremy L. Caradonna, *Sustainability: A History* (Oxford University Press, 2014), 89–111.

71. Myint-U, *Peacemaker*, 101.

72. Nkruma's fall is detailed in Susan Williams, *White Malice: The CIA and the Covert Recolonization of Africa* (PublicAffairs, 2021), 491–95. On the fate of modernization theory, see Ekbladh, *Great American Mission*, 226–56; Bradley Simpson, *Economists with Guns: Authoritarian Development and U.S.-Indonesian Relations, 1960–1968* (Stanford University Press, 2008). For UN Trade and Development (UNCTAD), see Martin Thomas, *The End of Empires and a World Remade: A Global History of Decolonization* (Princeton University Press, 2024), 289–91.

73. Jorge Luis Borges, "The Moon," in *Dreamtigers* (University of Texas Press, 1964), 64.

74. David Macey, *Frantz Fanon: A Biography* (Verso, 2000), 152–54.

75. Frantz Fanon and Charles Geronimi, "L'hospitalisation de jour en psychiatrie, valeur et limites," (1959), in Frantz Fanon, *Écrits sur l'aliénation et la liberté* (La Découverte, 2015), 425.

76. Frantz Fanon, "Écoute homme blanc!, de Richard Wright," in Frantz Fanon, *Écrits sur l'aliénation et la liberté* (La Découverte, 2015), 524–26; Macey, *Frantz Fanon*, 277.

77. Frantz Fanon, *The Wretched of the Earth* (Grove, 2004), 10, 68.

78. Fanon, *Wretched of the Earth*, 232, 238.

79. Che Guevara, "Farewell letter from Che to Fidel Castro," Havana, April 1, 1965. Accessed January 24, 2026, https://www.marxists.org/archive/guevara/1965/04/01.htm.

80. Edmundo Desnoes, *Memorias del subdesarrollo* (UNEAC, 1965), 14.

81. United Nations, Department of Economic and Social Affairs, *Proceedings of the World Population Conference, Belgrade, 30 August–10 September 1965*, vol. 1 (United Nations, 1967), 27.

82. David Sepkoski, *Catastrophic Thinking: Extinction and the Value of Diversity from Darwin to the Anthropocene* (University of Chicago Press, 2020); Thomas Robertson, *The Malthusian Moment: Global Population Growth and the Birth of American Environmentalism* (Rutgers University Press, 2012), 36–56.

83. Matthew Connelly, *Fatal Misconception: The Struggle to Control World Population* (Harvard University Press, 2008), 121; Alison Bashford, *Global Population: History, Geopolitics, and Life on Earth* (Columbia University Press, 2014), 269–79.

84. Amna Qayyum, "The Demographic State: Population, Global Biopolitics, and Decolonization in South Asia, 1947–71" (PhD diss., Princeton University, 2021), chap. 3; Jason Burke, "India Mass Sterilisation: Women Were 'Forced' into Camps, Say Relatives," *The Guardian*, November 14, 2014, https://www.theguardian.com/world/2014/nov/12/india-sterilisation-deaths-women-forced-camps-relatives.

85. H. Scott Gordon, "The Economic Theory of the Common-Property Resource: The Fishery," *Journal of Political Economy*, 62:2 (April 1954), 124–42; Adam Rome, "'Give Earth a Chance': The Environmental Movement and the Sixties," *The Journal of American History*, 90:2 (September 2003), 525–54.

86. Garrett Hardin, "Interstellar Migration and the Population Problem," *Journal of Heredity*, 50:2 (March–April 1959), 68–70.

87. Garrett Hardin, "The Tragedy of the Commons" *Science*, 162:3859 (December 13, 1968), 1243–48; Carl Jay Bajema, "Garrett James Hardin: Ecologist, Educator, Ethicist and Environmentalist," *Population and Environment*, 12:3 (March 1991), 193–212; Fabien Locher, "Cold War Pastures: Garrett Hardin and the 'Tragedy of the Commons,'" *Revue d'histoire modern et contemporaine*, 60:1 (2013), 7–36.

88. Al Reinert, "The Blue Marble Shot," *The Atlantic*, April 12, 2011, https://www.theatlantic.com/technology/archive/2011/04/the-blue-marble-shot-our-first-complete-photograph-of-earth/237167/; Benjamin Lazier, "Earthrise; or, the Globalization of the World Picture," *American Historical Review*, 116:3 (June 2011), 602–30.

89. Sabine Höhler, *Spaceship Earth in the Environmental Age, 1960–1990* (Pickering & Chatto, 2015), 8–16.

90. Arthur Hopcraft, *Born to Hunger* (Houghton Mifflin, 1968), x, 44.

91. Claude Cookman, "Gilles Caron's Coverage of the Crisis in Biafra," *Visual Communication Quarterly*, 15:4 (November 2008), 226–42; Lasse Heerten, *The Biafran War and Postcolonial Humanitarianism: Spectacles of Suffering* (Cambridge University Press, 2017).

92. Paul R. Ehrlich, *The Population Bomb* (Sierra Club/Ballantine, 1968), 15.

93. Paul Sabin, *The Bet: Paul Ehrlich, Julian Simon, and Our Gamble over Earth's Future* (Yale University Press, 2015), 1.

Chapter Five

1. Raymond Vernon, *Sovereignty at Bay: The Multinational Spread of US Enterprises* (Basic Books 1971), 3.

2. Donella H. Meadows, Dennis Meadows, Jørgen Randers, William Behrens, and Janine Delaunay, *The Limits to Growth: A Report for the Club of Rome's Project on the Predicament of*

Mankind (Signet 1972); Matthias Schmelzer, "'Born in the Corridors of the OECD': The Forgotten Origins of the Club of Rome, Transnational Networks, and the 1970s in Global History," *Journal of Global History*, 12:1 (2017), 26–48; Mauricio Schoijet, "Limits to Growth and the Rise of Catastrophism," *Environmental History*, 4:4 (October 1999), 515–30; Stephen J. Macekura, *The Mismeasure of Progress: Economic Growth and Its Critics* (University of Chicago Press, 2020), 104–8.

3. Elke Seefried, "Towards the Limits to Growth? The Book and Its Reception in West Germany and Britain, 1972–73," *German Historical Institute London Bulletin*, 33:1 (May 2011), 3–37.

4. Giuseppe La Barca, *International Trade in the 1970s: The US, the EC, and the Growing Pressure of Protectionism* (Bloomsbury, 2013); Christy Thornton, *Revolution in Development: Mexico and the Governance of the Global Economy* (University of California Press, 2021).

5. Allen J. Matusow, "Richard Nixon and the Failed War Against the Trading World," *Diplomatic History* 27:5 (November 2003), 769.

6. Daniel Yergin, *The Prize: The Epic Quest for Oil, Money & Power* (Simon & Schuster, 1991), 573, 579. For the Soviet read on the developing crisis in mid-1973 and alliances with Sadat, see Sergey Radchenko, *To Run the World: The Kremlin's Cold War Bid for Global Power* (Cambridge University Press, 2024), 392–95.

7. Meg Jacobs, *Panic at the Pumps: The Energy Crisis and the Transformation of American Politics in the 1970s* (Hill and Wang, 2016), 212.

8. Victor McFarland, *Oil Powers: A History of the US-Saudi Alliance* (Columbia University Press, 2020), 138.

9. McFarland, *Oil Powers*, 7.

10. Eric Helleiner, *States and the Reemergence of Global Finance: From Bretton Woods to the 1990s* (Cornell University Press, 1994), 103.

11. William R. Cline, *International Debt: Systemic Risk and Policy Response* (MIT Press, 1984), 11.

12. Robert O. Keohane and Joseph Nye, *Power and Interdependence* (Harper Collins, 1989), 7.

13. Quinn Slobodian, *Globalists: The End of Empire and the Birth of Neoliberalism* (Harvard University Press, 2018).

14. Cline, *International Debt*, 11; Timothy Mitchell, *Carbon Democracy: Political Power in the Age of Oil* (Verso, 2011), 171–84.

15. Jeronim, Perović, *Fuel and Power: Energy, Trade, and Russian Foreign Relations from Lenin to Putin* (Cambridge University Press, 2024), 112, 119, 193–204. A decade earlier, the same consumers howled when the recently elected government of Ronald Reagan announced sanctions on steel pipes and pipeline technology exports to the USSR as part of the "second Cold War." That was a short-lived declaration of economic warfare. By 1984, the grid that integrated Siberia and Western Europe was integrated.

16. Oliver Bullough, *Butler to the World: How Britain Helps the World's Worst People Launder Money, Commit Crimes, and Get Away with Anything* (St. Martin's Press, 2022), 51.

17. For general data, see Gabriel Zucman, *The Hidden Wealth of Nations: The Scourge of Tax Havens* (University of Chicago Press, 2013).

18. Robert Devlin, *Debt Crisis in Latin America* (Princeton University Press, 1989). See also Carlos F. Díaz-Alejandro, "The Post 1971 International Financial System and the Less

Developed Countries," in *A World Divided*, ed. G. K. Helleiner (Cambridge University Press, 1976), 177–205.

19. Carlos F. Díaz-Alejandro, "Good-Bye Financial Repression, Hello Financial Crash," *Journal of Development Economics* 19 (1985): 1–24; Albert Fishlow, "Coping with the Creeping Crisis of Debt," in *Politics and Economics of External Debt Crisis*, ed. M. S. Wionczek, (Westview Press, 1985), 100–111.

20. United Nations Economic Commission for Latin America and the Caribbean, *Statistical Yearbook for Latin America and the Caribbean* (United Nations, 1986), 514–15; Robert Cumby and Richard Levich, "Definitions and Magnitudes: On the Definition and Magnitude of Recent Capital Flight," in *Capital Flight and Third World Debt*, Donald Lessard and John Williamson (Institute for International Economics, 1987), 27–67.

21. Helleiner, *States and the Reemergence of Global Finance*, 146.

22. Helen Thompson, *China and the Mortgaging of America* (Palgrave, 2010), 8–9.

23. Peter S. Goodman, *Davos Man: How the Billionaires Devoured the World* (Mariner Books, 2022), 106–9.

24. "Multinationals: The Retreat of the Global Company," *Economist*, January 28, 2017, 19.

25. Karen Ho, *Liquidated: An Ethnography of Wall Street* (Duke University Press, 2009), 302–3; on meritocracy's self-rewarding propensities, see Michael Sandel, *The Tyranny of Merit: What's Become of the Common Good?* (Farrar, Straus and Giroux, 2020).

26. Richard Baldwin, *The Great Convergence: Information Technology and the New Globalization* (Harvard University Press, 2016).

27. Elizabeth O'Brien Ingleson, *Made in China: What US-China Interests Converged to Transform Global Trade* (Harvard University Press, 2024) for an important overview of the shifting division of labor between the United States and China, arguing that the reversal of roles can be dated back to the 1970s. See esp. 148–49 and on Don King, 181–82.

28. Peter E. Hamilton, *Made in Hong Kong: Transpacific Networks and a New History of Globalization* (Columbia University Press, 2021), 220–22.

29. Branko Milanovic, *Global Inequality: A New Approach for the Age of Globalization* (Harvard University Press, 2016), 18–20.

30. Alvin Toffler, *Future Shock* (Random House, 1970), 75.

31. Marc Levinson, *The Box: How the Shipping Container Made the World Smaller and the World Economy Bigger* (Princeton University Press, 2006), 211, 233–34.

32. Dara Orenstein, *Out of Stock: The Warehouse in the History of Capitalism* (University of Chicago Press, 2019), 3; John D. Kasarda and Greg Lindsay, *Aerotropolis: The Way We'll Live Next* (Farrar, Straus and Giroux, 2011); Gillian Hart, *Disabling Globalization: Places of Power in Post-Apartheid South Africa* (University of California Press, 2002), 166–69, 198–99.

33. Alice Amsden, *The Rise of "the Rest": Challenges to the West from Late-Industrializing Economies* (Oxford University Press, 2001); Deepak Nayyar, "Industrialization in Developing Asia Since 1970: Why Technology, Learning, and Innovation Matter," *Innovation and Development*, 11:2/3 (2021), 366; Robert Baldwin, *The Great Convergence: Information Technology and the New Globalization* (Harvard University Press, 2016), 85–91.

34. Javier Blas and Jack Farchy, *The World For Sale: Money, Power, and the Traders Who Barter the Earth's Resources* (Oxford University Press, 2021), 235–37; "Trafigura: A Toxic Journey,"

Amnesty International, April 11, 2016, https://www.amnesty.org/en/latest/news/2016/04/trafigura-a-toxic-journey/.

35. Daniel Yergin, *The Quest: Energy, Security, and the Remaking of the Modern World* (Penguin, 2012), 163, 193; John L. Brooke, *Climate Change and the Course of Global History: A Rough Journey* (Cambridge University Press, 2014), 543.

36. Calculated from the "Global Carbon Atlas," Global Carbon Project, , accessed January 31, 2026, http://www.globalcarbonatlas.org/en/content/welcome-carbon-atlas. See in particular the pages referring to regional carbon emissions over time.

37. Amitav Ghosh, *The Great Derangement: Climate Change and the Unthinkable* (University of Chicago Press, 2016), 87–89.

38. Sergey Radchenko, *Unwanted Visionaries: The Soviet Failure in Asia at the End of the Cold War* (Oxford University Press, 2014), 163, 177.

39. Boutros Boutros-Ghali, "An Agenda for Peace: Preventive Diplomacy, Peacemaking, and Peace-Keeping," *International Relations*, 11:3 (1992), 201. On mercenarism, see Sean McFate, *The Modern Mercenary: Private Armies and What They Mean for World Order* (Oxford University Press, 2014), 70 on peacekeeping.

40. Peter S. Goodman, *How the World Ran Out of Everything: Inside the Global Supply Chain* (Mariner Books, 2024), 30–32.

41. Thomas Friedman, *The World Is Flat: A Brief History of the 21st Century* (Farrar, Straus and Giroux, 2005), 8.

42. Theodore Levitt, "The Globalization of Markets," *Harvard Business Review*, May/June 1983, https://hbr.org/1983/05/the-globalization-of-markets.

43. Hernando de Soto, *The Mystery of Capital: Why Capitalism Triumphs in the West and Fails Everywhere Else* (Basic Books, 2000).

44. James Atlas, "What Is Fukuyama Saying? And to Whom Is He Saying It?" *New York Times*, October 22, 1989, http://www.nytimes.com/1989/10/22/magazine/what-is-fukuyama-saying-and-to-whom-is-he-saying-it.html?src=pm&pagewanted=2.

45. Francis Fukuyama, "The End of History?," *The National Interest*, 16 (Summer 1989), 3–18.

46. Strobe Talbott, "American Abroad: The Beginning of Nonsense," *Time*, September 11, 1989, https://time.com/archive/6703410/america-abroad-the-beginning-of-nonsense/.

47. Radchenko, *Unwanted Visionaries*, esp. 3–4 for a child's-eye view from Sakhalin Island.

48. Lea Ypi, *Free: A Child and a Country at the End of History* (W. W. Norton, 2022), 184.

49. John Williamson, "The Strange History of the Washington Consensus," *Journal of Post Keynesian Economics*, 27:2 (Winter 2004–5), 195–206.

50. Cited in Richard W. Franke and Barbara H. Chasin, *Seeds of Famine: Ecological Destruction and the Development Dilemma in the West African Sahel* (Universe Books, 1980), 1, 5; Boureima Alpha Gado, *Une histoire des famines au Sahel: Études des grandes crises alimentaires (XIXe-XXe siècles)* (L'Harmattan, 1993); Jeremy Swift, "Sahelian Pastoralists: Underdevelopment, Desertification and Famine," *Annual Review of Anthropology*, 6 (1977), 457–78.

51. Franke and Chasin, *Seeds of Famine*, 96–97.

52. And yet, in 1973, the American government spent $50 million to resettle Soviet Jews, about $1,500 per capita. For West Africa, the total relief spending for some twenty-two million drought victims came to less than $5. Laurie Wiseberg, "Can the Sahel Survive? Prospects for

Longer-Term Planning and Development," in *The Politics of Natural Disaster: The Case of the Sahel Drought*, ed. Michael Glantz (Praeger, 1976), 113.

53. Sebastião Salgado, *Sahel: The End of the Road* (University of California Press, 2004); "*The Salt of the Earth:* Sebastião Salgado's Own Way of Seeing," *Gerryco23* (blog), August 1, 2015, https://gerryco23.wordpress.com/2015/08/01/the-salt-of-the-earth-sebastiao-salgados-own-way-of-seeing/.

54. The story is recounted in William Shawcross, *The Quality of Mercy: Cambodia, Holocaust, and Modern Conscience* (Simon & Schuster, 1984), 123, 188–90.

55. Guy Debord, *The Society of the Spectacle* (Zone Books, 1994).

56. Susan Sontag, *On Photography* (Farrar, Straus and Giroux, 1977); Daniel Schreiber, *Susan Sontag: A Biography* (Northwestern University Press, 2014), 139–44.

57. Sontag, *On Photography*, 9.

58. Sontag, *On Photography*, 19.

59. Sontag, *On Photography*, 19, 97.

60. Carolyn J. Dean, *The Fragility of Empathy After the Holocaust* (Cornell University Press, 2004), 5–13. For general histories of eyewitnessing practices in visual representation, see Peter Burke, *Eyewitnessing: The Uses of Images as Historical Evidence* (Reaktion Books, 2001), and Jeremy Adelman, "Don't Look Away," *Aeon*, September 13, 2013, https://aeon.co/essays/does-photography-make-us-act-or-inure-us-to-despair.

61. Margaret E. Keck and Kathryn Sikkink, *Activists Beyond Borders* (Cornell University Press, 1998), 89–92.

62. Amaya's testimony can be read on Meiselas's website, which features a selection of her Mozote photos. "El Salvador Mazote," Susan Meiselas: Photographer, accessed 26 January, 2026, https://www.susanmeiselas.com/el-salvador-mozote.

63. Leigh Binford, *The El Mozote Massacre: Human Rights and Global Implications* (University of Arizona Press, 2016), 58–59.

64. Kathryn Sikkink, *The Justice Cascade: How Human Rights Prosecutions Are Changing World Politics* (W. W. Norton, 2011).

65. Jacobo Timerman, preface to *With Friends Like These: The Americas Watch Report on Human Rights and U.S. Policy in Latin America*, ed. Cynthia Brown (Pantheon, 1985), xi; Aryeh Neier, "Recommendations," in *With Friends Like These*, 233–35, 243. More generally, see Samuel Moyn, *The Last Utopia: Human Rights in History* (Harvard University Press, 2010).

66. Radchenko, *To Run the World*, 437.

67. Michael Cotey Morgan, *The Final Act: The Helsinki Accords and the Transformation of the Cold War* (Princeton University Press, 2018), 208, 219; William Korey, *The Promises We Keep: Human Rights, the Helsinki Process, and American Foreign Policy* (St. Martin's Press, 1993), 2, 336.

68. Peter Redfield, *Life in Crisis: The Ethical Journey of Doctors Without Borders* (University of California Press, 2013), 12.

69. It also led to a historiographic shift to push back the origins of modern human rights to eighteenth-century debates about embodied autonomy. See Lynn Hunt, *Inventing Human Rights* (W. W. Norton, 2007), 65–67.

70. Henry Shue, *Basic Rights: Subsistence, Affluence, and U.S. Foreign Policy* (Princeton University Press, 1980). Henry Shue, interview with author, Oxford, March 26, 2016.

71. Cited in David Scheffer, *All the Missing Souls: A Personal History of the War Crimes Tribunals* (Princeton University Press, 2012), 143.

72. David Scheffer, *All the Missing Souls*, 4.

73. Charles R. Beitz, *Political Theory and International Relations* (Princeton University Press, 1979), 6; Charles R. Beitz, *The Idea of Human Rights* (Oxford University Press, 2009), 43. On crimes against peace, see William Schabas, *Unimaginable Atrocities: Justice, Politics, and Rights at the War Crimes Tribunals* (Oxford University Press, 2012), 2–4.

74. David Rieff, *A Bed for the Night: Humanitarianism in Crisis* (Simon & Schuster, 2002), 36–37.

75. William D. Clark, interview by Patricia Blair, World Bank Group Oral History Program, The World Bank/IFC Archives, October 4–5, 1983, 20, https://documents1.worldbank.org/curated/en/571041468337173687/pdf/789640v20TRN0C0on010October04001983.pdf.

76. Willy Brandt, "Opening Address," speech by chairman of the Independent Commission on International Development Issues, delivered at Gymnich Castle (Erftstadt, Germany, December 9, 1977), 11, https://timeline.worldbank.org/content/dam/sites/timeline/docs/migrated/event50-Brandt-BrandtSpeech1977-1557709.pdf.

77. William D. Clark, interview, 22.

78. *North-South: A Programme for Survival* (Pan, 1980), 20–21, and esp. chap. 1.

79. R. T. Maddock, "The Arms Race in the 1980s," in *The Political Economy of the Arms Race* (Palgrave, 1990), 180–202.

80. Gunnar Myrdal, "International Inequality and Foreign Aid in Retrospect," in *Pioneers in Development*, ed. Gerald M. Meier and Dudley Seers (Oxford University Press, 1984), 163.

81. David Sepkoski, *Catastrophic Thinking*, 170–71, 194–96; Lawrence Badash, *A Nuclear Winter's Tale: Science and Politics in the 1980s* (MIT Press, 2009), 3, 63–77.

82. Badash, *Nuclear Winter's Tale*, 121.

83. Keck and Sikkink, *Activists Beyond Borders*, 121; Dale Jamieson, *Reason in a Dark Time: Why the Struggle Against Climate Change Failed and What It Means for Our Future* (Oxford University Press, 2014), 161–62.

84. Stephen J. Macekura, *Of Limits and Growth: The Rise of Global Sustainable Development in the Twentieth Century* (Cambridge University Press, 2015), 103.

85. John Harte and Robert H. Socolow, *Patient Earth: The Problems of Urban Blight, Population Control, Resource Management, Conservation, the Ecological Impact of the Military, and Alternative Uses of Our Land* (Holt, Rinehart and Winston, 1971).

86. Macekura, *Of Limits and Growth*, 124–25.

87. Paul Warde, Libby Robin, and Sverker Sörlin, *The Environment: A History of the Idea* (Johns Hopkins University Press, 2018), 122–23; Macekura, *Of Limits and Growth*, 222.

88. Will Steffen, Katherine Richardson, Johan Rockström, and Hans Joachim Schellnhuber, "The Emergence and Evolution of Earth System Science," *Nature*, 1:1 (January 2020), 1–10; Matthias Dörries, "The Politics of Atmospheric Sciences: 'Nuclear Winter' and Global Climate Change," *Osiris*, 26:1 (2011), 198–223.

89. Spencer Weart, *The Discovery of Global Warming* (Harvard University Press, 2008), 38, 84, 87.

90. Peter Wadhams, *A Farewell to Ice* (Allen Lane, 2017).

91. Pamela E. Mack, *Viewing the Earth: The Social Construction of the Landsat Satellite System* (MIT Press, 1990), 27, 129.

92. On the debate about road building and deforestation in the Amazon, especially involving NGO pressure on global creditors, see Macekura, *Of Limits and Growth*, 206–9.

93. Seth Garfield, *In Search of the Amazon: Brazil, the United States, and the Nature of a Region* (Duke University Press, 2013), 219; Susanna Hecht and Alexander Cockburn, *The Fate of the Forest: Developers, Destroyers, and Defenders of the Amazon* (Verso, 1989), 37.

94. G. E. Likens and F. H. Bormann, "Acid Rain: A Serious Regional Environmental Problem." *Science*, 184 (1974), 1176–79; Michael Oppenheimer, conversation with author, November 24, 2015.

95. Ann-Kristin Bergquist and Thomas David, "Beyond Planetary Limits! The International Chamber of Commerce, the United Nations, and the Invention of Sustainable Development," *Business History Review*, 97:3 (Autumn 2023), 481–511.

96. On the role of NGOs, see Julie Fisher, *The Road from Rio: Sustainable Development and the Nongovernmental Movement in the Third World* (Praeger, 1993); Garfield, *In Search of the Amazon*, 218.

97. For a searing critique, see Dieter Helm, *The Carbon Crunch: How We're Getting Climate Change Wrong—and How to Fix It* (Yale University Press, 2012), 9–13.

Chapter Six

1. Neil Irwin, "Heroes of the Crisis, Paid in Rage," Business, *New York Times*, September 16, 2018, 7; "IMF Survey," International Monetary Fund, September 1, 2010, https://www.imf.org/en/News/Articles/2015/09/28/04/53/sonew090210a.

2. Rita Abrahamsen, Jean-François Drolet, Michael C. Williams, Srdjan Vucetic, Karin Narita, and Alexandra Gheciu, *World of the Right: Radical Conservatism and Global Order* (Cambridge University Press, 2024), 2.

3. Chris Buckley, David Kirkpatrick, Amy Qin, and Javier Hernández, "25 Days That Changed the World," *New York Times*, December 30, 2020, https://www.nytimes.com/2020/12/30/world/asia/china-coronavirus.html?action=click&module=Well&pgtype=Homepage&section=World%20News.

4. Xi Jinping, "Speech During the Study of the Novel Coronavirus Pneumonia Epidemic," speech, Standing Committee of the Political Bureau of the Central Committee to Study the Response to the New Coronavirus Epidemic, February 3, 2020, https://www.qstheory.cn/dukan/qs/2020-02/15/c_1125572832.htm.

5. Pankaj Mishra, *The Age of Anger: A History of the Present* (Farrar, Straus and Giroux, 2017); Barbara F. Walter, *How Civil Wars Start: And How to Stop Them* (Crown, 2022).

6. Mauro Guillén, *The Architecture of Collapse* (Oxford University Press, 2015).

7. Albert O. Hirschman: *Exit, Voice, and Loyalty: Responses to Decline in Firms, Organizations, and States* (Harvard University Press, 1970); Jerome Roos, *Why Not Default? The Political Economy of Sovereign Debt* (Princeton University Press, 2019), esp. 225–34.

8. Walter Scheidel, *The Great Leveler: Violence and the History of Inequality from the Stone Age to the Twenty-First Century* (Princeton University Press, 2017).

9. "Les Français, les gilets jaunes et les mesures annoncées par Edouard Philippe," Sondage ELABE pour BFMTV, December 5, 2018, https://web.archive.org/web/20190110020502/https://elabe.fr/wp-content/uploads/2018/12/rapport_20181205_elabe_bfmtv_les-francais-les-gilets-jaunes-et-les-mesures-annoncees-par-edouard-philippe.pdf.

10. "Confidence in Institutions," Gallup, n.d., accessed February 1, 2026, https://news.gallup.com/poll/1597/confidence-institutions.aspx.

11. *2023 Edelman Trust Barometer: Global Report,* Edelman, n.d., accessed 1 February, 2026, https://www.edelman.com/sites/g/files/aatuss191/files/2023-01/2023%20Edelman%20Trust%20Barometer%20Global%20Report.pdf.

12. For the full text, see Tola Onanuga, "Emergency Budget: George Osborne's Speech in Full," *The Guardian,* June 22, 2010, https://www.theguardian.com/uk/2010/jun/22/emergency-budget-full-speech-text.

13. Nelson D. Schwartz, "The Recovery Was a Disaster All Over Again," *New York Times,* September 16, 2018, Business Section, 3; Thomas Piketty, *Capital in the Twenty-First Century* (Harvard University Press, 2014).

14. "Michael Moore Warns Trump Victory Would Be Biggest F—You Ever Recorded," *CBS News,* October 25, 2016, https://www.cbsnews.com/losangeles/news/michael-moore-warns-trump-victory-would-be-biggest-f-you-ever-recorded/.

15. Esther Addley, "Occupy Movement: From Local Action to a Global Howl of Protest," *The Guardian,* October 17, 2011, https://www.theguardian.com/world/2011/oct/17/occupy-movement-global-protest.

16. Jeronim Perović, *Fuel and Power: Energy, Trade, and Russian Foreign Relations from Lenin to Putin* (Cambridge University Press, 2024), 205.

17. George Soros, "A New Policy to Rescue Ukraine," *New York Review,* February 5, 2015, https://www.nybooks.com/articles/2015/02/05/new-policy-rescue-ukraine/.

18. Watch action footage here: "Putin in Crimea: Leader Dives on Black Sea Shipwreck in Mini-sub," *The Guardian,* August 18, 2015, https://www.bbc.co.uk/news/av/world-europe-33979708.

19. Nina Tannenwald, "Is Using Nuclear Weapons Still Taboo?," *Foreign Policy,* July 1, 2022, https://foreignpolicy.com/2022/07/01/nuclear-war-taboo-arms-control-russia-ukraine-deterrence/.

20. James Acton, codirector of the nuclear policy programme at the Carnegie Endowment for International Peace, quoted in Amy MacKinnon, Max Seddon, and Ian Bott, "A World Without Nuclear Arms Control Begins this Week," *Financial Times,* February 2, 2026, https://www.ft.com/content/fd1d2e57-dce7-489d-956a-22b839cfadd8.

21. Marc Santora, "Kharkiv Is Unbreakable," *New York Times,* April 24, 2024, https://www.nytimes.com/2024/04/24/world/europe/ukraine-kharkiv-russia-glide-bombs.html.

22. Samuel Charap and Sergey Radchenko, "The Talks That Could Have Ended the War in Ukraine," *Foreign Affairs,* April 16, 2024, https://www.foreignaffairs.com/ukraine/talks-could-have-ended-war-ukraine.

23. "Boris Johnson Visits Ukraine," *BBC News,* April 9, 2022, https://www.bbc.com/pidgin/tori-61052458.

24. Lydia Polgreen, "He Was the Face and Voice of Gaza. Israel Assassinated Him," *New York Times,* August 21, 2025, https://www.nytimes.com/2025/08/21/opinion/israel-al-sharif-killing-gaza.html.

25. See, for instance, Geoffrey Fowler, "You Have the Right to Film Police," *Washington Post*, April 22, 2021, https://www.washingtonpost.com/technology/2021/04/22/how-to-film-police-smartphone/. The Global History Lab at Cambridge also teaches classes on the use of personal phones as documentary, rapid-response history tools.

26. Nathan Jurgenson, *The Social Photo: On Photography and Social Media* (Verso, 2019).

27. Daniel Yergin, *The New Map: Energy, Climate, and the Clash of Nations* (Penguin, 2020), 117.

28. Javier Blas and Jack Farchy, *The World for Sale: Money, Power, and the Traders Who Barter the Earth's Resources* (Oxford University Press, 2020), 245–47.

29. Blas and Farchy, *World for Sale*, 248.

30. Blas and Farchy, *World for Sale*, 294–96.

31. Itamar Rabinovich and Carmit Valensi, *Syrian Requiem: The Civil War and Its Aftermath* (Princeton University Press, 2021), 36.

32. Fawaz A. Gerges, *ISIS: A History* (Princeton University Press, 2016), 2–3.

33. Hasan Kattan, interview by author, September 19, 2025.

34. Francesco D'Orazio, "Journey of an Image," in *The Iconic Image on Social Media: A Rapid Response to the Death of Aylan Kurdi*, ed. F. Vis and O. Goriunova (Sheffield: Visual Social Media Lab, 2015), 11; James Verini, *They Will Have to Die Now: Mosul and the Fall of the Caliphate* (W. W. Norton, 2019), 97–98.

35. Peter Pomerantsev, *This Is Not Propaganda: Adventures in the War Against Reality* (Faber & Faber, 2019), 176–77.

36. Emma Loop, "Canada's Political Leaders Got Emotional When Talking About Alan Kurdi," *Buzzfeed*, September 3, 2015, https://www.buzzfeed.com/emmaloop/heres-what-canadas-political-leaders-said-about-the-countrys#.trLPd5gM5d.

37. Michael Walzer, *Spheres of Justice: A Defense of Pluralism and Equality* (Basic Books, 1983), 33.

38. Charles T. Call, *Why Peace Fails: The Causes and Prevention of Civil War Recurrence* (Georgetown University Press, 2012), 3.

39. Jean-Marie Guéhenno, *The Fog of Peace* (Brookings, 2015), 62.

40. "Why Israel Must Hold Itself to Account," *The Economist*, August 9, 2025, https://www.economist.com/leaders/2025/08/07/why-israel-must-hold-itself-to-account?ppccampaignID=17210591673&ppcadID&gclsrc=aw.ds&gad_source=1&gad_campaignid=17210596221.

41. Julie Michelle Klinger, *Rare Earth Frontiers: From Terrestrial Subsoils to Lunar Landscapes* (Cornell University Press, 2017), 58; Henry Farrell and Abraham Newman, "Weaponized Interdependence: How Global Economic Networks Shape State Coercion," *International Security*, 44:1 (2019), 42–79.

42. For more on her reflections, see Amy Elizabeth Robinson, "Listening to the Loved One: Wildfire, Community, and Ambiguous Loss," in *Red Flag Warning: Mutual Aid and Survival in California's Fire Country*, ed. Dani Burlison and Margaret Elysia Garcia (AK Press, 2025).

43. T. J. Demos, *Against the Anthropocene: Visual Culture and Environment Today* (Sternberg Press, 2017), 19.

44. Cristina Mittermeier, "Starving-Polar-Bear Photographer Recalls What Went Wrong," *National Geographic*, December 10, 2017, https://www.nationalgeographic.com/magazine/article/explore-through-the-lens-starving-polar-bear-photo.

45. Mark C. Serreze, *Brave New Arctic: The Untold Story of the Melting North* (Princeton University Press, 2018), 24.

46. Paolo Pellegrin, "The Deceptive Beauty of the Changing Antarctic," *Magnum*, April 16, 2018, https://www.magnumphotos.com/newsroom/environment/paolo-pellegrin-antarctic-climate-change/?utm_source=Magnum+Photos&utm_campaign=1caafe7712-EMAIL_CAMPAIGN_2018_04_20&utm_m edium=email&utm_term=0_8b268cbf2c-1caafe7712-4760981&mc_cid=1caafe7712&mc_eid=fa22ea8753.

47. On the diffusion, see Lara Bullens, "How France's 'Great Replacement' Theory Conquered the Global Far Right," *France 24*, August 11, 2021, https://www.france24.com/en/europe/20211108-how-the-french-great-replacement-theory-conquered-the-far-right.

48. Ivan Krastev and Stephen Holmes, *The Light That Failed: A Reckoning* (Penguin, 2020). On the global tide of reaction, see Abrahamsen, Drolet, Williams, Vucetic, Narita, and Gheciu, *World of the Right*.

49. Jeremy Adelman, "Why the Idea That the World Is in Terminal Decline Is So Dangerous," *Aeon*, November 1, 2017, https://aeon.co/ideas/why-the-idea-that-the-world-is-in-terminal-decline-is-so-dangerous.

50. "Why They're Wrong," *The Economist*, October 1, 2016, 11.

51. Verini, *They Will Have to Die Now* (W. W. Norton, 2019), 79.

52. Mukul Kesavan, "Murderous Majorities," *New York Review of Books*, January 18, 2018, 37–38.

53. Quoted in Patrick Kingsley, *The New Odyssey: The Story of the Twenty-First Century Refugee Crisis* (Liveright, 2016), 18, 260.

54. Alison Smale, "After Assaults in Cologne, Merkel Proposes Tougher Asylum Laws," *New York Times*, January 10, 2016, 6; "Cologne Attacks: Pegida and Police Clash at Migrant Protest," *BBC News*, January 9, 2016, https://www.bbc.co.uk/news/world-europe-35274105.

55. Stephen Castle and Aurelien Breeden, "Channel Tunnel Has Become a Choke Point in the World Migration Crisis," *New York Times*, July 30, 2015, A6.

56. Helen Thompson, *Disorder: Hard Times in the 21st Century* (Oxford University Press, 2022), 155.

57. Richard Hall, "How the Brexit Campaign Used Refugees to Scare Voters," *PRI*, June 24, 2016, https://www.pri.org/stories/2016-06-24/how-brexit-campaign-used-refugees-scare-voters. It is worth noting that not all Brexiteers agreed with this nativist fearmongering. See Tom McTague, *Between the Waves: The Hidden History of a Very British Revolution, 1945–2016* (Picador, 2025), 452-453.

58. Goodman, *Davos Man*, 115.

59. Jonathan Freedland, "A Howl of Rage," *New York Review of Books*, August 18, 2016, 4–6.

60. Paul Gilroy, *Postcolonial Melancholia* (Columbia University Press, 2006).

61. Based on SIPRI Military Expenditure Database, Stockholm International Peace Research Institute, compiled by World Bank. https://data.worldbank.org/indicator/MS.MIL.XPND.GD.ZS. Accessed 1 February 2026.

62. *Trade in Services for Development*, World Trade Organization, 2023, https://www.wto.org/english/res_e/publications_e/trade_in_serv_devpt_e.htm; Richard Baldwin, *The Globotics Upheaval: Globalization, Robotics, and the Future of Work* (Oxford University Press, 2019).

63. Peter Hessler, "Manufacturing Diplomacy," *New Yorker*, March 15, 2021, 50.

64. Jeremy Adelman and Caitlin Zaloom, "Migrant Lives, Global Stories," *Public Books*, February 21, 2022, https://www.publicbooks.org/migrant-lives-global-stories/.

65. Based on United States Census Bureau data compiled by the Migration Policy Institute, accessed 1 February, 2026, https://www.migrationpolicy.org/programs/data-hub/charts/immigrant-population-over-time.

66. Hein de Haas, Mathias Czaika, Marie-Laurence Flahaux, Edo Mahendra, Katharina Natter, Simona Vezzoli, and Maria Villares-Varela, "International Migration: Trends, Determinants, and Policy Effects," *Population and Development Review*, 45:4 (2019), 885–922.

67. De Haas et al., "International Migration, 885–922.

68. Yannis Behrakis, "Greece: Witnessing the Migration Crisis," *Reuters: The Wider Image*, added December 7, 2015, https://widerimage.reuters.com/story/greece-witnessing-the-migration-crisis.

69. Sadiq Amini, "Where Did the Afghan Refugees Go?" *The Interpreter*, November 10, 2023, https://www.lowyinstitute.org/the-interpreter/where-did-afghan-refugees-go-where-next.

70. Lydia Polgreen, "I Went to Dubai and Caught a Glimpse of the Future," *New York Times*, March 11, 2025, https://www.nytimes.com/2025/03/11/opinion/dubai-migration-trump.html?smid=nytcore-ios-share&referringSource=articleShare; Hein de Haas, *How Migration Really Works* (Penguin, 2024).

71. "Anything to Stop the Migrants," *The Economist*, August 18, 2018.

Coda

1. Howard Eiland and Michael W. Jennings, *Walter Benjamin: A Critical Life* (Harvard University Press, 2014), 650–51.

2. *Walter Benjamin: Selected Writings*, eds. Howard Eiland and Michael W. Jennings, vol. 4, *1938–1940* (Harvard University Press, 2003), 392.

3. Hannah Arendt, "Walter Benjamin, 1892–1940," in her *Men in Dark Times* (Harcourt, Brace & World, 1968), 172.

4. Arendt, "Walter Benjamin," 174.

5. David Wallace-Wells, *The Uninhabitable Earth: Life After Warming* (Duggan Books, 2019), 226.

6. Start, for instance, with a recognition of what two authors call the principle of subsidiarity, of a multiscalar governance structure that reflects back a compound of mixed systems that don't conform to illusory universal or monolithic form. See Jonathan S. Blake and Nils Gilman, *Children of a Modest Star: Planetary Thinking for an Age of Crises* (Stanford University Press, 2024), 111–12.

Acknowledgments

1. Emmanuel Levinas, "No Identity," in *L'Ephémère* 13 (1970), 27–44. Reprinted in *Humanisme de l'autre homme* (Fata Morgana, 1972), 83–101. Cited in Michael Ignatieff, *On Consolation: Finding Solace in Dark Times* (Metropolitan Books, 2021), 234.

INDEX

Page numbers in *italics* refer to figures and tables.

A NOTE ON THE TYPE

This book has been composed in Arno, an Old-style serif typeface in the classic Venetian tradition, designed by Robert Slimbach at Adobe.